THE CRISIS MEETERS

Business Response to Social Crises

Also by Irving S. Michelman

BUSINESS AT BAY: CRITICS AND HERETICS OF AMERICAN BUSINESS

CONSUMER FINANCE: A CASE HISTORY IN AMERICAN BUSINESS

First Published 1973
AUGUSTUS M. KELLEY • *PUBLISHERS*
Clifton, New Jersey 07012

Library of Congress Cataloging in Publication Data

Michelman, Irving S
The crisis meeters.

Includes bibliographical references.
1. Business and politics--United States--History.
2. United States--Politics and government--20th century. I. Title.
JK467.M53 320.9'73'09 73-4914
ISBN 0-678-01320-9

PRINTED IN THE UNITED STATES OF AMERICA
by SENTRY PRESS, NEW YORK, N. Y. 10013

THE CRISIS MEETERS

Business Response to Social Crises

by
IRVING S. MICHELMAN

With Introduction by
DORE SCHARY

AUGUSTUS M. KELLEY • *PUBLISHERS*
New Jersey 1973

To David and Michael

Contents

Foreword

This is the story of how a gallery of businessmen responded to certain twentieth century non-business social crises. There are, as might be expected, rogues in this gallery, cast in the role of reactionary that comes so naturally to powerful men of business. Tom Girdler, of Republic Steel and the "Memorial Day Massacre" in Chicago, is a case in point.

At the other extreme are businessmen who have assumed the role of statesmen in meeting their particular crises. Myron C. Taylor, Chairman of U.S. Steel, won his toga by his audacious recognition of unions in the late thirties. True the government and the sit-down strikers in the General Motors plants had more or less written the final script for this convulsive movement which went far beyond the normal concerns of business. It took the action of a lofty conservative like Taylor, however, to legitimize the radical social stirrings of labor and avert a worse crisis.

This brings to mind how central the business role is to American history. We are a business civilization, for better or worse, and our particular abilities in mass production, invention and efficiency have served us well, as one used to say, in war and peace. Business institutions have changed drastically in this century. A nation of local stores and small plants has evolved into one of chain stores and large plants. Subtler changes have been the inescapable lock-in between business and government (after the quaint trial marriage of the NRA experiment) and the rise of a new managerial class possessing only minority stock ownership.

These managers, the new technological elite, carry the hopes of both political theorists and business school deans as the agents who might invest a berserk technology with a quality of life as well as a quantity of goods. Their new role is to pay attention to corporate responsibility even at the expense of maximizing short-run profits. One can extend sympathy — but not too much — to men charged with achieving such contradictory goals. In the context of the times, with government itself accepting the same mandate and depending on business for its fulfillment, the charge is reasonable.

In any event the charge is related to a level of ideal expectations arising from a past history of deeds and misdeeds, and here is where we return to our gallery of businessmen. The new executive, trying hard to become a humanist and generalist as well as technician in preparation for his awesome responsibilities, may well consider how previous executives met moral decisions in the social arena. How did the business class respond to America's first irresponsible war? In the business celebrations of the twenties, is there a lesson to observe from the Sacco and Vanzetti case, when business itself was charged with complicity in establishing the atmosphere of prejudice which apparently permeated into the Massachusetts courtroom? How enlightened was the business reaction to Franklin D. Roosevelt when that self-styled savior of capitalism vigorously responded to its death throes in the early days of the New Deal? At what point should a movie mogul or even a production boss resist the public clamor to take away the right to work from so-called Un-Americans? Where does one lay his own job on the line over an "outside" issue?

Of course clear cut answers for personal behavior under stress are as elusive here as elsewhere. The perspective of time helps establish a consensus of what is considered right and wrong. It also distorts the available choices by viewing past situations from new levels of ethics. There is in addition that tyranny of history which chains men to their times, making Jacob Coxey of Coxey's Army, for example, an eccentric rather than a prophetic businessman-economist with a program for meeting unemployment.

The gallery therefore includes well-intentioned men of business caught in moral dilemmas, damned by critics whichever way they turned during a particular social crisis, men like Mark Hanna, Andrew Carnegie and Henry Atkinson at the turn of the century, Governor Alvan T. Fuller of Massachusetts in the twenties, James P. Warburg in the thirties, Dore Schary in mid-century and Robert S. McNamara a few years back. In crisis situations generally beyond their control, these men, intelligent, ambivalent, able to see both sides of difficult questions, responded with originality and a substantial amount of courage. Quite diverse otherwise, they possessed in common an enlightened humanist temperament through which they filtered their decisions. Whether they were right or wrong is a matter for the reader to decide for himself as the crises are presented with special emphasis on the business point of view. If there is a lesson to be drawn, let it be this: An open-minded, humane temperament, based on a sense of history and civilization, will serve well as the key ingredient for the businessman's response to social crises.

My thanks are expressed to Professor Ernest R. May, Harvard's distinguished authority on imperialism, for his suggestions and for his review of the Spanish-American War period; Francis Russell, the noted writer and historian, for correspondence on his specialty, the Sacco-Vanzetti case, on which we amiably disagree; Neil H. Jacoby, former Dean of the UCLA Graduate School of Management and Eisenhower Economic Adviser, for comments on the New Deal and NRA sections; Professor John Hutchinson, UCLA Industrial Relations specialist, for his sharp analysis of my chapter on the labor crises; Philip Dunne, screen-writer and director, for his first-hand recollections of the Hollywood blacklist period; Marx

Leva, former Assistant Secretary of Defense, for incisive contributions to the analysis of the military-industrial complex; and to Augustus M. Kelley for editorial advice.

It is a privilege to have this book introduced by Dore Schary, a man of letters and action, who has done what many businessmen wish to do, that is, keep young, keep relevant, keep engaged. Mr. Schary himself is a "case history" in this book, faced with crisis decisions which would damn him either way he moved. His reliance on innate decency and his dedication to civil rights no doubt sustained him.

Once again my wife heard it all and read it all with loving patience.

IRVING S. MICHELMAN

Los Angeles, California, 1972

Introduction

by

DORE SCHARY

The book you are about to read is unique and refreshing. It is not a "how-to" or a "then-I-read" book, but rather, what I believe to be a superb examination of the play of power in big business and the use of such power in times of crisis.

My evaluation is based on my personal experiences with people of some substance who have wielded power in politics, big business, community affairs, philanthropy (yes, power is a factor even in good causes) and, of course, in motion pictures and the theatre. In any case, I believe that Mr. Michelman's book is a thoughtful and original piece of work.

During my 40-year career, I have held positions of substantial power and exercised that power sometimes rightfully and other times wrongfully. I have been elevated to opportunity by men of power and many times cut down to size by power plays I could on occasion identify and on other occasions by circumstances the nature of which I cannot understand even today.

My contacts with movie titans Nicholas Schenck, the Warner brothers, Louis B. Mayer, Y. Frank Freeman, Harry Cohn, Barney Balaban, Darryl Zanuck and Howard Hughes lasted over a long stretch of years. In politics, I have known Presidents Truman, Kennedy and Johnson and I worked diligently for Adlai Stevenson, Hubert Humphrey, Robert Kennedy, a number of other Senators and Mayor John V. Lindsay. Among public figures and industrialists, I have known Paul Hoffman, Louis Wolfson, Ralph Bunche, Roy Wilkins, Whitney Young, Eleanor Roosevelt and Golda Meir. My friends include many athletes, scores and scores of doctors and lawyers, a regiment of labor leaders and hundreds of colleagues in the arenas of Hollywood, Broadway and Madison Avenue.

All of these people share one thing — they hold or held power. In lesser or greater degree, it is true, but they have had power and used it and if they do not employ it well, they fall. Inevitably they become crisis meeters.

Power is never static — it shifts with each crisis and with each crisis the power base is diminished or widened. As I write this, a group of young people in the lobby of the Doral Hotel in Miami have just angrily attacked their candidate, George McGovern. They were rude and hot-headed — McGovern was patient and cool. It was a demonstration by a man who knows how to use power. By firmness, candor and no-nonsense, no stammering — he won the confrontation. It was a meeting of crisis that has given him added strength.

In business, which is the subject of Mr. Michelman's book, a power game is played by the same rules that apply to every activity of human life. The chessmen have a different design, but the goal is the same — checkmate — which in Arabic and Hebrew is "sheik-mate," meaning "the King is dead."

Obviously, other meanings are implied: win the game; get the head man out; get the other man's job; marry the man you want; marry the boss's daughter; win the big poker pot of the evening.

More — the "king" is your biggest competitor or perhaps the little one who wants to be big. Or the designer who must be wrenched from one firm to yours. Perhaps it is pursuing the architect who will build the stately dome in Xanadu that will carry the owner's name until it turns to dust. Power is a huge game of monopoly, but the money is real and the sites on Park Place are real and even Zeckendorf can lose a bankroll.

Sewell Avery loses his seat behind a big desk as two soldiers lift him up and out. Edsel Ford is defeated by a business he doesn't like and by a band of industrial hoodlums who in turn lose their ballgame, the Ford plant and their jobs to Edsel's son, Henry Jr., who settles the score in a fine display of power demonstrating that unless authority carries with it the muscle to use power, it is useless.

Big business has begun to assume its responsibility to the people it serves and to the people who serve it. But big business didn't become self-educated. Essentially, it was taught by the power of labor. The ogres and goblins feared by big business only 40 years ago have been stripped of the costumes that business designed for them those many years ago. No one seriously believes that unemployment insurance, health and death benefits, the 40-hour week, social security, long vacations and other fringe benefits will ever disappear. And with all these additional expenses, big business is healthier than it's ever been. Its profits are staggering and its potential ever-increasing. In the field of big business, the power struggle is never-ending. Not just between the two chief forces — management and labor — but within the two rival camps.

John Lewis, Walter Reuther, George Meany, Jimmy Hoffa and the minions who followed them waged their power fights inside labor so that they in turn could stand up and fight the powers behind big business. Mr. Michelman brings the historical labor-business crisis to vivid life.

There are three basic colorations to power, or better yet, three kinds of power — by aggression (Attila, Ghengis Khan, Napoleon, Hitler), by authority (Lincoln, F.D.R., Churchill), by persuasion (Moses, Jesus Christ, Mohammed, Gandhi). In big business, these three types of power are represented. The robber barons — Hill,

Astor, Harriman, and Jay Gould — struck savagely for what they wanted. Others used mainly authority to achieve what they wanted and some few, such as the industrialists Swope and Taylor, perfected the tools of persuasion and understanding.

There is no denying that often these three attitudes are combined in one person but in the main, they have different champions.

Mr. Michelman deals with business history that is not only illuminating but also entertaining. There is a lack of literature about the personality of big business and this book should be widely welcomed as a valuable addition to that sparse library.

Chapter 1

Free Silver and Free Cuba

Part I: *Sound Money*

In late 1969, Walt W. Rostow, President Johnson's powerful advisor on Vietnam, faced an unfriendly audience of members of the American Historical Assoication. As a University of Texas professor, Rostow offered the view that we first established our foothold in Asia quite by accident when the Philippine Islands were taken from Spain following the Spanish-American War.

"Your presentation of the period 1898 to 1900 is based on fallacious facts," stated a 36 year old assistant professor of history at New York University. Other historians heckled Rostow until Professor Arthur M. Schlesinger, Jr. reminded them about Voltaire and the privilege of dissent. "Look," Rostow's parting comment, "I've seen a lot of revisionists come and go."

One of the revisions historians have made about this absurd little war is that business and economic interests were not the chief warmakers after all. In fact, the one briefly sane group in America to resist the hysteria that engulfed the nation turns out to be the business community. It scores infinitely better in this respect than the church, the press, the politicians and, at the zero end of the scale, the completely silent college students.

Imagine Republican Senator Mason of Illinois damning in the Senate "the unpatriotic Wall Street speculators who would not let the nation do its duty to humanity" and this before the sinking in February 1898 of the *Maine*, one of the nation's prized new battleships, though second-class. Consider the plight of the urbane, witty Chauncey Depew, president of the New York Central and soon to be its Senator, who made a plea for peace at the dinner of the New York Republican Club on the evening of March 26, 1898. The nation's most noted after-dinner speaker was rudely interrupted by a pro-war partisan who was roundly cheered by the Republicans and carried about the room in triumph. This news was reported by William Randolph Hearst's unscrupulously martial New York *Journal*, which gallantly allowed Depew a *riposte* the next morning: "I find that the most warlike gentlemen are the ministers. At the dinner my good friend Rev. Dr. Duffield was anxious to start a war at 5 o'clock this morning."[1]

There was nothing humorous in the situation for the young Assistant Secretary of the Navy, Theodore Roosevelt, attending a dinner of the Gridiron Club in Washington on the same evening. Grinding his teeth and shaking his fist in the face of Mark Hanna, Republican National Committee Chairman, Senator from Ohio and President-maker of William B. McKinley, he is pictured by historians as shouting: "We will have this war for the liberation of Cuba, Senator Hanna, in spite of the timidity of the commercial classes."[2]

In all fairness, Rostow was correct. The immediate objective of the war was to intervene in the Cuban rebellion and free Cuba from Spanish tyranny. Part of the strategy of the hundred days' war was to pursue that portion of Spain's decrepit Navy not posted to Cuba but known to be holed up in Manila Bay, a good 10,000 miles the other way. Roosevelt again enters the picture. Literally bursting for war, he had been instrumental in appointing Commodore Dewey to command the Asiatic Squadron with orders to lay in wait for an attack on the Philippines. The orders were dispatched by Roosevelt on the day off of his cautious superior, Secretary of the Navy Long, who had reluctantly accepted Roosevelt as his assistant in order to please that other bellicose Harvard man, Senator Henry Cabot Lodge. By the time Dewey triumphed over the Spanish fleet on May 1, Roosevelt had transformed himself into Colonel of the Rough Riders, impatiently awaiting transportation to Cuba. He was on his way to San Juan Hill and thence to the White House to become the first President of a United States recognized as a world and colonial power.

Roosevelt was all purpose and action. McKinley was the man of accident and ambivalence in foreign affairs, justifying the Rostow thesis. A solid, fine-looking nineteenth century man, McKinley was the image of the actor Robert Morley in the latter's characterization of missionary brother to Katherine Hepburn in the movie *The African Queen.* Aside from the strong physical resemblance, there are other common elements binding the movie to history. Certainly the element of mission was embraced by American imperialists. And the idea of England and Germany carving up Africa was not lost on our national thought. Let McKinley speak for himself as he tells a group of visiting clergymen how we ended up with the Philippines (and Guam and Puerto Rico) instead of just freeing Cuba:

> The truth is I didn't want the Philippines, and when they came to us, as a gift from the gods, I did not know what to do with them. When the Spanish War broke out, Dewey was at Hongkong, and I ordered him to go to Manila and to capture or destroy the Spanish fleet. . . . But that was as far as I thought then.
>
> . . . . I thought first we would take only Manila; then Luzon; then other islands, perhaps, also. I walked the floor of the White House night after night until midnight; and I am not ashamed to tell you, gentlemen, that I went down on my knees and prayed Almighty God for light and guidance more than one night. And one night

> it came to me this way — I don't know how it was, but it came: (1) That we could not give them back to Spain — that would be cowardly and dishonorable; (2) that we could not turn them over to France or Germany — our commercial rivals in the Orient — that would be bad business and discreditable; (3) that we could not leave them to themselves — they were unfit for self-government — and they would soon have anarchy and misrule over there worse than Spain's was; and (4) that there was nothing left for us to do but to take them all, and to educate the Filipinos, and uplift and civilize and Christianize them, and by God's grace to do the best we could by them. . . . And then I went to bed, and went to sleep, and slept soundly, and the next morning I sent for the chief engineer of the War Department (our map-maker) and I told him to put the Philippines on the map of the United States . . . and there they are, and there they will stay while I am President![3]

Since our point of view is to examine how business reacted to the war and thereby gain insight into the actions and thoughts of predecessor businessmen, we can well start with McKinley. He was the candidate of big business, elected in 1896 over the people's candidate, William Jennings Bryan, by the largest majority since Horace Greeley went down to defeat before Ulysses S. Grant in 1872. These were the years of Republican ascendancy in the White House. The Grand Old Party had long since left the radicalism attending its birth pangs over slavery and was well on its way to becoming the party of big business and finance.

A party of privilege and conservatism could hardly take its ascendancy for granted as the century rushed to an end. The growth of cities, the waves of immigration, the dominance of factories over farms, the violence against labor, the bitterness in the unreconstructed South, the crass "spoils system" of the politicians, the dubious ethics and rush to consolidations of the business system — all conspired to unseat the party in power. Our undistracted ancestors were refreshingly intense about political and economic issues and took their right to vote seriously. As a result, the close popular votes among Democrats and Republicans belied the generally large electoral vote differences. Already the Republicans had yielded the White House twice to Grover Cleveland, a superior President of character and capacity who had attracted the vote of many independent Republicans, including a large number of smaller businessmen, for his "reform" Administrations in 1884 and 1892. These swing voters were known as "Mugwumps" (an Algonquin Indian term of no particular relevance) and they would carry their consciences to the Anti-Imperialist cause during McKinley's regime, after the war.

It is possible that future historians will compare the national mood surrounding the election of 1896 with that of 1968. There is a similarity in the pre-election experiences of the defeated parties. Just as Richard Nixon led the Republicans to victory after Lyndon Johnson had split the Democrats over Vietnam, so McKinley restored the Republicans to power after Cleveland split his party over the momentous — in those days — repeal of the Silver Purchase Act. On the other hand, Cleveland's downfall was also propelled by the severe Panic of 1893 whereas Johnson presided over prosperity. In terms of national mood, one can uncover psychic strains beyond those caused by a depression. The common symptom in both elections might well be that they took place during historically high periods of dissent. Dissent in turn produced its share of fear. Fear induced what is now known as backlash and backlash had significant political results.

If you were a comfortable businessman in one of the North Central or Northeastern states in 1896, you would have had the uncomfortable feeling that the dissent had reached alarming proportions and must be stopped at all costs. It was bad enough that the Populist candidate for President, General James B. Weaver, had polled over one million votes in 1892 and that at least a dozen Populists were in the House and Senate. Now the Democrats had dumped the estimable and right-thinking Mr. Cleveland, whose Administrations differed from the Republicans only on such issues as the amount of protection in the tariff, and had made an unholy alliance with the Populists themselves. With an apostate wealthy businessman like John P. Altgeld, the Illinois Governor who had just pardoned some of the Haymarket Massacre anarchists, drafting the party platform, the Democratic convention had nominated the "wild radical" Bryan on an unsound money program.

II

Free silver! The phrase is one of the great self-deluding economic slogans of American political history. For several decades we have been unblessed with these slogans which are generally born in depressions when men desperately seek panaceas. Of course, slogans persist in times of war and in the making of Presidents, especially in a country drenched with advertising techniques. But one has to go back to Dr. Francis Townsend and his Townsend Plan of "$200 a Month for Everyone Over Sixty," to Father Coughlin and his "Gentile Silver" (a direct mutant of Populism with its silver obsession) and to Huey Long's "Every Man a King" for that touch of rascality — that desire for something for nothing — which Americans seem to delight in when pouncing upon economic nostrums. The power of the phrase was felt even in foreign affairs, forcing the Republicans to take a harder line on Spain in the election of 1896, lest the Democrats ride to victory with the staggering combination of "Free Silver *and* Free Cuba."

Probably every rural schoolboy, especially if he were a son of the Middle Border states, knew more about the silver question than we can hope to learn from the confusing history books. He heard about it at the supper table, at the town meeting and in the church. It was also present in the schools as he learned to declaim the famous "Cross of Gold" speech of the great Boy Orator, William Jennings Bryan. In the 1890's you were either a "Goldbug" or a "Silverbug" or a "Straddlebug" on this Burning Issue and you wore your bug-pin on your heart accordingly. If you didn't quite understand the monetary theory involved, you responded emotionally in relation to your class, region and self-interest. You were either for "free silver" or for "sound money."

Free silver meant the unlimited coinage by the U.S. Mint of all the white metal presented to it by the eager silver-mining capitalists of the Western states who were cynically financing a good deal of the anti-capitalist agitation of their neighbors on the farms. It was the farming class which seethed with discontent in the nineties, spilling over into Populism, America's first great protest movement. Although the farming class was about to inherit a rare cycle of relative stability and prosperity, starting quite accidentally in the age of McKinley itself, in the mid-nineties it was racked with failure and frustration. To get a perspective on the importance of the farming class at this time, consider these statistics. The population of the country was approximately 70 million. Of the 29 million "breadwinners," over 10 million were in agriculture, by far the chief occupational category of Americans even in this great era of industrial revolution and enterprise. There were over 5,700,000 farms in operation (there are less than 3 million now) and 60% of the entire country lived in areas of fewer than 2,500 persons. America was still basically small-town, white and Protestant, especially beyond the North Atlantic and North Central regions. Moreover, the farmer had a venerated place in the hearts of his countrymen. He was the self-sufficient God-fearing, well-read yeoman of virtue and toil, embodying the early Jeffersonian ideals of property and responsibility. His sons and cousins in the cities of big business, finance capitalism and stock exchanges *paid attention* to the farm vote. (The new Populism associated with Senator McGovern's candidacy constitutes quite a different coalition, that of the discontented and alienated throughout the country, with only minor representation in the farm regions. His attacks on the misuse of business power, however, go straight back to the 1890's.)

How did these generally sound and conservative folk who knew the value of a dollar become addicted to free silver? It may seem strange to Americans who understand one economic hazard more thoroughly than any other, inflation, to recognize that what the farmers and the Democrats of 1896 wanted from free silver was exactly that condition.

The farmer had performed prodigious feats between 1860 and 1896. As the frontier expanded west of the Mississippi and north of the Missouri over 400 million new acres yielded to his plow and America's wheatlands became the breadbasket for a good portion of the earth. America's unrestrained, ebullient and unplanned growth, however, was attended by frequent cycles of good times and hard times, of boom and bust in an age of *laissez-faire* economics. Not only had droughts and grasshopper plagues tormented the more arid states but also a sustained period of price reductions, related to overproduction and an inadequate and immobile money supply in this pre-Federal Reserve banking period, made life desperate for hundreds of thousands of farmers. To the extent that Washington was involved in the economy, it was for protective tariffs for manufacturers reflecting a horrified interest in the colonialism by which European powers were satisfying their overproduced markets. Thus the farmer sold his crops for less dollars, paid more for his tariff-protected machinery and monopolized-railroad freight and became convinced he was getting squeezed out of his share of the land of opportunity by the Eastern industrialists and money interests.

Now that farming had become a complicated business itself, requiring extensive investment in land and equipment, the farmer was continually in debt. If he borrowed $1,000 with the intention of paying back the loan with the proceeds of 1,000 bushels of wheat he conceivably would have to come up with 2,000 bushels of wheat for the same $1,000. Every penny that contributed to this price deflation, caused by "sound money" presumably decreed by the scarcity of gold and a limited currency supply, was a thorn in his flesh, creatively raised to his brow by the Prairie Avenger Bryan.

Farm mortgaging was a primitive affair in those days. The government was completely uninvolved, although it had exceeded a good many twentieth century socialist countries with its lavish handout of homesteads to farming pioneers, a scandalous portion of which landed in the hands of speculators and railroads. Mortgages were available only for short-term periods and generally carried ruinous rates of interest reflecting the high risks involved. They were for the most part held by Eastern mortgage companies, known as "loan sharks" by the farmers, who had an active dislike for all financial institutions at the time. As prices fell by half for the products of one-crop wheat and corn farmers in the West and cotton farmers in the South between 1885 and 1890, foreclosures poured upon them. In the South share-cropping generally succeeded farm ownership and by 1880 one-fourth of all American farms were operated by tenants. It was an easy mental transition for the hard-working agriculturist to regard himself as a latter day serf or exploited agrarian peasant without the help of foreign ideology. Actually a case could be made that agriculture in many of the new states served the great Eastern manufacturing states somewhat as colonial India served England, providing cheap raw materials and foodstuffs in exchange for high-priced finished articles, thus producing handsome profits for further industrial expansion.[4] The theoreticians of the Populists, however, needed little inspiration from Marx and Engels in preparing the wild charges of conspiracy with which they would frighten the Eastern Establishment.

To top it all, the severe Panic of 1893, as depressions were known in those days, fell upon the hapless Cleveland in his second term and served as a prelude to the election of 1896. America was afflicted by panics after the Civil War, the more severe ones falling in 1865, 1873-1879, 1884 and 1893. They each ran their course to recovery without government aid, the overall economy gaining great periods of grace from the open frontier, the railroads that crossed the country, the stimulation of new inventions and heavy industry, the ambitions of great enterprisers and the availability of cheap immigrant labor. Since there were no built-in price rigidities arising from inflexible labor contracts, panics were the greatest price deflators of all, accelerating the deflation the farmers detested. By the end of 1893, 642 of the country's banks had closed, one-fourth of its heavy industry was shut down, 22,500 miles of railroads were in the hands of receivers and about two million people were unemployed.

The siren call of inflation through the unlimited coinage of silver attracted many respectable adherents in addition to those on the farm. It found antecedents in Lincoln's financing a portion of the

Civil War with the issuance of paper money called "greenbacks." These greenbacks were used to pay the soldiers and were also accepted as legal tender at face value for the purchase of government bonds. Yet until 1879 they were backed only by the credit of the government and were not redeemable in gold or silver specie any more than the currency we carry in our pocketbooks today. Peter Cooper, a respected New York industrialist and philanthropist, ran for President on the Greenback Party ticket in 1876 and two years later the Greenback-Labor Party coalition sponsored candidates who polled over a million votes from people who wanted greenbacks kept in circulation. Now silver inflation was regarded as less radical than paper money inflation in the great cause of raising prices.

It was the Republican Administration of "Little Ben" Harrison, between the two Cleveland Administrations, that passed the Sherman Silver Purchase Act of 1890. This Act directed the Treasury to buy 4.5 million ounces of silver each month, which was estimated to equal the entire domestic silver production, and to pay for it with Treasury notes redeemable either in gold or silver. The Treasury had no intention of coining the bullion and did all its redeeming in gold, so this Act seemed to serve no one in particular except the silver-miners, although it was passed to placate the voters of the Western states. There was little inflation possible without "cheap money" coming into circulation and cheap money could only arrive from actually coining silver at the old legal ratio of "16 to 1" established in a previous bi-metallic period when Andrew Jackson was President. 16 to 1 meant that a silver dollar would be coined containing 16 times as much silver as there was gold in a gold dollar. Perhaps the piping schoolboy orating the "Cross of Gold" speech is needed here to spell it out but the essence of the matter is that silver was worth only about *half* that amount of gold on the free market in the nineties. Thus the coined silver dollar would be more or less a fifty cents dollar, handy for paying off mortgages and for doubling the price of farm products but a source of shock for bondholders, bankers, foreign investors and other devotees of sound money and low wages. Yet the repeal of the innocuous Silver Purchase Act in 1893, forced through Congress by Cleveland himself as he desperately tried to stem the drain of gold from the Treasury during the panic years, resulted in the most heated passions. "Pitchfork Ben" Tillman, a one-eyed demagogue Populist from South Carolina then running successfully for the Senate, portrayed the typical Populist combination of religion, militancy and black humor by exploding: "When Judas betrayed Christ his heart was not blacker than this scoundrel Cleveland in deceiving the Democracy. . . . He is an old bag of beef and I am going to Washington with a pitchfork and prod him in his old fat ribs." (By 1899 the two antagonists were joined together as Vice Presidents of the Anti-Imperialist League, a strange result of the country's adventures in foreign affairs, no less gaudy than its economic twists and involving silver once again.) Grover Cleveland must have wondered if his difficult second term was worth it all. Dominated by the business conservatives in his party, fresh from four years of money-making with Wall Street lawyers and bankers, he could have only dim visions of the youthful, lusty years in the taverns of Buffalo where he relaxed with the common people. Ironically he might muse that although he was recruited for his second term by industrialists like Henry Villard, a liberal railroad king, because of his sound money instincts as well as his reform image, the party chieftains hedged their bet by giving the Vice Presidency to an outright free silver man, Adlai E. Stevenson of Illinois.

III

The activities of two successful businessmen of the period help bring the business world into focus although these men would be surprised to find themselves matched for any purpose. Henry Villard entered political history in 1891 by persuading Cleveland to run again to serve Villard's frantic need to protect his adopted country and his Northern Pacific railroad against the silver whirlwind. Jacob A. Coxey marched from Massillon, Ohio on Easter Sunday, 1894, his destination Washington. Villard was a Railroad Baron, a talented German emigrant who combined President-making with frequent trips to Germany where he had consulted with Prince von Bismarck himself on American affairs.[5] Coxey, frail and forty, the prosperous owner of a stone quarry near Massillon, appointed himself General of Coxey's Army as he prepared his unemployed soldiers for the march on Washington.

Henry Villard was a New Yorker and an outstanding member of the important German community which formed a large part of the first wave of immigration to America. Prior to 1883, over 95 per cent of America's immigrants came from northern and western Europe. The German citizens were particularly prominent both in the cities and in states like Wisconsin and Missouri. They generally shared a liberal sentiment reflecting the European revolts of 1830 and 1848 which contributed to their arrival in the first place. Villard came to America in 1853 and was a distinguished reporter in the Civil War. When he made his money in railroads he continued this interest by buying control of the New York *Evening Post* and helping to subsidize the *Nation*, both influential Mugwump-reform publications which opposed the war with Spain and the ensuing territorial annexation. He married the daughter of the uncompromising abolitionist editor William Lloyd Garrison, bequeathing her surname to his son Oswald Garrison Villard who edited the *Nation* with distinction until 1933.

Villard gained control of the Northern Pacific in 1881. This was the road that Jay Cooke had over-financed with $100 million of bonds sold at home and abroad after the Civil War, resulting in the great crash of Cooke's banking firm and the Panic of 1873. Villard himself lost control when the Northern Pacific went into bankruptcy in 1883 but regained it in 1889, an experience that made him particularly responsive to the need for financial stability, especially in relation to international finance where gold was the acknowledged standard. Besides owning a fortune in railroad and industrial securities, Villard was also the agent for some leading German banks which had invested heavily in American industry. On their behalf as well as his own, he wanted to make sure that American securities would continue to be payable in gold, not in silver or paper. In his mind an actual crisis condition faced capitalism.

In 1891 he made a tour of his line, which ran through the Populist states, and concluded that a currency crisis and panic were inevitable if the silver movement could not be diverted. Since the Republicans were saddled with Congressman McKinley's Tariff of 1890 which was so unpopular with the masses of voters and since the banking interests were fed up with an Administration that could pass the Silver Purchase Act, campaign funds would dry up and the cold little Harrison was sure to be defeated. The question that rang in his mind was what could be expected from the Democrats with their large number of free silver legislators?

In true Mugwump-reform fashion, aided by a sharp survival instinct, this man who had been an Abolitionist Republican stalwart from the very birth of the party decided to place principle above party and bolt to the Democrats—that is, the Gold Democrats of Grover Cleveland. In his memoirs the journalist turned businessman states the case for what was good for the Northern Pacific as being good for the country:

> . . . there was one way of saving the country and the road from a ruinous catastrophe, viz., by the earliest possible repeal of the Silver Purchase Act, and the election of a President in 1892 who could be relied on to exert executive influence for the repeal of the Act as well as for the establishment of the gold standard.

With the dapper William C. Whitney, a regular Democrat of great wealth and political genius, taking over as party boss and campaign manager, the generously funded Cleveland won the nomination, dissuaded the Silver Democrats from splitting the party and gained a comfortable 400,000 plurality over Harrison. August Belmont, another magnate in the regular Democrat fold, brought in ample funds from Wall Street. The taming of the Democrats was understood to be good strategy throughout the business world as Cleveland assumed his dismal tasks. They would include repeal of the Silver Purchase Act, several humiliating pilgrimages to J. P. Morgan & Co. to bail out the gold drain on the Treasury through the *private* sale of government bonds and the harsh action of calling out government troops to subdue the Pullman strikers in 1894. (Henry Villard's liberal *Nation* on the last item darkly hinted that the government might have to cope with the insurrection of the railway workers "in the old-fashioned way . . . to shoot them down."[6]) To top it all, Cleveland would be faced in this term with some major foreign policy decisions, including Cuba. In these his strength of character brought him some historical redemption.

One of Villard's suppliers, Andrew Carnegie, the most successful industrialist in America, also breathed easier with Cleveland's election. The canny Scotsman, bearing lightly on his conscience his complicity in the shooting of his Homestead steelworkers by Pinkerton strikebreakers only a few months earlier, was anxious to continue his travels abroad where he lived in a castle and deprecated the Europeans for their lack of democracy. "We have nothing to fear," chortled Carnegie, who had stayed in the Republican party but gave only a paltry $10,000 to Harrison's campaign, "Cleveland is a pretty good fellow." Then, correctly viewing Cleveland as a straw man even on tariff reductions, he added: "People will now think the Protected Manufacturers are attended to and will stop agitating. Off to Venice tomorrow."[7]

Meanwhile the Populists turned in a million votes for their third party candidate, General James B. Weaver, reminding everyone that silver was down but not out.

IV

Generals were great successes as politicians following the Civil War. Grant had two terms. Hayes was a Union General and so were Garfield and Harrison. Jacob S. Coxey understandably became General of the army of the unemployed. There is something appealing about this derby-hatted man with his spectacles and drooping mustache, in coat and vest, umbrella in hand, leading his raggle-taggle army in the time-honored tactic of petition and grievance on to the quaking Capitol of the discontented nation.

The winter of 1894 had been one of extreme suffering throughout the country. Tens of thousands of unemployed had banded together in small groups to forage for food and shelter, tramps on the move as in all depressions. Ominously there came reports of "industrial armies" and "agrarian anarchists" planning to march on Washington under the strange device of Coxey's Army. Now with the thaw of Spring, out of work miners, lumbermen and farm hands from the far West commandeered trains, threw off uncooperative crews and made their way across the continent, a sad turnabout for the frontier spirit. James Hill, president of the Great Northern, wrote urgently to Cleveland, whose campaigns he had supported in the same manner as Henry Villard, warning of the breakdown of law and order and estimating that at least 25,000 persons "of the worst class—men who do not want to work for a living" were converging on the Capitol.[8] These sub-armies, led by men with names such as Kelly and Fry of California and Fitzgerald of Massachusetts, were indeed on their way to a rendezvous with Coxey, but in pitifully small numbers.

What kind of a man was Coxey, who frightened a nation? He was a money crank, a gentle, patriotic and God-stricken businessman who should not have frightened anyone. Children and dogs understood this and applauded the exotic army, out of step behind the American flag.

Coxey was a Greenbacker, not yet a Populist or free silver man, who believed that "there's nothing wrong with this country that money can't cure." In his way he was quite a remarkable economist, in a day when most professional economists were ministers teaching their subject as a branch of moral philosophy, archaic and erroneous, in the universities. His plan was in essence a vast public works project to end the depression, involving hiring the unemployed at $1.50 per day — subsistence income at the time — to build roads throughout the country. Intelligent and able, he had issued pamphlets at his own expense since 1892. The bill would have the national government issue $500 million of paper money to states, counties and municipalities which in turn would issue their bonds to the government as security for the government loans. As the roads were built they would provide employment and improved transportation. The depression would be ended as the wages flowed through the economy and stimulated production. Unable to comprehend a permanent national debt, especially since no income tax was then available from individuals or corporations to extinguish it, Coxey also provided for the states to pay back the loans over a period of twenty-five years. Thus even the suspect greenbacks could be retired after serving their useful purpose. Since he hated the Eastern money interests and their gold obsession, Coxey stipulated that the government loans were to be non-interest bearing, a fatal flaw for attracting respectable support assuming any flaw was needed.

A $500 million addition to national spending for a country whose total federal revenues (all from tariffs, customs and the like) averaged $300 million during Cleveland's second term, with net expenditures kept nicely in balance regardless of the depression, was beneath notice of serious people in 1894. Actually the national debt was still below $1 billion at the time, in spite of Cleveland's frantic bond issues to buy more gold for the Treasury. There was no point in hoping that Coxey's fellow Ohioans, such as Senator Foraker, the railroad Senator, or Governor McKinley, recently defeated for re-election to Congress, would support his heresy. It was too much even for Senator Peffer of Kansas, the bearded-to-the-waist Populist apparition whom the *Nation* noted in 1891 was elected as a "revolutionary" dedicated to large distributions of money by the government to the people.[9] But Peffer agreed to introduce the Good Roads Bill in Congress, explaining that while he did not favor its passage, he thought it merited consideration.[10] As for public works projects for the unemployed, stronger minds than Peffer's boggled at the thought. Back in 1887, Cleveland had vetoed a $10,000 appropriation by Congress for drought-stricken farmers. "Though the people support the government," he said, "the government should not support the people."

So Coxey, successful quarry-owner and prophetic Keynesian, decided to meet the crisis of government inaction by direct action of his own. He would lead a non-violent protest march to Washington, a "petition in boots," and here some of the comedy enters the picture. Carl Browne, a radical from Iowa, emerged as publicist and second in command and soon colored the movement with the greasepaint of his own carnival personality. Once a vendor of Kickapoo Indian Blood remedy, Browne wore a ten-gallon hat and a buckskin jacket with silver buttons inscribed "FREE." Having sold the old-time religion as well, he named the movement "the Commonweal of Christ," mounted a white horse and reincarnated himself as the "Cerebellum of Christ." Under such auspices, a ragtail assortment of odds and ends rallied to the banner, including a Pittsburgh astrologer, a man known as the Great Unknown, a veiled lady, a Cherokee Indian who ate only oatmeal and a trumpet player named Windy Oliver. Perhaps Coxey was more crafty than naive, with a businessman's instinct for the lurid advertising of his day, since the reporters flocked to the scene and bathed it in good-humored publicity. Finally the march set forth from Massillon, a few hundred men led by a flag-carrying Negro and a seven-piece band playing the Commonweal hymn:

We're marching on Washington
To right the nation's wrongs.

Standard-bearers carried banners with the motto: "Peace on Earth, Good Will to Men. But Death to Interest on Bonds." Coxey himself rode in a buggy with Mrs. Coxey, who bore in her arms their infant, named with rare commitment Legal Tender Coxey.

His marchers were "patriots, not bummers," Coxey told the press, as the Commonwealers made their way through Pennsylvania and Maryland, enlisting considerable sympathy and handouts along the way. By now the marchers numbered about five hundred and a nervous Congress went into a special session on April 18 to discuss Coxey's Army. Editorialists saw the incendiary behind the clown and advocated "strict and stern repression" to protect the Capitol and its lawmakers. Wealthy persons were reported leaving Washington with their families, unsure of the resolve of the government to meet the threat with adequate force. In New York, Bishop Greer denounced Coxey in a fiery sermon as "an enemy of the people," perhaps having in mind the title of the recent play by Ibsen, an author equally unpopular with many turn-of-the-century conservative clergy. The New York *Evening Post* declared Coxey an imbecile.[11]

Now the army was at the Capitol gates and Congress continued its debate. Receive the petition in a friendly fashion, urged the newly elected Populists. Never, thundered the eminent Senator Hoar of Massachusetts, traditional home of dissenters, it would mean 65 million people dictated to by a minority of five or ten thousand. Meanwhile, Attorney General Olney, also from Massachusetts and one of the harsher men who have held that office, reported to Cleveland on the revelations of the two spies he had planted in the army as far back as Massillon. Only the prompt use of U. S. Marshals and regular troops in the Western states, he advised, had prevented the movement from taking over more trains and "matching the march of the Paris mob on Versailles."[12] The routing of the Commonwealers was a warm-up for Olney's strategy in subduing the Pullman strikers a few months later. Here federal troops would be deployed, without being requested by the uncooperative Governor Altgeld or by the courts. They were pressed into use by Olney on the novel grounds that the strikers were in conspiracy to restrain trade, violating the new Sherman Antitrust Act of 1890 which supposedly had been passed to limit business monopolies, not trade unions. Protect us from friends in the White House, some far-seeing business leaders might have mused, although the thoughts of businessmen, like most others, were limited by the context of the times.

Meanwhile Coxey had negotiated with the police authorities of the District of Columbia for a permit to parade peacefully to the Capitol where he would present his petition to Congress for the Good Roads Bill. The permission was refused. Nevertheless on May 1, Coxey's Army marched up Pennsylvania Avenue to the Capitol, led by bagpipers who put the estimated 20,000 spectators in a friendly frame of mind. This was hardly a May Day parade of the European type, led as it was by the mild bourgeois parents and infant in the buggy and by Coxey's seventeen year old daughter on a cream-colored horse as the goddess of peace. Another goddess of peace, an actress from Philadelphia, draped herself in the American flag. Since the country was a few years away from its furious debate over the possibility of war with Spain, the emphasis on peace was for its own sake.

On reaching the Capitol area, Coxey found himself barred by massed police who refused him permission to read his written protest. Coxey tipped his hat to the police commander and protested the orders. Then handing the statement to newsmen he and some followers hurried towards the Capitol steps. Mounted police charged them and a minor riot ensued. In five minutes it was all over but at least fifty marchers and spectators had been injured. Coxey and a few of his lieutenants were each fined five dollars and sentenced to twenty days in jail, charged with walking on the grass of the Capitol. Without its General, the army dissolved along with the nation's fears of insurrection. Coxey returned to Ohio, where he ran unsuccessfully for Congress on the Populist ticket. In 1932 he was the Farmer-Labor party candidate for President. He died in 1951, age ninety-seven. There are too few Don Quixotes in the American tradition. Hopefully he marches now with Yankee Doodle, Johnny Appleseed and Rip Van Winkle, similar blithe spirits invented by a nation with too low a tolerance for live eccentrics.

V

Coxey's vindication came with the New Deal, when deficit financing, public works and the denunciation of bankers all became official government policy. In addition, the establishment of the Federal Reserve System in 1913 was a recognition of Coxey's instinct for an expanding and mobile money supply. Finally the preference for some creeping inflation against the stagnation of deflated prices has become firmly established in economic theory for modern industrial states.

In his Army days, Coxey had still other significance. He illustrates, for example, that the business class possessed strong rival divisions of its own. The independent businessman did not identify his interests with those of the industrial magnates, much as he sometimes admired them. He was just as likely to be more radical, especially on the inflation or tariff issues, or more conservative in relation to labor. The smaller industrialists generally feared the size of the "trusts," a convenient description for giants in any industry. They suspected that big business would not only eliminate them but would also make an accommodation with big labor against their interests. The soon to be founded National Association of Manufacturers excluded big business at the start and was violently anti-labor.[13]

The magnates, on the other hand, learning their lessons from the bloody strikes of Coxey's era, now helped establish and support the National Civic Federation where they sat down with conservative labor leaders like Samuel Gompers to promote labor-management peace. The point is that in spite of Populist rhetoric about class antagonism, the business class had an extensive pluralism of its own, so that even Bryan would bid for business support in his quest for the Presidency. Labor itself, battered and broken, disowned the European pattern of class conflict, resulting in another curious surprise for the election of 1896. Labor simply did not fall into the open arms of the Democrat-Populists, preferring to get at reform and recognition under more respectable auspices. The Populists returned the snobbery, uncovering a strain of conservatism that took a leery view of labor's uprising. There were other Populist contradictions, such as a mean streak of nativism and anti-Semitism.

One further tune from Coxey's distant drummer deserves notice. The march he led was a symbolic turn to Washington, an open request for government intervention in economic affairs against all the conventional wisdom of the times. As such it marked a major change in the American farmer's creed as expressed in the Populist program. Heretofore the farmer was the rugged individualist nourished on the Lockean philosophy of natural rights and non-interference which presently served the business forces so well in all three branches of government. Now the agrarian folk had a different vision, strangled as they thought themselves to be by a railroad web and money kings beyond the concept of Locke. In brief where they formerly wanted controls, if any, limited to the rights of states, they now turned to Washington to redress their economic disadvantages. It is a nice illustration of the great capacity of American institutions, business and agricultural alike, to compromise with their established myths, from free silver to free enterprise, as the need arises.

The Populist platform as adopted at its historic convention in Omaha in 1892, seems mild enough from the safe vantage point of history. The central demand and emotional rallying point was for currency expansion through free silver. Then came such planks as government ownership of railroads, telegraph and telephone systems, a graduated income tax, a government warehouse for financing and storing perishable crops, direct election of Senators, the initiative and the referendum and postal savings banks. Aside from the startling emphasis on economic reforms as the responsibility of national government, the real threat of the Populists arose from the wild oratory of their colorful leaders. It was this side of Populism that frightened the business community and caused it to write off the Democratic party after it nominated Bryan in 1896.

There was Ignatius Donnelly, a silvery-bearded, cracked spellbinder from Minnesota who emphasized the conspiracy syndrome that has degraded American politics over the years. He actually wrote into the 1892 platform, on the subject of Eastern bankers: "A vast conspiracy against mankind has been organized. . . . If not met and overthrown at once it forebodes terrible social convulsions, the destruction of civilization, or the establishment of an absolute despotism." If names alone could frighten, there was "Sockless Jerry" Simpson of Kansas and "Pitchfork Ben" Tillman of South Carolina to rant at the business interests and draw headlines in the spectacular newspapers. But who would expect a lady to shout: "What you farmers need is to raise less corn and more *Hell!*"? It was Mrs. Mary E. Lease, the Kansas Pythoness, statuesque and shrill, outdoing Donnelly at the Omaha convention:

> Wall Street owns the country. . . . The great common people of this country are slaves, and monopoly is the master. The West and South are bound and prostrate before the manufacturing East. . . . The parties lie to us and the political speakers mislead us. . . . The politicians said

> we suffered from overproduction when 10,000 little children, so statistics tell us, starve to death every year in the United States, and over 100,000 shop girls in New York are forced to sell their virtue for the bread their niggardly wages deny them!

This may have been the time of President Harrison but it was also the time of Queen Victoria and such statistics must have had considerable impact. By 1897, young William Randolph Hearst was playing a similar game in his New York *Journal*, as he cynically tried to create a circulation-building war with Spain. One Evangeline Cisneros, a Cuban girl, had been jailed for defending her honor against a Spanish officer. One million American women, including the President's mother, had signed a *Journal* petition for her release, the paper claimed. Finally a Hearst reporter, who had probably made up the story in the first place, announced he had aided her to escape from jail.[14]

VI

In such an atmosphere of discontent and depression, of poverty amidst plenty, of failed national dreams, of farmers and small businessmen losing their status and security before the forces of industrialism, William Jennings Bryan appeared at the Chicago convention of 1896.

Of all the great convention speeches, surely Bryan's "Cross of Gold" is the one lovers of American history find most fascinating. Who would not want to be one of the immortal 20,000 who heard it? Imagine the young Nebraskan ex-Congressman, only thirty-six, planning to capture the nomination of one of the great parties by applying his magnetic voice to the dubious merits of free silver. Only three weeks before he had attended the Republican convention in St. Louis accredited as journalist-editor of the Omaha *World-Herald*. There he had happily observed thirty-four delegates led by Senator Teller of Colorado, a silver-mining millionaire, walk out when gold was nailed to the platform. Now the strategy was to fuse the Democrats, Populists and dissident Republicans into a mighty uprising of the common people that would sweep him into the White House. In his *Memoirs*, he tells how he and his wife wrote thousands of letters to delegates beforehand and how carefully he nursed the striking metaphor with which the speech would end.

Since the speech, like Bryan's intellect, was more form than substance, more heart than brain, one might as well enjoy the sensual aspects of the great oration as it has been passed down to us. First, the sight of the man himself, muscular and solid, bounding to the rostrum on a hot summer afternoon. Those who saw the youthful Bryan tell about his presence, the impression of suppressed power, the mane of black hair, the mien of the Roman Senator. He was as typical an American as his times could produce, nourished by the steel engravings of the great political heroes and debaters who stared down on him from the walls of country schools — Jefferson, Webster, Lincoln, Henry Clay. He was the humble, small-town lawyer so gifted with uncommon eloquence that his flaw, lack of profundity, hardly showed. In his photographs, the man looks supremely intelligent with frontal lobes generously outsized, as though holding back wonderful thoughts for the multitudes. Though practically nothing Bryan wrote or said has passed the test of time, Vachel Lindsay is endlessly quoted in the history books for his Bryan of sight and sound:

> Prairie avenger, mountain lion,
> Bryan, Bryan, Bryan, Bryan,
> Gigantic troubadour, speaking like a siege gun,
> Smashing Plymouth Rock with his boulders from the
>   West.

Actually the voice was a splendid baritone, not a siege gun. And Bryan was more Puritan than the New Englanders, caught up as they were with their stocks and bonds and children working long hours on the looms. Bryan was embarrassingly fundamentalist, believing to the end in the rock of ages rather than the age of rocks, but from his Bible he derived integrity and the King James English of the speeches which he at least wrote himself. It is tempting to ridicule "The Great Commoner," thrice rejected by the American people for the Presidency, but Henry Steele Commager reminds us that "he had an understanding of the psychology of his own kind that has never been surpassed and inspired such devotion in them as few other American statesmen have been able to command."[15]

The delegates hushed as the voice lifted them above sordid politics:

> The humblest citizen in all the land, when clad in the armor of a righteous cause, is stronger than all the hosts of error. I come to speak to you in defense of a cause as holy as the cause of liberty — the cause of humanity.

Repeatedly he glorifies the frontiersman, the hardy pioneer who made the desert blossom as the rose, "the people who rear their children next to Nature's heart, where they can mingle their voices with the voices of the birds. . . ." But the voice saves its big tones for the economic issues, for this is after all a speech about money, although the word itself is carefully avoided. A bold idea is launched. Is the following a socialistic demand for a redistribution of wealth, or a forerunner of Herbert Hoover's "trickle-down" theory of recovery as against Keynesian-New Deal "purchasing power"?

> There are those who believe that, if you will only legislate to make the well-to-do prosperous, their prosperity will leak through on those below. The Democratic idea, however, is that if you legislate to make the masses prosperous, their prosperity will find its way up through every class which rests upon them.

Of course it was neither, just the vague promises of a politician, although sincerely felt. Bryan was completely shallow as an economist in the sense that he was unable to frame a reasonable program for the injustices he so accurately sensed. On the other hand, he was no socialist as the Republicans would charge. To the extent that he was against business, he was against big business and the big capitalists. It was they who had merged business with government, demeaning the stalwart farmers, country lawyers, small shopkeepers and artisans with their trusts, their dear money and their gaudy consumption. This was the Populist distinction between the producing, small businessmen and farmers and the nonproducing financiers, speculators, and monopolists. It was a distinction that also beguiled the mind of a very subtle professional economist, Thorstein Veblen, working away that year in founder John D. Rockefeller's nearby University of Chicago on *The Theory of the Leisure Class*.[16]

The voice then made a bid for business sympathy, remembering that an American President can be elected only by a wide range of voters. Turning to the Gold Democrats, whose preceding speakers had accused the Silverites of "disturbing business," it said:

> . . . we reply that you have disturbed our business interests by your course. We say to you that you have made the definition of a business man too limited in its application. The man who is employed for wages is as much a business man as his employer, the attorney in a country town is as much a business man as the corporation counsel in a great metropolis; the merchant at the cross-roads store is as much a business man as the merchant of New York; the farmer who goes forth in the morning and toils all day — who begins in the spring and toils all summer — and who by the application of brain and muscle to the natural resources of the country creates wealth, is as much a business man as the man who goes upon the board of trade and bets upon the price of grain; the miners who go down a thousand feet into the earth . . . and bring forth from their hiding places the precious metals to be poured into the channels of trade are as much business men as the few financial magnates who, in a back room, corner the money of the world. We come to speak for this broader class of business men.

From such irrelevant reasoning, the masterful voice turned to the orator's art of wave and breaker, of crash and cymbal:

> We have petitioned, and our petitions have been scorned;

> we have entreatied and our entreaties have been disregarded; we have begged, and they have mocked when our calamity came. We beg no longer; we entreat no more; we petition no more. . . . *We defy them!*

According to reports, the defy was thrown to the audience by the speaker's entire body in a movement of superb disdain. There must have been cheers to the rafters and then a portentous silence, for what wonderful sounds would follow? This was the still moment Bryan had chosen for his great peroration, the inspired crucifixion scene. To understand it, one must recognize that Bryan now throws in England as another enemy to fight. In doing so, he was able to make silver the standard of patriotism, gold of disloyalty. This ultranationalism, or "jingoism," as we will discuss later, weaves the tale of free silver and free Cuba into one context. The Populists, contrary to the usual posture of reformists, were blatant nationalists who for the most part irresponsibly supported the Cuban adventure and the Philippine annexation. England, home of international bankers, was also the traditional enemy of the United States, having oppressed the infant republic in 1776, burnt the White House in the War of 1812 and aided the Confederacy in the Civil War. Within the last year, Cleveland and his overbearing Secretary of State, Richard Olney, recently promoted from Attorney General, had pulled the lion's tail with alarming brinksmanship. The issue was over the boundary between Venezuela and British Guiana. Taking the side of Venezuela on the grounds of the Monroe Doctrine, the United States demanded the dispute be submitted to arbitration under American auspices. Lord Salisbury haughtily took four months to answer for his Queen, whereupon Cleveland, seeking some political capital for his disastrous second term, all but threatened war. Salisbury sensibly retreated, having enough troubles with Germany and South Africa. Cleveland won great applause, especially from the noisy foreign policy expansionists. Midwest America never fully recovered from its Anglophobia, which Bryan exploited. The Republicans in St. Louis had talked of a bi-metallic conference with England, knowing that it would fail, and Bryan's preceding speakers had just suggested it for the Democrats. With this in mind, let the voice continue:

> If they dare to come out in the open . . . we will fight them to the uttermost. Having behind us the producing masses of this nation and the world, supported by the commercial interests, the laboring interests, and the toilers everywhere, we will answer their demand for a gold standard by saying to them: *You shall not press down upon the brow of labor this crown of thorns, you shall not crucify mankind upon a cross of gold.*

Pandemonium. It was Bryan all the way on the fifth ballot. Still, after the speech, Governor Altgeld had turned to Clarence Darrow, a young Chicago attorney who had defended Eugene Debs, the jailed Pullman strike leader, to ask, "What *did* he say, anyway?"[17]

VII

While the Bryanites saw in England the hand of gold conspiracy, the opposition turned to France to seek an adequate explanation for the stunning revolution in Chicago. Senator Vilas of Wisconsin, a Cleveland Cabinet Officer, asked the Chicago convention if "Perhaps somewhere in this country there lurks a Robespierre, a Danton, a Marat?" Soon the Republicans were specific about the new Jacobins. They were Bryan, Altgeld and Debs, with Tillman and his pitchfork a suitable alternate, offering America the prospect of the Revolutionary Terrors of 1793. *Harper's Weekly* was adept at this comparison and for good measure evoked Roman treachery as well. One of its typical cartoons shows Altgeld as a wild-eyed Catiline bearing the label "Repudiation" (meaning the repudiation of gold as the back-up for currency) and carrying the torch of "Anarchy." The mask he holds in front of his face is the silver-coined image of Bryan. Theodore Roosevelt, still in his thirties and winning his spurs in Republican politics, made a speech in Chicago in which he termed the upright Altgeld as "one who condones and encourages the most infamous of murders . . . and would substitute for the government of Washington and Lincoln . . . a red government of lawlessness and dishonesty as fantastic and vicious as the Paris Commune. . . ."[18] It was natural that the approaching reign of terror be discussed in the Union League Clubs, which had been formed in the Civil War to aid soldier relief and recruit volunteers. Now they had become Republican establishment clubs in major cities. In the Cleveland club, Mark Hanna puffed on his cigar and snorted: "There won't be a revolution. You're just a lot of damn fools."[19]

Bluff, outspoken, tough-minded, tolerant Mark Hanna. In the scales of history, he measures up as an admirable man, if not a superior man, among the business personalities of his times. Not a baron, he was still a captain of industry, building up a Great Lakes complex of coal and iron ore, merchant fleets, banking and street railways employing 6,000 men with whom he never lost touch. A sensitive man who keenly felt the vicious newspaper attacks on "Dollar Mark" Hanna, he might enjoy the irony that the same newspapers, if surviving, daily quote Hanna Mining on the New York Stock Exchange pages. Not an intellectual, he loved Shakespeare, leading to ownership of the Cleveland opera house and a willing acceptance of the role of Warwick to the man he made President. An unabashed believer in business prosperity as the prime role of government, of combinations and size and protective tariffs as having merit in an age of cutthroat industrialism, he saw Bryan's nomination as a crisis for the country. A drive for power, coupled with an affection for McKinley, inspired Mark Hanna to meet this crisis by creating a "steamroller" campaign such as the country had never seen and thereafter could never escape. Because he was a complex businessman, something of a heretic among his fellow capitalists as well as a man who would flaunt public opinion by denouncing the proposed war with Spain, Mark Hanna is our guide to the election of 1896.

Hanna grew up in Cleveland with John D. Rockefeller, whom he recalled as a man "mad about money, but sane in other things." He married into the prosperous Rhodes family and built the Rhodes business into his own flourishing enterprise. His brother-in-law was the distinguished historian James Ford Rhodes, whose history of the period includes personal insight into Hanna's character. With a fortune of six million hard, deflated dollars to his name, Mark Hanna at age fifty-seven decided in 1895 to retire from active business and become a President-maker. To this effort he devoted all the relentless drive he had shown in business, reinforced by a complete belief in his product, William B. McKinley. He had first met McKinley years before when the young ex-Major obtained freedom for a group of strikers in one of Hanna's plants who had been given prison sentences for rioting. Always tolerant about labor's aspirations to combine in the form of unions, just as business combined to stabilize its fortunes, Hanna was ahead of his times and scornful of reactionary magnates. When George Pullman refused to arbitrate the great national strike of 1894, Hanna announced: "A man who doesn't meet his men half-way is a God-damn fool!" The words reached Pullman, but Hanna knew his man and still succeeded in getting a campaign contribution from him in 1896. Later Hanna served as President of the National Civic Federation, a labor-management group, and was emissary for President Roosevelt in forcing recalcitrant mine operators to submit to T.R.'s demands for arbitration as T.R. enlarged the scope of the Presidency beyond the world of Cleveland and McKinley.

Since McKinley, something of a statue in search of a pedestal (in William Allen White's estimation), had a creditable pro-labor record in Ohio politics, Mark Hanna's sympathy for him is understandable. His feelings were actually highly personal: "I love that man," he once said, "he is the best man I have ever known."

His love extended to bailing out his candidate from potential bankruptcy. The depression that sent Coxey's Army from Massillon to Washington reached into high places as well as low, and Governor McKinley found himself unable to make good on $130,000 of notes previously endorsed for a ruined business associate. This was on the eve of McKinley's bid for re-election as Governor in 1893, an essential step towards becoming the next soldier-Republican President from the key state of Ohio. Mark Hanna took charge and arranged a secret syndicate of compassionate millionaires to pay off the debts, including Hanna, Myron T. Herrick, John Hay, Andrew Carnegie, Henry Frick, Philander C. Knox, Charles Taft and Judge William Day, a group producing several future Cabinet members and ambassadors.[20] The story is that McKinley was not allowed to know the names of his benefactors. Even more curious is why the Bryan forces, including William Randolph Hearst and his sleuths, could not uncover such a bombshell and perhaps change the course of history.

Having preserved his investment and anticipated a return to power of the party of business in 1896, Hanna paraded his reelected Governor up and down the country at his own expense. Long before the party conventions of 1896, Hanna had widely advertised his candidate on billboards and barns as "The Advance Agent of Prosperity," on the sound marketing principle of giving the people what they want. But candidates are elected by a majority of party delegates and Mark Hanna was not counting on the capitulation of the established regional Republican bosses in the East, powerful chieftains like "Easy Boss" Platt in New York and Matt Quay in Philadelphia. Accordingly Hanna moved to Thomasville, Georgia at the beginning of 1895.

There in his winter home, with the Governor paying him an extended visit, Hanna went about the business of securing the more than 200 Republican delegates from the Solid Democratic South. These gentlemen, including a large number of Negroes, represented something like the "rotten boroughs" of England. They were noticed only at election time and never were they so generously and prematurely canvassed as by Hanna.

Viewing Hanna's activity in the South with stubborn aloofness was Thomas B. Reed, Congressman from Maine and former Speaker of the House. Far superior to McKinley in intellect and vision, he saw his chances for the nomination vanishing under Hanna's steamroller. Reed was one of the most attractive statesmen in American history, leaving a record for political courage of the type that John F. Kennedy described among Senators in *Profiles of Courage.* In Reed's case, these instances included a prodigious stand against the movement towards war with Spain after McKinley was elected and Reed became Speaker once again. The stand for conscience continued through opposition to the Administration over the annexation of Hawaii and the Philippines, whereupon Reed refused to run again for the House he had dominated so long. "They were for me until the buying started," Reed complained of Hanna's Southern strategy. To Roosevelt, who was backing Reed's candidacy as the best gold standard man available at the time, the disillusioned candidate wrote: "In a word, my dear boy, I am tired of this thing and want to be sure that my debts won't have to be paid by a syndicate (a reference to McKinley) . . . moreover, the receding grapes seem to ooze with acid and the whole thing is a farce."[21] Ironically, had Hanna chosen to back Reed instead of McKinley, the war with Spain, which Hanna opposed, almost certainly would not have been fought. But Reed was too cynical, witty and self-righteous to become the businessman's candidate. When another hopeful declared in the House that he would rather be right than President, Reed assured him he would never be either. Of Hanna's McKinley, he quipped: "He has no more backbone than a chocolate eclair."

It is only fair, then, to show Hanna's flaws as well as his virtues. Cynical about the power of money as Reed was about the weaknesses of men, Hanna was a discreet briber of city councils for traction franchises and of delegates for political favors. To his credit, his conduct was superior measured against the standards of the times and his hypocrisy quotient almost non-existent. As a result of the latter, he has on record some startling statements, such as the time he remarked that "all questions of government in a democracy are questions of money."[22] The businessman of today, owing allegiance to conflicting claims of maximized profits, social responsibility, the nation and his alienated sons, to name a few, must pause with astonishment at the robust self-esteem with which Mark Hanna and his class viewed themselves. How incredible to think that in the 1880's Mark Hanna organized the Business Men's Republican Club. It was established so that Cleveland capitalists could confine their prestige to one party and have a good time in the process, such as torchlight parades of businessmen which Hanna led himself.[23] Next consider the climax of the McKinley campaign in New

York on October 31, 1896. A parade of 150,000 Sound Money Republicans saw trade associations marching in formation, their banners identifying them as lawyers, railroad officials and, according to the New York *World* of the next day, stockbrokers and clerks who passed before the Union League Club cheering and shouting: "We want Morgan!" It is inconceivable that Wall Streeters would parade for any cause today, unless protected by their new friends, the hard-hats. At any rate, Mark Hanna was the epitome of a business type now as prehistoric as the imperious Morgan and the Robber Barons themselves. Norman Hapgood, a contemporary of Hanna's, observed in 1920: "Mark Hanna's era marked a climax in the easy defiance by the strong. I well remember the charming bulldog manner in which Hanna took up the defence of unlimited monopoly. . . . It was a note that can never be sounded quite so fearlessly again."[24] Like Churchill, Hanna represented the end of an era.

VIII

Some students of politics see the election of 1896 as a duel between Bryan and Hanna rather than between Bryan and McKinley. Certainly Hanna, now the Chairman of the Republican National Committee, was a born strategist, working hand in glove with the cautious McKinley, to whom he delivered the nomination on the first ballot. There was no sense in trying to match Bryan's stupendous itinerary. The Boy Orator carried the tireless voice over 18,000 miles, where it made 600 speeches before at least five million listeners in three months. McKinley was assigned a "front porch" campaign, receiving with dignity thousands of organized delegations travelling below cost on the friendly railroads to Canton, Ohio, where they heard platitudes about the return of prosperity and sound money. "What we want . . . is a return to the good times of years ago. We want good prices and good wages, and when we have them we want them to be paid in good money . . . in dollars worth one hundred cents each," they were told. To this would be added a sober thought bound to strike home in a basically conservative nation, rich or poor. "In America we spurn all class distinctions. We are all equal citizens and equal in privilege and prosperity."

With McKinley calm and cool on the front porch, Hanna fired at Bryan the guns of propaganda, an inundation of printed material, advertising, posters and banners beyond imagination for Presidential campaigns. Herbert Croly, Hanna's admiring biographer, and Herman Kohlsaat, a Chicago publisher who was a member of McKinley's inner circle, have described this flood of "educational material" in detail. Over 120 million copies of 275 pamphlets, printed in English, Italian, German, Swedish, Polish, Yiddish, Greek and other languages were distributed. Speeches of McKinley supporters poured forth in the millions. Newspaper mats and stories flooded the press, along with learned threats about the effects of inflation from the famed academic economist at the University of Chicago, J. Laurence Laughlin. Speakers' bureaus were organized with the business efficiency of a Rockefeller, sending out firebrands like Theodore Roosevelt and ministers like Dr. Parkhurst to raise the cry of anarchy. The capitalist class rushed to the barricades with admirable vigor, perhaps victimized by its own propaganda, for Bryan's obsession with free silver was enough to defeat him in itself. Mark Hanna was trusted as a man who would not waste political contributions in overhead or careless bookkeeping. He turned fund-raising into a systematic assessment, for example, a levy of one-quarter of one per cent of capital was requested from banks and trust companies. Moreover it was well known that he was contributing a substantial fortune of his own to the cause. The war chest ended up with so much money that Hanna had to stop taking it. No one knows for sure how much was raised. It was somewhere between $5 million and $10 million but at least ten times as much as the Bryan forces spent.

The *coup de grâce* for Bryan was something more sinister, a whispering campaign that Hanna did not authorize but which he did not hinder. Toward the end of September, when reports had Bryan in the lead, employers used the type of subtle coercion that lawmakers have only recently learned to outlaw in labor and civil rights legislation. Large orders were given to manufacturers and shipbuilders with the publicized proviso that they would be cancelled if Bryan were elected. Mortgage agents from the great Eastern insurance companies informed farmers that mortgages would be renewed at longer terms and lower rates if McKinley were elected. Railroads, the largest industrial employer in America, enclosed threats in payroll envelopes about what would happen if Bryan won. Some banks added clauses requiring payment in gold to their promissory notes. The movement rose to a pitch as Election Day approached for the job-hungry nation. "Men, vote as you please," was a typical message across the country, "but if Bryan is elected tomorrow the whistle will not blow." The Democratic National Committee Chairman howled. Hanna blandly denied the accusations as absurd. Bryan took note of the intimidation and advised workmen to conceal their intentions, even march in Republican parades if necessary, but vote Democratic. Senator Teller, of Colorado, representing the mining interests who were the mainstay of Bryan's treasury, was disheartened. "Boys, I am afraid this beats us," he was quoted in the New York *World*, "If I were a working man and had nothing but my job, I am afraid when I came to vote I would think of Mollie and the babies."

Was the democratic process subverted when Bryan won only 176 out of 447 electoral votes? Probably not. Bryan's style was made to order for speaking from the back of a train, under the stars, and he reached more Americans in person than any previous candidate. A counter-offensive equal to Hanna's expenditures would not have worked and would have affected his underdog image. Other candidates have won with the nation's press and vested interests vilifying them. Besides, Bryan had many factors in his favor. The country was in the midst of a depression to be exceeded only by the 1930's, a perfect situation for the party with a new economic program. As far as pamphlets are concerned, a most extraordinary pamphlet by William Hope Harvey, entitled *Coin's Financial School*, literally swept the country, giving Silverites just enough economic double-talk to make the money issue a credible mania. Harvey named himself "Coin" Harvey, perhaps in touching tribute to little Legal Tender Coxey. As Coin Harvey, he engaged in fictitious dialogues with famous Goldbugs ranging from Lyman J. Gage, President of the First National Bank of Chicago, to the humorless J. Laurence Laughlin, who was infuriated at the rousing verbal defeats Coin Harvey administered to him and the others in the 155 page pamphlet. Coin Harvey was the Tom Paine of the free silver movement and his *Coin's Financial School* singed the brains of the silver men of 1896 as *Common Sense* did those of the minutemen of 1776. Financed by Bryan's silver-mining lobbies, at least one million copies were sold or given away.

In the end one must conclude that Bryan lost essentially because the city laborer, even the unemployed city laborer, believed in the Mark Hannas and McKinleys more than in the Bryans and Altgelds, at least for the time being. No one really doubted that the depression would end by itself and there was a general feeling of confidence and pride in the American future. Interestingly enough, McKinley did bring prosperity, the typically unplanned prosperity which this favored nation has stumbled upon so many times. New worldwide gold discoveries helped inflate prices. Famines in Europe called for our farm crops. The Spanish-American War did its part. Business confidence inspired a nation of businessmen to expand, combine, invent and promote with fantastic success. Bryan's election was definitely not in the national interest in 1896.

"God's in his heaven, all's right with the world," was the telegram Mark Hanna sent his friend in Canton. Both men being Victorian gentlemen, destined to see only a few years of the portentous twentieth century, the quotation from Browning's *Pippa Passes* was apt enough. Now they and their friends could share relief that the business community had passed through its crisis. Herman Kohlsaat described the joy in the Union League Club of Chicago late that night:

> . . . one of the world's greatest merchants started the old boyhood game of "Follow the Leader." He was joined by bank presidents, merchants, Chicago's foremost men; they went over sofas, chairs, tables, upstairs and downstairs and wound up dancing in each other's arms.[25]

Part II: *A Taste for Empire*

BUZZARDS FEAST ON THE COWARDICE OF THE WHITE HOUSE

Hanna and His Crew Have Scored Another Victory in "Havana Massacre" Scare

> Behind the bay cob with a bang tail there dashed up to the White House this morning a syndicate (Author's note: Was this a reference to McKinley's bailing out?) buzzard. He sprang out of the vehicle, handed the reins to a groundling and strode into the White House to seek his prey. It was Mark Hanna. Other buzzards stooped from their eyrise and joined the feast.[26]

With this purple prose, dateline April 6, 1898, young Willie Hearst's New York *Journal*, a present to him from his silver-mining father, strained to unleash the dogs of war. The "Havana Massacre" was a reference to the possible massacre of American residents in Havana if war were declared before their evacuation. In fact, McKinley had used this threat to stall off the declaration of war for a few more days of negotiation, showing a telegram from Consul General Lee to the hawks in Congress to prove his point.[27]

"An absurd yarn," manufactured by Hanna, scoffed the *Journal.* Then, throwing more punches at the business community for its pacifism, the article continued: "There is a rumor to the effect that the Rothschilds and the Standard Oil Company are to have a chance to try a game of auriferous inducements on the Spanish statesmen. From now until Monday is a long cry for the moneyed men and in the four days intervening they will have a chance to switch the situation to suit themselves." Here again the *Journal* was on the right track but, of course, editorializing the news in one of the most irresponsible episodes of American journalism. McKinley, desperately trying to avoid the war in the face of what seemed to be the hysterical demands of the entire nation, had discreetly allowed New York's Archbishop Ireland to seek the good offices of the Pope (a daring move for the President of a generally anti-Catholic nation), and, equally daring, had invited aid from the House of Rothschild.[28] The *Wall Street Journal* saw the good sense of buying one's way out of trouble. Commenting on the rumors to the effect that Spain might sell Cuba and that J. P. Morgan's return from Europe was connected with financing the purchase, it stated on March 31, "There is much satisfaction expressed in Wall Street at the prospects of having Cuba free, because it is believed that this will take one of the most disturbing factors out of the situation. . . . Even if $200 million is the indemnity demanded it is a sum which the United States could well afford, to get rid of the trouble."[29]

But Cuba was not for sale and the tottering Spanish government, finally willing to do everything the United States asked, except to grant Cuba independence instead of the proposed autonomy status such as Canada had with England, was swept into conflict with the inexplicably war-mad Yankees. After all, how could Spanish punctilio cope with Senator Henry Cabot Lodge's party politics and monetary fears? Known as the "scholar in politics," the erudite Lodge had advocated territorial expansion on highly intellectual and historical grounds such as manifest destiny, the significance of sea power and a place for the United States among the great nations. Yet in the spring of 1898, he was capable of writing to the President:

> If the war in Cuba drags on through the summer with nothing done we shall go down in the greatest defeat ever known. . . . I know that it is easily and properly said that to bring on or even to threaten war for political reasons is a crime and I quite agree. But to sacrifice a great party and bring free silver upon the country for a wrong policy is hardly less odious. On a great broad question like this, I believe profoundly in the popular instinct and what that instinct is no one who goes out among the people . . . can doubt for a moment.[30]

II

Historians have had a busy time seeking to explain the war with Spain and the subsequent annexations of Hawaii, Puerto Rico, Guam and the Philippines within a year. Theories range all the way from Richard Hofstadter's emphasis on the "psychic crisis" resulting from middle class anxiety over the depression and flood of immigration[31] to Ernest May's speculative "social-science" assessment of the influence of European role models on our policy makers.[32] Since the war and even the ensuing annexations were temporary aberrations, not repeated in our history in any comparable manner until Vietnam, a review of some of these reasons should be helpful. At the same time, since our attention is directed towards the business community in times of crisis, its unexpected good conduct should be certified.

First of all, there was a strong tradition of anti-colonialism, or anti-imperialism, as the phrase was used in the nineteenth century, in a nation which had to throw off the yoke of England before it could exist. The Founding Fathers were quite specific about the dangers of foreign entanglements and the young Republic considered the eternal wars of Europe over possessions an example to be strenuously avoided in the new world. In 1821 John Quincy Adams stated once more the case against foreign adventures for America. His words must have rung in the ears of his grandson, Charles Francis Adams, Jr., a noted businessman and Mugwump reformer who was one of the most important of the anti-imperialists:

> The frontlet upon her brows would no longer beam with the ineffable splendor of freedom and independence; but in its stead would soon be substituted an imperial diadem, flashing in false and tarnished lustre the murky radiance of dominion and power. She might become the dictatress of the world; she would no longer be the ruler of her own spirit.[33]

America did not view this warning as applying to its westward movement, as the Indians and Mexicans could testify. What was not taken by force or annexation was taken by purchase, from Louisiana to Oregon to Alaska, but a war for extra-continental territory was unthinkable for most people. The keystone of American foreign policy was the Monroe Doctrine of 1823. It notified Europe to give up hopes for any further colonization or interference in our hemisphere. No island outposts were deemed to be necessary for enforcing this message.

Still the marvelous sweep to the shores of the Pacific by pioneers, explorers, businessmen, prospectors, missionaries and railroaders, all under the most difficult circumstances, was not likely to deflate the American ego. Another tradition continued along with anti-colonialism. It was the "manifest destiny" of Americans to conquer their own continent and become a giant of wealth and power. The actual phrase was a late arrival, first used in 1845 by an obscure journalist named John L. O'Sullivan who had in mind the manifest destiny of the Southern states to extend slavery to new frontiers.[34] One of these frontiers, incidentally, was Cuba, then a slave-owning territory. Upon this island Southern adventurers, with Cuban allies, descended in 1850-1851 in a fiasco of invasion to be repeated at the Bay of Pigs in 1961. Fifty Southern invaders, many from leading families in the South, were shot or strangled on the beach by the Spanish defenders. President Pierce a few years later thereupon condoned a cloak and dagger scheme to blackmail Spain into selling Cuba to the United States for $120 million but was forced to retreat by Northern free-soilers.

A good phrase cannot be kept down, however, particularly one with such orotund internal rhyming and Calvinist determinism to recommend it. Back it came, the slavery overtones forgotten, in the writings of expansionists of the 1890's. The Republican party, responding to the idea more eagerly than the Cleveland Democratic opposition, included in its 1892 platform a call for "the achievement of the manifest destiny of the republic in its broadest sense." President McKinley, his ear always close to the ground for a consensus cliché, is reported to have said, when Hawaiian annexation was revived after Dewey's victory at Manila Bay: "We need Hawaii just as much and a good deal more than we did California. It is manifest destiny."[35] Like most political slogans, this one served not only as a substitute for thinking but several masters as well. In the years before the Spanish-American War it found employment endorsing the *mission* of America to bring the virtues of democracy and freedom to the world, certainly to Cuba, ninety-five miles away. Mission, like crusade, has a long history in warfare.

Unfortunately a large portion of the clergy appropriated the mission concept. This made it all the more difficult for the business community, beneficiaries of staunch free enterprise support from the clergy, to think independently when the crisis came. Typical was the Reverend Josiah Strong and his book *Our Country*. Grafting from the reigning intellectual favorite, Charles Darwin, the concept of "survival of the fittest," Strong described the destiny of the Anglo-Saxons. Led by the Americans, they were to accomplish God's will by conquering Latin America, the Pacific areas and Africa. One book cannot make a war any more than one newspaper. Yet the fact that 130,000 copies of this book were sold by 1891, provoking practically no opposition in spite of its claptrap thinking, indicates the surge of expansionist fervor under respectable auspices.

The most important book providing an underlying intellectual structure for going to war, or at least for expansion, was Captain Alfred Thayer Mahan's *The Influence of Sea Power on History*, published in 1890. Mahan was the Rickover of his time, forcing his way to the top of his profession by the power of his intellect.

As president of the newly established Naval War College, he had plenty of time for lectures and research in the New York Public Library, as our actual ships afloat were hardly a match for the Chilean navy, let alone Spain's. Writing with Olympian authority, Mahan preached the importance of sea power for the earth-bound world of his time, that whoever is master of the sea is master of the situation, holding the key to history. It was sea power, blockading the coast of France, that defeated Napoleon, inspiring Mahan's magisterial lesson: "Those far distant, storm-beaten ships, upon which the Grand Army never looked, stood between it and dominion of the world."

His books and articles struck a responsive chord at home and abroad. Harvard and Yale gave him degrees and so did Oxford and Cambridge. Kaiser Wilhelm II, worried about the "Yellow Peril" of Japan, placed copies on board every ship of the German navy. Japan responded by making it a text for its military and naval colleges. Beginning in 1890, a good deal in response to Mahan's pressure, Congress reluctantly authorized the beginnings of a big navy. Four first-class battleships were completed by 1896, some of them a match for Britain's first-line fleet. America was ready for a naval war, preferably "a splendid little war," as John Hay, our Ambassador to England, would later pompously describe it.

Mahan was specific about the course America should take. Not only must America have a great merchant fleet, it must also have a navy capable of defending this fleet, and strategic bases all over the world to shelter and service the navy. The long-planned Isthmian Canal in Panama should be accelerated to link America's far-flung coasts. To protect the canal, indeed to fortify the Monroe Doctrine, bases in the Caribbean, with Cuba first choice, were a necessity. In the Pacific, Hawaii and even the Philippines were essential for promoting trade with the Orient and protecting our coast from invasion. Mahan did not specify how we were to obtain these possessions, except to offer the kind of ambiguous advice McKinley would later follow. Obtain them "by righteous means," he wrote, "but don't dodge them when flung at our head."[36]

The ripe fruit America had been ducking was Hawaii. For many years the Hawaiians had been trying to annex their islands to the United States, under the leadership of its missionary families converted to a businessmen's oligarchy. After Japan defeated China in their war of 1895, these families were particularly concerned about their minority position, as well as the new tariffs on their sugar exports, practically all of which went to America. Only Cleveland's stubborn rectitude on the matter had prevented annexation in 1893 after the Americans had deposed the Hawaiian Queen Liliuoakalani with the highly irregular aid of U.S. Marines as Harrison's Administration ended. McKinley, who was a non-expansionist, felt his backbone stiffen at the thought of America's anti-imperialist tradition and the business community's aversion for unsettling foreign policies. As a result, he continued Cleveland's stand on both Hawaii and Cuba. In the latter island, a new revolt had broken out in 1895 by the poverty-stricken Cubans, hit hard by the American depression and the rising tariffs on their sugar exports. In addition Spain had fired on an American merchant vessel and the *insurrectos* were burning American-owned sugar plantations. An important group of Senators joined Lodge in clamoring for war, including Senator Morgan of Alabama, Democratic Chairman of the Foreign Relations Committee. Since the humanitarian aspect of the insurrection had not yet caught fire, McKinley stood firm in his inaugural address: "We want no wars of conquest; we must avoid the temptation of aggression."

Lodge and Roosevelt were inflamed by Mahan's theories. Lodge, son-in-law of an Admiral and descendant of a family that had made its fortune in clipper ships and the China trade, preached them relentlessly in the Senate. It is difficult today to read the arrogant and often racist statements of these young upper-class Americans without being repelled. President Eliot regarded them as "degenerate sons of Harvard." Now they were joined by another elite young man, Albert Beveridge of Indiana, an orator of the magnitude of Bryan, who would soon enter the Senate while still in his thirties and meanwhile outdid all his colleagues in outrageous warmongering. This brilliant young man, an authority on American history and destined to become a leader of the Progressive reform movement, linked the Midwest to the Eastern expansionists. He was capable of saying the following in a Boston speech just before war was declared:

> We are a conquering race. . . . We must obey our blood and occupy new markets in new lands. . . . It is the Almighty's infinite plan . . . debased civilizations and decaying races are to disappear before the higher civilization of the nobler and more virile types of man . . .[37]

In their defense one can only call up the old virtues of patriotism and note the keen awareness of these men that twentieth century America could no longer remain isolationist. It must also be granted that their words were worse than their deeds. America took its spoils from Spain and then surprised the world by turning its back on further territorial expansion. The young jingo Roosevelt might well have become our first Imperial President. As it turned out he was not a Napoleon but only a perennial member of the Harvard boxing team.

III

> We don't want to fight, but by jingo if we do,
> We've got the ships, we've got the men, and
> we've got the money too!

English music-hall audiences cheered on their imperialists with this ballad, bringing "jingo" into the language as a term for chauvinists and super-patriots. In America the vaudeville audiences were cheering Maggie Cline as she sang "Throw Him Down, McCloskey." Each time Miss Cline came to the title line, it was customary for the people backstage to throw something, whatever they could get their hands on, down to the floor with a crash. In front the audience reinforced the explosion with a roar of its own. Only a slight nudge was needed to turn the cheers towards the troops.

It is to the English model that one should look for a final strand in the cultural pattern making America's war and annexations understandable. For all their old enmity, Americans and Englishmen were forging a bond that would be decisive in world history. The showdown over Venezuela actually made the mother country realize that it must be allied with America, partners in the Atlantic community against the new threats of Germany and Russia. English statesmen accordingly did not push the cause of archaic Spain's imperial possessions and soon after the war made a bid for future support by giving up their interests in the Isthmian Canal through the signing of the Hay-Pauncefote treaty. For their part, Americans, foresworn of the glitter of aristocracy, monarchy and empire, could not help admiring England's special capacity in these fields. They married their daughters into titled families and acknowledged the superiority of English literary figures and philosophers in their schools and colleges. There was a general recognition that England had style and culture somewhat lacking in America, although her charms were not apparent to Irish-Americans and fanatic Silverites. Now England was at the very zenith of her history as the grand old Queen celebrated her Diamond Jubilee in 1897 with enough pomp and ceremony to thrill the world. Mark Twain watched the procession with typical American irony and envy: "Yes," he said, "the English are mentioned in Scripture—'Blessed are the meek for they shall inherit the earth.'"

Destined by geography to be a great seafaring nation, England had become the leading colonizer of the modern world. Her earth-hunger reflected full-bodied imperialism, the need to find new markets unavailable at home and overseas purchasers for surplus manufactured goods. This nation of shopkeepers and aristocrats had an additional item to export, her surplus sons, many of whom sought escape from the laws of primogeniture. None of these items applied to the American experience.

Yet the resurgence of the virtues of imperialism in English thought and statecraft, coming to a rush in the 1880's, directly affected Americans who were still in thrall to the English model. Both countries needed a fresh subscription to the half-truths and deceptions that made it possible for democracies at home to force their government on peoples abroad. Imperialism had been held in low esteem by a great many influential people in mid-nineteenth century England. After all Adam Smith, her leading economic philosopher, had long ago stated that colonies were a drain on the mother country and that America and trade should both be free. The success of the American experiment seemed to prove that a colony could flourish on its own far better than under the restrictive hand of empire and provide even greater trade and markets for England. Queen Victoria's reign marked the growth of the English Liberal party under the long dominance of the moralizing anti-colonialist William Ewart Gladstone, who went so far as to advocate Home Rule for the Irish. Another favorite Englishman in America was John Bright, a great orator in the Commons who had supported the Union cause during the Civil War and opposed colonies to the extent of suggesting Canada should join the United States. Among the younger English Parliamentary leaders, James Bryce, the most informed writer of the period on America and friend of its leading citizens, was thoroughly anti-colonial. Though England continued to pick up possessions, particularly under Disraeli's Tory leadership, the concept of imperialism was at a low ebb following our Civil War. This may help explain why President Grant's treaty to annex the Dominican Republic in 1869, based on an "expansion of markets" theory fed to the simple-minded President by conniving speculators, failed to get Senate approval. But America's sharp turns from isolationism to interventionism and back to isolationism were destined to proceed quickly enough.

Now a new age of imperialism appeared in England and on the Continent as well. How busy the map-makers must have been between 1870 and 1898 when Britain added 4 million square miles and 88 million people to its empire, Germany a million square miles and 40 million subjects, Belgium 900,000 square miles and 30 million people and Portugal 800,000 square miles and 9 million inhabitants! France deserves special mention for its subjugation of 40 million colonials in this brief period. When Jules Ferry became

Prime Minister in 1883 he sent troops to Hanoi, conquered Tonkin, now North Vietnam, and added it to French Indochina.

The motives were varied but everyone understood they were tied in with power and profit, as much as with military and naval strategy. France sought prestige as well as its share of what was left. Leopold of the Belgians talked about a great civilizing mission and removing the shackles of slavery from the Congo. Bismarck, who had been anti-colonial, realistically decided to grab as much as he could for Germany. The English leaders described themselves as duty bound to bring civilization and commerce to the uncivilized world, of assuming "the white man's burden," a phrase which rings so strangely in contemporary ears. Americans looking for England to take the lead in denouncing this dangerous race were chilled with disappointment. Gladstone ended his career aggressively sustaining imperialism, having cruelly bombarded Alexandria and dispatched troops a thousand miles south of Cairo to defeat at Omdurman. Other former anti-imperialists, such as Randolph Churchill and the young "radical," Joseph Chamberlain, both married to American wives, shocked their admirers by their full conversion to the imperialist faith. Lord Rosebery, an ally of John Bright in earlier years, now attacked the Conservatives for not being imperialist enough and became the Liberal Prime Minister in 1892-1895. In spite of the continuing tradition of anti-imperialism in England as well as in America, the plain fact is that England was more fully committed to imperialism than ever at the time of America's first tentative experiment with it. Americans like Roosevelt, Lodge, Beveridge and Hay, who were frequent visitors to England, received the strongest reinforcement for their doctrines from the admired English example. Since American businessmen were equally fascinated with England and considered her their chief commercial rival, such opposition as they expressed is somewhat remarkable.

IV

A distinguishing feature of the new European imperialism was its candid admission of economic necessity, especially for the highly industrialized countries. Americans like Lodge, Beveridge, and Mahan diligently included this argument for expansion. When applied to areas like Hawaii, the Philippines and Cuba, however, it appears to be a bid for support from the disinterested and unalarmed American business community. Advocates of armaments and defense have never been known for highly objective arguments. If one will grant that their words need not be taken at face value, the expansionists were offering exotic and vague trade as an inducement for the forceful acquisition of islands needed to withstand the sea power of the restless Great Powers. After all, the populations involved were small, the raw materials insignificant, the marketing power unimportant and the prospects of emigration fanciful. Andrew Carnegie, the leading businessman among the anti-imperialists, scoffed at the notion that trade would follow the flag. Canada, a British colony, traded more with America than with England. An "open-door" policy for all nations, along with reasonably free trade and freedom of the seas, would suffice to let America continue to lead the world in exports without the cost and shame of imperialism.[38] Of course there were business interests and journals thoroughly enticed by the offer, especially after the war was declared and won so painlessly. Yet as Julius Pratt, the historian who has done more than anyone else to clear the record about the business community's responsibility for the Spanish-American war, has declared: "The need of American business for colonial markets and fields for investment was discovered not by businessmen but by historians and other intellectuals, by journalists and politicians."[39]

In Europe the situation was quite different. If only for historical interest, capitalist businessmen might consider how European turn-of-the-century imperialism provided a stock argument for Marxist theoreticians. Since economic necessity admittedly was driving capitalist countries to colonial conquest, harsh criticism from the school of economic determinism could be expected. This would be doubly so when prodigious financier-adventurers like Cecil Rhodes appeared in Africa as a central driving force for imperialism compared with the reluctant businessmen of America. Keir Hardie, one of the first Socialists in the House of Commons, attacked the economic motivations he saw behind the Boer War of 1899: "A capitalist's war, begotten by capitalist's money, lied into being by a perjured mercenary capitalist press and fathered by the unscrupulous politicians, themselves the merest tool of the capitalists."[40] No such statements came from America's Populist leaders, who rather enjoyed the Spanish-American War along with the thought of William Jennings Bryan participating in the bright blue uniform of the Nebraska mounted volunteers.

Karl Marx had predicted the end of capitalism almost fifty years earlier while working away in the British Museum. It was Lenin, however, who heard in the clashes of imperialism the death rattle of capitalism and wove it into basic Marxist doctrine. Strangely enough, Lenin's mentor on imperialism was in large part a modest, frail English economist named John A. Hobson who died in 1940, perhaps as surprised as anyone at the inexorable doom of capitalism Lenin derived from the speculative reasoning of Hobson's *Imperialism*, published in 1902. Briefly, Hobson wrestled with the problem of surplus funds seeking investment just as surplus goods sought purchasers. The capitalists owned all these funds, accumulated in the classical Marxian pattern of the rich getting richer. Unable to invest the money at home where the poor didn't earn enough to take surplus goods off the market, Dutch, German, French, English and other capitalists had to invest their money in foreign markets, creating new purchasers as well as a return on their capital. Governments in turn were forced to accommodate this overwhelming economic need by plundering other countries. In the infallible Lenin version wars and then the revolution would inevitably follow.

This is a far cry from Free Silver and Free Cuba but the coin of imperialism has been so debased that the word's several meanings must be kept in mind. In a brief seventy years, practically all of the world's imperial possessions have been liquidated by the Great Powers. Marxists for thirty years have been calling America's foreign policy "imperialism" and our friends "imperialist lackeys." Russia has demonstrated a remarkable ability to draw countries like Czechosolvakia and Hungary into an imperial system without the slightest obedience to Hobson's or Lenin's rules. The rules have been outmoded by the emergence of great middle-class purchasing groups with heroic consumption abilities for domestic production. Private foreign investments, however, are more massive than ever, ten times as much as at the end of World War II. Territorial expansion does not follow these dollars but our foreign policy does not ignore their safety. In turn Europeans like Servan-Schreiber uncover the "challenge" of the American multi-national corporation as a new kind of imperialism. Future historians of empire may find this significant, along with the race for space and the custody of the oceans. Meanwhile Cuba persists as a thorn in our flesh.

V

"A sort of bellicose fury has seized the American nation," the French ambassador notified Paris after the sinking of the *Maine* on February 15, 1898.[41] "Ambition, interest, land-hunger, pride, the mere joy of fighting, whatever it may be," acknowledged the Washington *Post*, a few months later, "the taste of Empire is in the mouth of the people even as the taste of blood in the jungle."[42]

The jungle metaphor seems premature in a nation not yet exposed to two World Wars, genocide, the bomb and television. Yet our streak of violence is well known, from vigilantes to Ku Klux Klan, from ghetto to campus (". . . as American as cherry pie," Rap Brown told us). There is at least a "paranoid style" to be found in American politics, states Richard Hofstadter, who offers as an example 1898.[43]

With Freud barely out of medical school in that year, the record would reveal few if any references to the "psychic crisis" Hofstadter so well describes. William James, the Harvard psychologist and philosopher, recognized the warlike symptoms clearly enough. Aware of mankind's innate aggressiveness and hostility—the "discontents" Freud would note as being repressed by civilization—James optimistically hoped for their release in substitutes known as moral equivalents. But sports and bad theater, even the hanging in effigy of Spanish statesmen and McKinley himself, were a poor stand-in for action against a European, Catholic tyranny. America was also a nation of churchgoers and a great many of its moral shepherds were whipping up the hysteria by their commitment to the indisputable humanitarian reasons involved. After all, Spain had been traditionally cruel in quelling the revolt, especially under a General known as "Butcher" Weyler, whose 200,000 Spanish troops were bogged down by disease and the frustrations of guerilla warfare. The Cubans were in desperate condition, with at least a hundred thousand reported to be in concentration camps. Still war would not have been declared without the pressure of emotion, let alone the passion for adventure in men like Roosevelt of the Rough Rider period. William James was moved to the point of agony. How was it possible, he wrote to a friend on June 15, 1898, that "a nation's ideals could be changed in the twinkling of an eye," that America could "puke up its ancient soul . . . in five minutes without a wink of squeamishness."[44] A year later McKinley confessed: "But for the inflamed state of public opinion, and the fact that Congress could not be held in check, a peaceful solution might have been had."[45]

Thus the business community was presented with a crisis of decision. The pressures for war arose from the prospect of our national security lying naked before the imperial rush of the Great Powers, at least so they were told. The party of business faced eviction from the White House by free silver Democrats and Populists as their leader Bryan charged the Republicans with inhumane inertia for the same reasons of commercial greed exhibited on inflation. The church, the press and the discontented were loudly represented in the clamor for war. McKinley, the man of consensus, stubbornly lagged behind some of the ablest leaders of his own party, but his convictions slipped rapidly as the war clouds gathered over the sunken *Maine* and its 252 sailors. Finally, the theorists of expansion offered the business community the sugar-coating of markets and profits along with their thinly veiled disdain for the timid commercial classes.

Under the circumstances the remarkable thing is that businessmen offered any resistance at all. Perhaps not too much should be made of it as they all closed ranks once war was declared. Still the resistance was unique and can be examined in its two parts, first on Cuba itself and second, in the dissent over annexation of the Philippines.

At the outset, one should draw some boundaries around the word "businessmen." At one end there would be the men of Wall Street and their web of magnates and industrialists. At the other end the small town merchants endowed with the rural attitudes and prejudices of their environment. William A. Williams in his *Roots of the Modern American Empire* calls attention to the vigorous expansionist sentiment existing among farm owners and produce merchants. The Sunday congregations that prayed for "Free Cuba" included a significant number of small businessmen, grocers, druggists, livery operators and the like. On the other hand, the anti-imperialists included people not usually identified with business, such as college presidents and lawyers, in short, what is today called the Establishment. It is generally agreed that the greater part of the small proprietors and clerical employees in the cities and in the country were jingoes while the big proprietors and executives were likely to be anti-jingo.

Mark Hanna, McKinley's closest and most influential adviser, expressed a hard-headed, unemotional businessman's point of view from the start. Herbert Croly explains in his biography that for Hanna "the outbreak of war seemed to imperil the whole policy of domestic amelioration which he placed before every other object of political action."[46] Hanna had allowed McKinley to hoist the near senile Senator John Sherman into the Secretary of State's position—an indication of the lowly estate of foreign policy in those days—so that he himself could be elected Senator by the compliant Ohio legislature. There in the Senate Hanna hoped to serve his President and help keep him out of trouble over Cuba and other diversions from prosperity. Thomas Beer, son of William Beer, a lawyer-lobbyist for the J. P. Morgan banking and insurance interests, has written a perceptive biography of Hanna including personal recollections of Hanna and his friends. "Remember," Hanna told a young lady, "that my folks were Quakers. War is just a damn nuisance." To another he said that of course the Cubans were being mistreated and he was strongly in favor of their freedom. But he emphasized: "I hate the thought of a war. You don't know what a big war is like. Suppose the French come in with Spain against us?"[47] Once McKinley asked Congress for the resolution that was in effect a declaration of war, Hanna joined up realistically and supported his President all the way, including the backroom planning for Senate approval of the Philippine annexation treaty. Ironically, Hanna and Speaker Reed were in fact the greatest foes of the expansion policy. It was Hanna, however, as a spokesman for Wall Street and puppeteer of McKinley, who was consistently denounced in the press and pulpit. Pouncing on his long ears and Irish countenance, Hearst's Homer Davenport and the *Verdict* magazine's George Luks dealt him devastating and basically false cartoon violence over a period of years. He had the distinction of being criticized first as a dove by Davenport and later as a hawk by Luks.

A glance through the New York newspapers preceding the war reveals the business community's nightmare experience as peace-lovers. On April 7, the New York State Chamber of Commerce sent a resolution to McKinley intended to massage his backbone by decrying the possible war and strongly backing McKinley's efforts to avoid it. On May 5, 1898, at its 130th annual meeting, the Chamber passed another resolution which poignantly summarizes the turn of events:

> It is easy to understand the feeling of dazed surprise which overspread the mercantile and financial community when it found itself suddenly called upon to face the serious embarrassments and possible dangers of a war with a maritime power over a question that had not come very near to its own life. As long as there was hope of bringing about a permanent settlement of the questions in dispute by peaceful means, it was natural and becoming that the influence of this Chamber should have been thrown strongly in the scale in favor of a solution of the problem by the resources of diplomacy. But, for loyal Americans, the day has gone by for the discussion of that aspect of the trouble, except as an historical question . . .[48]

The significance of this resolution, which seems to have escaped the historians concerned with the question, is especially apparent when note is taken of the committee involved in its preparation. It includes J. Pierpont Morgan, Abram S. Hewitt, August Belmont, John D. Rockefeller, the banker Levi P. Morton and Macy's Isidor Straus. No rambling about manifest destiny, no acknowledgment of mission, no concern with the markets and commercial survival offered by expansionists high and low. In seconding the resolution Abram S. Hewitt, son-in-law of Peter Cooper, iron-master and Congressman, friend of John Bright and Lord Bryce, spoke as follows:

> . . . They could never be made to understand that we do not desire to add to our territorial possessions and our responsibilities. . . . When the final victory comes, they will be made to see that neither the Government of this country nor the people of this country will take advantage of the situation to add one foot of territory to its already ample domain (Great Applause).[49]

Among the tycoons who felt the sting of the warmongers was Philip D. Armour, the Chicago meat-packer, who had pleaded for moderation. On April 7, a few weeks before the die was cast, Hearst's *Journal* published an editorial:

> WHEN MR. ARMOUR WOULD DECLARE WAR
> If Spanish troops were to invade the stockyards and drive off Mr. Armour's hogs, then Mr. Armour would rage and fume and call upon the United States Government to avenge the wrong. If a Spanish fleet were to find its way into Lake Michigan and were to drop shells on the roof of Mr. Armour's house, Mr. Armour would not be a peace angel for more than a minute. . . . But when sailors, American sailors who have gone to sea in a battleship to protect the meat he sends abroad to feed the European armies, when American sailors are murdered in their sleep, when their bones rot and the kites fly over the flag they carried, there must be no war.[50]

This reference to the *Maine*, incidentally, was after a McKinley investigating committee had found no conclusive evidence to determine whether a Spanish submarine mine or its own engine room problems had exploded the *Maine*. Samuel Eliot Morison, America's great historian and part-time Admiral, reports that a further inquiry in 1911 established it was a mine. "Although it is still a mystery who set and fired the mine," Morison writes, "it is difficult to conceive what interest any Spaniard might have had in doing it, and easy to imagine that a Cuban rebel would have planned it, in order to get the United States involved with Spain."[51] The Cuban "Junta" was indeed active in the United States in the 1890's. In 1897 an Illinois printer sued the Junta for payment for bonds of the proposed Cuban government he had manufactured for them. At least two Senators, including Mason of Illinois, the denouncer of Wall Street's lack of patriotism, were found to have been given some of these bonds![52]

The New York *Journal* was obviously riding the war issue in a reckless manner. When the New York *Times*, however, sought to justify the proposed war on the grounds of humanity, another distinguished businessman, George Foster Peabody, wrote a letter of objection. The *Times* thereupon printed a pro-war editorial shifting from humanity to self-defense as the issue at stake: "The time has come for Spain to quit this hemisphere."[53] All in all, the forces for peace were being completely routed.

In this light it is only simple justice that some of the historical criticisms of the business community have been subject to revision. Harold Faulkner, for example, claimed in 1924 that the "great cause for the war" was the fact that the United States "was sufficiently advanced for financial imperialism," implying the war was fought for markets and new fields for investment. Twenty-seven years later this distinguished economic historian stated in *The Decline of Laissez Faire* that "the point of view taken by certain economic historians that the United States went to war with Spain for economic reasons seems not warranted by the evidence."[54]

Julius Pratt, the University of Buffalo historian, deserves credit for a thorough examination of the printed record bearing on the question. For his *Expansionists of 1898*, Pratt laboriously sifted through a large number of financial and trade periodicals before concluding that the business community was distinguished by its anti-war sentiment. Prosperity was returning, exports were at a record high and the connection between the war advocates and the Silverites, who believed that war would somehow advance the cause of silver, was viewed as rank hypocrisy. There were petitions by affected businessmen calling McKinley's attention to a $300 million loss in trade between Cuba and the United States in the three years prior to 1898 and the need for arbitration to end the conflict. War was not offered as a solution, in spite of widespread destruction of American property. Business interests were, of course, concerned with increasing sales, particularly in foreign trade, but colonies did not enter their considerations, regardless of the grand plans on their behalf by the expansionists.

Pratt does note a strong shift in sentiment in the business journals as reason finally lost its hold on the nation. When Senator Proctor, who owned Vermont marble quarries, made a trip to Cuba in March and reported in the Senate the terrible suffering of the *reconcentrados* as justification for intervention, the unflappable Speaker Reed snapped: "Proctor's position might have been expected. A war will make a large market for gravestones."[55] The *Wall Street Journal*, however, reported a change in business sentiment as a result of Proctor's statements, "as many of them expressed it, they made the blood boil." The *American Banker* changed to a considerably less peaceful position as a result of Proctor's speech, although still hoping the Cubans would accept Spain's offer of autonomy. Finally, interest in the sugar-coating penetrated the business camp as Austria-Hungary talked about European protective measures against American trade and the Germans and Russians occupied ports in China. The latter event agitated the hitherto anti-imperialist *Journal of Commerce* to launch a drive for an "open door" policy in the Orient which was vigorously taken up by Chambers of Commerce from New York to San Francisco.[56] Though American trade with China was less than two per cent of total foreign trade, the potential 400 million purchasers were viewed as being lost to the Europeans.

From here it was an easy step for affected business interests to covet the Philippines when Commodore Dewey dropped them in McKinley's lap.

VI

On February 6, 1899, the Senate ratified the treaty of Paris, by which the United States acquired from Spain Guam in the Marianas, Puerto Rico in the Caribbean and the Philippines in the Orient. Cuba, the object of the fighting in the first place, could not be acquired. Senator Teller had authorized an amendment to the war resolutions forbidding its acquisition and so it became nominally independent under American supervision. The United States circumspectly paid $20 million for the Philippines, as McKinley, now a full-fledged expansionist, urged his treaty commissioners to keep the prize. Hawaii had already been annexed in 1898.

An awkward obstacle to our diplomacy arose from the fact that the young Filipino rebel leader, Emilio Aguinaldo, returned from exile in Hong Kong and proclaimed himself President of the Philippine Republic on July 1. McKinley's troops arrived a few months later and the disillusioned Aguinaldo began to realize that the Filipinos were to receive only a change in masters. By the time the Senate ratified the treaty with a two-vote margin, General Arthur MacArthur was at war with Aguinaldo. Before it was over, more than 200,000 Filipinos would die in the futile guerilla struggle. America would lose more men than in the Spanish-American War and would be involved in atrocities against the "little brown brothers."

This was the background for the Anti-Imperialist League, the most important wartime dissent movement prior to Vietnam. Sharing Aguinaldo's disillusionment was an impressive and varied group, many of whom dropped old animosities to join the common cause. The movement started, as might be expected, in Boston, conscience of the nation, with stern Mugwump descendants of the Pilgrims, such as Gamaliel Bradford and Erving Winslow, among its founders. Most of the officers of the League were older men, estranged from the ideas of Lodge and Roosevelt. President of the League was George A. Boutwell, eighty years old, former Massachusetts Governor and Senator and Secretary of the Treasury under Grant. It is the 41 vice-presidents, however, who present such a vivid panorama of turn-of-the-century history that one wishes they could all have assembled at least once around the same table. There would be Grover Cleveland and opposite him the unpredictable "Pitchfork Ben" Tillman; Andrew Carnegie next to Samuel Gompers, the labor leader; John Sherman, McKinley's Secretary of State, who had resigned in protest before the war; Donelson Caffrey, the Louisiana Senator and sugar planter; J. G. Carlisle, Cleveland's Secretary of the Treasury who had dealt with Morgan; New York's fiery Congressman Bourke Cockran, allied with Patrick Collins and Patrick Ford in hatred of imperialism, especially as applied to the Irish and William Graham Sumner, Yale's great conservative sociologist, who wrote such papers as *The Conquest of the United States by Spain.* College presidents included Henry Wade Rogers of Northwestern, Herman von Holst of Chicago and David Starr Jordan of Stanford. Among the ministers were Thomas Wentworth Higginson, the old abolitionist, and C. H. Parkhurst, the vice investigator in New York. Felix Adler, destined to found the Ethical Culture Society, was the only Jew besides Gompers among the genteel reformers, dissident Republicans (former President Harrison was a member) and Cleveland Democrats who dominated this group. In addition to Carnegie, businessmen vice-presidents included Charles Francis Adams, Jr., who had been a railroad president, Hazen Pingree, self-made millionaire reformer who became Governor of Michigan, Samuel Bowles, publisher of the Springfield *Republican* and Edward Atkinson.

Andrew Carnegie was one of the most articulate and thoughtful businessmen in American history. Five feet two inches tall, with flaxen hair and spaded beard surrounding wide-apart blue eyes, the Scottish immigrant boy had become rich enough to be a law unto himself in 1899, his wealth increasing annually by ten to twenty million tax-free, hard dollars. Only J. P. Morgan was able to finance the sale of Carnegie's great steel works and Carnegie made sure he would by discreetly threatening to run some vital Morgan interests into the ground. The result was the first billion dollar corporation, U. S. Steel, organized in 1900. It paid $500 million for the Carnegie works of which about 50 per cent went to Carnegie personally. Eventually he bequeathed $350 million to his charitable foundations. This sort of man was a major catch for the anti-imperialists. Not only was his cash on the line but his pen directed a steady flow of letters to McKinley and articles to the magazines and press. Something akin to George Bernard Shaw's Andrew Undershaft, the paradoxical munitions magnate in *Major Barbara*, Carnegie was unpredictably original. How can you fault a man who would write as merrily as Shaw himself: "It will be a great mistake for the community to shoot the millionaires, for they are the bees that make the most honey and contribute most to the hive even after they have gorged themselves full. . . ."?[57] He preached pacifism and left a fortune to its cause, yet made sure he got his share of the big naval armor plate orders. He argued for the choice of free trade over colonies while drafting a good part of McKinley's protective tariff of 1890. About as appalled as anyone could be at the thought of Bryan in the White House, he now welcomed him as a comrade in the Anti-Imperialist League and offered to back him against McKinley in 1900 if only Bryan would give up free silver.

No one dared question the patriotism of this "Star Spangled Scotsman," who lectured his friend, Prime Minister Gladstone, about Britain's need to ship the Royal Family back to Germany and adopt the American system of government. As soon as he sensed the Administration was bent on keeping the Philippines, he attacked imperialism vigorously, predicting the abandonment of democratic principles and the bloody role of oppressor in those islands. When Whitelaw Reid, publisher of the New York *Herald Tribune* and a Treaty of Paris Commissioner, invited him to a reception for the Commissioners, he wrote:

> Unfortunately I shall be in Pittsburgh the evening of your reception for the signers of the *War* Treaty with

> Spain, not the Peace. It is a matter of congratulations, however, that you seem to have about finished your work of civilizing the Filipinos. It is thought that about 8000 of them have been completely civilized and sent to Heaven. I hope you like it.[58]

The dissent expressed over the Philippines was sharp and unrestrained. Yet it provoked no threats from the Administration, perhaps because of its bi-partisan nature and the eminence of its leaders. Carnegie closed one of his letters to McKinley with: "Your friend personally; but the bitterest enemy you have officially, as far as I know."[59] Ironically, Carnegie threatened to turn the labor vote against McKinley if he persisted in annexation, deluding himself that he could be a labor spokesman after the tragedy of Homestead. Still, the anti-imperialist period was Andrew Carnegie's finest hour, as the man of great wealth faced the moral crisis of his nation with passionate conviction and closely reasoned arguments. Finley P. Dunne's "Mr. Dooley" was impressed by Carnegie's uncompromising stand: "So I suppose, Hinnissy, we'll have to stay and do the best we can, an' lave Andrew Carnegie secede fr'm th' Union."[60]

Edward Atkinson provides a different personality to round out our post-mortem of businessmen in non-business crisis situations. Atkinson, a Bostonian of moderate income, was a corporation and trade association executive in a day when most of the business-talking was done by owners rather than executives. Atkinson was something of an engaging crank, whose *forte* was statistics which he was forever manufacturing for his speeches and articles. Because he had so much to say, he is one of the few minor businessmen used as a sounding board for the period. Edward Chase Kirkland, for example, constantly turns to Atkinson in his *Dream and Thought in the Business Community, 1860-1900*, although the thread of the book necessarily hangs on larger fry.

Though Atkinson was as prickly a rebel as the anti-imperialists could produce, he was totally conservative in his economics and admiration for the Establishment. His statistics would help produce a "natural history of industry," as he put it.[61] This museum-exhibit approach to business easily led to a veneration for the "natural laws" of economics which men of privilege were invoking from both Darwin and the Supreme Court to justify the trusts and other inequities of the day.

There was none of the patrician disdain for business in Atkinson that Charles Francis Adams, Jr., another prize catch of the anti-imperialists, exhibited. Though Adams had deigned to go in and out of the railroad business, the direct descendant of two Presidents shared the weary envy of his brothers Henry and Brooks towards the new plutocracy. Only an Adams of Boston could write in his *Autobiography:*

> I have known, and known tolerably well, a good many "successful" men — "big" financially — men famous during the last half-century; and a less interesting crowd I do not care to encounter. Not one that I have ever known would I care to meet again, either in this world or the next; nor is one of them associated in my mind with the ideas of humor, thought or refinement. A set of mere money-getters and traders, they were essentially unattractive and uninteresting.[62]

As Adams was a snob, Atkinson was something of a Babbitt, happily engaged in the fight for democratic principles so long as they were neatly isolated from radical economics. Just as Babbitt rose to righteous fury against the vigilantes of Zenith, Atkinson came into his own over the Philippines. He had always been an advocate of a small army and navy, not only for peaceful reasons but also because he had calculated the cost to be excessive. How far away from Admiral Mahan is Atkinson in a letter to Treasury Secretary Fairchild in 1885, in which he expresses gratification that the whiskey tax alone covered all naval costs: "The navy floats on beer — when we have any navy to float — and a surplus over."[63] There is writing talent in such a statement and Atkinson's pen was soon ready to engage the sword. In 1899 he became editor of his own *The Anti-Imperialist*, described by Thomas Wentworth Higginson as "the most elaborate single battery which the war-party had to encounter."[64]

Tall, massively built and handsomely bearded, Atkinson's business life centered on cotton manufacturing and the presidency of a Boston mutual fire insurance company. His other life was in his constant enthusiasms, ranging from tariff reformer to sound money advocate, statistician, public speaker, dietician and inventor of the Aladdin Oven, a kerosene pressure cooker he hoped would somehow end poverty. A man of such diversity might inspire limited confidence and Charles Francis Adams, Jr. drily observed that Atkinson "was always in evidence."[65] Still this warmhearted Bostonian's opinions were heard in the highest circles, frequently in Senate hearings and before university audiences. He was a trustee of Massachusetts Institute of Technology and received an L.L.D. from the University of South Carolina, honors which helped assuage the blow of not having attended Harvard or any other college.

The Boston branch of the League was founded in Atkinson's office. As its vice-president, he continued his stream of letters to McKinley and launched fierce attacks on the Administration in his *Anti-Imperialist* articles bearing such titles as "The Cost of a National Crime" and "The Hell of War and its Penalties." In the latter, the careless statistician shocked the public by detailing the susceptibility of troops in tropical areas to malaria, leprosy and especially venereal disease. Over half the British troops in Hong Kong, he claimed, had this rarely mentioned affliction. "The way has already become plain for the youth of the land to avoid disease and death in the tropics," he concluded, "by refusing to volunteer or enlist in the army or navy of the United States."[66] Since Atkinson had compiled an ingenious mailing list for his pamphlets that included all members of Congress, leading clergymen, mayors and civic and trade organizations throughout the country, his assaults soon made him obnoxious to the Administration.

In time he became embarrasing to the League, which issued statements to the effect that he was acting on his own and not in his capacity as a League officer. But the stage had already been set for Atkinson's great scene, a confrontation with the government itself. Noting Administration reports that his writings had stirred up discontent among the troops in Manila, he thanked Washington for the valuable idea and asked for five hundred names and addresses of soldiers and officers to receive his pamphlets. Failing to receive the lists, he then let it be known he had mailed pamphlets to Admiral Dewey and other dignitaries in the Philippines for distribution. The Postmaster General rose to the bait and seized the pamphlets from the mail sacks in San Francisco. Overnight Atkinson became a national celebrity and 135,000 of his pamphlets were eventually in circulation. A wary Administration did not repeat the blunder and the seventy-two year old Massachusetts Mugwump waited in vain to be arrested for sedition.

VII

The election of 1900 saw McKinley soundly defeat Bryan again. In some ways the election could be regarded as a mandate for imperialism in view of Bryan's affiliation with the anti-imperialists but again the issue was clouded by Bryan's obsession with free silver. Within a few years all the vigor was gone from the movement as the rebels were defeated and the United States pursued its reasonably enlightened colonial administration of the Philippines.

In 1934, Congress acted to give independence, after a transitional commonwealth period, to its far-flung possession, thus proving the anti-imperialists wrong in their gloomy predictions of the course of empire. In fact the gift was accelerated by American commercial interests who wanted a tariff wall against competitive Philippine products and by isolationists who wanted an end to the military commitment. Yet history continued to bind the islands to America. There is the well-staged photo of General Douglas MacArthur splashing ashore at Leyte Island in 1944 with the summons: "People of the Philippines, I have returned." Soon the Japanese were evicted and on July 4, 1946, full independence was granted to the Philippines. In 1951, a Philippine-American mutual defense treaty was signed and in 1954 the Philippines joined us in the Southeast Asia security treaty (SEATO). Still the Philippines have managed to overcome excessive sentiment attached to the second mother country. In spite of more than a billion dollars spent in the past twenty years by America in the Philippines, President Johnson had to pay over $40 million to hire a Filipino construction battalion to go to Vietnam and the American embassy in Manila is constantly replacing its windows. A shade from the past startled Americans in 1964 when the news of the death of Aguinaldo was reported, age ninety-four.

What lesson can be drawn from the role of businessmen in the Spanish-American War? No lesson, perhaps, but at least a dividend of humor. It is droll, after all, that the materialist businessmen did not want war and for the perfectly sound reason that it would not be profitable. Businessmen are resigned to hearing themselves described as warmongers. They may therefore be excused for being amused at their unlikely role in America's most popular war, forced by a bloodthirsty Congress on a most reluctant President.

Second, history suggests a comparison with America's least popular war, conducted by four Presidents without benefit of official Congressional authority. The magnitude of the Vietnam episode in terms of a world power struggle and shattering discord at home makes the comparison with the earlier aberration unworthy. Still there is a modest record of organized dissent in the business community over Vietnam which will have at least a footnote in history. The Business Executives Move for Vietnam Peace has the distinction of being purely business-sponsored and yet unable to gain any significant public support from big business. A possible deduction would be that only a small businessman or an individual controlling a public company can afford to take an unpopular stand on such an issue. At any rate, this organization, which has managed to raise only about $100,000 a year since 1968, presents a sound and respectable platform for its arguments because of its business credentials. These arguments emphasize that Vietnam is a bad investment on which any intelligent business executive would cut his losses as soon as possible. Being cool business executives, its supporters must subdue the moral passion that excited their predecessors in the Anti-Imperialist League. Yet one feels certain this passion is repressed only for strategic reasons in an age of public relations. Ironically, the organization's leaders feel that they have great support among corporate executives in big business whom they call "secret patriots," unable to pierce the veil of corporate anonymity. For example, in 1970, 25,000 top executives were mailed a statement by a star witness against Vietnam, retired Marine Corps Commandant General David M. Shoup, and asked to comment. The mailing was sponsored by the Businessmens Education Fund, an offshoot of the anti-war group, devoted to the long range policy of concern with the type of national priorities that results in a "military-industrial complex." Of 1,700 replies, some 1,000 executives from the nation's 500 largest corporations said they agreed with General Shoup but would not let their names be used.[67]

Many top executives have, of course, dissented publicly on the course of our Vietnam policy, most noticeably Louis B. Lundborg, former Chairman of the Bank of America, whose statements include this balance-sheet type of analysis expected from business leaders: "An end to the war would be good, not bad, for American business. War is, as we say in business, a low-yield operation."[68] The final verdict, however, will probably show that American businessmen were for the most part quite willing to leave dissent to the younger members of the family. Though trying to enter the thoughts of youth is a high-risk matter, it is likely the children would have preferred their fathers in the office to speak out as dissenters themselves if possible. In this sense they would have responded to Mark Twain's sentiments at the height of the anti-imperialist debate. The great humorist, so struck by business ambitions that he lost practically all his money backing a linotype machine invention, spoke about a clergyman who had attacked him publicly:

> He said that if I had my just deserts I should be dangling from a lamp-post somewhere. . . . He hadn't anything personal against me, except that I was a traitor. . . . It would be an entirely different question if the country's life were in danger, its existence at stake; then . . . we could all come forward and stand by the flag and stop thinking about whether the nation was right or wrong; but when there is no question that the nation is any way in danger, but only some little war away off, then it may

> be that on the question of politics the nation is divided, half-patriot and half-traitors, and no man can tell which from which.[69]

What conclusions can be reached about the moral fiber of our businessmen forbears at the turn of the century? Perhaps it was easier to flout the Establishment in those days before massive organizations took over. Certainly businessmen did not hesitate to tell off their Presidents in their colorful contemporary rhetoric. The issues perhaps were not momentous. First an incredible national debate over free silver and then an unnecessary war to free one island and annex another touched the lives of some randomly selected men of business, Henry Villard, Jacob Coxey, Mark Hanna, Andrew Carnegie and Edward Atkinson. Yet how can one really reconstruct the past to measure the depth of their personal crises? As Anthony Eden reminds us about passing judgment on France under occupation, only those who were there can really know what it was like.

Footnotes

[1] The clipping is in Volume 4 of the Scrapbooks of the Spanish-American War collected by J. Wilstach, in the New York Public Library.

[2] The story is quoted in Henry F. Pringle, *Theodore Roosevelt* (New York, 1931), p. 179 and also in Mark Sullivan, *Our Times* (New York, 1922), Vol. II, p. 378. In the Wilstach Collection, however, a New York *World* clipping with dateline Washington, D.C., March 27, 1898, gives a different and presumably more accurate version: ". . . Mark Hanna was present at the dinner. Looking squarely at the Senator from Ohio, Mr. Roosevelt said that the interests of the business world and of financiers might be paramount in the Senate, but they would not be paramount with the American people and if anyone wanted to stand in their way outside of the Senate he was welcome to try the experiment."

[3] Quoted from Foster Rhea Dulles, *America's Rise to World Power* (New York, 1954), p. 51.

[4] Lewis Corey, *The Decline of American Capitalism* (New York, 1934), p. 51.

[5] Ernest R. May, *Imperial Democracy* (New York, 1961), p. 59 fn.

[6] *The Nation*, July 5, 1894, p. 1.

[7] G. B. Harvey, *Henry Clay Frick the Man* (New York, 1928), p. 157.

[8] Quoted in Matthew Josephson, *The Politicos* (New York, 1938), pp. 561-562, from the Cleveland Papers, letter of May 5, 1894.

[9] *The Nation*, February 5, 1891, p. 104.

[10] Russel B. Nye, *Midwestern Progressive Politics* (Harper Torchbook Edition, New York, 1965), p. 92.

[11] Josephson, *op. cit.*, pp. 564-565.

[12] *Ibid.*, p. 563.

[13] Robert H. Wiebe, *Businessmen and Reform* (Cambridge, 1962), pp. 20-31.

[14] May, *op. cit.*, p. 134.

[15] Henry Steele Commager, *The American Mind* (New Haven, 1950), p. 347.

[16] Irving S. Michelman, *Business at Bay* (New York, 1969), pp. 35 ff.

[17] Quoted in Ray Ginger, *The Bending Cross: A Biography of Eugene Debs* (Rutgers University Press, 1949), p. 188.

[18] Josephson, *op. cit.*, p. 700.

[19] Thomas Beer, *Hanna* (New York, 1929), p. 24.

[20] C. S. Olcott, *The Life of William McKinley* (New York, 1916), Vol. I, pp. 289-292.

[21] Quoted in Barbara Tuchman, *The Proud Tower* (New York, 1966), p. 144, from Henry F. Pringle, *Theodore Roosevelt* (New York, 1920), p. 159.

[22] Beer, *op. cit.*, p. 168.

[23] Herbert Croly, *Marcus Alonzo Hanna* (New York, 1912), pp. 115 ff.

[24] Norman Hapgood, *The Advancing Hour* (New York, 1920), pp. 76-77.

[25] Josephson, *op. cit.*, p. 708.

[26] New York *Journal*, April 7, 1898, p. 1, Wilstach Collection, *op. cit.*

[27] May, *op. cit.*, pp. 152-159.

[28] *Ibid.*

[29] Quoted in Julius W. Pratt, *Expansionists of 1898* (Baltimore, 1936), p. 247.

[30] May, *op. cit.*, pp. 146-147.

[31] Richard Hofstadter, *The Paranoid Style in American Politics* (New York, 1967, Vintage Books Edition), pp. 145-187.

[32] Ernest R. May, *American Imperialism: A Speculative Essay* (New York, 1968), Chapter 7.

[33] Quoted in Robert L. Beisner, *Twelve Against Empire: The Anti-Imperialists 1898-1900* (New York, 1968), p. ix.

[34] Pratt, *op. cit.*, p. 1.

[35] Olcott, *op. cit.*, Vol. I, p. 379.

[36] Quoted in Pratt, *op. cit.*, p. 15, from *Atlantic Monthly*, September 1893.

[37] Claude Bowers, *Beveridge and the Progressive Era* (New York, 1932), p. 69.

[38] Beisner, *op. cit.*, pp. 178-179.

[39] Pratt, *op. cit.*, p. 22.

[40] Heinz Gollwitzer, *Europe in the Age of Imperialism 1880-1914* (New York, 1969), p. 215.

[41] May, *Imperial Democracy, op. cit.*, p. 143.

[42] Quoted in Dulles, *op. cit.*, p. 38, from edition of June 14, 1898.

[43] Hofstadter, *op. cit.*, pp. 3-40.

[44] Quoted in Samuel E. Morison, Frederick Merk and Frank Friedel, *Dissent in Three American Wars* (Cambridge, 1970), pp. 90-92, from a letter to Henry Lee Higginson of September 18, 1900. Beisner, *op. cit.*, p. 48, quotes the same phrase in an earlier letter to Francois Pillon.

[45] Samuel E. Morison, *The Oxford History of the American People* (New York, 1965), p. 801.

[46] Croly, *op. cit.*, p. 278.

[47] Beer, *op. cit.*, p. 554 and 548.

[48] Wilstach Collection, New York Public Library, *op. cit.*, New York *World*, May 6, 1898.

[49] *Ibid.*

[50] *Ibid.*, New York *Journal*, April 7, 1898.

[51] Morison, *op. cit.*, p. 800.

[52] May, *op. cit.*, p. 51, quoting Cuban diplomatic correspondence of January 16, 1898.

[53] Wilstach Collection, *op. cit.*, New York *Times* of April 4, 1898.

[54] Harold U. Faulkner, *The Decline of Laissez Faire* (New York, 1951), p. 15.

[55] Tuchman, *op. cit.*, p. 150.

[56] Pratt, *op. cit.*, pp. 246-247.

[57] Quoted in Edward C. Kirkland, *Dream & Thought in the Business Community 1860-1900* (Chicago, 1964, Quadrangle edition), pp. 156-157.

[58] Beisner, *op. cit.*, 1. 175.

[59] *Ibid.*, p. 181.

[60] (Finley Peter Dunne), *Mr. Dooley in the Hearts of His Countrymen* (Boston, 1899), pp. 6-7.

[61] Kirkland, *op. cit.*, pp. 17-18.

[62] Beisner, *op. cit.*, p. 13.

[63] Kirkland, *op. cit.*, p. 119, from Atkinson Papers of Massachusetts Historical Society.

[64] Beisner, *op. cit.*, p. 87.

[65] *Ibid.*, p. 89.

[66] Edward Atkinson, *The Anti-Imperialist*, May 27, 1899, pp. 17-35.

[67] New York *Times*, May 30, 1970.

[68] *Time*, July 31, 1970, p. 66.

[69] Morison, Merk and Friedel, *op. cit.*, p. 95, quoting from John Edikian *et al.*, eds., *After Dinner Speeches at the Lotos Club* (New York, 1911), pp. 14-15.

Chapter 2

Those Anarchistic Bastards

> In the middle of the journey of our life, I came to myself in a dark wood where the straight way was lost.

With these words, the poet Dante begins the descent into the Inferno in his *Divine Comedy*, written about 1300. Now hear the words reported to have been said by Bartolomeo Vanzetti a few months before he and Nicola Sacco were electrocuted on August 23, 1927:

> If it had not been for these things, I might have live out my life talking at street corners to scorning men. I might have die, unmarked, unknown, a failure. Now we are not a failure. This is our career and our triumph. Never in our full life could we hope to do such work for tolerance, for justice, for man's understanding of man as now we do by accident. Our words — our lives — our pains —

> nothing! The taking of our lives — lives of a good shoemaker and a poor fish-peddler — all! That last moment belongs to us — that agony is our triumph.[1]

At the beginning of their middle life, in their early thirties, Sacco and Vanzetti, without a shred of crime in their previous history, were found guilty of a payroll robbery and murder on April 15, 1920 in South Braintree, Massachusetts. Their seven years of trials and appeals finally engaged the attention of the entire world. When the switch was thrown at Charlestown prison, the humble compatriots of the elegant Dante became immortal in their own right, legendary characters in a new kind of American tragedy. Across the Atlantic an ancient and corrupt Europe howled at the thought of an unfair, prejudiced trial even for the least of America's immigrants. The new world, man's last great hope, must not be allowed to repeat the errors of the old world. It could not have its own Dreyfus case! Mussolini himself, suppressor of everything the confessed anarchists stood for, entered his protests, joining the Pope and the proletarians, the intellectuals and the aristocratic Marquis de Ferrante, his Boston Consul, in denouncing a bewildered Massachusetts. The Bay State, whose courts and judges had not hung any witches since 1692, understandably resented the overseas attention being paid to its venerated judicial system. This further jeopardized the chances of pardon for the convicted men.

Appropriately, Massachusetts' great Senator, Henry Cabot Lodge, the firebrand of expansion and internationalism in 1898, had recently capped his career by leading the fight against Wilson and his League of Nations, thus turning the nation's back against Europe as America sought a "return to normalcy" after the strains of World War I. In the White House, the state's leading citizen, Calvin Coolidge, was characteristically silent, accepting no phone calls about the case. Having reached the White House by forbidding a Boston police strike, he could hardly be expected to believe in the innocence of two anarchists and strike leaders. When the girls of Smith College participated in a daring rally on behalf of Sacco and Vanzetti in April, 1927, Coolidge's Northampton townspeople broke it up with unexpected small-town violence. Granville Hicks, on the Smith faculty and a rally organizer, came to an important conclusion in 1946 which seems valid as history. It was not, Hicks sorrowfully admitted, just the rich and powerful who were against the two Italians:

> It was also the doctors, the lawyers, the shopkeepers, the farmers, the workers. It was practically all my neighbors in Northampton except for the other members of the college faculty.[2]

Now, over forty years later, America has a new series of trials in which the political overtones involve the minds of thoughtful citizens more than the underlying acts themselves. There are the Chicago conspirators who faced Judge Julius Hoffman, Dr. Spock and his fellow draft advisers, the Berrigan priests at Catonsville and Harrisburg, the Oakland Seven, the New Haven Nine and the others that will follow. Nothing could be further from the Smith incident than the experience in New Haven, another New England college community, in April 1970. Again the issue was over a fair trial for unpopular defendants in a period of fear and backlash caused to a large extent by the actions of the group to which the defendants belonged. The change in community temper is incredibly marked. President Kingman Brewster of Yale, a trained attorney, encouraging his faculty and students to take a position on the New Haven Nine trial, concerning the murder of Panther Alex Rackley by his own fellow Panthers, stated publicly:

> . . . I am appalled and ashamed that things have come to such a pass that I am skeptical of the ability of black revolutionaries to achieve a fair trial anywhere in the United States. In large measure the atmosphere has been created by police actions and prosecutions against the Panthers in many parts of the country. It is also one more inheritance from centuries of racist discrimination and oppression. . . .[3]

The specific unfairness which caused the rumpus at New Haven, incidentally, was the six months contempt of court sentence meted out to two Panther functionaries over reading a note from defendant Bobby Seale in court. (The unhappy Judge Mulvey withdrew the sentence when Yale immediately reacted.) Herbert Ehrmann, at the time the last living defense attorney for Sacco and Vanzetti, would have shed tears of gall over the irony of this situation, having passionately believed since 1926 in the monstrous unfairness of his clients' trial, ranging all the way from colossal prejudice, harassment on cross-examination, tampering with evidence, preparation of witnesses and suppression of vital information to general miscarriage of justice by the officials involved. Yet to imagine President Lowell of Harvard, who held the lives of the defendants in his hands at the final moment, capable of substituting "Italian anarchists" for "black revolutionaries" in President Brewster's above statement, would call for the wildest stretch of the imagination. One can only conclude this digression by noting that regardless of the fairness of President Brewster's remarks, with their apparent moral overkill to placate a seething student body and black faculty, times have indeed changed for unpopular defendants in the courts. Not only did Yale subsequently open its dormitories to feed and bed thousands of May Day Panther demonstrators gathered in New Haven but Yale's alumni kept their cool and their President intact. The townspeople apparently went about their business, happy and relieved that no store windows were broken, either by Panthers or students.

Granted these new defendants stand a better chance of obtaining a fair trial, assuming the charges, such as those in the Chicago trial, make sense in the first place, none of them are likely to produce a figure so attractive and fascinating as Bartolomeo Vanzetti, the fiercely mustached one with the piercing eyes, the noble cranium and the fantastically flawed eloquence derived from his self-education behind bars. Robert Oppenheimer and Alger Hiss were equally if not more important in the political dimensions and tragic elements of their trials but their cold intelligence and escaped martyrdom alone make them no match for the fish peddler and the shoemaker. Only men as humble as Sacco and Vanzetti could inspire their supporters — and eventually themselves — into accepting the ultimate comparison, the crucifixion itself. More than any other American trial, the Sacco-Vanzetti case produced a legacy of plays, novels and poetry. As the years fly by, however, it appears that Ben Shahn's belatedly recognized gouaches and serigraphs will be regarded as the major artistic creation of the trial, particularly with the completion of the great mosaic mural reproducing his central work, "The Passion of Sacco and Vanzetti," on an outside wall of a Syracuse University building in 1967. Shahn relates that he was painting in Paris in 1925, imitating Cezanne and the Parisian school, when he noted the agitation in Europe over the convicted men. Returning to the United States, he joined the pickets in Boston and suddenly came to the realization that his destiny was to become a painter in the cause of social justice. "Even as a youngster," he is quoted, "I always regretted not having lived in some great historic time; the time of Lincoln or Washington, or even during the crucifixion. Then suddenly it came to me — this was a crucifixion — right in front of my eyes."[4] Like Dante, Shahn came face to face with himself in his middle life, in this case with fortunate results.

II

The business class has been charged with railroading Sacco and Vanzetti to the electric chair because they were anarchists. Since the business class is an abstraction and the judicial system, if any institution, bears the burden of electrocuting apparently innocent men, the business class can reasonably claim clean hands. This would be particularly in order since the accusation against the business class, or more particularly the capitalist class, was part of the deliberate strategy of the worldwide Communist and left-wing labor organizations which attached themselves to the case. It was not an even exchange. While instigating and exploiting international criticism of capitalist America's violation of civil liberties, the Communists contributed to the Sacco-Vanzetti Defense Committee a paltry $6,000, according to the fund's treasurer, Aldino Felicani.[5] The young typesetter, faithful anarchist friend of the accused, kept the books in the most meticulous business style and eventually became an admired and revered printing press entrepreneur in Boston.

It appears certain that a great deal of money was raised by various fronts that never reached the cause. At the same time one should reject the impression that the mass protest meetings at home and abroad depended on Communist manipulation. After all, the matter was easily recognized without propaganda as a great human drama. The seven years wait and the electric chair itself were regarded as cruel and unusual punishment. The case was widely, and for the most part accurately, reported in the leading newspapers and magazines of the world as legitimate news. As for Russia, that nation was still reeling from its own revolution, too busy liquidating its domestic dissenters, including anarchists, to be doing much international plotting. In America, the recently born Communist party, legal but harassed, was split into two factions totalling less than 60,000 members. The I.W.W.— the "Wobblies"— America's only home-grown labor party with genuine class warfare convictions, were down to a declining membership of 35,000. They were also on the run from sheriffs and state anti-radical laws as they spun out the last days of their rather romantic, hand to mouth "working stiffs" existence. Neither of these groups had money to spare for Sacco and Vanzetti.

Over three hundred thousand dollars were spent in seven years for trial and appeal expense, press releases and pamphlets, defense experts, the search for witnesses and tracing of new evidence.[6] This money came from sources more concerned with justice and fair play for two simple laborers than with the dialectical analysis of the inevitable fate of alien homicide suspects in Massachusetts courts during the death struggles of capitalism.

The funds would include a substantial amount from the small treasuries of some of the more adventurous unions, particularly those with a soft spot for Fred Moore, the conniving radical lawyer of the first years of the defense. (The union leaders in turn may have only vaguely realized that American business leaders in the twenties viewed anarchists primarily as a threat to their successful fight to contain the growth of unionism rather than as a challenge to the established political order.)

Next there would be modest contributors from the intellectuals. These artists, writers and professors no doubt put their meager resources on the line with a mental assist from their traditional anti-business sentiment. Unless captured by the radicals, however, as John Dos Passos temporarily was, their animosity would be on cultural grounds, certainly not implacably political.

Finally, there would be the gifts in cash or in service from the liberals and conservatives of the Establishment itself, those who believed in defending unpopular causes involving personal liberties regardless of the propaganda and wild charges from less sincere partisans. Add to this the support from the non-political American Civil Liberties Union and similar organizations such as the Ligue des Droits de l'Homme in France and the informal accounting, as gathered from the responsible Sacco-Vanzetti literature, is reasonably complete. The funds appear to be untainted, especially since principal supporters such as Felix Frankfurter and Aldino Felicani carefully resisted Moore's deviousness and the Communists' efforts to take over the fund-raising and otherwise infiltrate the Defense Committee. Of course, the support from men like Frankfurter, Dos Passos, Heywood Broun and Walter Lippmann, priceless to the defense, cost nothing.

One widow's mite must be added, the small gifts of Italians in numbers large enough to account for one-third of the funds received by the Defense Committee. The Italians, especially those of New England, were generous with their hard-earned dollars. Still politically weak, ethnically separated and toiling at the lowest paid jobs, they were, like most immigrants, basically conservative, finding Calvin Coolidge's business-dominated America far superior to the monarchs and dictators they had fled. In their efforts to emulate their Yankee superiors, they must have regarded the troublesome anarchists with a baleful eye but they did not renounce them. The entire Plymouth Italian community apparently revered the bachelor Vanzetti as a saintly man. Sacco, with his beautiful titian-haired Rosina, his son Dante and new baby Ines, made up a family of unusual diligence at work and harmony at home in the town of Stoughton. At any rate, the professed peaceful anarchism of the accused, however at odds with the rash of bombings plaguing the nation at the time, did not prevent an outpouring of more than fifty Italian alibi witnesses on their behalf. These folk included many as conservative and respectable as the late George Apley himself, but all were scorned as hopeless perjurors by District Attorney Katzmann, as the record clearly shows.

Since some formidably persistent doubts have been raised about the innocence of the two men, particularly Sacco, the support of the Italian community must be kept in mind for the "whole picture" of the case, which seems to be the only vantage point remaining for those seeking an answer for their own minds. Katzmann needled the jury to disregard defense witnesses, both as to alibis and identification, on the grounds of unreliability and their drawing together as Italians. "Some of those Italians up there told you what to say?" was a typical harsh question thrown through an interpreter at Mrs. Margaret Fiochi, a Plymouth resident for twenty-two years and wife of a veteran railroad worker.[7] She was one of fourteen who testified that Vanzetti delivered eels to their homes on December 24, 1919, the day he was supposed to have attempted another payroll robbery in Bridgewater, preceding the South Braintree crime. To convict Vanzetti, as they did, the Plymouth jurors had to believe that none of these religious people bought their day-before-Christmas eels (an important Italian tradition) from the atheistic fish-peddler and his boy assistant, Beltrando Brini, now a high school principal in Quincy, Massachusetts, who swears passionately to Vanzetti's innocence.[8]

The implication that the witnesses were all bound by some kind of Mafia tradition to lie for men who flouted their religious and political sensibilities should arouse some reasonable doubt in a murky case involving life and death. This is one reason why supporters of the men feel that prejudice was the real criminal. Indeed the credibility of these witnesses in both trials is enhanced by their moral courage, as well as their apparent tolerance, inasmuch as at least four employees claim they were summarily dismissed from their factory jobs when their testimony against Sacco and Vanzetti wavered under examination by the District Attorney.[9]

Rather than accept the conspiracy of perjury theory, one wonders how such close-knit, almost tribal communities as those Italian enclaves of a half-century ago would not have quickly learned the truth and cast out the guilty ones.

From the higher rungs of the Italian immigrant ladder appeared an able young lawyer from Pittsburgh, Michael Angelo Musmanno, who rushed to their defense in the closing years. He stayed on to write about them and plead for their vindication until his death in 1971 as a Supreme Court Justice in Pennsylvania and leading Italian-American citizen. Only a few years before he had been in Milan to testify on behalf of the families of Sacco and Vanzetti in a libel suit against a German author who had charged the men with being guilty. [10] Still wrapped in mystery and emotion, the Sacco-Vanzetti case is a case that simply will not die.

IV

Prejudice — the word calls for instant denials and defenses. Who would admit he pre-judges anyone or anything? Common sense and common law point the same way — a man is innocent until proved guilty. Wait until all the evidence is in. Judge Webster Thayer, pinched, frozen-faced Yankee elder, who asked his presiding judge to give him the South Braintree case with full realization of its loaded significance,[11] made it plain for the record that prejudice was not allowed in his court. In his charge to the jury in the Dedham courthouse, where both Sacco and Vanzetti (Sacco had not been indicted in the Plymouth trial as he was at work on the day involved) were convicted for the South Braintree crime, he stated on July 14, 1921:

> Let me repeat to you what I said to another jury in a similar case: Let your eyes be blinded to every ray of sympathy or prejudice but let them ever be willing to receive the beautiful sunshine of truth, of reason, and sound judgment, and let your ears be deaf to every sound of public opinion or public clamor, if there be any, either in favor

> or against these defendants. Let them always be listening for the sweet voices of conscience and of sacred and solemn duty efficiently and fearlessly performed. The law grants to every person the same rights and privileges . . .[12]

Some readers will be prejudiced against the Judge's pompous, antiquarian flow of English and unconsciously give thanks they never appeared before him. Prejudice is insidious, as human a flaw as envy and selfishness. As a social phenomenon, however, it tends to periodic peaks. We have had three peaks of prejudice, each stimulated by fear and hysteria, in twentieth century America. The contemporary backlash against students and blacks was preceded by the nightmare world of Senator Joseph McCarthy. Attorney General A. Mitchell Palmer's anti-Red scare, probably the most inexcusable of the three episodes, hung over America at the time of Sacco and Vanzetti's arrest.

Businessmen and business standards set the style for America of the twenties. It was the age of business triumphant, when Harding and Coolidge and Hoover, just before the deluge, presided in the White House somewhat as Chairmen of the Board of the United States. "The business of America is business," said Coolidge, and flappers, movie stars, bootleggers, college kids in raccoon coats, Babbitts in small business and bond salesmen in big business all agreed. There was reason for satisfaction in the business world. The business class had come out of the doghouse it occupied under Theodore Roosevelt, with his patrician disregard for businessmen, and Woodrow Wilson, the moralizing professor who had carried on the Progressive reform movement with its endless federal regulations, including the fiercely resisted Federal Reserve control of the banking system. It is hard to believe the claim of many historians, such as Richard Hofstadter, that anti-business sentiment in the muckraking period at the turn of the century reached a level exceeding that of the New Deal.[13] At any rate, by the twenties the patient had achieved a miraculous rehabilitation.

The good will towards business was not undeserved. Business, particularly the ominously feared big business, had produced an incredible arsenal in record time to turn the scales of history and defeat the German war machine. Then after a modest post-war depression which seemed to end by itself, without meddling from Washington, America's turned-on industrial apparatus poured forth hordes of consumer products for its pleasure-loving, city-centered, growing middle class. We see it differently now because we know that as these citizens patronized the glamorous stores and marched to the movies and ballrooms by the millions once a week, they would march right on to breadlines and marathon dance contests where free food was enough to attract participants. In the twenties, the few professors and economists who recognized that such a lopsided, undirected economy, doomed by speculative mania and poorly distributed purchasing power, would end in depression, were treated as unwelcome guests at the great board meetings in the White House. As in Victorian England, people and politicians simply could not see the utterly different world laying in wait for them. This is a merciful condition for those close enough to the top but it induces smugness, which in turn fosters prejudice.

Prejudice among business men? The businessman is glad to sell all comers and reward all employees according to merit regardless of race, religion or previous condition of servitude. Besides, prejudice is a personal vice that cannot stand the tests of the market place and the maximizing of profit. Today's businessman is realistic enough to pass by such claims. He adjusts to state and federal fair employment regulations with moderate good humor and an awareness that his old enemies the unions are the new repositories of discrimination. If he has personal prejudices, or even controversial convictions, he is likely to mask them with the most appropriate public relations. As for unions, they are here to stay, corporate giants as strong as business itself. They can no longer be exorcised by charges of radicalism. Revolutionaries are recognized as a political or counter-cultural force, more likely to be found on the campus than on the picket lines. The beards and bombs belong to the sons of businessmen, not to foreigners, or as the word was then used, aliens.

It was not so in the twenties. Henry Ford was the great business hero of that decade and he was as prejudiced as a man could be. The great wizard of the auto industry was the prime mover in putting 23 million autos on the road in 1929 compared with 7 million in 1919. Much of the prosperity of the twenties was due to his genius and his inspired raising of wages to $5 for a nine-hour day in 1914, against the wishes of his competitors. Ford's prejudice was not against blacks or even foreign born radicals. He was a pioneer in giving blacks economic opportunity. The Russians, putting aside their anti-capitalist faith in favor of technological faith, beat a path to his factories. One of the ironies of business history is the thought of Henry Ford hosting seventy Soviet engineers inside his Dearborn plant one day in 1932 while 3,000 unemployed workers demonstrated on the outside.

Ford's prejudice was centered against bankers and Jews. In 1920 he established the Dearborn *Independent*, which soon became America's leading anti-Semitic journal and the first under respectable auspices. To his credit, Ford responded to a libel suit in 1927 by apologizing to the Jewish people for everything the *Independent* had said about them and for republishing the fake "Protocols of the Elders of Zion." The point is that a leading manufacturer could, in the same time span of the Sacco-Vanzetti case, attack an important minority and get away with it, both in sales and national prestige.

In fact the twenties were an intolerant and law-breaking period, despite the prim Coolidge hibernating in the White House as a stand-in for the nation's conscience and morality. Hate literature abounded, especially against the Catholics, accusing the Knights of Columbus, for example, of indulging in obscene rites. America's own knights of the nightsheets, the disreputable Ku Klux Klan, came back to life in the twenties, especially in the North and the West, not just the South. The Klan elected governors in Oklahoma and Oregon, and in 1924 practically took over Indiana. Its membership reached five million as it perpetrated its bizarre mixture of 100% white, Protestant Americanism and sadistically inspired puritanism and anti-intellectualism. Fortunately the Klan went into decline in the late twenties, not so much because of criticism from high places as the disgraceful revelations of graft and rape on the part of its "Grand Dragons" such as David Stephenson of Indiana. The Klan's membership list was appropriately invisible but there is no question that it attracted at this time an inordinate number of small businessmen, the filling station operators, Main Street store-owners and real estate agents whose mood reflected sourness and anger at the invasion of chain stores and foreign born merchants threatening their status in their home territory.

Congressmen as well as Klan reacted to the new isolationism by taking another look at the immigration laws. Hordes of destitute Europeans, uprooted by the ravages of war, had been flocking to the United States, more than 800,000 in the year ending June 30, 1921 alone. Over two-thirds of these were from Southern and Eastern Europe, with Italians represented in very substantial numbers. After an Emergency Quota Act in 1921 to shut the door, the 1923 Immigration Act deliberately discriminated against Southern and Eastern Europeans on the basis of arbitrary national origins quotas. Great Britain and Northern Ireland, for example, could now send 65,721 a year to America as against 5,802 from Italy. Called "Dagos" and "Wops," many of them digging ditches, generally slow in becoming naturalized citizens, embarrassed by their notorious gangsters and anarchists, the Italians must have wrily observed Columbus Day in the Promised Land. The officially sanctioned prejudice was not lost on the average American's mentality.

Now comes the final disreputable condition of the early twenties, the one that closely relates to the Sacco-Vanzetti case, the anti-Red raids of Attorney General A. Mitchell Palmer. Like Judge Thayer, District Attorney Katzmann, President Lowell and even the well-intentioned businessman-Governor of Massachusetts, Alvan T. Fuller, Palmer ends up on the debit side of history's ledger. There may be ultimate vindication for the others if Sacco and Vanzetti turn out to be guilty after all, but Palmer appears to be beyond redemption.

Palmer's mistake was in giving the people and the Congress what they wanted, a crushing drive against the "Reds." As with McKinley in the Spanish-American War, tremendous pressure poured forth from the wellsprings of democracy to take action inconsistent with democratic traditions. Add to this the lure of Presidential ambitions and Palmer's transition from a liberal Congressman and friend of labor to a despotic Attorney General is explainable.

He had first been elected to Congress in 1908 with the support of Pennsylvania steelworkers, coal miners and clay-pit laborers, including a large core of recent immigrants. In 1919, as Wilson's third Attorney General, he regarded himself as a "radical friend of labor." In this role he refused to emulate predecessors, such as McKinley's Olney, by intervening in the massive strikes, involving four million workers in 1919 alone, which were exasperating post-war America. This problem of strikes with its attendant fear of radicals in the labor movement is a major indictment that can be laid at the door of the business community. It explains why the business community went along so easily with the anti-Red hysteria which in turn affected the fairness of the Sacco-Vanzetti trial. To this extent, the dominant business community is a silent witness at the trial, a role of course far less culpable than that assigned to it by the radical exploiters of the case. In retrospect, the business community failed to measure up to a high level of responsibility in the twenties, first, because it so blindly fought labor and its strikers in an effort to ward off unionism and second, by joining in the anti-radical hysteria to discredit labor regardless of other motives. United States Steel, for example, was able to stall off unions for another fifteen years by charging its 1919 strike was Communist led instead of a genuine grievance. It finally broke the strike, after fourteen were killed in Gary, Indiana, by starving out the workers with strikebreakers and state and federal troops.

Palmer did not have to be anti-labor to ride the whirlwind against the radicals. A series of bombings, the mad specialty of anarchists rather than organized labor, frightened the nation into demands for repression. Palmer had been on the job only three months when a bomb burst outside his Washington residence, destroying the ground floor and scattering part of the clumsy bomber's remains on Assistant Secretary of the Navy Franklin D. Roosevelt's nearby lawn. Also scattered along the street were copies of an anarchist manifesto entitled "Plain Words," promising death to government officials. A year later, the typesetters for this pamphlet were identified as two members of the New York branch of Sacco and Vanzetti's loosely organized anarchist group. In fact Vanzetti had just returned from a visit to New York to report on the fortunes of the detained typesetters when he was arrested as a suspect for the recent payroll murders. In the few days between Vanzetti's return from New York and his arrest on May 5, 1920, Andrea Salsedo, one of the typesetters, fell, jumped or was pushed out of the fourteenth floor window of the Manhattan Department of Justice office at 21 Park Row. The claim of the Massachusetts anarchists that this was the real reason why they were carrying guns at the time of the arrest failed to convince the jury, which apparently accepted the prosecutor's suggestion that they were on their way to another robbery in the same neighborhood.

The bombing of Palmer's house was preceded by the discovery in the New York Post Office of sixteen bomb packages addressed to a group of citizens and officials ranging all the way from John D. Rockefeller, Sr. to Supreme Court Justice Oliver Wendell Holmes. In June of 1919 seven explosions in five eastern cities gutted homes, buildings and a rectory. Although the police could not trace the perpetrators, the common assumption deemed the action a declaration of war by Red bombers without fine distinctions as to which faction of the political left, let alone anarchists, was actually involved. The newspapers did their part with headlines typically stating. RED PERIL HERE and REDS DIRECT STRIKE. By the time Palmer's raids had been accomplished even the New York *Times* and the Washington *Post* had joined in praise of the Attorney General's actions. The two family favorite magazines, *Life* (at that time a cartoon and humor magazine) and the *Literary Digest*, constantly portrayed a composite radical of disheveled appearance, ape-like posture, a sputtering bomb in hand and wearing Russian boots, about to assault the female Statue of Liberty. His label was usually "Bolsheviki," "Commie," or "Anarchist" and the apparition was enough to frighten businessmen as well as small children. The businessman could not be blamed for remembering that the anarchist Alexander Berkman, now freed from prison, had invaded Henry Clay Frick's office only twenty-seven years ago during the Homestead strike and almost succeeded in stabbing Frick to death. In March 1927 when the fever had subsided but Sacco and Vanzetti were about to exhaust all appeals, Felix Frankfurter reminded the business community of its participation in the national hysteria. He also offered as evidence of how intense the feeling was the thought that it could have affected Boston businessmen the way it did. Frankfurter brought the matter up in his famous *Atlantic Monthly* article which sounded the final alarm to non-radicals to prevent injustice. Alertly presenting the evidence in the words of John F. Moors, a partner in the brokerage firm of Cabot and Moors, rather than from his own suspect Harvard sanctuary, Frankfurter wrote:

> Boston was one of the worst centers of this lawlessness and hysteria. Its proximity to industrial communities having a large proportion of foreign labor and a history of past industrial conflicts lent to the lawless activities of the government officials the widespread support of influential public opinion. One of the leading citizens of Boston, Mr. John F. Moors, himself a banker, has called attention to the fact that the "hysteria against 'the reds' was so great, at the time when these men were convicted, that even the most substantial bankers in the city were carried away to the extent of paying for full-page advertisements about the red peril." (Frankfurter quoted from Moors' letter to the *Boston Herald* of November 3, 1926.)[14]

"I was shouted at from every editorial sanctum in America from sea to sea," Palmer later bitterly complained, "I was preached upon from every pulpit; I was urged to do something now, and do it quick and in a way that would bring results." The United States Senate in the fall of 1919 unanimously demanded a reason for Palmer's inaction and implied he might be removed from his post, a bitter threat to his well-known Presidential ambitions. Meanwhile the dying Wilson, who had earlier cautioned him to show restraint, offered little support for his Attorney General's hesitation.

With this background, Palmer's infamous actions gain credibility. Having swallowed anarchist literature hook, line and sinker, Palmer screeched into action to save the country from revolution. A wartime addition to the immigration code had outlawed anarchism in all forms. Aliens who violated the code, even by subscribing to anarchist publications, could be arrested and deported. It was as deadly efficient as anything the Communists themselves could dream up. Immigration officers under the Department of Labor would conduct the brief hearings and ship the aliens out on the next boat. A warrant to show that some part of the immigration code had been violated dispensed with the Bill of Rights and required only a mimeograph machine for its production. Appeals would be practically impossible for the terrified aliens, now being listed in elaborate cross-card files by Palmer's new General Intelligence Division of the Department of Justice, headed by a twenty-four year old attorney named J. Edgar Hoover.

On November 7, 1919, federal agents and local police raided the Russian People's House in New York City and similar centers in nine other eastern cities, netting four hundred and fifty suspects. Before the night was over, half were released as innocent but by morning Palmer had become a national hero in most of the nation's press. By December, Palmer had secured deportation orders for 249 Russians, including Alexander Berkman and his friend Emma Goldman. They were packed into an ancient army transport and delivered to Russia by way of Finland in January, 1920. The Finns were at war with Russia but arranged a short truce in order to carry out this strange return of human cargo according to the international protocol which seems to persist through all regimes.

Now Palmer shifted into high gear. With the Secretary of Labor on sick leave, he induced the Secretary's weak assistant to change Rule 22 of the deportation hearings procedure so that it was no longer necessary for arresting officers to inform aliens of either their right to counsel or what the charges were against them. Next, 3,000 warrants were printed with blank spaces for the aliens who were to be granted a free trip home.

On the night of January 2, 1920 an all-out raid took place in thirty-three cities in twenty-three states. The knock on the door in the middle of the night, the blinding flash of light, the brutal dragging of men from their homes and beds all took place fifty years ago. By midnight the 3,000 warrants had been used up. In many cases the names were entered long after arrest. An estimated 2,000 additional suspects were picked up without any charges at all.

When the smoke had cleared, thoughtful Americans began to realize the cure exceeded the disease. The National Council of Churches, already branded as Red-sympathizing, bravely started an investigation. So did the more sensible administrators in the Department of Labor, particularly Louis C. Post, who immediately cancelled 2,000 of the warrants as defective and finally whittled down over 4,000 suspects to 556 deportees. Palmer asked Congress to impeach Post as a Communist sympathizer but Post was found capable of acting as he did without such leanings. He was returned to his duties after a month-long hearing. An interesting protest occurred in Detroit where nearly eight hundred had been arrested with less than four hundred warrants issued. The missing warrants arrived two weeks after the raid. A group of Detroit businessmen under the leadership of the five and ten magnate, S. S. Kresge, distinguished themselves by immediately investigating the raids and blasting the authorities.

Boston as we have noted had a high place in the raid plans and was expected to cast up a fine catch. Sacco and Vanzetti, unless they were actually cold-blooded killers as charged, must have had chills of goose flesh at the sight of gangs of their compatriots marched through the streets of Boston in chains to be jammed into the underheated and overcrowded prison on Deer Island in Boston Harbor. Why they weren't included is a mystery since they were known to be active anarchists, guilty at least of being on the subscription lists of the *Cronaca Sovversiva*, the leading anarchist journal edited by the recently deported Luigi Galleani, for whom Sacco and Vanzetti professed great admiration. Two of the Department of Justice investigators in the Boston area, Fred Weyand and Lawrence Letherman, later gave affidavits to the defense that they had given this information to the District Attorney as part of a professional trade-off arrangement. They supplied the affidavits voluntarily because they could not conceive of the shoe edger and fish peddler being guilty of what they regarded as distinctly professional gang crimes and they did not want to see innocent men electrocuted. The disclosure of this secret arrangement was particularly embarrassing to District Attorney Katzmann, who had claimed, with Judge Thayer's approval, that his relentless examination of the defendants' anarchism during the trial was for the purpose of making them prove they really were frightened radicals. Otherwise their gun-toting and lying upon arrest would be evidence of "consciousness of guilt," which it was his duty to establish. Of course, Katzmann and everyone else in the courthouse knew they were genuine anarchists. The District Attorney's line of questioning simply insured their conviction either way. The jury could not help regarding them as both anarchists and criminals in relation to the small arsenal found on their persons at the time of arrest, although anarchism was not supposed to be an issue in the trial.

Approximately one thousand Massachusetts radicals were picked up in the January raid and over four hundred were placed in the Deer Island prison. In this instance the Bay State immediately struck a strong blow for liberty. Federal Judge George W. Anderson soon cleaned out the jails to the last man on the grounds that every principle of justice and fair dealing had been violated in relation to warrants for arrest, detention of the accused and the so-called "hearings" granted them. Twelve nationally known lawyers, headed by Felix Frankfurter, Roscoe Pound and Zechariah Chaffee of the Harvard Law School, formed a national investigating committee that combed the entire scope of the raids and came up with a devastating indictment of Palmer and the Department of Justice. The real danger to the country, they stated, was not the possibility of a revolution as much as Palmer's abuse of federal power. Ticking off the Constitutional Amendments scrapped in the raids with a meticulous gathering of the evidence, they helped turn public opinion against Palmer, whose political hopes were soon beyond repair.

Had Sacco and Vanzetti been picked up and deported, one of the world's great trials would never have occurred. Instead on April 15, they presumably suddenly became full-fledged gunmen, carrying out a double murder and robbery, unmasked in broad daylight, in front of two shoe factories within a few miles of their own steady places of employment. And both men were promptly and cheerfully at work the first thing the morning after.

Americans saddened by the breakdown of trust and unity in the Vietnam period may well ponder over the sickness of our society after World War I. What caused the rash of strikes, the isolation from the ideals of the League of Nations, the repression of civil liberties, the violent race riots in Cleveland and Washington, the bigotry of the Klan and the surrender to hysteria against a truly weak leftist opposition? Was it really the recognition of an implacable showdown between the rich and the poor, the powerful and the weak, the privileged and the deprived? "All right, we are two nations," snarled John Dos Passos, a member of the upper class himself and a man who recorded events with the sharp eye of a reporter as well as a moralist. Could the allegiance to one nation become a mockery over a symbolic case such as Sacco and Vanzetti's, which shocked Dos Passos into making this statement? The class warfare explanation simply does not hold up, particularly from the viewpoint of history which has seen labor develop into a self-conscious middle class. There was no sinister alignment, even in the twenties, of the vested interests in the form of a plutocracy, such as European and South American countries regularly brought forth. On the other hand, there has been the indisputable record of practically every abuse in power, every lapse in tolerance, finally resulting in new reforms and new levels of public morality. Without the abuses, there could perhaps be no reforms. The test of the nation has been its ability to come to its senses given time. It is the time factor, of course, which is held in disrepute by the present generation of blacks and youths, with their new views of space and relativity.

Certainly the bomb-throwing itself was enough to frighten a good portion of the nation and discredit the trend towards political liberalism. In addition one may as well recognize America is hardly immune to mob psychology and violent prejudice. It has a distinct record of violence and anti-intellectualism. Everything can happen here. That it doesn't happen is a credit to the government structure, the more enlightened leaders and the good sense of the citizens in the long run.

Wars of course are the most powerful agents of national unity and national sickness. The backwash and let down after World War I was a setting for fear and irrationality. Apparently no American war was so popular while it lasted and unpopular as an aftermath. Laborers came back to underpaid jobs in a period of inflation, business faced a depression and a deluded group of bomb-throwers captured the headlines. Samuel Eliot Morison, who, as a young Harvard history professor, was one of the first to lend his distinguished name to the Sacco-Vanzetti defense, is still puzzled about our post World War I aberrations. He has recently concluded that a good deal of it was a boomerang from the excessive propaganda whipped up against the Germans. When the war ended abruptly before even half our soldiers had seen action, there was a mood of frustration, a large part of which siphoned off against the Red menace.[15] At any rate, it is clear that a nation can easily lose its bearings. Still Sacco and Vanzetti must have thought of Judge Anderson and the Harvard law professors as equals in some measure to their anarchist demigods. How else can one explain their blithe plans to have run an anarchist meeting the week after their arrest, to raise funds for Salsedo and his fellow printer Elia?

V

> Proletarians, you have fought all the wars. You have worked for all the owners. You have wandered over all the countries. Have you harvested the fruits of your labors, the price of your victories? Does the future promise you anything? Have you found a piece of land where you can live like a human being and die like a human being? On these questions, on this argument, and on this

> theme, the struggle for existence, Bartolomeo Vanzetti will speak. Hour______Day______Hall______Admission free. Freedom of discussion to all. Take the ladies with you.

On the night of their arrest in a trolley car in Brockton on May 5, 1920, Vanzetti's above ingenuously pencilled draft in Italian for a printed notice was found in Sacco's pocket. It was pure Vanzetti, combining romantic, half-baked questions, a reminder about freedom of discussion and a rather gallant invitation to the ladies. Aside from an insight into the man's personality, it bears on the "consciousness of guilt" which was a prime factor in the jury's decision.

When arrested, Sacco and Vanzetti were returning from an evening visit to a neighborhood garage. They and two fellow anarchists had been refused delivery of a car whose license plates had lapsed. The garage owner had been alerted to notify the police of any request for the car as one Boda, the owner, was an anarchist. The Bridgewater police chief, Michael Stewart, who emerges as something of a Toonerville cop in this case, had been advised by a dim-witted informer with access to a "crime detector machine" to watch for an anarchist with a car kept in a shed if he wanted to catch the payroll murderers. Stewart, who had recently taken part in Palmer's Red raids, figured that a man named Coacci and his friend Boda met the vision in the machine and set the trap for the arrest of anyone coming for Boda's auto. Only Sacco and Vanzetti were indicted from among the four, including Boda and his friend Orciani, who called at the garage, since they carried guns and had to establish alibis for April 15.

Herbert Ehrmann, in his final comprehensive summary of the case, published in late 1969 a few months before his death, poses the question:

> . . . Experienced police detectives, had only to ask themselves a few questions. Would robbers in possession of two or more automobiles and a variety of number plates (a switch of cars had been employed in the South Braintree crime) seek to take out and use a broken-down old

> Overland which did not even have a 1920 registration? Would such men ride around in interurban streetcars? Would highwaymen in possession of nearly sixteen thou-and dollars, recently stolen, have any interest in the picayune process of collecting coins in dribs and drabs? Would they risk displaying themselves to make appeals at public meetings to obtain the kind of small change customarily produced?[16]

This type of nagging question is typical of the case and perhaps will never be answered to everyone's satisfaction. In our speculative treatment of the case as a social phenomenon, with the business class dragged in as one of the accused, its complex development, involving a 6,400 page total transcript, can only be selectively considered. One aspect that springs from Vanzetti's premature note, the nature of his anarchism, is worthy of analysis. Not only should such a loosely used word be reviewed by followers of the case but also anarchism gains new interest by the historical leap which brings it to the campus today. In a dominantly business society, businessmen with their great prestige and indirect influence on political matters, can well afford to philosophize about revolutionary matters. In the first place, by their personal actions they have already accomplished not only an industrial revolution but also a social revolution, as represented by our reasonably successful modern capitalism. Secondly, there is now another dominant institution in our society, hardly recognized in the twenties, the eight and one-half million college students and their faculties, who, to an important degree, rebel against much of our established society's values, including business values. In this context, businessmen can review their reaction to the crisis of the twenties.

That a wing of the Boston anarchists had a self-image quite different from the bomb-throwing Bolsheviki is apparent in the appeal of the friends of Sacco and Vanzetti a few days after their arrest. These men, who whiled away their Sundays in the "Italian Independent Naturalization Club of East Boston," naively expected the full shelter of the law for their pursuit of ideals which were on the surface consistent with America's official aspirations. The hastily organized defense committee, assembled when the accused were informed they were murder rather than anarchist suspects, consisted of their typesetter friend Aldino Felicani (what is the attraction between typesetters and revolutionaries?) and sixteen other East Boston anarchists. The others were all skilled workers, one a building contractor, but they must have shared some rejection of American life, some disillusion with the land they had adopted. At any rate, the following from their Italian pamphlet, entitled "Men of Good Will," is curiously disarming for those who might believe a man electrocuted as a criminal is as good as a man electrocuted as an anarchist:

> Two of our active good friends and comrades . . . have become involved in one of those tragic, dark legal plots in which innocence has all the semblance of guilt, and honesty has the hypocritical mask put on by the subtlest of rogues. . . . In a country where subversive ideas are persecuted with Inquisitorial fury, anarchists are beyond the pale. . . . . We are convinced that an attempt is being made, through the persons of Sacco and Vanzetti, to strike at all subversive elements and their libertarian ideas. A sentence . . . would serve, in the hands of our enemies, to show that lovers of liberty are common criminals and that their ideas are not entitled to any of the civil freedoms. . . . We face a severe, a terrible test.[17]

If anarchists were beyond the pale, they had a worldwide epidemic of bombings and assassinations to blame. Yet these Bostonian lovers of liberty were apparently convinced they did not have to share the guilt for that faction of the movement. Anarchists could be talkers and writers, or "quietists," as Sacco and Vanzetti's group appeared to be, or "activists" who composed a murderous rogue's gallery of their own. In this context, Sacco and Vanzetti perhaps saw themselves in league with men like Tolstoy, Gandhi or even Boston's own Henry David Thoreau, each of whom had a touch of anarchy in his soul in respect to a decided distaste for organization and authority. But inevitably the movement, for all its Utopian ideals, led to its dark side, the "propaganda of the deed." This call to arms from the anarchist vocabulary meant the violent, often suicidal, murder of an authority figure for symbolic or propagandist purposes. The difference between Harvey Lee Oswald, James Earl Ray and Sirhan Sirhan and the traditional anarchist killers is that the former apparently acted as lone wolves in slaying their authority figures rather than as agents prepared to die for a universal political creed.

Most Americans of the twenties still remembered the assassination of President McKinley in 1901 by the demented Leon Czolgosz, who rationalized his deed, insofar as he was capable of doing so, by the anarchist doctrines which had inflamed his mind. This tragedy was the culmination of a series of assassinations in Europe. The liberal Spanish Prime Minister Canovas, who might have enabled McKinley to avert the Spanish-American war, was shot in 1897. President Carnot of France was stabbed to death by an Italian anarchist in 1894, who gave the usual cry "Long live anarchy," which Sacco himself proclaimed from the electric chair. The melancholy and beautiful Empress Elizabeth of Austria was assassinated by an anarchist with a home-made dagger as she walked by a lake in Geneva in 1898. King Umberto of Italy fell before another anarchist in 1900.

In 1886 the crowned heads of Europe looked aghast at America where a sensational trial for murder revolved around our own anarchists. In the midst of a violent labor conflict over the eight-hour day, centering in Chicago, August Spies, an anarchist German-language newspaper editor, charged that "the police and militia, the bloodhounds of capitalism, are ready to murder" and suggested meeting the bullets with dynamite. A protest meeting over two strikers killed in a clash with police soon followed in Haymarket Square on May 4. At the last minute, the peaceful meeting erupted into chaos and a bomb killed seven charging policemen. Eight anarchists were arrested without direct evidence proving their guilt. Spies, for example, was hanged for inciting the crime through his journal. Altogether four were hanged, one committed suicide and three went to prison. Anarchism became a word of horror in America, associated with foreigners and labor incendiaries. It was even used to smear political figures of the stature of Bryan and Altgeld. When the latter had the temerity to pardon the three prisoners, he went into public oblivion.

Under these circumstances it would take a bold mind to join the East Boston anarchist group. One might conjecture as to why so many of the laborers who carried the black flag of anarchism were foreigners. Perhaps their naive concept of an unregulated, no-boss factory stemmed from the more primitive working conditions in their own factories and farms in the small towns of southern Europe, where family or even tribal enterprise still existed. Its utter impossibility in advanced industrial countries patterned by technology and mass production limited its appeal to native Americans, so that anarchy and foreigners were more or less synonymous. The Communists, dedicated to the machine quite as much as Americans themselves, quickly parted company with the anarchists in their midst, who were disciples of Bakunin.

An undisciplined giant of a man, sprung from the Russian landowning class, Mikail Bakunin fostered a cult of violence and destruction that helped launch the terrorist side of the anarchist movement. Yet the anarchist program, decentralized, anti-statist, anti-party, anti-bureaucratic, looking for spontaneous combustion from the down-trodden workers, was a ridiculous concept, even with its handy bombers, for tough Communist theoreticians such as Marx, Lenin and Stalin. Marx fought Bakunin from the start and Lenin and Stalin slaughtered anarchists from the Ukraine to the plains of the Spanish Civil War. Castro in Cuba and Gomulka in Poland have followed suit.

The true believers among the anarchists in turn condemned the Russian Revolution as a betrayal. They saw no difference between corporation capitalism and state capitalism. It is not too far-fetched to surmise that an orthodox anarchist would feel more at home with Adam Smith's free-form economics, Jefferson's independent agrarian yeomen and the hippies in a commune than under the thumb of a Russian five-year plan. Vanzetti certainly was not a Communist. He regarded Lenin as a traitor to the Revolution[18] and in one of his letters from prison, he states didactically:

> . . . In Russia this happened: The Czarism was destroyed by a revolution; part of the owners were expropriated; a party took the power, stopped the continuation of expropriation and appropriated to itself that part of the social wealth which had already been expropriated by the people. From that moment the revolution began its regression and a few leaders of a small party became the only and real rulers of the land.[19]

Not that Vanzetti and his less imaginative friend Sacco were not revolutionaries. They burned with revolutionary ardor in the sense of making the world over quickly on Utopian terms. Certainly they believed that control had to be wrested from the capitalist class which they identified, as the Marxists did, with oppression and wars. It would take a highly civilized capitalist to regard the personal problems of such men with equanimity. On the other hand, tolerance for unfriendly ideas has its own strong tradition in America.

There seems to be no record of either man advocating terrorism in speech or in writing. One would have to have access to their innermost thoughts to determine at what point they would condone "the propaganda of the deed," but their thoughts were not on trial. In an atmosphere of anti-Red hysteria in America in the twenties, not many people, including twelve good Norfolk County jurors, would be making fine distinctions about degrees of anarchism more suitable for anarchist debating societies. Even there a debate could not be guaranteed. One of Vanzetti's heroes, Enrico Malatesta, a firebrand anarchist always in and out of European jails, was almost shot to death by another hot-headed Italian anarchist. The charge: Malatesta leaned too much toward Marxism, in respect to his zeal for organization, for a pure anarchist.

Another fiery typesetter and printer, Pierre Joseph Proudhon (1809-1865), was a more appropriate mentor for Vanzetti. Proudhon was his intellectual hero. "Proudhon has illuminated me," he wrote happily to one of his faithful lady correspondents, most of them Boston Establishment wives who were touchingly loyal to both men to the very end.[20] Translating Proudhon's *The War and the Peace* into English from an Italian edition became a labor of love in Charlestown prison that helped keep Vanzetti's feverish mind generally on the sane side.

No government at all was the best government for Proudhon, who coined the phrase "an-archy" for his waiting type fonts. This was one step beyond Calvin Coolidge's subsequent opinion that "the best government is the least government," for it could do even without the Boston police department let alone all the other inspectors and regulators spawned by a complex society. Ironically, this type of thought, romantic and anti-scientific, springs up again in the plea of the young: "I am not an IBM card. Do not punch me, mutilate me or process me." Such a put-on phrase would have delighted Proudhon who answered his own question "What is property?" with the famous answer "Property is theft." It was a clever way of provoking thought about the sequence of events and laws that had taken property from the many and deposited it in the protected hands of the few. In a similar vein to "God is dead," archly offered by today's theologians, Proudhon had stated "God is evil," thus taking on both heaven and earth.

Proudhon was Bakunin's teacher and together they were the first prophets of the movement, beginning about the time of the revolutionary year of 1848. But Proudhon was a man of reason who earnestly believed, unlike Bakunin, that man could be persuaded to bring about a stateless society through reason and not by violence. A man of peasant stock, son of a French innkeeper, Proudhon felt an innate sympathy for artisans and workmen and these men in turn responded to his authority. Austere and hard-working, his example for both Sacco and Vanzetti is quite understandable. To the degree it bears on their tendency towards violence, it should be noted that Proudhon was a rather unwilling revolutionary. He disapproved of conspiracy and never endorsed terrorism. He was no parlor socialist, however, and his words were bombastic enough: "To be governed . . . is under pretext of the public good to be exploited, monopolized, embezzled, robbed, and then at the least protest or word of complaint, to be fined, harassed, vilified, beaten up, bludgeoned, disarmed, judged, condemned, imprisoned, shot, garroted, deported, sold, betrayed, swindled, deceived, outraged, dishonored . . . and imagine that among us there are democrats who believe government to be good, socialists who in the name of liberty, equality and fraternity support this ignominy, proletarians who offer themselves as candidates for President of the Republic! What hypocrisy!" Whatever one can say about the absurdity of the anarchist ideal (George Bernard Shaw met it head on in an 1893 tract called *The Impossibilities of Anarchism)*, one must also note that it is the creed of angry men, whether quietist or activist.

Shaw was fascinated by the third major prophet of anarchism, Prince Piotr Kropotkin, who died at the age of seventy-nine in 1921, the year of the South Braintree trial. It is noteworthy that this trinity of anarchists, unlike Danton, Marat and Robespierre, each lived to a ripe old age. Though experienced with jails, they were careful to let others do the killing their preaching ultimately inspired. "He was amiable to the point of saintliness," wrote Shaw, "and with his full beard and lovable expression might have been a shepherd from the Delectable Mountains."[21] The shepherd was not above urging consideration of the "dagger, gun and dynamite" in the pages of *La Révolte*, which he edited in France at one point of his colorful career, but generally his violence was rhetorical. Somehow or other — perhaps it was because he was a genuine Russian prince — Kropotkin managed to become lionized by his own enemies in the turn-of-the-century world. He had studied under Proudhon but enjoyed his own luster as a noted geographer, which brought him recognition in the scientific world. Latching on to Darwinian theory, he produced a somewhat more logical economic doctrine than either Proudhon or Bakunin had been able to devise. The capitalists were wrong, he stated, in contending that Darwin's tooth and claw analysis of survival justified the competitive ethic. On the contrary, he found from his own expeditions to the Siberian steppes that basically a spirit of cooperation existed among the species, which man could achieve in communal settings. His book

Mutual Aid was widely noted and generally applauded. Kropotkin is the founding father most highly regarded by those student anarchists who have taken the trouble to do their homework. He is considered an advocate of participatory democracy, which appeals to today's anti-authoritarian youth, with his call for "a society . . . regulated by mutual agreements . . . not petrified by law, routine or superstition but continually developing. . . ."[22]

This scientific anarchist, once a page to the Czar, like Tolstoy in love with the peasants, was honored by the bourgeois world he threatened to strike. There is an amusing story that Kropotkin refused to rise to toast the King at a dinner of the Royal Geographers Society, whereupon the dinner chairman proposed another toast, "Long live Prince Kropotkin" and the whole assemblage rose in his honor. He was invited to lecture at the Lowell Institute in Boston in 1901 and was entertained by Mrs. Potter Palmer in her new Gothic castle on the North Shore when he reached Chicago. Herbert Marcuse, today's leading philosopher of the left, also finds the heavy hand of the state repressive both in capitalist and communist countries. He has complained about the tendency of America to domesticate and popularize her critics. It results in society becoming "one-dimensional," without the cutting edge of substantive choices being considered, he feels. Kropotkin was a case in point.

But our survey of Sacco and Vanzetti's anarchist heroes cannot terminate on such a cheerful note. There were monsters who contaminated the movement beyond redemption, men in love with death and destruction, misguided zealots ready to take the lives of innocent judges, personal enemies and bureaucrats as well as tyrants. Francois Ravachol was such a person in France in the 1890's, covering his criminal streak with the cause of anarchism as he went singing to the guillotine. The movement created a haven and a sense of mission for the terrorist who hated society personally, who would not hesitate to blow himself up to even the score. Because it did not disown the "propaganda of the deed," whatever moral authority the official movement possessed (there were International Anarchist Congresses in the 1880's) soon dissipated. By the time it was apparent that the appalling slums and disparities of the Victorian world were no longer hopeless for those at the bottom, anarchism persisted only in rare offshoots such as the East Boston local of Sacco and Vanzetti. There it found a mixture of disillusionment with America, frustrated intellectualism and sentimental attachment to the firebrands and vendettas of the old country. Central to its existence was the fact that most of its members were laborers in a country still lacking a strong labor movement, where strikers for an eight-hour day were harshly repressed. Perhaps also the movement provided the secret, conspiratorial side of life denied its members by their Yankee neighbors in their Masonic, Odd Fellows, Elks, Eagles, Moose and other anthropomorphic lodges.

How the dark side of anarchism revived once again in the hands of native-born affluent children of the great universities is still another question. Ironically, Sacco in his cross-examination took occasion to lecture the jury about how children such as his Dante would never be allowed to go to Harvard College.[23] The jurors, who for the most part must have had the same idea about their own children, considering Harvard as it was at the time, no doubt were unsympathetic about sons of anarchists at Harvard.

VI

We are now ready to enter the Dedham courtroom. If we believe the trial was unfair, we had better concentrate on the judge and the District Attorney, rather than the jury, for evidence of prejudice and unfair play. The jury was unanimous in reaching its verdict on the first poll in a distressingly few hours after a seven-week trial. These twelve men were prejudiced but only to the extent society as a whole was prejudiced at the time. The theory of the jury system holds that at least one or more of them would have had the good sense and conscience to vote against sending innocent men to death regardless of social pressures. That is, unless the judicial system itself misled them.

Actually Fred Moore for the defense probably made a major mistake in challenging every prospective juror who had even the slightest connection with the world of capitalism, except for some minor real estate men. This extended to challenging intelligent young men who worked in brokerage houses or banks, to the intense annoyance of his co-counsels, the McAnarney brothers, solid Massachusetts attorneys who had been hired to bolster the appearance of the flashy labor lawyer but were kept in subordinate roles. Over seven hundred veniremen had to be dragooned from the highways and byways of Dedham and surrounding towns before the jury was finally selected. Moore failed to realize that the humbler types he approved were less likely to be objective about his clients' radicalism than the more educated business people he challenged. As it was, he unwittingly let slip through Walter Ripley, a former chief of police of Quincy, who became foreman of the jury. In a supplementary motion for a new trial argued two years later, the defense produced an affidavit from an old and reputable friend of Ripley who swore that the latter had told him just before the trial, "Damn them, they ought to hang anyway!"[24] Ripley had died before the affidavit was obtained. On the other hand, John Dever, a twenty-seven year old clothing clerk at Filene's, was inspired by the case to become a lawyer and to write his unpublished memoirs of his jury experience. Francis Russell, a noted historian whose *Tragedy in Dedham* (1962) reluctantly finds Sacco guilty and Vanzetti innocent, quotes from the posthumous manuscript to the effect that prejudice did not affect the jury's deliberations.[25]

Returning to Judge Thayer, his antagonism for Moore from the very start is understandable. In many ways, Moore was just about the worst possible lawyer for the defense of Sacco and Vanzetti. Imported at the outset by their radical friends through Carlo Tresca, the New York anarchist leader, and his friend Elizabeth Gurley Flynn, Moore succeeded in becoming one of the most disliked men in Massachusetts as the trial progressed. A maverick lawyer from California who had shown some success in winning cases for the "Wobblies," Moore was the first to see the symbolic class struggle possibilities of the case. According to Eugene Lyons, then in the leftist phase of a long and creditable career as a journalist that would finally land him on the political right, Moore played the case like a virtuoso. Whatever he may have felt about the innocence of his clients, the broader goal of exploiting them, raising and spending large sums on their behalf and securing his own fame was his paramount concern. Lyons, for example, was sent by Moore immediately to Italy to drum up support from leftists and members of the Italian Parliament, which was the start of European concern for the accused men.[26] Wearing long hair at a time when it was distinctly out of fashion, Moore sprawled over the courtroom without a coat and in front of the courthouse without shoes. Though his clients' lives were at stake and the District Attorney was exhibiting cunning and ferocity beyond the call of duty, Moore's subsequent efforts to get Commonwealth witnesses to change their stories were highly unethical to say the least. In addition, between the Plymouth and Dedham trials, he foolishly started negotiations with a Mrs. de Falco, who represented she could buy off the District Attorney. He then changed course and swore out a warrant for her arrest, which resulted in the District Attorney having to take the stand. The case was dismissed after making the front pages but Moore could not have had a more unfriendly judge and District Attorney greeting him at Dedham.

Rosina Sacco cried with distress at the conduct of Moore whom she distrusted from the start, feeling the small donations of the Italian supporters were going to the wrong man. The McAnarney brothers offered to refund their fee if they could take over but Moore clung to his position. William Thompson, a friend of the McAnarneys, was called in by them during the jury selection to confirm their feeling that so many sparks were already flying between Moore and Judge Thayer a miscarriage of justice was inevitable. Thompson later recalled for the Lowell Committee that he told the brothers, "Your goose is cooked."[27] The unfortunate metaphor for men who would die in the electric chair six years later was probably lost on these Establishment lawyers who were passionately convinced of the innocence of the accused. Otherwise they would not have touched the case.

Finally Sacco, incensed at the exploitation of the case and at odds with Moore, demanded in 1924 that he be removed. The Defense

Committee, also at the breaking point with Moore, agreed and he was eased out in favor of William Thompson as general counsel. Later both Felix Frankfurter and Thompson laid great emphasis on Moore's damage to the cause of the accused men, given the demonstrated predisposition of Judge Thayer against radicals in the first place. They insisted that the conflict could not help being communicated to the jury.

Moore's entrance in the case had the fatal element of tragedy in the sense that he was the gift of friends. Similarly Vanzetti's experience with John P. Vahey, produced by the local politician among the Italians for his Plymouth trial, was fatal. Vanzetti did not take the stand in his own defense because, he later stated, Vahey thought he had an iron-clad alibi (the day-before-Christmas sale of eels) and would suffer from cross-examination about his anarchism. The failure to testify in his own behalf may have resulted in his conviction at Plymouth, which thereupon branded him as a convict for attempted payroll robbery at the ensuing Dedham trial rather than a man of good character and unblemished record. At any rate, Governor Fuller regarded the failure to testify as highly significant and as sufficient evidence of guilt to weigh against the chances of pardon for both men.[28] Conceivably the decision was up to Vanzetti and not his attorney who set forth the choice. Yet at that time Vanzetti's English was rudimentary, the case was unknown and he relied on his attorney. He felt his suspicions were confirmed when Vahey a few years later became the law partner of District Attorney Katzmann, who, like Thayer, officiated at both Plymouth and Dedham. Ironic mistakes of strategy and choice of counsel thus joined the other circumstances which seemed to bear down relentlessly in the Greek manner on the doomed men.

Moore's exit from Boston sustained the tragic theme. Divorced during the case and broke, his life's work snatched from his hands in midstream, he started out alone for California in an old car stocked with little tin signs IF YOU CAN READ THIS, YOU'RE TOO DAMNED CLOSE, which he hoped to sell at filling stations to pay his way back. He died of cancer shortly after the execution but not before telling his friend Upton Sinclair that "Sacco was probably, Vanzetti possibly guilty."[29] Sinclair at the time was writing his novel *Boston*, based on the case, and was not shaken in his own faith in their innocence, as Moore had added that he had not the slightest hint of this from either man. Supporters of the defense, including Moore's divorced wife, claim that Moore's statement reflected resentment over his treatment. Eugene Lyons has added to the mystery by claiming that Moore's investigations had led to the trail of a certain criminal group at which point the "Italian anarchist members of the Committee called him in and ordered him to 'lay off.' They wouldn't say why."[30] Along the same line Max Eastman quoted Carlo Tresca as saying Sacco was guilty and Vanzetti was not, shortly before Tresca was assassinated in 1943.[31] Men like Ehrmann and Judge Musmanno rejected the split-guilt theory as hearsay and improbable.[32]

But Judge Thayer's prejudice showed brightly aside from his natural dislike for Fred Moore. As careful as he was to create an official record of the case that would defy reversal in a higher court, he was careless in his frequent discussions of the case on the outside. As a result, when death loomed for the defendants, a surprising array of affidavits from the Judge's own world of business, law and clubs arose to confront him.

We can start with some rather amusing testimony from a proper Bostonian named George U. Crocker who told the Lowell Committee how Judge Thayer became first a crashing and then an ominous bore about the case.

> Q. (By Mr. Thompson) Oh, yes. Do you recollect while the trial of the Sacco case was going on, being approached by Judge Thayer in the University Club? A. I do.
>
> Q. Now, will you state in your own words what you recollect about that matter? Please state as fully and carefully as you can. A. Well, the first time, one evening, this gentleman approached me, called me by name and I didn't recollect having met him before, but he began talking to me and told me how we must protect ourselves against reds, then he began to talk about this Sacco — Sacco and

Vanzetti case. I finally realized he was the presiding judge in the case and he talked to me a great deal about it until I got away. He told me a good deal about their being reds and anarchists and how we must protect —

Q. (By President Stratton) What did he say? A. I cannot remember exactly the words he used, but to the effect that we must protect ourselves against them, there were so many reds in the country, and he had a couple of them up in the trial at which he was presiding.

Q. (By President Lowell) How far along was the trial? A. I don't know. Why perhaps halfways through the trial. I don't know.

(By President Lowell) It lasted seven weeks.

Q. (By Judge Grant) You mean the trial? A. It took seven weeks.

(By Mr. Crocker) And he talked to me several times along the same lines. He told me about the evidence somewhat, and I got away from him as soon as I could. One morning at breakfast, it was on the morning when he delivered his charge, he was living at the University Club at that time. He either signalled me to come over to his table, or I was at breakfast and he came in and sat down, and he began to talk again about this trial and it went in one ear and out, because I didn't want to have anything to do with him. In part he talked about the counsel for the defense in the argument for the defense, and I don't know what it was. I didn't like to listen to it. Then he pulled out of his pocket a paper which he said was part of his charge and he said "Now Moore said so and so yesterday in his argument to the jury and I want to read you part of the charge I am going to deliver. That will hold him," etc.

Q. (By President Lowell) It would what "hold him"? A. Hold him.

Q. (By President Lowell) Hold him.

Q. (By Judge Grant) Where? A. It would hold him. It was an answer to his argument, McAnarney's argument and he talked and I was very uncomfortable and I got away as soon as I could, and I avoided in the future all talk with him about the case. In fact, I spoke to the head

> waiter or stewart [*semble*, steward] at the Club "For Heaven's sake, don't put me with that man." Of course I can't remember all he said, but the circumstances impressed it upon my memory, but I can't remember any definite language that he used, except that matter of McAnarney's argument and his answer to him and didn't I think it would hold him.[33]

Next a legitimate humorist, Robert Benchley, entered the case in dead seriousness. On his own initiative, he breached the rules of clubmen and gentlemen by supplying the following sworn statement to the Lowell Committee on July 13, 1927:

> My name is Robert Benchley. I reside in the City of New York. I am Dramatic Editor of "Life." I was brought up in the City of Worcester, Massachusetts, and am acquainted with many people there, among others with Mr. Loring Coes, with whom I have been on friendly terms for many years. In the year 1921, during the trial of Sacco and Vanzetti before Judge Webster Thayer in the Superior Court at Dedham, Mrs. Benchley and I were visiting Mr. and Mrs. Loring Coes in Worcester. During this visit, on a day which I think must have been a Saturday or Sunday, I was sitting in an automobile with Mrs. Benchley and Mrs. Coes outside the Worcester Golf Club waiting for Mr. Coes to come out. When Mr. Coes came out and got into the automobile he told us what Judge Thayer, who was in the club, had just said in his presence and in the presence of several others about Sacco and Vanzetti. The account by Mr. Coes of these remarks of Judge Thayer made a vivid impression upon my mind, and I remember them with considerable distinctness. Mr. Coes told us that Judge Thayer, whom he referred to as "Web," had just been telling what he Judge Thayer intended to do to Sacco and Vanzetti, whom Judge Thayer referred to as "those bastards down there." Mr. Coes said that Judge Thayer had referred to Sacco and Vanzetti as bolsheviki who were "trying to intimidate him," and had said that "he would get them good and proper." Mr.

> Coes said that Judge Thayer had told him and the other men that a "bunch of parlor radicals were trying to get these guys off and trying to bring pressure to bear on the Bench," and that he "would show them and would get those guys hanged," and that he, Judge Thayer, "would also like to hang a few dozen of the radicals." Mr. Coes said that Judge Thayer added that "no bolsheviki could intimidate Web Thayer," and that he added in substance that Worcester would be proud of having such a defender as Judge Thayer. I am informed and believe and therefore allege that Mr. Coes has within a few days been requested by Mr. Thompson, counsel for Sacco and Vanzetti, to make an affidavit as to the remarks of Judge Thayer which I have mentioned and has refused to do so on the ground that it is difficult for him to remember what happened so long ago, and that he is disinclined to make the effort because Judge Thayer is an old friend of himself and his family. I am also informed and believe and therefore allege that in October, 1926, Mr. Coes was thrown from his horse and sustained a injury from which he has not yet entirely recovered.[34]

Coes indignantly issued a statement to the press denying Benchley's remarks, showing particular annoyance with the inference that the fall from the horse had affected his memory. Benchley's affidavit has no legal standing, of course, but what possible motivation could he have had for lying about what he heard Coes say?

Finally in November 1924, a short time after Judge Thayer had denied motions for a new trial, he spoke with James P. Richardson, professor of law and political science at Dartmouth, where he attended a football game of his alma mater. Ten days after the men were sentenced to death, on April 19, 1927, Professor Richardson wrote a letter to Governor Fuller which resulted in the following testimony before the Lowell Committee:

> A. Judge Thayer met [me] on the field with a group about. He spoke to me by name. He has known me for a long time. He immediately went into the subject of the

> Sacco-Vanzetti case; he referred at once to the motions which had been pending before him, and which he within a short time disposed of. My recollection is, I don't know, but Mr. Ranney is probably correct, would have been that some of these motions had been decided on shortly before this conversation.
>
> Q. (By Mr. Ranney) That is right, all decided. A. (By Prof. Richardson) All had been decided, probably a short time before. Judge Thayer said as near as I can remember, "Did you see what I did with those anarchistic bastards the other day. I guess that will hold them for a while."
>
> Q. (By Mr. Thompson) Yes? A. Let them go to the Supreme Court now and see what they can get out of them."
>
> Q. Yes? A. There was more of the same sort.
>
> Q. Yes? A. Well, there was more of the same sort. My recollection is fairly accurate.[35]

A minor incident from the maligned business world attaches to the Richardson testimony. As if type-cast for a play, some Dartmouth alumni thereupon wired an offer of $10,000 to the college if President Hopkins would discharge Professor Richardson. Perhaps this was the inspiration for James Thurber's and Elliot Nugent's hit *The Male Animal*, which ran on Broadway in 1939 and later became a popular movie. In what must seem a hopelessly antiquated setting for today's collegians, a young English professor is about to be fired by a neolithic Chairman of the Board of Trustees at Midwestern University. The reason — he proposes to read to his class Vanzetti's "That agony is our triumph" statement at a time when other professors have just been forced out as "Reds." It is the big football weekend and the young professor's wife is having second thoughts about an old beau who was a football hero. The play ends as she prepares to follow her husband to his showdown, aware that the male animal has more important qualities than athletic prowess.

Thus the trial, like all great trials, began to enter the fabric of the nation's myths and legends. Yet the Lowell Committee, appointed by the earnest Governor upon pressure of Bishop Lawrence and other distinguished figures to make sure justice was being served, had the following to say about Judge Thayer's indiscretions:

> From all that has come to us we are forced to conclude that the judge was indiscreet in conversations with outsiders during the trial. He ought not to have talked about the case off the bench, and doing so was a grave breach of official decorum. But we do not believe that he used some of the expressions attributed to him, and we think that there is an exaggeration in what the persons to whom he spoke remember. Furthermore, we believe that such indiscretions in conversation did not affect his conduct at the trial or the opinions of the jury, who indeed so stated to the Committee.[36]

For many, the epitome of the wise, conservative Boston lawyer is Joseph N. Welch, the kindly looking defense counsel whose moral indignation was most responsible for destroying Senator Joseph McCarthy's public image at the Senate hearings on his conduct. Here is Joseph Welch's estimate of Judge Thayer:

> I also knew Judge Webster Thayer. I have tried cases before him. I have sat in his lobby and heard him discuss the Sacco and Vanzetti case. It is clear he believed Sacco and Vanzetti to be guilty. It is also clear that this was not merely an intellectual conclusion on his part, but a passionate dedication to the proposition that the two of them were to die. It was unfortunate that under Massachusetts law one man and only one man could grant Sacco and Vanzetti a new trial. That man was Judge Thayer. After the jury verdict, Judge Thayer's rulings on the various motions for a new trial were as fatal and as conclusive as was throwing the switch at their execution. But Judge Thayer was beyond persuasion. He was not to be moved by reason. He was, in this case, incapable of showing mercy. This is not to say he was wrong. It is only to describe him.
>
> I have always thought that the great tragedy of the

> Sacco-Vanzetti case was that it happened to be assigned to Judge Thayer. I think almost any other judge would have granted a new trial.[37]

Only Thayer could grant a new trial because in the Massachusetts appeal system the Supreme Judicial Court confined itself to reviewing the law and not the facts of a case. Within that limitation, the defendants were whipsawed by the technical rules of the review court, which caused it first to disregard consideration of facts which to all intents and purposes involved the law and second to grant the widest discretion to a lower court judge in his conduct of the case. In fact, as Thompson plaintively called to the attention of the Lowell Committee, no Massachusetts judge had yet been found to have abused his discretionary capacity. Thus the decision of Judge Thayer, for example, that the discovery of a new witness to the South Braintree crime, Roy Gould, constituted only an additional defense witness not worthy of causing a new trial, was deemed a matter of his proper discretion. The agonized defense had tracked down and produced Gould after the trial was over. He was the only witness close enough to the crime to have a hole shot through his coat at a distance of five to ten feet, having been shot at by a bandit aiming directly at him as he stood in the street. Gould stated categorically that Sacco was not the man sitting next to the driver. He could have been a star witness at a new trial to offset the prosecution's major identifiers of Sacco, two flustered female bookkeepers who placed him next to the driver from their vantage point behind the factory office windows. (Francis Russell has written to the author that Gould was one of Moore's "bribed witnesses." Still, he was shot, at close range, by the murderers.)

Similarly a most unusual reversal of testimony arose from the deposition of Captain Proctor, the state police ballistics expert, that he had practically perjured himself during the trial by pre-arrangement with District Attorney Katzmann. The jurors heard the following question and answer against a background of acceptance by both sides that "Bullet No. 3," a fatal bullet, had been fired from a Colt automatic 32 calibre pistol. Sacco had been carrying such a gun at the time of arrest.

Q. Have you any opinion as to whether No. 3 was fired from the Colt automatic which is in evidence?
A. I have.
Q. And what is your opinion? A. My opinion is that it is consistent with being fired by that pistol.[38]

Two years later Proctor had second thoughts and recanted. He swore that the District Attorney had asked him to assert the bullet passed through Sacco's pistol. "The District Attorney desired to ask me that question, but I had repeatedly told him that if he did I should be obliged to answer in the negative. Had I been asked the question: Whether I had found any affirmative evidence whatever that this so-called mortal bullet had passed through this particular Sacco's pistol, I should have answered then, as I do now, without hesitation in the negative."[39]

In denying a new trial on this evidence, Judge Thayer asserted in effect that the jury had understood the mealy-mouthed answer of Captain Proctor, who died shortly after the date of his affidavit. Yet Judge Thayer himself had explicitly charged the jury to the effect that Proctor had testified the fatal bullet went through Sacco's pistol before sending them out for their decision. The Supreme Judicial Court in turn declined to disturb Judge Thayer's finding of fact on the Proctor motion for a new trial, affirming its rule that "the question of granting a new trial, even in a capital case, ordinarily rests in the sound discretion of the court."[40]

The Proctor affidavit, which was not denied by Katzmann, was one of the factors that led Felix Frankfurter to write his impassioned *Atlantic Monthly* article which played such an important part in bringing high level support to the defendants. It was also instrumental in causing the *Boston Herald* to publish a Pulitzer prize-winning editorial on October 26, 1926 demanding a new trial. Whatever the real answer is to the critical ballistics evidence — each side produced an array of experts to cancel out the other — it appears that Judge Thayer and not the Supreme Judicial Court bears the responsibility for a miscarriage of justice if indeed there was one. In the area of discretionary rulings, which was the area

Library of Congress

Edward Atkinson. About 1898. A businessman who risked jail over retention of the Philippines after the Spanish-American War.

Ohio Historical Society

Mark Hanna (left). The Ohio millionaire, who also objected to the Spanish-American War, entertains President and Mrs. McKinley (right) at dinner at his home.

THANKSGIVING.

"For What We Are About To Receive, May The Lord Make Us Truly Thankful."

Ohio Historical Society

Mark Hanna and President McKinley. As seen in *Puck* magazine. They dine on the platter of "Sound Money," a Burning Issue around which businessmen rallied to defeat William Jennings Bryan.

Library of Congress

Andrew Carnegie. The irrepressible steel baron who upbraided McKinley for going to war with Spain. Shown with peace advocates in 1913 protesting the advent of World War I.

Library of Congress

Coxey's Army. Led by "General" Jacob Coxey, a respectable quarry owner and amateur economist, the army of the unemployed marches on Washington in 1894.

United Press International

Sacco (right) and Vanzetti (left). The Massachusetts anarchists, convicted of payroll robbery and murder during the anti-Red scare after World War I, talk with Mrs. Sacco in the Norfolk County Courthouse, 1923.

Chicago Historical Society
Reprinted courtesy Chicago Tribune

The New Deal. As seen by cartoonist Carey Orr, reflecting the views of the majority of big business and the nation's press in 1936.

United Press International

The great NRA parade of September 13, 1933, when 500,000 New Yorkers marched for an economic principle involving price-fixing and wages and hours controls. From left, Grover Whalen, General Hugh S. Johnson, Governor Herbert H. Lehman.

in which Thayer's alleged prejudice could roam far and wide, he was in fact irreversible. In 1939 Massachusetts finally enacted changes in its laws to remedy the inability of the Supreme Judicial Court to review all the facts in a capital case.[41]

Judge Thayer, like Attorney General Palmer, eventually was rejected by the society he wanted to protect in an excess of vigilante spirit. There were no promotions or peace in store for him. Harassed by cranks and threats, he died in 1933, seven months after a bomb had wrecked his garage and part of his residence. One of the jurors also had his home completely destroyed back in 1927 as the execution neared and Judge Thayer lived in apprehension of his turn. Supreme Court Chief Justice Taft himself had openly congratulated the Lowell Committee's Judge Grant on his support of the Commonwealth, taking the occasion for some malicious digs at Felix Frankfurter. As death overtook the frosty little judge from Worcester, he could contemplate Frankfurter a power in Washington and on his way to the Supreme Court in the great social upheaval created by the depression. Wall street had finally been laid low but not by the outrageous bombing on September 16, 1920 which killed forty people, undoubtedly priming Judge Thayer for his role in the tragedy at Dedham.

The intellectuals, the artists and writers all turned sharply towards liberalism and a questioning of the old values as the economic system literally fell to pieces. Not only Sacco and Vanzetti but the entire class of business and privilege somehow became victims of the case which was looked upon as a symbol of an old order responsible for the present distress. Thayer was pursued bitterly by Maxwell Anderson who depicted him as the haunted judge in the play *Winterset*, roaming the streets as a tragic King Lear in search of the truth. Ben Shahn enshrined him in his gouaches and mural as a cold face of death behind the courthouse window.

The literary legacy matched the historical legacy of opprobrium for Judge Thayer, which in turn frequently extends into the realm of inaccuracy. In 1970 *The American Heritage History of the 20's and 30's* appeared with the statement that Judge Thayer unabashedly instructed the Plymouth jury about Vanzetti that "although he may not actually have committed the crime (he) is nevertheless morally culpable because he is the enemy of our existing institutions."[42] This is whole cloth and will not be found in the record of the case. It is too preposterous for the canny Thayer himself to have uttered in court. Nor is it offered by Ehrmann or Professor Edmund Morgan and Louis Joughin, whose *The Legacy of Sacco and Vanzetti* is the other exhaustive critique of the case in favor of the accused. Morgan and Joughin explain the currency of such comments in the fact that most of the pages of Thayer's charge to the Plymouth jury are missing from the record. They quote as an example of mis-statement Lyons' 1927 book on the case to the effect that friends of the defendants reported Thayer said, "The defendant's ideals are cognate with the crime."[43] Judge Thayer obviously should not be condemned by hearsay from a prejudiced source.

VI

District Attorney Frederick Gunn Katzmann was a self-made man from a poor family who had worked his way through Harvard and then Boston University Law School at night. A successful Republican politician in his late forties, he approached his job in a workmanlike fashion, unconcerned with the desire for publicity and need for approval that seemed to characterize Judge Thayer, then close to retirement age. His brother Percy had successfully defended an anarchist named Zagroff before Judge Thayer in April 1920, the month of the South Braintree crime. Curiously this showed that a Dedham jury could act fairly enough. It refused to convict on the charge of "advocating anarchy" because there was only talk and no violence involved. Thayer denounced the jurors after they brought in their verdict but Percy Katzmann had won his case. As with his brother, Fred Katzmann's approach to a trial was to view it as all part of the job. Some corners might be cut but the main idea was to win the case. A good record of convictions would eventually mean a judgeship or even the attorney-generalship. Katzmann was confident, ruthless and enjoyed confronting his adversary, especially under the protective wing of Judge Thayer. The transcript speaks for itself. Here Katzmann cross-examines Vanzetti at Dedham:

> Q. (By Mr. Katzmann) So you left Plymouth, Mr. Vanzetti, in May, 1917, to dodge the draft, did you? A. Yes, sir.
>
> Q. And you stayed away, did you not, until the class in which men of your age came had all been drawn in the draft? Is that true? A. Not exactly.
>
> Q. What part of it isn't true? A. It isn't true because men of my condition were never compelled to be a soldier.
>
> Q. No men of your condition were compelled to be soldiers? A. Yes, sir.
>
> Q. Were you physically unable to be a soldier? A. I don't speak of the physical condition. I speak of civil condition. [He was an alien.]
>
> Q. Were you physically sound? A. I hope so.
>
> Q. Do you know? A. I ought to be.
>
> Q. Did you believe you were? A. Yes, sir.
>
> Q. Physically sound as you were, and after you had been in this country since 1908? A. Yes, sir.
>
> Q. When this country was at war, you ran away so you would not have to fight as a soldier? A. Yes.
>
> Q. Is that true? A. It is true.
>
> * * *
>
> Q. And are you that man, Mr. Vanzetti, that on May 9th was going to address a meeting down at Brockton to your fellow citizens, saying: "You have fought in the wars, and you have worked for capitalists, and tried their ways?" Are you the man, sir, that was going to address the returned soldiers? A. Yes, sir.
>
> Q. You were going to advise in a public meeting men who had gone to war? Are you that man? A. Yes, sir, I am that man, not the man you want me, but I am that man.[44]
>
> * * *

No doubt Katzmann recognized that Vanzetti was the subtler of the two defendants, more able to keep his restraint and sense the traps being laid out for him. He therefore saved his ammunition for the stubborn and doctrinaire Sacco, who finally rewarded him with a rambling speech for the jury's benefit.

Q. (By Mr. Katzmann) Did you say yesterday you love a free country? A. (By Sacco) Yes, sir.

Q. Did you love this country in the month of May, 1917? A. I did not say,— I don't want to say I did not love this country.

Q. Did you love this country in the month of 1917? A. If you can, Mr. Katzmann, if you give me that,— I could explain —

Q. Did you understand that question? A. Yes.

Q. Then will you please answer it? A. I can't answer in one word.

Q. You can't say whether you loved the United States of America one week before the day you enlisted for the first draft? A. I can't say in one word, Mr. Katzmann.

Q. You can't tell this jury whether you loved the country or not?

MR. MOORE. I object to that.

A. I could explain that, yes, if I loved —

Q. What? A. I could explain that, yes, if I loved, if you give me a chance.

Q. I ask you first to answer that question. Did you love this United States of America in May, 1917? A. I can't answer in one word.

* * *

Q. There are two words you can use, Mr. Sacco, yes or no. Which one is it? A. Yes.

Q. And in order to show your love for this United States of America when she was about to call upon you to become a soldier you ran away to Mexico?

MR. JEREMIAH MCANARNEY. Wait.

THE COURT. Did you?

Q. Did you run away to Mexico?

THE COURT. He has not said he ran away to Mexico. Did you go?

Q. Did you go to Mexico to avoid being a soldier for this country that you loved? A. Yes.

Q. You went under an assumed name? A. No.

Q. Didn't you take the name of Mosmacotelli? A. Yes.

Q. That is not your name, is it? A. No.

Q. How long did you remain under the name of Mosmacotelli? A. Until I got a job over to Mr. Kelley's.

Q. When was that? A. The armistice.

Q. After the war was practically over? A. Yes, sir.

* * *

Q. Then, for the first time, after May, 1917, did you become known as Sacco again? A. Yes, sir.

Q. Was it for the reason that you desired to avoid service that when you came back in four months you went to Cambridge instead of to Milford? A. For the reason for not to get in the army.

Q. So as to avoid getting in the army. A. Another reason why, I did not want no chance to get arrested and one year in prison.

Q. Did you want to get arrested and spend one year in prison for dodging the draft. Is that it? A. Yes.

Q. Did you love your country when you came back from Mexico? A. The first time?

THE COURT. Which country did you say? You said —

Q. United States of America, your adopted country? A. I did not say already.

Q. When you came back. I asked you. That was before you went. A. I don't think I could change my opinion in three months.

Q. You still loved America, did you? A. I should say yes.

Q. And is that your idea of showing your love for this Country? A. (Witness hesitates.)

Q. Is that your idea of showing your love for America? A. Yes.

Q. And would it be your idea of showing your love for your wife that when she needed you you ran away from her? A. I did not run away from her.

MR. MOORE. I object.

THE WITNESS. I was going to come after if I need her.

THE COURT. He may answer. Simply on the question of credibility, that is all.

Q. Would it be your idea of love for your wife that you were to run away from her when she needed you?

MR. JEREMIAH MCANARNEY. Pardon me. I ask for an exception on that.

THE COURT. Excluded. One may not run away. He has not admitted he ran away.

Q. Then I will ask you, didn't you run away from Milford so as to avoid being a soldier for the United States? A. I did not run away.

Q. You mean you walked away? A. Yes.

Q. You don't understand me when I say "run away," do you? A. That is vulgar.

Q. That is vulgar? A. You can say a little intelligent, Mr. Katzmann.

Q. Don't you think going away from your country is a vulgar thing to do when she needs you? A. I don't believe in war.

Q. You don't believe in war? A. No, sir.

Q. Do you think it is a cowardly thing to do what you did? A. No, sir.

Q. Do you think it is a brave thing to do what you did? A. Yes, sir.

Q. Do you think it would be a brave thing to go away from your own wife? A. No.

Q. When she needed you? A. No.

* * *

Q. Is Italy a free country? Is it a republic? A. Republic, yes.

Q. You love free countries, don't you? A. I should say yes.

Q. Why didn't you stay down in Mexico? A. Well, first thing, I could not get my trade over there. I had to do any other job.

Q. Don't they work with a pick and shovel in Mexico? A. Yes.

Q. Haven't you worked with a pick and shovel in this country? A. I did.

Q. Why didn't you stay there, down there in that free country and work with a pick and shovel? A. I don't think I did sacrifice to learn a job to go to pick and shovel in Mexico.

Q. Is it because,— is your love for the United States of America commensurate with the amount of money you can get in this country per week? A. Better conditions, yes.

Q. Better country to make money, isn't it? A. Yes.

Q. Mr. Sacco, that is the extent of your love for this country, isn't it, measured in dollars and cents?

MR. JEREMIAH MCANARNEY. If your Honor please, I object to this particular question.

THE COURT. You opened up this whole subject.

* * *

Q. What is the reason you came back from Mexico if you did not love money, then? A. The first reason is all against my nature, is all different food over there, different nature, anyway.

Q. That is the first reason. It is against your nature. The food isn't right. A. Food, and many other things.

Q. You stood it for four months, didn't you? A. Three months.

Q. Three months? A. Yes.

Q. You came back all right physically, didn't you? A. I should say yes.

Q. And you had Italian food there, didn't you? A. Yes, made by ourselves.

Q. You could have had it all the time if you sent for it, couldn't you? A. Not all the time, I don't know.

Q. Did you fail to have it at any time in the three months you were there? A. Yes, sir. Different.

Q. What is the difference about it? A. Oh, different food that we did not like.

Q. It was Italian food, wasn't it? A. No, sir.

Q. Didn't you say it was? A. Sometimes after.

Q. You could have had it all the time if you sent for it, couldn't you? A. Could have had beans sometimes and any other vegetable.

MR. KATZMANN. I ask that be stricken out and the witness required to answer the question.

Q. Could you have had it by sending for it? A. Could not get it all the time.

Q. Why couldn't you get it in Mexico the same as you get it here? A. I suppose Mexico is not very much industries as in this country.

Q. Couldn't you send to Boston to get Italian food sent to Monterey, Mexico? A. If I was a D. Rockefeller I will.

Q. Then, I take it, you came back to the United States first to get something to eat. Is that right? Something that you liked? A. No, not just for eat.

Q. Didn't you say that was the first reason? A. The first reason —

Q. Didn't you say that was the first reason? A. Yes.

Q. All right. That wasn't a reason of the heart, was it? A. The heart?

Q. Yes. A. No.

Q. That was a reason of the stomach, wasn't it? A. Not just for the stomach, but any other reason.

Q. I am talking first about the first reason. So, the first reason your love of America is founded upon is pleasing your stomach. Is that right? A. I will not say yes.[45]

* * *

Q. (By Mr. Katzmann) What did you mean when you said yesterday you loved a free country? A. First thing I came in this country —

Q. No, pardon me. What did you mean when you said yesterday you loved a free country? A. Give me a chance to explain.

Q. I am asking you to explain now.

* * *

When I was in Italy, a boy [Sacco began], I was a Republican, so I always thinking Republican has more chance to manage education, develop, to build some day his family, to raise the child and education, if you could. But that was my opinion; so when I came to this country I saw there was not what I was thinking before, but there was all the difference, because I been working in Italy not so hard as I been work in this country. I could live free there just as well. Work in the same condition, but not so hard, about seven or eight hours a day, better food. I mean genuine. Of course, over here is good food, because it is bigger country, to any those who got money to spend, not for the working and laboring class, and in Italy is more opportunity to laborer to eat vegetable, more fresh, and I came in this country. When I been started work here very hard and been work thirteen years, hard worker, I could not been afford much a family the way I did have the idea before. I could not put any money in the bank. I could no push my boy some to go to school and other things. I teach over here men who is with me. The free idea gives any man a chance to profess his own idea, not the supreme idea, not to give any person, not to be like Spain in position*, yes, about twenty centuries ago, but to give a chance to print and education, literature, free speech, that I see it was all wrong. I could see the best men, intelligent, education, they been arrested and sent to prison and died in prison for years and years without getting them out, and Debs, one of the great men in his country, he is in prison, still away in prison, because he is a Socialist. He wanted the laboring class to have better conditions and better living, more education, give a push his son if he could have a chance some day, but they put him in prison. Why? Because the capitalist class, they know, they are against that, because the capitalist class, they don't want our child to go to high school or to college or Harvard College. There would not be no chance, there would not be no,— they don't want the working class educationed; they want the working class to be a low all the times, be underfoot, and not to be up with the head. So, sometimes, you see, the Rockefellers, Morgans, they give fifty,— mean they give five hundred

* Author's note: Did he actually say "Inquisition"?

thousand dollars to Harvard College, they give a million dollars for another school. Everybody say, "Well, D. Rockefeller is a great man, the best in the country." I want to ask him who is going to Harvard College? What benefit the working class they will get by those million dollars they give by Rockefeller, D. Rockefellers. They won't get, the poor class, they won't have no chance to go to Harvard College because men who is getting $21 a week or $30 a week, I don't care if he gets $80 a week, if he gets a family of five children he can't live and send his child and go to Harvard College if he wants to eat anything nature will give him. If he wants to eat like a cow, and that is the best thing, but I want men to live like men. I like to get everything that nature will give best, because they belong,— we are not the friend of any other place, but we are belonging to nations. So that is why my idea has been changed. So that is why I love people who labor and work and see better conditions every day develop, makes no more war. We no want fight by the gun, and we don't want to destroy young men. The mother been suffering for building the young man. Some day need a little more bread, so when the time the mother get some bread or profit out of that boy, the Rockefellers, Morgans, and some of the peoples, high class, they send to war. Why? What is war? The war is not shoots like Abraham Lincoln's and Abe Jefferson, to fight for the free country, for the better education, to give chance to any other peoples, not the white people but the black and the others, because they believe and know they are mens like the rest, but they are war for the great millionaire. No war for the civilization of men. They are war for business, million dollars come on the side. What right we have to kill each other? I been work for the Irish, I have been working with the German fellow, with the French, many other peoples. I love them people just as I could love my wife, and my people for that did receive me. Why should I go kill them men? What he done to me? He never done anything, so I don't believe in no war. I want to destroy those guns. All I can say, the Government put

> the literature, give us educations. I remember in Italy, a long time ago, about sixty years ago, I should say, yes, about sixty years ago, the Government they could not control very much these two,— devilment went on, and robbery, so one of the government in the cabinet he says, "If you want to destroy those devilments, if you want to take off all those criminals, you ought to give a chance to Socialist literature, education of people, emancipation. That is why I destroy governments, boys." That is why my idea I love Socialists. That is why I like people who want education and living, building, who is good, just as much as they could. That is all.[46]

Having delivered this monologue, Sacco found himself seriously challenged at the level of a junior high school debating society by Katzmann. Why didn't he go back to Italy if the vegetables were fresher there? Did he love work as much as he loved this country? "Did you intend to condemn Harvard College?" (Judge Thayer instructed Sacco to answer the question over defense counsel's objection). Did he know that over one hundred thousand children attended the public schools of Boston? "I know millions don't go there," the bewildered young Italian, on trial for his life for murder, managed to reply.

VII

Governor Alvan T. Fuller was the model of the businessman turned public servant as the just reward for enterprise and ability. Only forty-nine in 1927, he had enjoyed a life of achievement and honors. Never had he anticipated being swept into one of the great trials of history, wherein the eyes of the world would look upon him as a sort of Puritan Pontius Pilate confronted by two of his humble Italian citizens. It must have been with a sigh of relief that he assigned a share of his burden to an Advisory Committee headed by a Lowell of Boston who was also the President of Harvard, itself an institution rivalling the Commonwealth.

Fuller was not a man to evade an issue and he conducted his

own investigation, sometimes working fourteen hours a day on the case, at the same time the Lowell Committee was conducting its inquiry. Often the witnesses would shuttle directly between his office and the Committee's in the State House. He visited the defendants at length in prison and generously remarked of Vanzetti, "What an attractive man!" Fuller's responsibility lay in whether or not a pardon should be granted. The Advisory Committee was to advise him on this question and he could take or leave its advice. He had the power to give Sacco and Vanzetti freedom, to commute their sentence to life imprisonment or allow their sentence to stand. He had appointed the Committee against the wishes of an estimated ninety per cent of the city's lawyers who felt the accused were guilty and that the outside clamor on their behalf was unwarranted.

Supporters of the defendants placed a good deal of their hope in Fuller's reputation as an independent man, an essential requirement for second-guessing the court system and flouting the overwhelming public opinion of his state. The independence sprung from his Horatio Alger rise to success after the early death of his father, a *Boston Globe* typesetter. He was a New England bicycle champion at sixteen and at eighteen had his own bicycle repair shop. Turning to automobiles, he became the head of a mammoth Packard agency with outlets throughout New England. His fortune was in the millions — some claimed he was the richest man in Boston — and he lived in a Beacon Street mansion hung with eighteenth century English masters. He had not had the time or money to go to college.

The pressures on Fuller must have been immense in 1927. There was always the threat of mad bombers. There were constant demonstrations and petitions in Boston. The worldwide protest meetings had long since left their left-wing launching pad and were propelled by a momentum of their own, fed by journalists and the love-hate tie binding Europe to upstart America. European critics had already cheered Sinclair Lewis' *Babbitt* when it appeared in 1922, confirming their suspicions that American civilization was dominated by bone-headed, reactionary businessmen. With large and sophisticated radical parties and newspapers harping on the issue, all shades of European opinion clamored for justice for Sacco and Vanzetti. Anatole France, Romain Rolland, Henri Barbusse and a dozen other leading French writers were joined by former Premier Caillaux and a voice from the past, Alfred Dreyfus himself. Thomas Mann, Fritz Kreisler, Albert Einstein and Paul Loebe, President of the Reichstag, were heard from Germany. John Galsworthy, H. G. Wells, Ramsay MacDonald and George Bernard Shaw expressed concern from England. It would be naive to assume that Fuller's independence would extend to shrugging off attacks from intellectuals of this order, let alone the great array of college presidents, ministers, writers and cultural figures in America. In his turn to President Lowell for advice, Fuller acknowledged intellectual authority as a final arbiter. European criticism may have been resented but it could not be ignored by this experienced businessman who had gone to Europe himself in 1899 to bring Boston its first imported autos.

Just before the execution, England's Harold Laski wrote to his famed correspondent, Justice Oliver Wendell Holmes: ". . . I wish I could make Fuller realize the immense damage his action has done to the good name of America. The case has stirred Europe as nothing since the Dreyfus case has done. And to me, at this instance, and with the reliance I have on the substantial accuracy of Felix's (Frankfurter's) picture, it seems that it is indeed another Dreyfus case."[47]

A reasonable claim has been made by David Felix, in *Protest: Sacco-Vanzetti and the Intellectuals*, that the intellectuals by and large were hoodwinked by Communist propaganda in the Sacco-Vanzetti case. This would be because of their eagerness to impute blame on authority and assign innocence to the underdog at the expense of judgment and the evidence.[48]

In attempting to associate ourselves with the choice confronting Governor Fuller, we should note there were two levels of criticism involved. The left-wing approach, typified by the Communists and domestic radicals such as Eugene Debs, saw the case as a conspiracy by the "mill-owning, labor-sweating malefactors of Massachusetts" and their "capitalist courts," to use Debs' words.[49] The intellectuals, however, rested their case on a different approach, typified by Frankfurter's sharp analysis, that here was simply an unfair trial, completely removed from conspiracy, that demanded a retrial on the basis of unusual prejudice in a past period, courtroom irregularities and new evidence. On this basis, Felix's charge against the intellectuals seems unwarranted, even if the men were guilty and the trial fair, as Felix seems to believe. Certainly the intellectuals were entitled to view, on their own initiative, an unfair trial in itself as a crime. Governor Fuller no doubt brushed aside the propaganda approach but must be granted credit for concern with the fairness of the trial as well as the guilt of the men. It was on this basis that distinguished Boston businessmen such as John F. Moors, A. Lincoln Filene, Carl Dreyfus, John Hays Hammond, Heman W. Burr and the most prestigious corporation lawyers such as Charles P. Curtis and Roland W. Boyden pressed for a review or clemency. At the same level, the American Federation of Labor demanded a new trial by resolutions in 1926 and in previous years for these two laborers who had little use for organized labor within their anarchist scheme. With these distinctions in mind, Governor Fuller's task comes into focus.

Yet Fuller must be measured in the light of his own prejudices and attitudes, which may have prevented him from regarding the period of the Palmer raids as one of undue hysteria likely to affect judges and juries. As a youthful Congressman from 1917 to 1921, he was a leader in the action which refused to seat Victor M. Berger, a Socialist from Milwaukee, who had been duly elected to the House, unseated and then refused again after winning a reelection. "Berger characterizes the action of the House as a 'crucifixion' and in a manner it is," stated Fuller. "It is the crucifixion of disloyalty — the nailing of sedition to the cross of free government, where the whole brood of Anarchists, Bolshevists, I.W.W.'s may see and read a solemn warning."[50] Still Fuller was an intelligent, able man with an eye on the White House and fully aware of Attorney General Palmer's eclipse on this issue long before 1927.

Another ominous portent for the defendants lay in an article

Fuller had written in *Success* magazine in December 1926 on "Why I Believe in Capital Punishment. ". . . I have particularly emphasized the strict enforcement of capital punishment for those who have taken human life. Friends, relatives, even newspapers are enlisted in a campaign to win over the sympathy of the man supremely charged by the Commonwealth with carrying out its laws. Sometimes for two or three weeks these assaults on his sense of justice may continue."[51] It is believed that Fuller did not have Sacco and Vanzetti in mind at the time but instead the tremendous local demands for clemency for three "carbarn bandits," guilty of murder beyond any doubts at all but good Irish Catholics whose mothers had gone down on their knees before him for mercy. In retrospect, having refused to save these bandits from the chair, he could hardly have extended mercy to representatives of a far less important voting bloc, still another fateful accident of timing pursuing the unlucky defendants. Still Fuller's reputation for independence was justified — he had refused to follow Senator Lodge's stand against the League of Nations — and his attention to the case was so conscientious that hope existed until the last moment. Herbert Ehrmann believes in the end Fuller's decision rested on two factors. He lost sight of the significance of the fairness of the trial in his businessman's determination to concentrate on the black and white issue of whether or not the men were guilty. Secondly, once the Lowell Committee supported the courts, he could hardly be expected to contradict its members and its august chairman, probably the only man in Massachusetts with the capacity to stare him down. In Ben Shahn's mural, Governor Fuller stands half-stage center, a small figure compared with the three pious Committee members holding lilies over the caskets of the dead men.

It is pointless to analyze too deeply the characters and motivations of the Committee members, three elderly gentlemen including Lowell, President Stratton of MIT and a retired judge named Robert Grant. Lowell dominated the Committee and prepared the report for the most part. Many see Lowell as a crusty old conservative, a world apart from today's college presidents. Yet he had been a lawyer in his youth and as a staunch defender of academic freedom had supported Harold Laski, a visiting Harvard professor, to the point of laying his own job on the line. Critics complain that Lowell could not see the possibility of error in the Massachusetts court system and that he was arrogant about believing the defendants' witnesses, most of whom were paraded before him. A good deal is made of his jubilation in proving from a newspaper story that a testimonial banquet for James T. Williams, editor of the *Boston Transcript*, was not held as asserted by a defense witness. Sacco had claimed to be in Boston getting a passport on April 15, 1920, the day of the payroll murders. Among his alibi witnesses was a Professor Guadagni, who testified he had coffee with him in Boston on that day. The professor had stated he remembered the date because a testimonial banquet was being tendered to Williams by the Italian community on the same day. Lowell, armed with a news clipping reporting the banquet was on May 13, set out to prove Guadagni a liar and badly shook the confidence of William Thompson when he produced the evidence. When Guadagni came back the next morning with a clipping from *La Notizia*, an Italian paper, proving there had been another banquet for Williams in an Italian church on April 15, Lowell apologized but excluded his error from the minutes of the hearings until pressured to insert them after the execution. In another hairbreadth adventure, Herbert Ehrmann set out to find evidence that Vanzetti's friends were not lying about the purchase of eels on December 24, 1919, the day of the Bridgewater robbery attempt which resulted in the Plymouth trial. Governor Fuller had remarked there was no evidence to back up the claim. By sheer luck Ehrmann tracked down an American Express Company receipt, after searching the records of all the fish dealers at the Boston piers, dated December 20, 1919 and showing a shipment of eels to Vanzetti. This would prove that Vanzetti had received the eels in time to prepare them for the day before Christmas sale. Neither Fuller nor Lowell were sufficiently impressed to accept this bolstering of the alibi. Fuller surprisingly stated to John F. Moors that Vanzetti could commit a crime in South Braintree at 7:30 in the morning and get to Plymouth in time to sell eels at 9:30.

In a handwritten letter to an inquirer dated September 13, 1933, Lowell stated the Committee had concluded Sacco and Vanzetti were guilty because of additional evidence not produced at the trial, such as the two new eye witnesses to the crime. Ehrmann has countered that not one of the reasons advanced by Lowell were presented in court and that these witnesses were actually rejected by the prosecution as uncertain. Lowell also states in his letter that one of the fatal bullets at South Braintree was so obsolete defense experts were unable to find specimens in the shops, yet Sacco had some in his pockets and pistol at time of arrest. Ehrmann replies that Shelley Braverman, a defense expert, was still able to buy the "obsolete" bullets in 1962. They had been discontinued during World War I but a large stock of supplies was still available in the twenties.[52] Thus the case refuses to be solved.

The major condemnation of Lowell seems to be an unwillingness to admit that Thayer's prejudice, if not hatred, was sufficient reason for a reprieve since it was too late for a new trial. But with a reprieve, Sacco and Vanzetti would have lost the martyrdom they finally accepted.

Were they guilty? Only a few people probably know for sure, such as Rosina Sacco and her son Dante. According to Francis Russell, Dante has recently refused his request for a statement about his father's innocence, which certainly does not prove anything. Francis Russell bases his final opinion on unofficial tests he obtained in 1961 with Sacco's forty-year old, rusty pistol in order to compare new bullet markings with the "fatal bullet" on a comparison microscope presumably better than was available in the twenties. Judge Musmanno indignantly rejected the circumstances surrounding Russell's test as well as the careless handling of the pistol and bullet since 1920, not to mention during the trial.[53]

Most history books and standard references refer to the case as a tragic miscarriage of justice in a shameful period of hysteria. The charge that the capitalist system conspired to suppress the men is recognized as propaganda just as it was by responsible people at the time. Yet the business community acted no better than society as a whole at the time, perhaps because of its unjustified fear of labor's drive for unionism. The writer recalls boyhood in a small western Massachusetts city in the twenties. His friend, Enzo Marinaro, whose print shop he liked to hang around in, told him tearfully one day he was being driven out of town by the Mayor and the local businessmen who wouldn't patronize him. The reason — he was a "Socialist" because his little Italian newspaper had been attacking Benito Mussolini. The writer wonders how local jurors would have treated the printer had he been circumstantially indicted in a brutal murder case.

In the end the evidence and the witnesses seem to cancel each other out and only the prejudice of the court and the character of the men stand in relief. Five men were in the South Braintree murder car but only two were ever apprehended or even identified, a most unusual circumstance for a capital crime in broad daylight. They carried guns, lied at the time of their arrest and couldn't get jurors to believe their alibis for either the guns or for where they were on the days involved. Yet none of the $15,776 payroll money was ever traced to them and their conduct after the crime made no sense for criminals. Most of the new evidence, such as the Ripley, Gould and Proctor motions have been mentioned. An alternate cast, the Morelli gang of Providence, was ingeniously produced by Ehrmann as a more likely group to be involved in professional robberies. One of the Morelli gangsters was available for robbery on that day and photos indicate he was the twin image of Sacco. Judge Thayer, the Supreme Judicial Court, the Lowell Committee and Governor Fuller rejected this motion for a new trial as well as the others.

The United States Supreme Court, with Justice Holmes himself involved, refused to review the case for lack of jurisdiction. Justice Brandeis disqualified himself because he had allowed Rosina and Dante Sacco to occupy his Dedham house during the trial and because he was the close friend of Mrs. Elizabeth Glendower Evans, the most active of the Boston ladies engaged in the defendants' support. In a recent reprint edition of the trial transcript, Supreme Court Justice William O. Douglas implies that if the case were presented to the Supreme Court today it would be heard as a result of Supreme Court precedents about unfair trials developed since the twenties.[54] Interestingly the cost of printing the original transcript in 1929, so that it could serve as a useful guide in schools and libraries, was quietly borne by a small group headed by John D. Rockefeller, Jr., son of Sacco's symbolic enemy.[55]

Shining through the whole case for friend and foe alike is Bartolomeo Vanzetti. Russell, Felix and others who challenge the popular sympathy for the defendants generously acknowledge Vanzetti was an uncommon man. William Thompson said the following:

> I went into this case as a Harvard man, a man of old American tradition, to help two aliens who had, I thought, been unjustly treated. I have arrived at a humbler attitude. . . . The Harvard graduate, the man of old American traditions, the established lawyer, is now quite ready to say that nowhere in his soul is there to be found the faith, the splendid gentility, which make the man, Bartolomeo Vanzetti.[56]

Footnotes

[1] The statement was taken down in a prison interview by Phil Stong of the North American Newspaper Alliance and reprinted in the *New York World* and other papers. The incident is described in "The Last Days of Sacco and Vanzetti," (Stong), in *The Aspirin Age*, edited by Isabel Leighton, (New York, 1949), pp. 169-189.

[2] Granville Hicks, *Small Town* (New York, 1946), p. 28.

[3] For a full quotation of President Brewster's generally misunderstood speech, see Francine duP. Gray, "The Panthers at Yale," *New York Review of Books* (June 4, 1970), pp. 29-36.

[4] Martin H. Bush, *Ben Shahn, The Passion of Sacco and Vanzetti* (Syracuse, 1968), p. 12.

[5] David Felix, *Protest: Sacco-Vanzetti and the Intellectuals* (Bloomington, 1965), p. 169.

[6] Louis Joughin and Edmund M. Morgan, *The Legacy of Sacco and Vanzetti* (New York, 1948), p. 235.

[7] Supp. Vol., 295. Sacco and Vanzetti reference works refer to the five volumes of the transcript of the Dedham trial, published by Henry Holt and Company, New York, in 1929 as "Holt," and the Supplementary Volume, also published by Holt in 1929 and containing related reports, as "Supplementary.")

[8] Herbert B. Ehrmann, *The Case That Will Not Die* (Boston, 1969), p. 142.

[9] *Ibid.*, p. 142.

[10] New York *Times*, July 11, 1967. (The author was found not guilty.)

[11] Francis Russell, *Tragedy in Dedham* (New York, 1962), pp. 127-128.

[12] Holt, Vol. II, pp. 2239-2264.

[13] Richard Hofstadter, "What Happened to the Antitrust Movement?" in Earl F. Cheit, ed., *The Business Establishment* (New York, 1964), p. 5.

[14] Felix Frankfurter, *The Case of Sacco and Vanzetti* (Boston, 1927), p. 43.

[15] Samuel Eliot Morison, *The Oxford History of the American People* (New York, 1965), pp. 885-886.

[16] Ehrmann, *op. cit.*, p. 49.

[17] Russell, *op. cit.*, p. 107.

[18] Frankfurter, Marion, and Gardner Jackson (eds.), *The Letters of Sacco and Vanzetti* (New York, 1928), letter to Alice Stone Blackwell, January 24, 1924, p. 16.

[19] *Ibid.*, letter to Leonard Abbott, November 25, 1926, pp. 213-214.

[20] *Ibid.*, letter to Mrs. Maude Pettyjohn, p. 188.

[21] Quoted in Barbara Tuchman, *The Proud Tower* (New York, 1962), p. 71.

[22] Paul Goodman, "The Black Flag of Anarchism," *New York Times Magazine*, July 18, 1968, pp. 10 ff.

[23] Holt, Vol. II, pp. 1876-1877.

[24] Holt, Vol. IV, p. 3579.

[25] Russell, *op. cit.*, p. 132.

[26] Eugene Lyons, *Assignment in Utopia* (New York, 1937), pp. 29-36.

[27] Ehrmann, *op. cit.*, p. 156.

[28] *Ibid.*, pp. 139, 535.

[29] Francis Russell, "Sacco-Vanzetti: The End of the Chapter," *National Review*, May 5, 1970, p. 461.

[30] Russell, *Tragedy in Dedham*, *op. cit.*, p. 462.

[31] Ehrmann, *op. cit.*, p. 403 fn., qu. Eastman in *National Review* of October 21, 1961.

[32] Michael A. Musmanno, "Was Sacco Guilty?" *The New Republic*, March 2, 1963, pp. 25 ff. Also Ehrmann, *op. cit.*, p. 403 fn.

[33] Holt, Vol. V, pp. 4968-4969.

[34] Holt, Vol. V, p. 4928.

[35] Holt, Vol. V, pp. 5067-5068.

[36] Holt, Vol. V, p. 5378.

[37] Herbert Ehrmann, *The Untried Case* (New York, 1960), foreword by Joseph N. Welch, pp. iii-iv.

[38] Holt, Vol. I, p. 896.

[39] Holt, Vol. IV, pp. 3641-3643.

[40] Holt, Vol. IV, pp. 4356-4357.

[41] Joughin and Morgan, *op. cit.*, pp. 316-317.

[42] *The American Heritage History of the 20's and 30's*, R. K. Andrist, ed., (New York, 1970), p. 149.

[43] Joughin and Morgan, *op. cit.*, qu. Eugene Lyons, *The Last Days of Sacco and Vanzetti* (New York, 1927), p. 64. Also see John Dos Passos, *Facing the Chair* (Boston, 1927), p. 57: "In his charge to the jury in the Plymouth trial Judge Thayer definitely said that the crime of highway robbery was consistent with Vanzetti's ideals of radicalism." Vanzetti himself, in his extemporaneous remarks upon being sentenced at Dedham, charged Judge Thayer with such a remark "to the best of my memory." (See Ehrmann, *The Case That Will Not Die*, *op. cit.*, p. 453.)

[44] Holt, Vol. II, p. 1737.

[45] Holt, Vol. II, pp. 1867-1873.

[46] Holt, Vol. II, pp. 1876-1877.

[47] Mark A. DeW. Howe, ed., *Holmes-Laski Letters* (Cambridge, 1954), vol. 2, pp. 900-999.

[48] Felix, *op. cit.*, pp. 241-249.

[49] "Eugene V. Debs to the Workers of America," included in Dos Passos, *op. cit.*, preface.

[50] Ehrmann, *op. cit.*, p. 532.

[51] *Ibid.*, p. 532.

[52] *Ibid.*, pp. 512-529.

[53] Musmanno, *op. cit.*, pp. 25-30.

[54] William O. Douglas, prefatory essay to *The Sacco-Vanzetti Case, A Transcript* (New York, 1969), Appel Reprints.

[55] Joughin and Morgan, *op. cit.*, p. 318.

[56] *Ibid.*, p. 511, qu. from *New York World* of May 15, 1927.

Chapter 3

That Man in the White House

On the last day of October 1936, Franklin D. Roosevelt closed his campaign for a second term with a wild and reckless denunciation of American business. Before a screaming audience in Madison Square Garden, the master politician jabbed at his opponent mercilessly preparatory to the knockout punch. But the opponent seemed to be some candidate from Wall Street rather than the mild, progressive Alf Landon, Republican Governor of Kansas. Ignoring Landon, Roosevelt inflamed the chanting crowd with downright Populist sentiments such as Kansans once used to vilify New Yorkers in Bryan's time. Reviewing the New Deal, he said:

> We had to struggle with the old enemies of peace — business and financial monopoly, speculation, reckless banking, class antagonisms, sectionalism, war profiteering. They had begun to consider the Government of the

> United States as a mere appendage to their own affairs. And we know that Government by organized money is as dangerous as Government by organized mob . . .

Now the President's voice hardened:

> *They are unanimous in their hatred for me — and I welcome this hatred.* I should like to have it said of my first Administration that in it the forces of selfishness and of lust for power met their match. I should like to have it said . . .

The cheers and cowbells drowned out the words. The champion was not about to waste his roundhouse blow. "Wait a moment," he shouted, and then:

> I should like to have it said of my second Administration that in it *these forces met their master.*

Here was FDR at his worst, wearing the mantle of the demagogue, flaying the business community for a depression it could hardly have instigated by itself and, finally, laying on the metaphor of mastery, as though the forces of business were to be brought to his heel. Granted that great crises cause great controversies and American political oratory knows no limits, it was still a bit too much. Ironically there was no need to pull out all the stops. The President was absolutely certain of a victory so overwhelming he would be all but crowned by Americans not living in Maine or Vermont. The forces of business had practically guaranteed the election with their fatuous assemblage of millionaires in the Liberty League applauding Al Smith in white tie and coattails as he linked the New Deal with Russian Communism. Where was the FDR who had greeted the organization of the Liberty League with high good humor and laughed his head off as their antics played into his hands?

Where indeed was the President who, infinitely complex as he was, had one undeniable characteristic, the *noblesse oblige* of the aristocrat which bound him to patrician reform of the Establishment but not to rabble-rousing? Where was the FDR who yearned for business approval, who accepted America as a business civilization, who believed intensely that he was saving capitalism in its time of extreme crisis? Where was the President who had initiated a honeymoon with business by placing it in the driver's seat of the National Recovery Administration and had been lukewarm to labor's cause in his practical emphasis on business recovery before union recognition? Where finally was the President whom historians now chide for failing to go far enough with government spending to end the depression because of his thrifty Dutch hang-up with a businesslike balancing of the budget?

The depression of the thirties that brought FDR to the Presidency was the greatest crisis the American business community ever faced. One can speculate that it is inconceivable an economic crisis of such magnitude — at least thirteen million people comprising one-third of all employees out of work and out of hope — would today result in another deal of emergency relief legislation and cautious experiments. In a brief forty years, the heritage of the Great Depression has been to lay the political responsibility for full employment squarely at the federal doorstep. Having yielded its old independence to the government for so long a period, the business community in a new crisis of such dimensions would probably acquiesce to the nationalization of basic industries, a step FDR emphatically rejected. Its fears of dictatorship have been largely dissipated by actual experience with securities and banking regulation, a managed currency, farm subsidies, wages and hours legislation, labor reforms, massive government welfare spending, high taxes and all the other dreaded programs initiated in the thirties. The point is not only to consider how slender a reed — full employment — fortifies capitalism against the claims of socialism in contemporary America but also to appreciate how undeserving it was for FDR to gather the hatred of a large part of the business community. For good measure, FDR himself felt the landed squire's patronizing disrespect for powerful men of business, especially the red-handed financial connivers of the day, and undoubtedly took some malicious pleasure in fighting back at the "fat cats" (he often used the term) who called him "a traitor to his class." Not immune to the conspiracy syndrome which has contributed to the paranoid side of American history, Roosevelt in 1937 even entertained the notion that a few thousand capitalists were conspiring to thwart the New Deal by deliberately prolonging the current recession, according to the diaries of Morgenthau and Ickes.[1] But FDR was too complex a man for even his closest associates to pin down in their diaries as he brilliantly improvised his plan of action. His conspirators could just as well be rejected suitors — now loved, now hated.

II

So much has been written about FDR, whose four terms spanned the nation's greatest peacetime and wartime crises, that new entrants are well advised to explore their own particular corner of his vast terrain. If we center on his relations with the business community of the New Deal period, three levels of confrontation may be noted. There are first of all his experiments and decisions affecting the economy, that realm of the nation where businessmen toil and which they somewhat reasonably feel they know best. Secondly there is the area of gut and viscera, where the men who give ulcers tend to boil over themselves when their traditional status and power are challenged. A third area, in which these levels become articulated in banquet speeches, trade association statements, country club gossip, newspaper editorials and occasional books, is the field of economic philosophy.

The New Deal sharpened discussions about economic philosophy to a degree unmatched since the turn of the century, when muckrakers attacked the arrogant post-Civil War business oligarchy. This oligarchy contained the so-called "Robber Barons," who had done so much for industrial expansion in their own vigorous way but were now recognized as anachronisms in need of restraint and regulation. The key word of the new order was "antitrust," a genuinely popular concept both in and out of Congress, which first appeared as legislation in 1890. The word itself survives as an anachronism looking backward to the time when any dominant enterprise or group of enterprises was known as a "trust," whether it was milk, sugar, money, steel, oil, or even, as the muckrakers contended, coffins.

Antitrust led to sophisticated arguments about the desirability of industrial size itself. Historians conveniently divide the sides of the debate, citing on the one hand the school of Justice Brandeis and Woodrow Wilson, with Thomas Jefferson and Andrew Jackson in the wings, who deplored big business as monopolistic and soul-stifling for the democracy. The rival school is symbolized by FDR's cousin Ted, who peered further into the new century and presumably advocated the benefits of regulated size while doing a bit of popular "trust-busting" himself. "Rural toryism," snorted Theodore Roosevelt about the Brandeisian fears. With regulatory commissions and even some light-handed government planning (easily learned in World War I), disciples of Roosevelt's "New Nationalism" foresaw a great nation of technology-ridden urban dwellers able to master and use their inescapably large institutions. As a corollary, it became evident if one could stand big business, one could also stand big, or central, government. This school, too, had its spirit in the wings, the only non-President other than Brandeis who achieved a political-economical label in the discussions, Alexander Hamilton.

One need only come up for air in modern America to realize the Hamiltonians have won the day. Antitrust persists, of course, as a bi-partisan political restraint on business monopoly but there has been little indeed of the breaking up of big units the Brandeisians (or "atomists," as some unwary philosophers used the pre-nuclear word), advocated. The old Justice won his point, too, in the cutting down to size of the "financial trust," the one he feared most because of its undercover power. From the days of young attorney Brandeis' bold attack on the manipulators of "other people's money," through the House's Pujo Investigating Committee hearings on Wall Street in 1912, the establishment of the Federal Reserve System in 1913, the Pecora Committee Senate investigations of the early 1930's, the Securities and Exchange laws of 1933 and 1934, the modification of the gold standard in the 1930's, the Banking Acts of 1933 and 1935 and the Temporary National Economic Committee investigation of 1937-1938, the financial community took one knock after another which reportedly moved control of financial matters from Wall Street to Washington.

The Progressive reform movement of Theodore Roosevelt and Woodrow Wilson expired under the distractions of World War I and a new era of business ascendancy triumphed in the 1920's. There was prosperity such as the nation had never known before, accompanied by Presidents and Cabinet officers who valued and appreciated the business giants pouring out the cornucopia of goods and services. The business of America was business, as its oracle Coolidge put it, and a Morgan partner was conceived to be certainly wiser and slightly more useful than the President himself. Wall Street had particular dignity. Its stock promoters were now called investment bankers as it poured shaky loans all over the world in its own version of foreign aid and borrowed six billions from its allied banks to finance the speculations of domestic investors. "Character" was the hallmark of the "sound, good fellows" who were stewards of this great trust, J. P. Morgan II had explained to the swarthy Pecora. Richard Whitney, President of the New York Stock Exchange ("a perfect institution," he told the Pecora men) and brother of a Morgan partner, must have mused on these words as he went to work in his customary striped pants and black coat. FDR's fellow Grotonian and Harvard man was soon to enter Sing Sing, another "traitor to his class."

III

FDR himself made an entry into the business world of the twenties with dreary results. There is no reason for expecting that a President of the United States should show business success among his credentials. This would eliminate Abraham Lincoln and Harry S. Truman in addition to FDR. Still, Roosevelt would have had an edge on the "unscrupulous money changers" he drove from the temple in his 1933 inaugural speech had his own record been more illustrious. John T. Flynn, an excellent financial reporter who helped Pecora establish the climate for securities regulation, later turned on FDR, "the country squire in the White House," and catalogued his business failures in a book received by an eager audience. Even more sympathetic writers, such as Daniel Fusfeld, in his *Economic Thought of Franklin D. Roosevelt*, score him low as a businessman. In the spirit of presenting a somewhat irrelevant side of Roosevelt, yet one of interest to business-minded people, some of his ventures may be recorded.

Roosevelt's father James had been a successful corporation vice-president and investor before retiring to Hyde Park to live on the substantial income of his own funds and his wife's inherited capital. A railroad executive, James had also made several bids for high stakes in money and power but failed each time. The most spectacular effort was his participation in forming a company to dig a canal across Nicaragua. Armed with Congressional permission and the blessings of President Cleveland, the company raised six million dollars, started construction and foundered in the depression of 1893. His father's comfortable escapes seem to have left FDR with no early animus against business and it is safe to assume this disposition was late-blooming, a result of the crash and depression. Instead the sheltered life of ponies, sailboats, governesses, trips abroad and exclusive schools gave him an awareness of the comforts of wealth and the privileges of property. Sure of his world and of his high station in life, particularly in his college years when TR was in the White House, Franklin went on to quick political success. Ambitious to make his name in public service, he became a State Senator, Assistant Secretary of the Navy under Woodrow Wilson (TR's old post) and Democratic Vice Presidential candidate in 1920 with Ohio's Governor Cox, all by the age of thirty-eight. Now there had to be a breathing spell before he could enter public life again at the propitious moment. Armed with his bar exam diploma (he had left Columbia Law School without a degree), FDR appropriately chose the twenties for his interlude as a businessman. Within eight months after the Cox defeat, he was stricken with polio, never to walk again, but in time he was courageously back in his Wall Street office, spiritually strengthened by the tragedy. There he dabbled in business and politics until becoming Governor of New

York in 1928, one step short of the "rendezvous with destiny" for both himself and the nation.

Actually FDR needed income in order to support his family in style without help from his doting mother. The combined fortunes of Elinor and Franklin at the time amounted to about $300,000, all invested in bonds, which brought the young couple close to $15,000 a year. A social friend, Van Lear Black, president of the Fidelity and Deposit Company of Baltimore and friendly to FDR's political aspirations for high office, solved his financial problems by making FDR a vice-president at $25,000 a year, a post which continued till 1928, and which often as not was filled by Louis Howe, the strange, dedicated President-maker who hitched his star to FDR even before the sickness at Campobello. The use of his name and connections were FDR's main contribution to the insurance company, which did a flourishing business in bonding construction jobs for builder-politicians. Ironically when his son James Roosevelt performed a similar function in Boston insurance circles, although with considerably more profit, Roosevelt detractors cried out in anguish, fortified by the tradition that a President's son must suffer from all sides.

With this kind of ample income, in terms of 1920 dollars, FDR's excursion into slightly balmy enterprises can be understood, especially in view of his exuberant optimism, experimental temperament and the wildcat atmosphere of downtown New York in that decade. In 1922 he bought control of a Maine lobster fishery that supplied many of the swank hotels and restaurants in the East. According to the records, it expanded sharply, then succumbed to mismanagement and bankruptcy in 1924, costing FDR a substantial loss. In general, FDR spread his risks, winning some, losing others, never backing any venture all the way, a symptomatic preview of one of his Presidential liabilities.

A winner was Photomaton, Incorporated, the first of the companies that produced the automatic photo slot machines, still to be found in air terminals and railroad stations. His Dutchess County neighbor Henry Morgenthau brought him into the company as a director and each sold his $3 stock at $17 in 1928.

The urge to cash in on vending machines spread to stockholdings and a directorship in a postage stamp machine company which in turn merged with several other companies to form Consolidated Automatic Merchandising Corporation. As a director of the latter, FDR saw it open a completely automatic United Cigar Store in Times Square as a widely publicized herald of the "automatic age in merchandising." Happily FDR left the firm long before it failed in the thirties, its promises of vast profits and an army of unemployed store clerks unfulfilled, at least from that source.

To round out the tale of enterprise, note must be taken of dry oil wells in California and Wyoming, a cattle ranch near Warm Springs, Georgia (where he of course lavished tremendous energies to make the baths self-sufficient on a non-profit basis), and a promotional plan for banks to sell twenty-year 3½% compounded income savings certificates.

For those who thought FDR entirely unversed in the currency problems that would vex the early New Deal, he could point to his service as the $10,000 a year president of United European Investors, which induced American and Canadian holders of German marks, plagued by runaway inflation, to turn them over to the corporation, which quickly invested them in German stocks as a hedge against inflation. Somehow it worked out to the investors' advantage and FDR sold out to his associates in 1926. Finally there was the American Investigation Corporation, FDR vice-president, investigating air transport by dirigible. The blue ribbon board included a Hanna, some Mellons, Owen D. Young of G.E., and, strangely, Cecil B. DeMille. The role of the former Assistant Secretary of the Navy was to get major financial aid from Washington for these rugged capitalists, who abandoned the grandiose scheme when the same was not forthcoming.[2]

The most significant part of FDR's business interlude was his presidency of the American Construction Council from 1922 to 1928. The Council was a super body representing 250 trade associations within the building industry. Its formation became desirable when the industry was reeling from the investigations of the Lockwood Commission in New York City, which revealed graft, monopoly, racketeering and price collusion. Not that this was anything remarkable in New York's history, but it was aggravated by the post-war depression of 1920-1921 which saw the industry particularly depressed and unprofitable. President Harding's energetic Secretary of Commerce, Herbert Hoover, decided with his wartime friend Franklin D. Roosevelt to do something about it. Together they launched the idea of the Council, with the usual ethical reasons stated in its platform plus the major objective "to stabilize the entire construction industry by eliminating the 'peak and valley' conditions, to the advantage of capital, labor and the public in general." For an industry facing heavy antitrust violations, this was a plaintive call for some way to stabilize without such violations, which of course is the perennial dilemma facing most of America's large industry.

Hoover's action was consistent with his vigorous leadership of the Department of Commerce which he often thought of as an extension of the Chamber of Commerce. FDR as a part-time lawyer and politician could not help finding the position congenial for fees and public exposure. Still, to be president of the Council involved endorsing a policy, one which strongly shaped FDR's developing economic philosophy and his relations with businessmen.

There was the Progressive faith in regulation inherited from his great influences, TR and Woodrow Wilson, as evidenced in FDR's statement: "If the members of the construction industry are unable to keep their own house in order, an exasperated public will someday regulate their house for them." There was also recognition by the young trade association executive of a generally unmentioned subject, one that had distinctly Hamiltonian overtones: "Muddling through has been the characteristic method employed by the construction industry for the past few years. There has been no system, no cooperation, no intensive national planning."[3]

But what kind of planning did FDR have in mind for his sick industry, plagued with chicanery and instability? It was the only kind of planning available short of what surely would be regarded as socialism, that is, the planning of private industry around its own table, with the sword of antitrust hanging over its head. Trade associations had become a major institutional force by the early twenties, with codes of fair practices and sharing of information replacing the old days of jugular competition and trade secrets. Often they were led by public-spirited leaders devoted to the welfare of their industries, though many, particularly in the utility business, were primarily lobbies. In spite of the fact that certain codes were found to violate antitrust laws, the movement was encouraged by Washington, particularly through the Department of Commerce and the Federal Trade Commission. The articles of faith of the associations incorporated the beginnings of the movement towards social responsibility on the part of business, as against the pursuit of profits alone, a Progressive ideal to which FDR readily subscribed. Within ninety days after taking office in 1933, FDR proposed legislation for the National Industrial Recovery Act, known as the NRA. It was to be a voluntary partnership between business and government to promote business recovery, based on operating codes. As he signed the ill-fated bill on June 16, FDR, only a few years away from business and the American Construction Council, blithely stated "history would regard it as the most far-reaching legislation ever enacted by the American Congress."

IV

Before he could turn to a plan for industrial recovery, before facing even the more pressing relief and farm problems, for that matter, FDR had to deal with a financial crisis, the crumbling of the nation's banks like a house of cards on the eve of his inauguration. Historians writing about the New Deal tend to be engulfed by the titanic personality of FDR himself, the dazzling quarterback who dominated the White House, Congress and practically all of the people, including businessmen, at the outset. Exceptions, of course, would be the President's intimate advisers, men like Raymond Moley, Rexford Tugwell, Henry Morgenthau and Harold Ickes, whose valuable but egotistical memoirs often picture FDR as a clumsy intruder in the midst of their own furious activities. To gain a fresh point of view and to support the theme of how businessmen reacted to crises, James P. Warburg, a banker, will be our guide to the banking crisis, the currency crisis and a strange round of love and hate for FDR himself.

Bankers suffered the greatest fall from grace under the New Deal. President Hoover had already seen five thousand banks crash by 1932, wiping out nine million savings and checking accounts involving four billion dollars. This was of course before banks had government deposit insurance and the drain of purchasing power of such magnitude, let alone the personal tragedies involved, exacerbated the depression almost beyond repair. Wall Street as well was in disrepute since the crash of 1929. Considering the money lost in stocks and in banks, practically everyone in the country could regard bankers as personal villains. After all they were the most pompous figures in the cities and towns throughout the nation, the symbols of money and the mysterious workings of economics which a stunned populace could not fathom. To millions, they were simply thieves who had taken away their money, foreclosed their farm and home mortgages, or called in their margin accounts. Part of the grim humor of the depression seems implausible today, when depositors simply wait for their FDIC checks when the rare bank goes under: "Don't tell my mother what I'm doing," a banker begs a friend, "she thinks I'm playing a piano in a sporting house." President Hoover finally turned on them himself, promoting a Senate investigation of Wall Street and its large New York bank connections in the spring of 1932. He could hardly have expected the scandalous mess the probe would uncover, especially after the election when Ferdinand Pecora took over as counsel. In short, bankers were among America's least favorite people.

When James Warburg returned from Europe in November 1932, it was just in time to cast a vote for Franklin D. Roosevelt. Jimmy Warburg, then age thirty-six, had been abroad on business as president of the International Acceptance Bank, a New York bank specializing in foreign business established by his father, Paul M. Warburg. Jimmy was a gilded scion of one of the great German-Jewish banking families, his roots tracing to Loebs and Schiffs as well as seven generations of Warburg merchant bankers in Germany, where he lived till age six. He was distinctly a member of "our crowd," as this network of families called themselves, but none could doubt Jimmy's abilities aside from his family connections. After achieving Phi Beta Kappa at Harvard and serving a brief stint as a Navy flier in World War I, Jimmy had modestly spent an apprenticeship at a Washington bank and then two industrious years with the First National Bank of Boston. There he turned his insatiable appetite for writing into some monographs on shoes and textiles and other First National specialties. This was the beginning of his reputation as an intellectual as well as a businessman. All in all he would produce about thirty books on economics and foreign affairs of varying quality and length in his lifetime, four of which were damaging broadsides launched at Franklin D. Roosevelt. When he died at age 72 in 1969, he had achieved recognition as a respected dissenting pamphleteer in the great eighteenth century tradition. A man of varied talents, he had also surmounted the stuffy banking tradition of the crowd in his engaging and high-spirited career.

Jimmy Warburg's secret life was that of a lyricist and *bon vivant* during the twenties following the Boston interlude. Always a man of words, he became lyricist, somewhat in self defense, to his wife Kay Swift, who transferred her energies from gentle piano compositions to hard-hitting musical comedy tunes. Together they produced several durable hits, including "Fine and Dandy," "Can This Be Love?" and "Can't We Be Friends?" The peak of their activity as the song-writing team of Kay Swift and Paul James was the writing of the entire score for *Fine and Dandy*, starring Joe Cook. The backers of this production in addition to Warburg were two future New Deal angels, Marshall Field and Averell Harriman. Though the show ran for over a year and grossed a million dollars, Warburg found he was outwitted by the producers' accounting practices and ended up reimbursing his partners largely out of his music royalties.

Eventually the interminable visits of show people such as Ira and George Gershwin to his New York apartment and summer home, coupled with night life, Sunday painting and early morning exercise of his horses, proved too far out for the young banker and his disapproving father. The marriage to Kay Swift terminated in 1934 and Warburg turned towards more sedate activities such as the boards of the Juilliard School of Music and the New York Philharmonic Society. One can surmise that this slightly raffish side of Warburg attracted him temperamentally to the New Deal. The atmosphere in Washington at the time was a heady mixture of intellectuals, professors and eccentrics such as had only been hinted at in TR's time. Certainly it was a great change from the low-brow poker-playing atmosphere of Harding, the middle-brow business climate of Coolidge, or the high-collar air of righteousness under Hoover. Though Roosevelt was hardly an aesthete, he had an instinctive graciousness towards the arts and to his great credit he backed Harry Hopkins in the valuable and humane Federal Theatre and Arts Projects as part of WPA. Still not many pipers entered the White House, though all the New Deal memoirs unite in telling how Tommy "The Cork" Corcoran, one of Frankfurter's young geniuses, would delight the President as he strolled around with his accordion, singing Irish ballads. An unlikely minstrel whom Warburg was to work closely with was Roosevelt's prize ex-Republican, Treasury Secretary William L. Woodin, former head of the American Car and Foundry Corporation. "Wee Willie" Woodin was an elfin little man of frail health and cheerful spirits who was literally to work himself to death during the financial crises of the early New Deal. Raymond Moley affectionately describes Woodin as half-artist and half-businessman, who would strum his guitar while pondering on grave decisions. In February 1934, when the silver advocates were gaining headway in their perennial demands, Moley heard Woodin tinkling on the piano late at night in the apartment they were sharing. Woodin said he was composing a lullaby. Moley suggested it be called "Lullaby to Silver." Woodin agreed and the composition was actually published under that name.[4]

Jimmy's desire for writing and public service found an example in Paul M. Warburg, who had married a Loeb and then become a partner in Kuhn, Loeb & Company, a firm which rivalled the House of Morgan in power and influence. Paul M. Warburg had been a great advocate of a central banking system for the United States and was a key figure in developing the Federal Reserve System, of which he could claim to be the "father" quite as much as Senators Glass and Aldrich. In 1914 he was appointed a member of the first Federal Reserve Board by President Wilson and he later wrote an important history of the new Federal Reserve System. After government service he became chairman of the board of the Bank of Manhattan, in which Warburg money had been invested. Paul M. Warburg's other claims to distinction had been to prophesy publicly the 1929 crash and to write some poetry, a field in which Jimmy also ventured.

Having warned others, Paul could be expected to follow his own advice and the Warburgs were surviving the depression in good shape. Now Jimmy, a Democrat, having done what he could abroad, was anxious to join the Roosevelt team. Roosevelt had already made speeches attacking Wall Street and its speculators, as well as calling for utility holding company regulation and general reforms in the banking system. Warburg was sophisticated enough to shrug off the attacks, probably convinced, as was Joseph P. Kennedy, another Wall Streeter, that such attacks were not only deserved but would help insure victory. He could recall that the creation of the Federal Reserve System had been roundly opposed by bankers and their economists.

Other than this, FDR was extremely conciliatory to businessmen, whose Republican votes were not yet in the bag. In general his campaign speeches were only vaguely inflammatory and as late as October 1932, his Pittsburgh speech, which now reads like a giant misprint, stated:

> The credit of the family depends chiefly on whether that family is living within its income and that is equally true of the nation. . . . I regard reduction in federal spending as one of the most important issues in the campaign. In my opinion it is the most direct and effective contribution that government can make to business.

The fact is Roosevelt, in common with most business leaders and economists, could not yet comprehend the concept of deficit financing as the way to spend the country out of the depression by stimulating purchasing power. This concept, later so widely connected with Keynes, was then practically unknown in Warburg's circle or among FDR's brain-trusters and, of course, was never to be wholly accepted by FDR. Although Roosevelt promised vigorous, experimental action in some of his campaign speeches and had been a pioneer in direct relief and work project relief as Governor of New York, no unsound theories of unbalanced budgets or currency inflation were allowed to jeopardize his bid for the Presidency. He did cover all the obvious national issues but the main thrust was to hammer away at Hoover's inactivity in response to the crisis. Reminiscing about the 1932 campaign, Tugwell recalls that he and his fellow brain-trusters, Moley and Berle, were embarrassed by such speeches as the one at Pittsburgh, which he thought "foolish beyond calculation." Still these amateurs had to reconcile themselves to the fact that Roosevelt the politician felt it was necessary to get elected before he could do anything at all about change.[5] To secure his nomination, he had repudiated his support of the League of Nations, under the prodding of William R. Hearst. As most analysts of FDR agree, he was exasperatingly both lion and fox.

Jimmy Warburg, with his grasp of economic theory, would not have blanched at temporary deficit spending. Neither would the concept of under-consumption rather than over-production as a cause of the depression have bothered him. This theory, which FDR had privately accepted in long discussions with his brain-trusters,[6] implied a lack of well-distributed purchasing power as the time-bomb of the twenties. Even accepting this theory, one still had a choice, either to lean towards restoration of business confidence through good conduct in the White House, which Hoover and the business community were now demanding from the new Administration, or to push for recovery through the spending and prodding of the central government. While Warburg was sympathetic to increased government action, his own economics were slanted towards restoring business confidence by avoiding currency manipulation, a heresy which was strongly in the air and somehow feared from Roosevelt. As a corollary, Warburg also possessed a basic belief, as Hoover did, that the cure of the depression required renewed international trade, lower tariffs and monetary cooperation instead of each country going it alone as economic nationalists. This was an international banker's point of view but not inimical to the domestic reforms promised by Roosevelt. Since FDR had not yet revealed his full hand on trade and currency, Warburg was curious about where the President stood as he maneuvered his own career towards Washington.

Actually Roosevelt had considerable support among the business community. It is surprising to note that 24% of all contributions above $1,000 to FDR in the 1932 campaign came from bankers and brokers.[7] From his New York days, FDR had generous business backing. A Business and Professional Men's League for Roosevelt was working away at full steam in 1932 under the chairmanship of Jesse I. Straus, the Macy's president who would be rewarded with the Ambassadorship to France. Herbert Lehman, of the prominent banking family, had been Roosevelt's Lieutenant Governor and was a very substantial contributor. Bernard Baruch put up $60,000, John J. Raskob of General Motors $25,000 and others like Henry Morgenthau, Marshall Field, Averell Harriman, Lincoln Filene, Owen D. Young, Vincent Astor, W. L. Woodin, Jesse Jones and Joseph P. Kennedy were generously involved. Even the House of Morgan, through its liberal Russell Leffingwell, a personal friend of FDR, was discreetly in the Roosevelt corner, although only to the extent of the one partner. After the election, Leffingwell was proposed by FDR's advisers for the post of Assistant Secretary of the Treasury. "No, we can't have 23 Wall Street," Roosevelt cannily decided, although he appreciated the chance to extend the olive branch towards business.[8] Nor could a Morgan man feel comfortable at FDR's elbow, with the Pecora investigation going full blast, culminating in the indignity of a midget being photographed in the lap of J. P. Morgan himself while securities regulation laws were being rushed through Congress.

One additional factor may have influenced Jimmy Warburg to flout Wall Street by joining the Administration. Sensitive to developments in Europe, where his uncle Aby still ran the Warburg bank in Hamburg, the astute Jimmy had come back from a long trip in 1930 convinced that Hitler was a menace who would soon come to power and plunge the world into war. Albert H. Wiggin, not yet ejected as president of the Chase bank for his stock-rigging and self-dealing, invited Warburg to lunch where he heard this preposterous news and promptly called Paul M. Warburg to warn him: "Your son is crazy. You ought to have him locked up." But Jimmy Warburg probably had a surer touch for foreign affairs than economic affairs and was not dissuaded. Although the Warburgs appeared, like the Rothschilds, to be beyond the reach of guttersnipe anti-Semitism, the complete distaste of FDR for such a sentiment must have appealed to him. Not only did the Hudson River aristocrat have the support of prominent Jews but he eagerly sought the counsel of advisers like Justice Brandeis and Felix Frankfurter. Furthermore he was completely at home with them, leading soon to charges by Roosevelt haters of international conspiracies and a flaw of Jewishness in FDR's family tree. Actually FDR was incapable of anti-Semitism or similar kinds of snobbery. History would reveal his best friends to have been the son of a harness maker (Harry Hopkins), a gnomelike reporter of no particular lineage (Louis Howe) and his neighboring Jew (Henry Morgenthau). At any rate, Jimmy Warburg, a man about town in New York's social set, was friendly with Jimmy Roosevelt, a similar type, who was then living in one of the cottages on the Westchester estate of Jimmy's uncle Felix Warburg. At Jimmy Warburg's request, the President's eldest son brought Raymond Moley, the number one brain-truster, to lunch at the bank. Soon Jimmy was in the President's circle as a financial expert, one of the few Wall Streeters the President would bring into his Administration.

V

"Ray Moley tells me," the President-elect beamed, "that you are the white sheep of Wall Street." The scene was FDR's home on New York's East 65th Street. It was the first week of February 1933. The interregnum was still in force, since inaugurations were then on March 3.

Warburg replied that the flattering distinction belonged more appropriately to his father, adding fatefully that a white sheep did not necessarily beget white lambs.

Roosevelt chuckled. "I didn't know you were a farmer like me. Anyway, I want you to work with Ray Moley on the banking and currency situations. . . . Which one of you gentlemen is Ikes?" "Ickes," corrected the man who was for years to be Secretary of the Interior.[9]

FDR in the first hundred days was superb, robustly confident, born to command, enlarged by the crisis as Churchill was when he once assumed the reins. "We have nothing to fear but fear itself," FDR assured the nation on Friday, inauguration day. After furious weekend preparations, he announced the closing of the nation's banks Monday morning and called Congress into special session on March 9. To buy a few days' time for Woodin to prepare an emergency banking bill providing for the orderly re-opening of the banks and to protect the nation's dwindling gold supply, he also issued an edict freezing gold in the vaults. Searching for authority for the bank closing and the gold freeze, Attorney General Cummings settled for the dubious power of the Trading with the Enemy Act of 1917. Not that it really mattered, but Jimmy could note that this wartime act had been amended in 1918 at the suggestion of Paul M. Warburg just in case the government might find it necessary to invoke a peacetime embargo on gold.[10] The martial authority for the bold action was appropriate. Washington had become a command post and the enemies were crisis and depression. Even the euphemism of a "bank holiday" was good psychological warfare. Added to the shattering totality of the move, which settled the matter once and for all, the holiday seemed to offer brighter prospects ahead.

When Moley called Jimmy Warburg to Washington on March 7 to help reopen the banks as soon as possible, Warburg found a bi-partisan band of stalwarts working around the clock in the Treasury building. Though FDR had refused Hoover's last minute request to come out for sound money and generally to repudiate the New Deal platform (in order to restore business confidence and stem the bank closings), he did sensibly allow his Treasury Department to work hand in hand with Hoover's ex-officials. Under Secretary Ogden Mills and Assistant Secretary Arthur Ballantine, along with some dedicated Federal Reserve Board officials, gave invaluable aid to Woodin while the nation, innocent of credit cards, went through the nightmare experience of closed banks. Actually Hoover's officials had already prepared standby plans for closing and re-opening the banks along the lines that finally evolved in the emergency. They had pressed Hoover to take this action prior to the inauguration but the sullen President, plagued with indecision, concentrated on making FDR issue retractions. Thus Hoover accomplished nothing in the crisis and lost his chance to share the great credit which FDR reaped. Hoover's rebuttal is on the record. In his memoirs twenty years later, he stated that Roosevelt's campaign oratory had caused the crisis and that the crisis was not severe enough to close all the banks.[11]

It is not generally realized that FDR's closing of the banks only added the final touch to closings that were already sweeping the nation under state auspices during February. By the afternoon of March 3, banks in twenty-four states were closed or restricting withdrawal of money. The Governors of Illinois and New York were finally persuaded to close their banks on March 4 and all the remaining states were in the process of doing so when FDR made his March 6 proclamation. Governor Lehman had also reluctantly closed the New York Stock Exchange over the weekend, against the objections of Richard Whitney and other financial leaders.

The state of panic on the part of depositors would have caused an intolerable run on an already dangerously depleted currency and gold supply, so that a complete suspension was inevitable. More than $2 billion of currency had been withdrawn in the current crisis, $700 million in the last week alone. Now the entire nation looked numbly towards Washington for action on a subject as dear to the hearts of its citizens as life and death, the safety of their money in the banks. It was the boldness and psychological mastery of the situation by FDR and his lieutenants that turned chaos into gaudy triumph.

Warburg aided the harassed Treasury and Federal Reserve officials as they prepared an Emergency Banking Act and started the tremendous task of certifying which banks could reopen at the end of the four-day holiday and what to do about shoring up the other banks. He could note with satisfaction that money cranks and radicals were excluded from the action and that scores of bewildered bankers were milling through the Treasury corridors, called in to give the stamp of legitimacy to the decisions of the feared new Administration. If he mused on what caused the rash of bank failures preceding the present depositors' panic, he would have emphasized the speculative mania of the twenties during which bankers invested billions in securities or in loans against securities. When the market crashed in 1929, banks became insolvent and closed their doors in a chain reaction.[12] But this hardly scratched the basic weakness in the system. Experts now point out there were too many banks outside the Federal Reserve or national banking system. These state banks were carelessly administered and tremendously undercapitalized. They provided the great majority of the 10,000 bank failures that occurred in the prosperous twenties as well as the thirties. From 1920 to 1932, 65 per cent of all closed banks had capital of less than $50,000 and most of these were in agricultural states where the depression hit first. By 1932, big city banks were going under until finally the banking system itself expired symbolically on the weekend of the inauguration. No doubt Hoover was correct to the extent that some of the panic, especially the gold withdrawals by the smart money men, was related to the certainty of FDR's victory. Speculators and hoarders wanted their gold out before the dollar might be devalued in an effort to raise prices.

Depositors don't panic, however, if their deposits are covered by government insurance. There was consideration of the same during these hectic days and Warburg, essentially conservative, was not then attracted to it. Since FDR and Woodin were also unalterably opposed to such insurance, it was not revived until the 1933 Banking Act a few months later. Even then FDR considered vetoing the 1933 Act because of this provision but finally let it stand.[13] Since FDIC insurance became one of the glories of the New Deal, one is tempted to speculate on the President's conflicting emotions, tempted by his experimental nature to support this ingenious plan but aware of the cries of socialism inherent in such government intervention. At this stage, FDR actually lagged behind the radical temper of his own Congress, not to mention the exasperated sentiments arising in the conservative heartland of America itself. "The fact is," the Akron *Beacon Journal* stated in a front page editorial on March 3, 1933, as Ohio banks crumbled, "the whole American business world is in a desperate situation and it may be saved only by heroic and instant action. Either take this course (federal guarantee of bank deposits) or confess that we are whipped, close the doors of our banks, stores and factories, and let chaos and revolution take their course, with all that these imply in the overthrow of American institutions."[14]

Actually the business community could have nothing but praise for FDR in the banking crisis. He allowed the Hoover officials to help shape the strategy and execution of the closing and re-opening. Planners and visionaries were excluded from the proceedings in favor of men like Woodin, Warburg, and Moley. Not that FDR didn't have a friendly ear for advisers like Tugwell, Adolf Berle, Frankfurter and even Brandeis, each of whom would have joyfully countenanced elaborate restructuring of the discredited banking system then and there, including a strong injection of nationalization. He simply preferred an orthodox rescue, quite consistent with his stance as the saver of capitalism. He also realized that more tinkering and reforms could come with further legislation, as they did with the Banking Acts of 1933 and 1935. Yet at the time, Congress might very well have nationalized the banks with as much dispatch and pleasure as it brought back beer a week later.

Some observers regret that FDR didn't produce more substantive changes for the banks in his hour of complete command. Tugwell's opinions in that respect are well-known but even Arthur Schlesinger, Jr., in *The Coming of the New Deal*, suggests that "the decision to save the system rather than change it had come about almost by inadvertence." Schlesinger states that FDR was anxious to get the support of the bankers and had no theorist of the stature of Keynes to brainstorm the larger reform.[15] Raymond Moley, however, insists that the FDR of 1933 was solidly in the corner of business and moderation and never gave a second thought to upsetting something so sacrosanct as banking.[16] "Capitalism," Moley states with the self-satisfaction of an accomplice, "was saved in eight days."[17] The irony of the difference between FDR's image and reality was not lost on contemporary critics less enamored with the capitalism of the thirties. "The President drove the money-changers out of the Capitol on March 4th," said Congressman Lemke of North Dakota, "and they were all back on the 9th."[18]

Lemke was referring to the opening of the special session of Congress on the 9th, which passed the Emergency Banking Bill with a whoop and holler, practically sight unseen, so it could be signed by FDR that night. The holiday had to be extended to the 13th, on which date the first group of the country's 18,000 banks would be opened. Progress reports had been issued by the Treasury Department and on Sunday night, March 12, FDR delivered his master stroke, a device of style and leadership completely his own, the first "fireside chat." Now the master politician and actor were fused to perfection. Like a kindly grandfather, he spoke to 60 million people over their 20 million radios. "I want to talk for a few minutes with the people of the United States about banking," he said as the whole nation paid attention to the unlikely subject. In twenty minutes he explained why the holiday had been declared, how some of the banks would open the next day and others later with government assistance. He emphasized how completely orthodox the entire plan had been and in front porch tones stated, "There is nothing complex, or radical, in the process." Then he advised depositors to bring their money back to the banks. "I can assure you that it is safer to keep your money in a reopened bank than under a mattress."

Warburg and the other men of high finance watched in wonder the next day as the people flocked to the banks to redeposit their currency, just as FDR had asked. By the end of March, over a billion dollars in currency, half of which was in gold coin, bullion or certificates, were returned to the banks. It was not even necessary to use the emergency supply of a new Federal Reserve bank note currency, not backed by gold, which had been dreamed up in the days and nights in the Treasury building. FDR had demonstrated what the financiers knew in their hearts, that any banking and currency system depends above all on a most illogical consideration, that of make-believe or public confidence, certainly not on the convertibility of paper into gold alone. On the other hand, FDR's advisers were not willing to let gold slip away. The Federal Reserve Board had announced on March 8 that lists of persons who had withdrawn gold since February 1 and failed to bring it back by March 13 would be published, which achieved the desired result. On April 5, the President issued an executive order forbidding the hoarding of gold, beginning some adventures with the sacred metal that would soon outrage the temporarily dazzled bankers and financiers.

VI

For some reason, men of the wide open spaces who were also gifted in finance appealed to FDR more than their counterparts in the East. Warburg as a Harvard man and Wall Street maverick made the inner circle but was welcomed as a rare exception. The real favorite financial men, Warburg noted, were Lewis Douglas, Director of the Budget and Jesse Jones, FDR's chairman of the Reconstruction Finance Corporation. A third Westerner, Marriner Eccles, the Mormon banker from Salt Lake City, had not yet arrived on the scene. When he appeared at the beginning of 1934, he quickly made his mark and became the superb Chairman of the Federal Reserve Board through all the remaining Roosevelt years.

Douglas was the fair-haired boy at the outset and FDR crowed about the lean, cowboy-handsome millionaire from Arizona whose family copper and banking wealth propelled him into Congress at an early age. Douglas, the President observed, added just the right conservative touch to the official family and was a real "find." Douglas's economics, however, were as traditional as the barter and wampum system of the Southwest Indians. He believed in every sentence of FDR's rash budget-balancing promises and was straining at the leash to put the Hoover administration to shame for its profligate spending.

Douglas was impervious to the blandishments of FDR's brain-trusters if indeed he ever listened to them. For close to a year, FDR had been coached by Moley, Berle, Tugwell and Frankfurter so that he was at least aware of the dilemma between budget-balancing and the stark human crisis that made it impossible for the time being. Any claims for a consistent approach to economics on FDR's part must rest on the genuinely humane and concerned temperament through which he filtered appeals to his free-wheeling intellect. But Douglas was a man of deep convictions who, like Hoover, thought in cosmic and eternal terms. Warburg watched in fascination as Douglas pressed for an Economy Act that would cut the salaries of government employees and lop off veterans' benefits. A man like Warburg naturally preferred budget-balancing but his common sense warned him of the irony of applying it to a prostrate economy in the amount of approximately a half billion dollars.

Today every schoolboy presumably knows deficit spending can be regarded as an instrument of enlightened public policy when the economy sags. The FDR of 1933, however, did not yet subscribe to this rationalization of the downgrading of thrift, though he had heard and talked about it. Two unsung American visionaries, William Trufant Foster and Waddill Catchings, an economist and a business executive respectively, had remarkably anticipated Keynes' basic concept without the erudite mathematics and rigamarole that would accompany Keynes' *General Treatise*, not due till 1936. Foster and Catchings had written to a disbelieving audience in the prosperous twenties, summing up their cure for the next depression with plain Yankee horse sense that was still pure Keynes: "When business looks rotten, more public spending." Their premise was simply that a depression in modern times would no longer wring itself out according to classical economic theories. Instead it would stay at bottom without government intervention and priming. The increased public debt would only be owed to the people itself and thus could be countenanced without excitement until paid back in good times. "Too good to be true," FDR is said to have written in his copy of Foster's *The Road to Plenty.* "You can't get something for nothing."[19]

Now the persuasive, attractive Arizonan was after FDR to cash in the promise he had exacted from the President in return for accepting the position of Director of the Budget.[20] His reasoning was high-sounding. The banking crisis had cast a shadow across the "credit of the United States" and a big Treasury debt refunding was scheduled momentarily. It was essential for the restoration of confidence that government expenditures be cut. With Moley, the most conservative of the brain-trusters, sitting at his side, Douglas drafted the Economy Bill along with FDR's accompanying message to Congress. The work was done during the bank holiday and was considered part of the official strategy for meeting the demand for confidence on the part of the business and banking community. By 1936 the President had a different attitude towards this perennial demand. "Confidence," he fumed, "don't they realize that I have to have confidence in them?" But on March 10, he delivered his message, including words that were to be thrown back at him over and over: "Too often in recent history liberal governments have been wrecked on rocks of loose fiscal policy."

It took a special kind of courage, even for a President with an overwhelming mandate from the people and a majority in Congress, to ask for pay slashes for federal employees and the authority to cut $400 million from scheduled veterans' payments, the same veterans who had been defeated by Hoover in their bonus march on Washington less than a year before. As Will Rogers said that week, "If he burned down the capitol, we would cheer and say 'well, we at least got a fire started.'" A reluctant Congress passed the bill, enticed by the parallel offering of the beer act. Douglas and his President had outdistanced Hoover himself. There is a sequel to this story for within a year Congress chipped away at the economy bill until it was all but repealed and by 1935 a $2 billion bonus was passed over FDR's half-hearted veto. By that time FDR was a confirmed spender although nostalgic about budget-balancing. Still in 1933, FDR was a hero to Douglas and had gone just about as far as a man could go to placate the world of business.

From his office by the Great Salt Lake, Marriner Eccles watched what he thought was consummate foolishness on the part of Roosevelt and his neighboring banker friend in the Budget office. Sharper and shrewder in economic thought than any man in the New Deal, including the sophisticated Warburg, Eccles could not comprehend ramming a deflationary bill through Congress at the bottom of a hopeless depression. As creative-minded as Douglas was fossil-minded, the self-educated Eccles had already preached the doctrine of creating purchasing power through government spending and deficit financing to break the back of the depression. At bankers' conventions and as a minority witness at a Senate Committee "lame duck" hearing on the depression in February 1933, this talented forty-two year old businessman had prescribed practically every workable New Deal remedy from massive public works projects, direct relief to states, deposit insurance, securities regulations, banking reform and welfare legislation to mortgage bailing-out agencies and a farm-allotment program.[21] It was not till the end of the year that he joined the Administration, by which time FDR's honeymoon with business was on the wane.

Another millionaire strolling through the corridors of power at the time was Jesse Jones, the monolithic white-haired Texan who looked and acted every inch the President himself. He was of particular interest to Warburg and his fellow bankers since he would write the final chapter on the banking crisis as head of the RFC.

Jones had come to Washington as one of the Democrats required by statute to be a board member of Hoover's new RFC in 1932. He had been in lumber, banking, real estate and newspapers, a typical "new money" wheeler-dealer with little sympathy for the cautious financiers of the East intent on preserving established fortunes. The Republican concept of the RFC proved too tame for his expansive energy and genuine desire to make American business hum at full throttle once again. He had been a friend of Roosevelt and now at age sixty grasped the chairmanship with joy. Unencumbered by economic doctrine, he simply regarded the RFC as a hugely effective temporary bank with which practical economic miracles could be performed. At Harvard, Professor Joseph Schumpeter, the economist who wrote of the gales of innovation launched by full-blooded private enterprise capitalists, must have viewed Jones' activities with disbelief. In the New Deal wonderland, here was a capitalist in bureaucrat's clothing, rousing the dormant economy with the ingeniously applied billions of a non-profit bank.

In fairness to Hoover, the ex-President's sponsorship of the RFC had been a brilliant stroke. Established by Congress to lend money to banks, insurance companies and railroads facing bankruptcy, it had performed great service in a brief time. Critics assailed its concern with institutions rather than people but within the context of Hoover's ideology it was a major concession against *laissez-faire*. The theory was that if the institutions were saved, at least jobs and investments would be preserved and the benefits would "trickle down" to the people accordingly. Some of the trickling raised eyebrows when it was learned that $90 million was lent to the Chicago bank of Charles G. Dawes, Coolidge's vice-president and an ex-member of the RFC board. Another 1932 loan of $23 million to the Missouri-Pacific Railroad, controlled by the daffy Van Sweringen brothers who were desperately in default to the Morgan interests, raised cries of favoritism. Still another $40 million went to the Bank of America, whose founder A. P. Giannini had just returned from Europe to reclaim his bank from the Eastern money men in a dramatic proxy fight. Ironically Hoover then personally requested A. P.'s support for the 1932 election and found him committed to FDR. It was a further example of the type of business support FDR was able to maintain from people who may not have liked the New Deal but were themselves in conflict with the *rentier*, or fixed income, attitude of men like Warburg's Wall Street colleagues. Thus Hoover's RFC was only a pale image of the mighty engine it would become in the New Deal. In July 1932, Congress passed a bill that would allow the RFC to make loans to states, municipalities, corporations and individuals. "Never before has so dangerous a suggestion been seriously made to our country," said Hoover as he vetoed the bill. Under Jones and the New Deal, *fifty billion dollars* were invested in an empire including mortgage agencies, the Commodity

Credit Corporation, the Electric Home and Farm Authority and an Export-Import Bank to spur foreign trade.

As new Chairman of the RFC, Jones found himself empowered to buy preferred stocks in banks rather than just lend them money, as a result of the emergency banking legislation. For the record, it now appears that Jones was so hostile to the idea of purchasing preferred stock in the banks that it took months of Federal Reserve Board and White House pressure to get him started on the program for which he later took such great credit.[22] Within this framework of inconsistency, or ability to change one's mind, which was so typical of the New Deal leaders, Jones finally wrapped up the banking crisis.

Although preferred stock rather than a loan was a much safer proposition for the weak banks, these banks refused to take advantage of the offer, fearing government control through the stock ownership. Anticipating a collapse of the banking structure all over again, just as business was reviving and would need additional bank credit, Jones, with FDR's encouragement, laid it on the line at the September 1933 meeting of the American Bankers Association. Speaking to the proud bankers, who had only a few months before vowed to fight deposit insurance legislation "to the last ditch," Jones stated bluntly: "Banks must provide credit . . . otherwise the government will. Be smart, for once. Take the government into partnership with you." Then, off the record: "Half the banks represented in this room are insolvent; and those of you representing these banks know it better than anyone else."

Meanwhile the new FDIC insurance program required a certificate of solvency by January 1, 1934 in order to qualify for membership. This harsh fact finally broke the resistance of banks needing RFC capital, as they could hardly expect to retain depositors without the FDIC seal. By 1935 the RFC had invested over one billion dollars in the preferred stocks of approximately half the banks in America. Bank failures became insignificant and eventually the billion dollars was practically all repaid. The crisis had been met by a combination of political leadership and psychology, government credit, reform legislation and dedicated public servants, including a goodly representation from the business community.

VII

Four days after the banks began to open, Jimmy Warburg picked up his morning New York *Times* to read he was about to be named Woodin's Under Secretary of the Treasury. Since he had no inkling of this news, he reviewed its significance with a banker's proper caution. Because he would deal with banks, he might possibly have a conflict of interest in view of the family's considerable Bank of Manhattan holdings, in which he had a contingent interest payable upon his widowed mother's death. A large block of bank stock was then unsalable at a decent price and the problem was conveyed to Woodin, Moley and FDR himself. One suspects that FDR recognized Warburg's reluctance as a hedge against cutting his Wall Street ties too sharply. At any rate, FDR amiably agreed to Jimmy's request that he be allowed to serve without salary or title for six months in whatever capacity the President wished. This suited the President's own Machiavellian tendency to cross lines of authority as the spirit moved. Warburg was given the immediate assignment of working on the agenda for the forthcoming World Economic Conference that Hoover had left in FDR's lap. As an afterthought, FDR asked Warburg to work with Moley on a business recovery plan and with Woodin on reform of the banking system. Filled with admiration for the new President who had the nation in the palm of his hand, Warburg immediately moved to the Carlton Hotel in Washington.

Warburg recognized that there were tremendous pressures on FDR both in and out of Congress to raise prices by making the dollar cheaper in terms of gold, in other words more dollars for the same weight of gold, or devaluation of the gold content of the dollar. A price increase reflecting inflation as we know it since World War II, that is, too many dollars chasing too few goods, aggravated by excessive wage pushes, was not even a possibility in the stagnant thirties. If prices were to be raised by cheapening the currency, it would be done through deliberate government "managing" of the price of gold, rather than allowing the dollar to reflect the fixed price of $20.67 per ounce. This was heresy for sound money men such as Lewis Douglas, firmly anchored to keeping the United States on the gold standard at all costs, and even to Warburg himself, who would permit only a very controlled round of devaluation.

Raising prices through the coining of silver, the issuing of paper money without gold convertibility or the devaluation of the dollar in terms of gold had elements of the great Populist fight of William Jennings Bryan all over again. The debtor class, represented most tragically by the foreclosed farmers, was in an ugly mood. With their products fetching rock bottom prices, how could they pay off mortgages and bank loans committed in the twenties when prices were high? (The answer, incidentally, would be found in government bailing-out agencies such as the Home Owners Loan Corporation and farm credit agencies rather than inflation itself.) On the other hand, mortgage holders and bond investors were delighted to receive payment in dollars that purchased more goods than ever, although even this group could hardly benefit from business and farm failures that jeopardized their principal. Added to the class conflict were psychological considerations. Depressions might end quicker when more money jingled in one's pockets since not all prices, for example rents and other fixed payments, increased at the same time. Conversely, international trade was presumed to depend on confidence in sound dollars.

Thus a nagging question concerned Warburg, as detailed in the diary he kept while the World Economic Conference, promoted by the internationally-minded Hoover, drew near. Did the Administration intend to make international recovery and currency stabilization a primary aim or did it intend to place domestic recovery through price increases first?[23]

The quarterback in the White House juggled this and a hundred other plays in his mercurial mind as he zigged and zagged down the field in the first hundred days. In order of urgency, domestic recovery far exceeded international cooperation and foreign policy on FDR's strategy list. On the very day that FDR was inaugurated, Hitler snatched dictatorial power from the frightened and senile von Hindenburg. Japan had already invaded Manchuria in 1931. The world was sliding into full-scale war but neither the President, the Congress nor the nation would countenance even a defensive arms build-up.

The world-wide depression, which in Germany helped bring about Hitler, created in America a pacifism that was not without certain minimum merits. Crime, except for some Bonnie and Clyde forays against the hated banks, was at a low level. A hitch-hike or a walk in the park was safe enough. Neighbors shared the common grief with thousands of kindnesses. Intellectual curiosity and receptiveness to new ideas flourished as the people endured not only massive unemployment but also dust bowl storms and one of the worst winters on record in 1933-1934. There was, however, a lurking violence beneath it all, though not against foreign menaces or even domestic Communism. The targets were the agents of a foundering capitalism, typified by the representatives of the banks and insurance companies enforcing the clauses of their contracts.

The city dwellers hung on in a state of apathy and despair, except for the bonus march and occasional strikes, but the farming states witnessed a raising of the pitchforks that was as near revolution in the American experience as anything since 1776. In conservative Iowa, for example, rope-swinging farmers came close to hanging a foreclosure Judge in one county and manhandled a sheriff and agent of a New York mortgage company in another. Throughout the state, hundreds of farmers would gather at foreclosure sales, bid in at $1.00 and return the properties to the former owners. A fiery leader had sprung up in this state named Milo Reno, who formed the Farmers' Holiday Association in 1932. The idea was to take a holiday from bringing the goods to market until prices at least matched the "cost of production." A thirty day embargo on shipments to Sioux City was enforced by blocked highways, smashed windshields and punctured tires. When state authorities put some of Reno's men in jail, a thousand farmers obtained their release under threat of storming the jail. The uprising was repeated in Nebraska,

Minnesota, even in Pennsylvania. Milo Reno was very much on Roosevelt's mind when he became President. Roosevelt's natural instincts flew to the farmer. He thought they had been badly neglected by Hoover and his 1932 campaign strategy depended on their support. Repeatedly he told his economic advisers that something had to be done about farm prices. Milo Reno had called for a national farmers' strike for May 13 and fear of its consequences was a major factor in FDR's gold heresy which so incensed the business establishment.

Thus the economic conference in London which FDR suddenly torpedoed on July 3, to the great consternation of Warburg and Moley, was doomed to failure from the start. By that time, FDR had committed himself to economic nationalism, convinced that price increases at home should not be strangled by international agreements on currency stabilization or a return to the gold standard. FDR had a global sense and was aware of the role of the United States in the world power structure. A big navy man, he had managed to include a fleet increase, as a business recovery measure, at the outset of his Administration. It was clear to him, however, that Hoover had delayed too long in meeting the crisis at home. Thus when Roosevelt casually extended diplomatic recognition to Russia in 1933, the objective was a new customer for American products and not a military alliance. Similarly a half million unemployed young people were gathered into the Civilian Conservation Corps as a result of the spectacular legislation following the inauguration but the atmosphere in the camps was one of scouting rather than supermen. The worst critics of FDR were generally content to raise the cry of economic dictatorship rather than the political kind. Even a high-minded critic such as Jimmy Warburg would soon be finding the end of freedom — if not the road to serfdom — in FDR's economic policies. When he further decided FDR was power-mad, Warburg made his fatal error.

For Warburg, being attached to the U.S. delegation to the London Economic Conference as economic adviser was first an exhilarating and then a traumatic experience. The exhilaration came from being on the world stage, matching wits with the frosty, white-bearded

Montague Norman, the wizard of the Bank of England, Ramsay MacDonald, England's Prime Minister who doubled as Conference chairman and lost his position partly as a result, the indestructible Hjalmar Schacht, who would brainstorm Hitler's economic autarchy, Edouard Herriot, recently a French Premier, T. V. Soong, the Harvard-educated representative from China and similar characters. The American delegation was quite mismatched, representing some of FDR's habitual whimsy in making appointments. Secretary of State Cordell Hull was its reluctant Chairman, unable to take with him FDR's backing for some conciliatory tariff reductions. Senator Key Pittman of Nevada was its clown. More often inebriated than not as protection against the London fog, Pittman shot up street lamps at night and acted the hayseed at the royal reception, apparently to the delight of the King and Queen.

The Conference is now but an unimportant footnote to history, lost in the tremendous farm and business recovery experiments launched in the "First New Deal," as FDR's first term is generally known. For those involved, however, FDR's pulling the rug from under it was a severe shock that started Moley, Douglas, Dean Acheson (the new Under Secretary of the Treasury) and Warburg on their way to the anti-Roosevelt shores, washing along with them their ranks of business admirers.

Moley, the most business-oriented of the brain-trusters, was the second most powerful man in the first months of the Administration and had been made Under Secretary of State for lack of any more suitable office. Arriving dramatically in mid-Conference, presumably bearing a message from FDR, he infuriated Hull's sense of pride by stealing the show. His message was only an innocuous affirmation that FDR would support a currency truce for at least the duration of the Conference, which Warburg and the others had regarded as their basic instructions from FDR in the first place. On July 3, FDR, his mind finally made up to back domestic price increases (the AAA and NRA had just been started) and not international currency agreements, sent his "bombshell" message to the Conference. Referring to the gold standard and currency agreements as the "old fetishes of international bankers," he said these ideas must be replaced "by efforts to plan national currencies with the objective of giving to those currencies a continuing purchasing power which does not vary greatly in terms of the commodities and need of modern civilization. Let me be frank in saying the United States seeks the same kind of a dollar which a generation hence will have the same purchasing and debt paying power as the dollar value we hope to attain in the near future. That objective means more to the good of other nations than a fixed ratio for a month or two in terms of the pound or franc . . ."

Warburg immediately resigned from the U.S. delegation, unsure what a commodity purchasing dollar might be but certain that he could not advise a delegation being second-guessed so capriciously from Washington. He was still a member of the team, however, far short of the boiling point he would register a few years later. "If Mr. Roosevelt had said in 1932 what he said to the London Conference in July 1933," he demanded of his fellow Democrats in his best-selling *Hell Bent for Election* in 1935, "do you think you would have voted for him?"[24]

Meanwhile the repudiated Moley quickly adopted the mood of FDR's nationalism. PERSONALLY BOW TO YOUR JUDGMENT WITH NO INCONSIDERABLE RELIEF, he cabled FDR but it was too late. Caught red-handed by Hull for having sent a supposedly confidential cable to FDR a few days later complaining about the intellectual quality of the American delegation, Moley soon resigned to become editor of Vincent Astor's new magazine *Today*. He capped his long career with position papers for Senator Goldwater's bid for the Presidency in 1966. Each of the original brain-trusters, Moley, Berle and Tugwell, were still writing away in their seventies and Moley's *The First New Deal*, published in 1966, lingers morbidly on the Conference. In it he tells how FDR spent the days of the bombshell message cruising on the *Indianapolis*, with Henry Morgenthau and Morgenthau's former Professor at Cornell, George Warren, among the distinguished supercargo. "It was subsequently shown that both of these individuals were desirous of deflating me," Moley writes of the inflating commodity dollar conspirators.[25] More to the point, Moley questions whether the breakup of the London Conference did not agitate "the blind nationalism which swept Europe" into World War II. Most historians agree that the collapse of the Conference and the failure of the ensuing Disarmament Conference marked the last chances of cooperative action to prevent war. "Henceforth international trade would be directed by national governments as a form of bloodless warfare," writes William E. Leuchtenberg. "In the very year that Hitler assumed power, the collapse of the Conference sapped the morale of the democratic opponents of fascism. Roosevelt's policies strengthened those forces in Britain and France which argued the futility of international parleys and celebrated the virtues of economic self-interest."[26] But the real bomb was Adolf Hitler, supreme over a vengeful Germany, with arch manipulators such as Hjalmar Schacht ready to bend monetary policy to the uses of a military state. As for America's business community, the threat of World War II was only vaguely sensed in the face of thirteen million unemployed. If the business community had to name a foreign threat, it would undoubtedly have been Russia, with its disturbing economic system. There was considerable admiration for strongmen dictators in the corporations and country clubs. The kindly Thomas Lamont of Morgan's had a photograph of his friend Mussolini on his office wall.[27] The trains were running on time in Italy and industrialists were enjoying the esteem of the military states. To his credit, FDR never shared this temptation with his fellow capitalists, whom he certainly helped save in war if not in peace.

Jimmy Warburg mused over his first misgivings about FDR's monetary policies as he sailed home from London that July. On April 18, FDR had called a group to the White House for an evening meeting presumably to discuss the Conference. With characteristic drama, the President abruptly announced he would take the United States off the gold standard the next day. The country had already been "off gold" since the embargo of March 6 and Warburg could see the sense of the move, although he hoped it would be only an interlude on the way to returning to a limited gold standard (such as we had until President Nixon's "bombshell" of August 1971 which suspended convertibility of the dollar into gold internationally) when circumstances permitted. FDR had already tipped off Woodin and Moley earlier in the busy day but for the others the news was a complete surprise. The morning papers had carried an impressive article by Walter Lippmann which pretty well summed up the President's options. The pressures for inflation were overwhelming, Lippmann noted. Between raising prices at home and maintaining the gold value of currency abroad, the gold standard was dispensable. "If the decision is taken to keep the dollar as the dearest currency in the world, then for as long as that experiment lasts, we must expect the American price level to be subjected to the forces of deflation . . . Where can such a policy end except in such revulsion of popular feeling as to make certain the acceptance by Congress of some scheme of really wild inflation?"[28]

Only Lewis Douglas, the defender of a balanced budget and of continued deflation as a burden to be bravely tolerated, was appalled at the news. Now he was about to receive another blockbuster. FDR flourished a printed copy of the Thomas Amendment to the Agricultural Adjustment Act. "I've just told Senator Thomas a few hours ago that I'll accept his amendment. Have it thoroughly rewritten," he directed Moley and Herbert Feis, the State Department economic expert, "and give them word to pass it." Then with a chuckle, he added, "Congratulate me!"[29]

There was no bloodier shirt to wave in the faces of sound money men than the Thomas Amendment. That very morning Warburg had been told by Moley the President would not accept it. As rewritten, it gave the President authority to bring about inflation by issuing $3 billion of greenbacks in exchange for government bonds, to fix the ratio of silver to gold and to provide for the free coinage of silver and reduction of gold content in the dollar by Presidential proclamation. Patiently the President explained he had no intention of using these powers carelessly. It was a matter of settling for permissive powers as in the Thomas Amendment or facing the fact that Congress would make them mandatory. "It gives me a birch rod to stand in the corner," FDR stated like a kindly schoolmaster.[30]

Warburg and the others in the room were aware of the pressures on the President. Senator Wheeler had tacked on an amendment to the same AAA bill which would finally bring into law Bryan's old obsession with free coinage of silver at a 16 to 1 ratio. It had been barely defeated by a weak ten votes. These votes were now held back only on condition the Thomas Amendment would become part of the urgent AAA legislation. The farmers were on a rampage and businessmen themselves had a strong organization demanding support for the amendment.

The Committee for the Nation was the imposing name of a group of business and farm leaders who had been badgering FDR to go off the gold standard and raise prices even before his inauguration, a striking example that the business community itself was divided on the great issue. Frank A. Vanderlip, its chairman, was a former Assistant Secretary of the Treasury and a former president of the National City Bank of New York. Though the Committee harbored some speculators and cranks, it also included James H. Rand, Jr., of Remington Rand, General Robert Wood and Lessing Rosenwald of Sears Roebuck, Vincent Bendix, Samuel J. Fels, Philip K. Wrigley and Frank Gannett. George le Blanc of New York's Equitable Trust was also involved, his specialty being persuading Father Coughlin to preach the virtues of devaluation to his entranced thirty-five million radio listeners. The Committee's economists were led by Professor Irving Fisher of Yale and George Warren. Fisher was the nation's most distinguished monetary theorist. Some comments from his letters to his family, published years later by his son, give insight into the hopes and fears swirling around the yellow metal for a previous generation held in thrall to it, or perhaps for professors speculating in stocks:

> *April 12, 1933.* The Committee for the Nation have been having their sessions all day both before and after seeing the President. He did not commit himself but I am confident that he is for reflation in some way or another . . .
> *April 19, 1933.* Now I *am* sure — so far as we ever can be sure of anything — that we are going to snap out of this depression fast. I am one of the happiest men of the world . . . It is evident that FDR has not until recently been sure which turn to take. Now that the right turn has been

> taken my work is over, except for details. My next big job is to raise money for ourselves. Probably we'll have to go to Sister again, but I hope that can be avoided. I have defaulted payments the last few weeks because I did not think it was fair to ask Sister for more money when there was a real chance that I never could pay it back. I mean that if FDR had followed (Carter) Glass we would have been pretty surely ruined. So could Allied Chemical, Sister and the U.S. Government . . . Today the peg which kept our dollar up in foreign exchanges has been pulled out. And lo! The stocks and commodities soar at once![31]

Of course, Fisher's hopes were premature and the depression continued to baffle politicians and professors alike until it ended years later with an assist from World War II. The point is the most formidable pressures were on FDR to take some kind of inflationary action. It is also clear that FDR had painstakingly arrived at his monetary decisions and experiments, whether right or wrong, and was not the economic lightweight that Warburg and a good deal of the business community patronizingly imagined. Yet on the night of April 18, as the various witnesses described it, FDR faced a palace revolt. "At the risk of being impudent," recalls Warburg, "I went so far as to say that I considered the passage of such a bill completely hare-brained and irresponsible, and that unless it were accompanied by a statement from the President that he had no intention of using the powers conferred, it would result in uncontrolled inflation and complete chaos . . . Moley was in one of his satanic moods . . . delighted by this dramatic move of the President and rather amused by my discomfiture . . . Hull never opened his trap. Pittman made sure we would buy silver . . . Feis looked as though he was going to throw up . . . Lew Douglas went to bat with me and Will Woodin, once he got through his head what it was all about, which took some time."[32]

Douglas may have been slow on the uptake but the Washington night air revived him as he and Warburg walked back to the Carlton Hotel. They discussed the calamity with Moley past midnight and then walked the streets into the morning. As they left Moley's room,

Douglas delivered a gem of irrelevancy: "This is the end," he said, "of western civilization."[33] The thought crystallized once again on August 30, 1934, when in resigning from the Administration, he predicted the same end in his letter to FDR if the budget continued to be unbalanced.

What actually did FDR do with his Thomas Amendment powers? True to his conservative nature, he never used the greenback provision. He stalled valiantly on the silver powers well into 1934, when Congress forced through a new Silver Purchase Act sufficient to please both the ghost of Bryan and the incredibly alive "Coin" Harvey, who had run for President against FDR on 16 to 1 in 1932. He used the gold content power to fix the price of gold at $35 an ounce in 1934, about $6 cheaper than the Thomas Amendment permitted. There it stayed until December 1971, when a "token" change to $38 per ounce was decreed by the Nixon Administration for purposes of International Monetary Fund settlements. But in reaching $35 an ounce, FDR and Professor Warren put the gold standard "on the booze," as Keynes described it, and lost Jimmy Warburg on the way.

IX

The story of FDR's playing with the price of gold at breakfast-time now figures prominently in the anti-Roosevelt repertoire. The best that can be said for the four month experiment is that it caused little harm and was cheerfully abandoned when it didn't work. It was not until many years later, in the Morgenthau diaries, that the zany scene was reported — FDR eating his soft-boiled eggs, usually in bed, with Professor Warren, Jesse Jones and Morgenthau helping to set the price of gold for the day. It really didn't matter what the price was so long as it was a little above the world price and the increase varied enough from day to day to foil the speculators. "Let's make it 21 cents today," FDR once said to the unhappy Morgenthau. "It's a lucky number because it's three times seven."

Ever since the crash of the London Conference, FDR had been chafing to do something about prices and keep the irate farmers at bay. The AAA was slow in getting started. On September 14, 1933, John Simpson, president of the National Farmers' Union, a moderate group compared with Milo Reno's Jacobins, wrote to FDR that "the people are overwhelmingly disappointed and disgusted with your program." It soon would be "an absolute failure."[34] FDR had given the assignment to find a way to inflate to a study group headed by Warburg after Professor Fisher's visions had been dashed by a sudden fall in prices in August. Meanwhile Morgenthau's Professor Warren was steadily making a convert of Roosevelt. Warburg was keenly aware of the rival camps and had met with Warren and Roosevelt at Hyde Park. Though he recognized Warren's sincerity, he dismissed the commodity dollar as a delusion.

Obviously we still don't have a dollar of steady purchasing power, however desirable that may be. The present generation spends a dollar which purchases about fifty per cent of the commodities it would buy in 1939, let alone 1933. We have experienced a long cycle of either creeping or galloping inflation ever since we came out of the Great Depression. The new idea is not to have a dollar that will buy the same amount of potatoes but to go along with inflation if it does not exceed productivity, meaning output per man hour, which presumably increases annually through efficiency. But the commodity dollar was a heady dream in 1933 when scarce dollars bought too many potatoes and the nation's debts in dollars tragically outweighed the dollar value of its assets, a plain case of insolvency in business terms, as FDR wrote in 1934.[35] The dollar was to be stabilized at the purchasing power of 1926, a year recalled nostalgically by the crisis-ridden Administration. Professor Warren beguiled FDR and himself with reams of charts and statistics which proved that the price of gold directly affected the price of commodities. The government would buy gold at gradually increasing prices. This would increase farm commodity prices, in terms of dollars, as the gold value of the dollar fell, in other words, monetary rather than "supply and demand" inflation. Both Keynes and the House of Morgan had applauded FDR on his April 19 gold decision. In turn Keynes reinforced Warburg by declaring Warren's theory a foolish idea when he met Warburg in London after the Conference. "There is no mathematical relation between the price of gold and the price of other things," Keynes lectured FDR in the press after the experiment started. Instead of an ideally managed currency in the Keynes formula, this was "more like a gold standard on the booze."

FDR was not a Keynes admirer then or later and he had more than enough domestic advisers on his hands. When Warburg's orthodox group failed to come up with anything but a suggested quick return to a modified gold standard, FDR felt it was time for another fireside chat. To his puzzled listeners, FDR amiably announced on October 21, 1933 that he was "authorizing the RFC to buy gold from time to time at prices to be determined by the Secretary of the Treasury and the President . . . thus continuing the move towards a managed currency." Though most of his listeners were as uncomprehending as the next generation during the gold crises of the 1960's, they had no trouble identifying the opposition. Wall Street and the banking community were outraged and a manifesto soon appeared signed by forty conventional economists. It was like McKinley-Bryan replayed when fifteen thousand people came to a meeting at New York's Hippodrome in November to hear a defense of inflation. Roosevelt's dubious torchbearers at the meeting were Senator Thomas, proud of the indirect effect of his amendment, and Father Coughlin, who within a year would turn viciously on "Franklin Double-Crossing Roosevelt" over silver.

The defection of a man as subtle and rational as Warburg, however, is of interest here rather than the well-known attacks on FDR from the right and the left. The first member of the gentlemen's club to resign was Dean Acheson, his mustaches bristling at FDR's cold orders to execute a policy which he plainly felt was illegal as well as ill-advised. Suspecting his fellow Grotonian had leaked his dissent to the press, FDR asked for his resignation before Acheson could submit it. Since Woodin was too ill to stay on, Morgenthau thus gained the office of Secretary of the Treasury. Perhaps because Warburg held no official office his opposition approached disloyalty. Using his privilege of easy access to the President, he had the opportunity for chin to chin argument against the Warren experiment.

FDR stated it was not just a case of marching farmers but his personal conviction that further deflation was the greater evil. Warburg then had the temerity to state that he might organize anti-inflation sentiment among the banks and life insurance companies. "I wouldn't like that," said FDR. Warburg sensed he had reached the point of no return as he beat a retreat from the Oval Room.

Wall Street had mixed emotions about the experiment, which started with domestic gold purchasing by the RFC. Since the nation was bent on inflation, stocks began to rise as a hedge against it, even though industry was still gasping for air. Though the dollar was driven down in terms of world currencies, domestic farm prices barely reacted, much to Warren's despair. When the theory next called for the RFC, through the New York Federal Reserve Bank, to outbid gold on the world market, the outraged central bankers of France and England predicted a collapse in the foreign exchange market and threatened retaliation. Meanwhile Warburg organized groups of businessmen and economists in New York and Chicago to protest and made good his threat to call on the life insurance presidents. Lewis Douglas somehow persuaded the American Federation of Labor to declare against inflation at a sound money meeting held on the same night as the Hippodrome spectacle. The anti-Administration fight came to a crescendo that November when people as diverse as Al Smith, Bernard Baruch and the presidents of General Motors, du Pont and Macy's announced their opposition to what Smith called "baloney dollars." On November 23, Warburg gained national publicity with a speech before the American Academy of Political Science in Philadelphia in which he discreetly lashed out at the President's advisers, including his fellow speakers Professor Fisher and Senator Thomas, rather than the President himself. Like a good politician, he still wanted at least a back door entrance to the White House and was not ready to become Wall Street's spokesman against FDR personally. Later Warburg concluded that Father Coughlin's intemperate showing at the Hippodrome was the most important factor turning public opinion against the Warren program.

It is more likely that even though public opinion was solidly behind the President, FDR simply realized the theory didn't work.

It was time to cashier Warren and turn to something else regardless of business opposition. The AAA and NRA were underway and a massive spending program, involving deficit financing, to stimulate jobs and purchasing power was about to be launched. This was enough action without the distraction of currency experiments. The President ended the gold-buying by establishing the price of gold at a fixed maximum of $35 per ounce, close to the open market price, and the country returned to a modified gold standard in January 1934. There were even some good effects. American farm exports spurted to countries heavy with dollars received from the sale of their gold. The mark-up in dollars for the Treasury's vast gold supply produced a bookkeeping profit which was transferred to a substantial currency stabilization fund. It was at least a better result than continued deflation and unrest, though dumb luck was mixed with the President's magician's instinct.

Although little harm had been done, the gold-buying episode aggravated the latent hostility between Roosevelt and the financial community, which now decided its suspicions about crackpots and professors in Washington had validity. The fragile bridge between FDR and business thus began to shake a mere nine months after the honeymoon. Jimmy Warburg, however, still had some reserve to draw on with his tolerant boss. After putting down Father Coughlin's economics in a radio-newspaper dialogue, Warburg was rewarded with an invitation to dine at the White House in January. "You have squashed some of the worst radicals and at the same time brought some of the conservatives nearer the middle," said FDR to the young banker who had openly defied him. Happily Warburg left Washington, dropped in at the Bank of Manhattan and embarked on a cruise ship for a vacation. Aboard he dashed off the first of the prodigal stream of books by New Deal insiders, published in May 1934 under the appropriate name *The Money Muddle*.

X

The book was a best seller, perhaps because so many people had so little money that even reading about it gave satisfaction. (How aptly the title compares with a best seller of the affluent 60's, *The Money Game.)* In the spirit of Harvard gamesmanship, Warburg rushed off a first copy to FDR. The President's answer testifies to his innate feeling for the underdog, the consistent passion of an inconsistent man:

> Please get yourself an obviously second-hand Ford car; put on your oldest clothes and start west for the Pacific Coast, undertaking beforehand not to speak on the entire trip with any banker or business executive (except gas stand owners), and to put up at no hotel where you have to pay more than $1.50 a night. After you get to the Coast go south and come back via the southern tier of States. If you start this trip about the first of September you will find the climate charming and the roads passable. Incidentally, you will save money because I am sure that living in New York must cost you a lot more than living in a Lizzie!
>
> When you have returned, re-write *The Money Muddle* and I will guarantee that it will run into many more editions![36]

Warburg did not take FDR's advice. Meanwhile as he estranged himself from the White House, he found his own home in disrepair. His marriage to Kay Swift had deteriorated, partly as a result of his frequent absences in Europe and Washington, and finally a divorce was undertaken. For solace he enjoyed the company of Phyllis Baldwin, a Westchester neighbor from a proper Roosevelt-hating family who was a liberal Republican herself, being co-leader of Manhattan's famed "Silk Stocking" Seventeenth Assembly District. Anyone seriously studying animosity to FDR will have to admit that family and social ties account for a strong bond, as perhaps they always do in political matters. The classic instance of the high-spirited snobbery which drew the rich together was Peter Arno's famous cartoon in the *New Yorker*. "Come along," a bright-eyed, mink-coated matron accompanied by mother, husband and insipid son calls out to friends in a Manhattan town house. "We're going to the Trans-Lux to hiss Roosevelt."

With such inspiration, and touched by the wine of success from his first effort, Warburg turned out still another 1934 book on the New Deal, called *It's Up to Us.* As the title implied, it was up to citizens to do something about key FDR measures such as the 1933 Banking Act, the NRA and the Gold Reserve Act of 1934. One wonders where FDR found the grace to acknowledge the second book from the busy author whose literary career depended on shooting holes in the New Deal:

> Many thanks for sending me the first edition of the new book. I have glanced through it today and I know you will not mind my saying that you interest me but leave me *freezing* because you do not offer specific alternatives or specific plans.
>
> I still wish you would take that trip in the flivver! You might stop at Hyde Park for luncheon on the way. . . .[37]

In fact Warburg was more interested in advocating the anti-New Deal philosophy of Henry Ford than in driving his product. Married to Phyllis Baldwin in April 1935, he was somewhat taken aback by the glowing reviews of *It's Up to Us* which praised his attack on the New Deal's vast assumption of powers. That wasn't quite what he meant but he quickly recognized his offspring as legitimate and went down the road to apostasy.

By the summer of 1935, Warburg had written a series of syndicated articles for the *New York Herald Tribune* which were published that year as a book entitled *Hell Bent for Election.* It was the political sensation of the year and sold almost a million copies. For the anti-Roosevelt forces, its slashing attack and impeccable authorship seemed a miraculous gift. It gave heart to those who anticipated the return of FDR to country squire in the forthcoming election.

All the intellectual dishonesty and personal animosity of partisan politics were embodied in the slim little book. In a chapter called "Words versus Deeds," Warburg matched the New Deal measures against a list of campaign promises and then shocked his readers by revealing the promises were those of Norman Thomas, the Socialist candidate, and not FDR. Thomas took a more realistic view of the President who had stolen his thunder and was responding to the crisis with a revived capitalism. "If Roosevelt has carried out the Socialist platform," Thomas lamented to the press, "he has carried it out on a stretcher."

The basic thrust of the book, however, was to raise the cry of dictatorship. FDR, Warburg in effect charged, was hell bent for dictatorship. Ignoring the fact that the developments in Germany, Italy and Austria were based on military take-overs in war-defeated countries where democratic governments had been unable or unwilling to meet their responsibilities for such things as unemployment, the author implied a similar fate for America. The reason would be the new centralized instruments of government with which the New Deal was fighting the depression. Under guise of giving the nation "a more abundant life," wrote Warburg, FDR headed a central federal bureaucracy with "complete dictatorial powers over all the factors that affect the economic and social life of the nation. . . . To accomplish this purpose means to substitute for the American form of government a central 'authoritarian' state along the lines of the various European experiments in Socialism and dictatorship. . . ."[38]

The last chapter, which Warburg later stated he wished he had never written, contained the unkindest cut of all, an attack on FDR's character and motivation. ". . . Mr. Roosevelt's individuality is such as to make him an ineffective and dangerous man in the White House, because his actions and intellectual processes are too greatly dominated by his emotions, and because his emotional drive is primarily an inordinate desire for popularity."[39]

If there were no more dinners at the White House, one could still attend the great dinner of the Liberty League, scheduled for January 25, 1936, at the beginning of the election year, in the Mayflower Hotel a few blocks away. It was inevitable that Jimmy Warburg's strange Odyssey would finally wash him to the distant shore.

Organized Roosevelt-hating by people who might have known better received an institutional framework with the forming of the Liberty League in August 1934. Here at last was an organization that would embrace disaffected conservative Democrats such as Al Smith and John W. Davis, FDR's defeated predecessor Presidential candidates, and top-level businessmen as well. The American Liberty League was definitely not anti-Roosevelt, Jouett Shouse, former Chairman of the Democratic National Committee and leading spirit of the new organization, announced with a straight face. Shouse's money base was provided by a corps of du Pont family members, reviving an old association between Shouse and the du Ponts in the recently expired Association against the Prohibition Amendment. By 1935 the League was at full speed, its non-partisan mask long discarded. It was spending twice as much money as the Republican party itself. Although it claimed 120,000 members, over half of its funds came from a few dozen bankers, industrialists and businessmen. In 1936, one-fourth of its funds came from the du Pont family alone, the greatest public extravagance of the famous family until "Motsey" Copeland, an extreme conservative of the 1970's, petitioned for his epic bankruptcy.[40]

Its roster of members included a Who's Who of American business leaders, men who had already led the United States Chamber of Commerce and National Association of Manufacturers into bitter anti-New Deal resolutions as the full meaning of the New Deal registered its impact. The business establishment was no longer willing to give up its traditional power over economic matters to the professors and experimenters in the White House. Since business conditions were substantially improving, most industrialists felt it was time to abandon the abject surrender to Washington of 1933 and to assert the claims of individual initiative and minimum government intervention once again. A 1935 "Soak the Rich" tax bill, as the Hearst press called it, was a vendetta against producers, many business leaders honestly felt. (Warburg in *Hell Bent for Election* had expressed shock at FDR's proposal to raise corporation income taxes from 13¾ per cent to as much as 16¾ per cent, even though the smaller corporations would get a reduction to 10¾ per cent.) The business community could draw moral support for its opposition from the striking down of the NRA in 1935 and a good part of the AAA in 1936 by the nine old men on the Supreme Court whom FDR so disrespectfully consigned to horses and buggies.

All in all by 1936 the lines were pretty well drawn for a cold war between Washington and business. The letters of Frankfurter and Roosevelt reveal that FDR leaned more than ever for comfort and praise upon the tough-minded Harvard professor, especially after the NRA debacle. Frankfurter had insisted that the round of business-government cooperation was a failure and urged FDR to face the facts. Once he understood that his overtures to business were being rebuffed, he could meet the opposition to his programs by stiffer taxes, antitrust suits and the "death sentence" for the type of utility holding companies Samuel Insull had used to fleece so many investors.[41] Many historians see this policy as a general change in direction from the business placating "First New Deal," whose strategists like Moley, Berle, Baruch and Hugh Johnson sat at FDR's elbow, raising high the hopes for cooperative, central planning implicit in the NRA. The "Second New Deal" presumably had a philosophy which emphasized a restoration of competition within a centrally defined social framework as the type of economic system that would end the depression and prevent undue concentration of economic power.[42] But the business community was not about to accept Frankfurter's Brandeisian philosophy for its very own in spite of the appropriated banner of competition. For their part, businessmen knew which kind of competition they wanted without Frankfurter's advice. More to the point they were upset about competition in the running of their affairs from the government itself. Add to this the tremendous surge of unionism sweeping the country as a result of the NRA labor provisions along with the ensuing National Labor Relations Act and one could hardly expect the business leadership not to put up a fight. The financial community was particularly hostile. The reforms of its banking and investment institutions were not yet appreciated and could hardly be accepted with good grace, having more or less been forced down its throat under public spotlight. Finally the barely understood, profligate spending for relief and social security measures, producing what was then considered totally irresponsible budget deficits, was enough to drive any man to the Liberty League. "Private fulminations and public carpings against the New Deal have become almost a routine of the business day," stated *Time* magazine on September 23, 1934. On April 27, 1936, *Time*'s opinion was more ominous. "Regardless of party and regardless of region today, with few exceptions members of the so-called Upper Class frankly hate Franklin Roosevelt." With practically every newspaper and business organization against him, with the late Huey Long, Doctor Townsend and Father Coughlin capable of launching a third party on the right, with the Communists and Socialists bitterly attacking him from the left, with dictators abroad and the Supreme Court at home adding to his woes, FDR had no one left but the people.

XI

In its few years of activity, the Liberty League specialized in printing well-prepared and seemingly effective pamphlets attacking specific New Deal programs. Business sponsorship could be expected to produce a high quality of propaganda and so it did. To its credit, the League's arguments excluded the personal smears and much of the distortion of the rabid anti-New Dealers, elevating the issues to that rare occurrence in democratic government, a reasonably logical debate over what passes for liberalism and conservatism at a given period in history. This was a time for taking a stand on a critical development in the historic role of the federal government. It was a period when business lost its prior status and independence, a time when the federal government intruded to become the senior and ultimately responsible partner in a new kind of "mixed" capitalism. There were real issues at stake in those years, unlike the 1960's when Barry Goldwater evoked a conservative role for government which no longer possessed credibility. Over five million pamphlets were distributed covering over a hundred subjects. The crusade was particularly effective on the college campuses, where hundreds of chapters were established by short-haired, job-concerned students whose conservative professors looked down their noses at Roosevelt and, if they had heard about him, Keynes. In addition the League poured out a continuous stream of editorials and news stories to the nation's newspapers. Jouett Shouse was always ready to make a speech deploring fiscal irresponsibility, scorning New Deal economic planning as dangerous and deceitful, or exposing government regulation of business as bad economics. A favorite Shouse speech was entitled: "You Owe Thirty-One Billion Dollars."

All this was in the Mark Hanna tradition but neither Mark Hanna, Dwight Eisenhower nor Richard Nixon would have allowed the incredible boner of the Mayflower dinner. It was a plain case of the best brains of business being sabotaged by the affair's dinner and program chairmen.

At the strictly formal gathering, wives were faithfully in attendance and guests well publicized and reported. A large part of the country's wealth — perhaps the largest collection of millionaires under one roof — was noted by the New York *Times* reporter, whose paper finally came over to Roosevelt, under Frankfurter's prodding,[43] before the election.

Jimmy Warburg, writer in residence for the anti-New Dealers, received excited applause as he joined the two thousand dinner guests. He could wave to Dean Acheson and Lewis Douglas, but not to Herbert Hoover, who had courageously decided not to endorse the League. Hoover's defeated opponent, Al Smith, had the rostrum all to himself as the main speaker. Incongruously attired in white tie, stiff collar and tails, the man whose public image was brown derby and bow tie delivered one of the silliest speeches in political history:

> I'm going to let you in on something. . . . How do you suppose this happened? The young brain-trusters caught the Socialists in swimming and they went away with their clothes. Now it is all right with me if they want to disguise themselves as Karl Marx or Lenin or any of the rest of that bunch, but I won't stand for their allowing them to march under the banner of Jefferson or Jackson or Cleveland. . . . There can only be one capitol, Washington or Moscow. There can only be the clear, pure fresh air of free America, or the foul breath of communistic Russia. There can be only one flag, the Stars and Stripes, or the

> flag of the godless Union of the Soviets. There can only be one national anthem, The Star Spangled Banner or the Internationale.

Arthur Krock of the New York *Times*, a Roosevelt critic, quickly recognized the dinner as a tremendous error that would make FDR more popular than ever with the voters. Alf Landon, the Republican candidate, later tried to disengage from the League's fatal embrace. Jimmy Warburg began to have second thoughts. With a sinking feeling he noted the business representatives who had resisted this type of logic, realistically sticking with FDR in spite of the glittering call to arms. Marriner Eccles had laughed off the Liberty League. Jesse Jones, Joseph P. Kennedy, Averell Harriman, Bernard Baruch, Gerard Swope of G.E., Thomas J. Watson of IBM, Edward A. Filene, Myron Taylor of U.S. Steel, Robert E. Wood of Sears Roebuck and Leffingwell of Morgan's were notable business leaders who still wanted to make the New Deal work and thought the concept of FDR as dictator outrageous. *Fortune*, already the most influential business magazine though only a few years old, in a December 1935 article entitled "The Case Against Roosevelt" concluded that it was "fairly evident to most disinterested critics" that the New Deal "has had the preservation of capitalism at all times in view."[44]

Now it was time for Jimmy Warburg to commit political suicide. Attached to the Landon-Knox campaign as a top strategist for Knox, he resigned in October 1936. Ostensibly his reason was Landon's refusal to advocate reciprocal trade treaties, which Warburg thought so necessary for international economic recovery. Unable to face the humiliation of informing FDR directly of his change of heart, Warburg notified Secretary of State Hull. Advising the reciprocal trade champion of his decision, he released the letter to the newspapers, perhaps conjuring a mental image of FDR's overpowering, vital face devouring the news at breakfast the next morning.

Indeed Jimmy Warburg had been carrying an image in his subconscious during the break with FDR and therein lies a tale that restores politics and economics to the human level once again. In a confession of Freudian impulses as unexpected as Richard Nixon's

Six Crises, Warburg's autobiographical *The Long Road Home*, published in 1964, explains his break with FDR in psychological terms. He could justify, he writes, his opposition to monetary experimentation, to deliberate inflation and economic nationalism, even legislation which turned out to be unconstitutional. But how could one explain the tasteless, ingrate attacks on the President himself? He found the answer on the psychoanalyst's couch. There he learned that he had entered Roosevelt's circle shortly after the death of his beloved father, that Roosevelt had become "in many ways a second father to whom I transferred much of the respect and admiration with which a young man needs to endow a father or a father figure." Unfortunately the surrogate father proceeded to attack precisely those touchstones for which his real father had lived. Even Warburg's debate with Marriner Eccles in opposition to the 1935 Banking Bill, which shifted monetary control away from New York and towards Washington, must have been traumatic. One might say that since Paul M. Warburg was the father of the Federal Reserve System, the Fed was in a way Jimmy's brother, adding a bit of fratricide to his guilts.

> My participation in banking reform, in a modernization of the gold standard and in a revision of certain aspects of the Federal Reserve System had, without my knowing it, given me an uncomfortable feeling of having taken part in the desecration of my father's life work even though my conscious reason informed me that those reforms were urgently necessary. . . . My substitute father had betrayed the beloved parent whose place he had to a certain extent taken.[45]

Finally this estimable man offers us a lesson in candor and self-insight rare in public figures: "In addition, my marriage into a Republican family had probably served to fortify my hostility to Roosevelt, providing praise and encouragement for my least praiseworthy attacks upon the President's personality. Hindsight forces me to suspect that a by no means admirable desire to show off before my wife and her family may have played a part."[46]

Thus Jimmy Warburg kept his theories up to date, becoming a Freudian and a Keynesian before either theory yielded to the revisions of a later decade. Eventually he divorced the Republican wife and married his secretary, living happily and productively until death in 1969. Did he ever make up with FDR? Of course, just as Dean Acheson and Lewis Douglas did. FDR had the aristocrat's perception for quality, the secure man's ability to forgive over such trifles as gold and white tie dinners, particularly if a little contrition were shown. Warburg became a strong supporter of FDR's wartime foreign policy. He helped establish the Fight for Freedom Committee in the Spring of 1941 and was one of the first to debate Lindbergh over the Allied chances. He served well as FDR's deputy director of the Office of War Information and devoted the rest of his life to studying and writing on foreign and economic policy. Many businessmen hated Roosevelt more but not so well.

Footnotes

[1] William E. Leuchtenberg, *Franklin Roosevelt and the New Deal* (New York, 1963), p. 248.

[2] Daniel Fusfeld, *The Economic Thought of Franklin D. Roosevelt and the Origins of the New Deal* (New York, 1956), pp. 101-116.

[3] *Ibid.*, p. 103.

[4] Raymond Moley, *The First New Deal* (New York, 1966), p. 172 and p. 299.

[5] Rexford G. Tugwell, *The Brains Trust* (New York, 1968), p. 473.

[6] *Ibid.*, p. 473.

[7] Leuchtenberg, *op. cit.*, p. 188.

[8] Moley, *op. cit.*, p. 81.

[9] James P. Warburg, *The Long Road Home: The Autobiography of a Maverick* (New York, 1964), p. 107.

[10] Moley, *op. cit.*, p. 157.

[11] Herbert Hoover, *Memoirs* (New York, 1951-1952), Vol. III, p. 213.

[12] Warburg, *op. cit.*, pp. 108-109.

[13] Moley, *op. cit.*, p. 175.

[14] William E. Leuchtenberg, *The New Deal: A Documentary History* (New York, 1968), p. 21.

[15] Arthur M. Schlesinger, Jr., *The Coming of the New Deal* (Boston, 1959), p. 5.

[16] Moley, *op. cit.*, pp. 178-179.

[17] Raymond Moley, *After Seven Years* (New York, 1939), p. 155.

[18] Leuchtenberg, *Franklin Roosevelt and the New Deal*, *op. cit.*, p. 44.

[19] Schlesinger, *op. cit.*, p. 136.

[20] Moley, *The First New Deal*, *op. cit.*, pp. 202-203.

[21] Irving S. Michelman, *Business at Bay: Critics and Heretics of American Business* (New York, 1969), pp. 99-146.

[22] Moley, *op. cit.*, p. 165.

[23] Warburg, *op. cit.*, p. 116.

[24] James P. Warburg, *Hell Bent for Election* (New York, 1935), p. 20.

[25] Moley, *op. cit.*, p. 453.

[26] Leuchtenberg, *op. cit.*, pp. 202-203.

[27] John Brooks, *Once in Golconda* (New York, 1969), p. 282.

[28] Walter Lippmann, *Interpretations: 1933-1935* (New York, 1936), pp. 50-53.

[29] Herbert Feis, *Characters in Crisis* (Boston, 1966), pp. 108-113.

[30] Warburg, *The Long Road Home*, *op. cit.*, p. 119.

[31] Irving Norton Fisher, *My Father, Irving Fisher* (New York, 1958), pp. 267-276.

[32] James P. Warburg, *Oral History Project at Columbia University*, qu. in Jordan Schwarz, *1933: Roosevelt's Decision: The United States Leaves the Gold Standard* (New York, 1969), p. 157.

[33] Warburg, *The Long Road Home*, *op. cit.*, p. 120; Moley, *op. cit.*, p. 302.

[34] Leuchtenberg, *op. cit.*, p. 78.

[35] Franklin D. Roosevelt, *On Our Way* (New York, 1934), pp. 58-63.

[36] Warburg, *op. cit.*, p. 159.

[37] *Ibid.*, p. 159.

[38] Warburg, *Hell Bent for Election*, *op. cit.*, p. 75.

[39] *Ibid.*, p. 75.

[40] George Wolfskill and John A. Hudson, *All but the People: Franklin D. Roosevelt and His Critics, 1933-1939* (New York, 1969), p. 161.

[41] Leuchtenberg, *op. cit.*, p. 150.

[42] Max Freedman, *Roosevelt & Frankfurter: Their Correspondence, 1928-1945* (New York, 1967), pp. 351-352.

[43] *Ibid.*, pp. 293-294; pp. 358-359.

[44] *Fortune Magazine*, "The Case Against Roosevelt," December, 1935, p. 107.

[45] Warburg, *The Long Road Home*, *op. cit.*, pp. 169-170.

[46] *Ibid.*, p. 170.

Chapter 4

The Blue Eagle Partnership

Early in September 1933, New Yorkers cheered the biggest parade in the city's history. Considering the Armistice parade after World War I and Lindbergh's triumphant processional in 1927, post-depression Americans may well ponder over the fact that this parade was in celebration of a new partnership between business and government. A nation of failed merchants and discredited politicians was being given another chance — a new deal — and in honor of the event a quarter million men and women were streaming down Fifth Avenue. It was the NRA parade, the National Recovery Administration more formally, and this was the culmination of other parades throughout the country. It had its own insignia, the Blue Eagle, a stark bird in the American Indian style whose talons grasped three thunderbolts on the right and a cogged wheel on the left. Although the NRA was only three months old, almost every American was able to translate the ideograph, a lightning assault by business and government which would make the wheels of industry hum once again.

The politicians as usual were in the reviewing stand. Before them the marchers came on and on, in praise of an economic concept rather than heroes or holidays. Boys in olive drab from the Civilian Conservation Corps camps, stockbrokers from the wreckage of Wall Street, delegations of life insurance salesmen, $14 a week department store clerks, newly resurrected beer and whisky people, even chorus girls, all were "doing their part" as called for by the legend underneath the Blue Eagle. "Happy Days Are Here Again" was a favorite theme of the bands but there was plenty of martial music. After all, this was war, a war on depression. FDR had declared war on the depression in his inaugural address. With at least twelve million unemployed, the depression was worse than war for a good portion of America.

It seemed fitting, then, that "the big cheese," as General Hugh S. Johnson, the NRA boss, liked to call himself, was the number one attraction on the reviewing stand. Governor Lehman was there, a sterling example of the type of businessman turned public servant and fervent New Dealer. Grover Whalen, the city's perennial greeter and salesman was there, at home with all the ballyhoo. Averell Harriman was on the stand as NRA state chairman. Yet all eyes strained towards Hugh Johnson, the second most publicized man in the nation for a gaudy, hectic two years that witnessed the greatest institutional experiment in American business history.

The photos show Johnson dressed in a rumpled, double-breasted suit, disarmingly civilian, his face square-jawed, worldly and pugnacious, the same type found in Roman busts and the annual reports of major corporations. He seems to be having trouble with his acknowledgement to the paraders. The right hand is raised more in Mussolini style than in the manner of his alma mater, West Point. Now there is no point in making out Hugh Johnson as a fascist since he simply wasn't one. Still the Mussolini complex lurked attractively for him, as it did for many American businessmen until the new Caesar turned into sawdust. For example, Johnson was intrigued with Mussolini's yoking of business and government under the concept of "corporate syndicalism." He once gave a copy of Rafaello Viglione's approving book, *The Corporate State*, to Secretary of Labor Frances Perkins, but this could certainly be justified in the interests of professional curiosity. Similarly, in June 1932, he produced a manifesto for curing the depression, representing the best thought of himself and his mentor, Bernard M. Baruch, to whom he was currently attached as a personal researcher and analyst. Baruch was then regarded as a kind of supernatural business sage, having been adviser to Presidents on business matters ever since his distinguished service to Wilson as Chief of the War Industries Board. Although Baruch may have been flattered by Johnson's fulsome praise for the contents of the manifesto, which included Baruch's diehard admonition to balance the budget at all costs, he could hardly have approved Johnson's pseudonym: "Muscleinny, Dictator pro tem." In fairness to Johnson, one should note the General's explanation, written in 1935: "Of course the idea of a dictator who sequestered Congress but left the courts open was only to show what he 'did' could really have been done constitutionally by Congress itself."[1]

Muscleinny was to go through some shattering experiences in his impossible job and finally on October 1, 1934, having been eased out by FDR, he found himself making a tearful farewell speech to his loyal legions of employees in the auditorium of the Department of Commerce building. "The NRA," said General Johnson, "was as great a social advance as has occurred on this earth since a gaunt and dusty Jew in Palestine declared, as a new principle in human relationship, 'The Kingdom of Heaven is within you.'" Struck by the comparison, Johnson observed in a welter of self-pity: "Very often the crucifixion of a man means more to the thing he is trying to do than all his living efforts." Finally he concluded with the last words of Madame Butterfly — in Italian — as she committed *harakari*, explaining the lyrics with the comment, "to those who know Mussolini only as a shining example (it) means roughly 'To die with honor when you no longer can live with honor.'"[2]

Whether his role model was Mussolini or Madame Butterfly, it should be obvious that at this point at least General Johnson was a liability to the NRA. One wonders whether a cooler General, for example Douglas MacArthur, who was also available, might have made NRA work. At any rate, Hugh Johnson had more in common with his other West Point classmate, George Patton, equally brilliant but erratic and possibly paranoid.

The story of NRA is Johnson's story more than FDR's. It was Johnson who was responsible for its brief period of success as well as its decline. Thus the flashback to Johnson at the New York parade is poignant when one considers that the job broke Johnson's health and stability. The newspapers complained about his "fascist salute" that day. *Time* even had a photograph to prove it. Johnson typically later countered, "but it wasn't my own arm in the photograph. I think it was the arm of Mayor O'Brien who stood beside me which had been faked onto my body."[3] Like the ambivalent scientist in the movie *Dr. Strangelove*, General Johnson had an arm that often reached for his own jugular.

II

Hugh Johnson is unexpectedly included in the list of FDR's original brain-trusters by Raymond Moley, the acknowledged den leader who assembled the group. As Bernard Baruch's representative, Johnson wrote speeches for the 1932 campaign on the farm relief program which weighed so heavily on FDR's mind. Moley considered his services important to FDR's victory and both Baruch and Johnson were rather impatiently awaiting their rewards when the NRA plum was placed in Johnson's hands. While the other brain-trusters were professors, Johnson's credentials were those of a desk-bound General in World War I followed by substantial experience as an authentic business executive. Thus he somewhat legitimately joins our group of businessmen reacting to national crises.

In his plaintive biography *The Blue Eagle from Egg to Earth*, written for *Redbook* magazine immediately after his Madame Butterfly performance, Johnson lingers sentimentally on his Oklahoma Territory boyhood and subsequent army life. These were passages of simple virtues and patriotism, unlike the harsh world of conflicting interest, fouled-up bureaucracy and constitutional dilemmas which doomed the NRA. Born in 1882 at Fort Scott, Kansas, "to the discordant accompaniment of bugle calls, whinnying cavalry horses and bawling top sergeants," the scrappy little boy from a modest family dreamed of West Point and finally made it. "Everybody in the world's a Rink-Stink but Hughie Johnson and he's all right," was the proud boyhood motto of this typical midwest product of turn-of-the-century America. His background was a world apart from the sheltered life and education of FDR. Yet suddenly the entire depression-struck nation was looking to these two men, rather than to the traditional captains of industry, to perform the miracle of restoring jobs for the army of unemployed.

After graduating from West Point as the youngest in his class but not otherwise distinguished, Johnson spent some routine military years in the Philippines and then in Mexico chasing Pancho Villa with General Pershing. During this interlude, he wrote boys' books as a sideline, featuring gallant West Pointers and picturesque top sergeants who spoke from the corners of their mouths. Johnson's vision of life was always in terms of heroes, villains, crusades and crises. Gruff though he was, affecting the tough cavalryman's pose, the General also believed in a romantic, chivalrous code of conduct. It was one of the weapons with which he bravely attempted to grace the behavior of stubborn business executives and labor leaders in the NRA days.

The Army recognized his talents and sent him to the University of California at Berkeley for a law degree and on to service in the Judge Advocate's office in Washington. When World War I approached, Johnson was tapped to produce the draft act which he did with aplomb, illegally printing thirty million registration forms and getting them ready to mail in anticipation of the passage of the law. His war service saw him attached to Bernard Baruch's War Industries Board as the Army representative, where his impatience helped cut through production log jams. Mustered out as a thirty-seven year old General, Johnson had his pick of executive jobs. He chose to follow George N. Peek, a farm expert and War Industries Board associate who would later head the AAA, to the Moline Plow Company. Peek was president and Johnson vice president and general counsel. This major farm equipment manufacturer managed to go bankrupt and through a hectic reorganization during the seven years of the prosperous twenties when Johnson was in effect running it. Turning his sword into a plowshare was a harrowing experience for the General. In retrospect he attributed the company's failure largely to "the savagery of competition throughout the field." On examining the NRA experiment, the businessman is reminded of the poor esteem in which competition, particularly cutthroat competition, which could end in closed factories, reduced purchasing power and sweatshop labor, was held by a growing body of public opinion. At any rate, Hugh Johnson never felt strange in the business world after Moline Plow. "When you add to these natural and normal difficulties of the business the burden to operate a great concern with the hot breath of the sheriff on your neck night and day for seven years," he wrote, "it may not be pleasant, but it is an industrial, financial and commercial schooling which no man could get in forty years of normal business experience."[4]

III

Every great institutional reform has an intellectual or philosophical history preceding the crisis which makes the reform, or in NRA's case, the attempt at reform, possible. An obvious precedent for the NRA was socialism. The word was taboo for Roosevelt, Johnson, Baruch and just about everyone else connected with NRA, but planning, one of the essentials of socialism, was acceptable enough in the emergency. The great example of successful economic planning in the American experience was the prodigious arsenal created under the auspices of the War Industries Board. This was a far more agreeable example to invoke than the profit-shattering Soviet experiment, which only a few important New

Dealers, such as Rexford Tugwell, dared to consider as a recommendation for massive planning.

Wartime industrial planning in turn owed its inspiration a good deal to Germany's total mobilization in 1914, as recorded in Walter Rathenau's influential book of that year, *Germany's Raw Materials Management.* Johnson and the other U.S. military men were admirers of this accomplishment of the defeated enemy. General Ludendorff, a special hero of Hugh Johnson, returned the compliment when he claimed that America's organized industrial might made the difference.

Another thread behind the NRA was some deep thinking on the part of American business leaders themselves. The most noteworthy programs were offered by Gerard Swope and Henry I. Harriman. Swope, president of General Electric, was very much in evidence during the New Deal years. Except for FDR's heresy in wanting to regulate the Stock Exchanges, Swope was a constant supporter of the President. One of Baruch's top men on the War Industries Board, Swope as early as 1931 had presented Herbert Hoover with "The Swope Plan." Swope advocated trade associations in each industry that would have compulsory membership for firms with fifty or more employees. Through these associations production and consumption would be coordinated and even prices would be stabilized. To accomplish the coordination, there would be uniform accounting practices and access to each company's books. Welfare plans such as pensions and unemployment insurance would be included and the whole system supervised by a national economic council. This was far beyond the publicly acknowledged trade association objective of "codes of fair competition." It was an outright bid to suspend antitrust legislation as had been done for the trade associations with government approval in World War I. Such advocacy might appear unseemly for the head of a company which even then had gained distinction as being one of the most habitual and unregenerate price-fixing offenders in American business history. But Swope was basically a humane business leader, offering an exchange of steady employment and flattened business cycles in return for his cartels and supreme council. Hoover ignored the

Swope plan, having righteously sparked his Federal Trade Commission to crack down on trade association conspiracies he sensed were getting out of hand.[5]

Henry I. Harriman, head of the New England Power Company, was more elaborate with his proposals, which carried the unusual prestige of Harriman's presidency of the United States Chamber of Commerce. In those unsettled times, Harriman and Swope still considered themselves as rugged enterprisers and sound capitalists. It was just that the times were too rugged for anyone to bear along under the status quo. Harriman, for example, was appalled at the idea of government spending through deficit financing to put men to work. Early in 1933, he advocated on behalf of the Chamber cutting $1 billion in government spending by reducing federal activities to the level of Coolidge's somnolent 1925 Administration.[6] On the other hand, a business-government partnership, originated and administered by the trade associations, could sustain prosperity and employment through intelligent planning, market sharing, a bit of price-fixing and an economic council at the summit, according to a 1932 Committee Report that must be unique in the Chamber's archives. Harriman had talked to FDR at length several times in 1932 and had been encouraged to submit his ideas formally. Immediately after the inauguration he presented Moley with "An Economic Program" which bore many similarities to the eventual NRA bill. In it he advocated that the antitrust laws be amended to provide trade associations with actual power to abolish unfair operating conditions, in effect to make the associations special deputies with power over erring competitors. The associations would require a majority vote to determine what was unfair and a government agency would have to approve the final regulations. There would also be permitted collective action among competitors to balance production with demand, again with a government agency given the opportunity to approve or reject the plan.

Harriman's proposal differed from Swope's in its emphasis on government agency surveillance. It also provided that the trade groups could regulate "such matters as maximum hours of labor and minimum rates of pay." Here indeed was a novel idea, far beyond Swope's vague promises of either a job or unemployment insurance for labor. It was a foregone conclusion that the Supreme Court would knock down national wages and hours legislation. Hence the alternative plan for business to make the handout to labor as a trade association gift, freed from the threat of antitrust prosecution for engaging in such trade-restraining activities. Significantly no mention of unions was contained in either proposal, it being assumed the moribund unions should continue to have the threat of antitrust aimed in their direction when necessary. It is interesting to note that few members of the tired and old-fashioned labor leadership at the time were excited about NRA or, for that matter, about minimum wages, either by law or through codes. Matthew Woll, vice president of the dominant American Federation of Labor, for example, opposed minimum wages. He reasoned that the minimum wages might somehow become the maximum wages and that once guaranteed, they would make laborers less interested in joining unions.[7]

There were, however, some alert and powerful labor leaders, such as John L. Lewis and Sidney Hillman, who were ready to join the generals and the executives in calling for business recovery through the national planning of business and government. Representing the chaotic and depressed coal and garment industries, they too wanted industry stability which they thought could come only from national action. Not very hopeful about national wages and hours legislation, they reasoned that industrial codes would at least protect the higher-wages employers from the ruthless competition of sweatshop operators. Senator Robert Wagner of New York, an eloquent champion of labor, placed his hopes for recovery primarily in public works projects but found the NRA concept a valid exercise in national economic planning. In addition he astutely saw the proposed legislation as an opportunity to trade off a guarantee for protected union organizing activities in return for the relaxation of the antitrust laws.

Thus a stream of forces was converging to give life to the ill-fated bill. Believers in national planning whose roots went all the way back to Theodore Roosevelt's vision of a strong and responsible central government; the Progressive inheritors of the Roosevelt tradition, such as Senator La Follette in Congress and Harold Ickes in the Cabinet; the dreamers and visionaries of a beneficent state, such as Rexford Tugwell and the philosopher John Dewey; practitioners from the War Industries Board who recalled what had already been done in a similar emergency; business leaders forced to drop *laissez faire* because of the gravity of the depression; labor leaders probing for the patronage of government; Congressmen exasperated with the old order and ready to rubber-stamp legislation during the fury of the First Hundred Days; and finally FDR himself.

Fond as he was of Wilson and Brandeis, FDR leaned towards Cousin Ted on the issues of bigness and destructive competition. Moreover he had been a part of the war production effort as Assistant Secretary of the Navy and had then immersed himself in trade association activities as President of the American Construction Council. Above all he looked upon himself as the man who should balance all interests, the mediator who would restore order and harmony among farmers, businessmen, laborers and consumers. He had helped the bankers open their doors. He had treated the farm sickness with the Agricultural Adjustment Act and a prescription of inflation. Now he must help business get on its feet with public works and institutional changes as well. FDR's anti-business sentiment at the time was primarily against the speculators and money-changers. He found it perfectly consistent to encourage Pecora's pitiless investigation of Wall Street and had already sent on March 29, 1933 a recommendation to Congress for drastic securities legislation. The regulation of stocks and bonds was only a policeman's reform to correct an obvious abuse and the anguished cries of Wall Street were brushed aside. The National Industrial Recovery Act, however, was conceived as a great voluntary partnership between business and government that might become the most notable achievement of his Administration. FDR was entirely happy to let business carry off the honors, to leave it fully entitled to its profits and new immunities if only it would do its part.

IV

On April 25, 1933 Hugh Johnson and Bernard Baruch, fresh from a hunting trip in South Carolina, ran into Raymond Moley in the lobby of Washington's Carlton Hotel. Moley, entranced by the legendary Baruch and his efficient gun-bearer, seized the opportunity to draw them into the plans for industrial recovery which he knew FDR impatiently awaited. Moley probably sensed that Baruch's protegé was a most desirable candidate for administrator of the proposed law. In his capacity as FDR's major-domo, Moley thereupon put him to work. As Johnson later wrote:

> He said that the draft of an Industrial Act was an immediate necessity and, recalling our many studies of the subject, our frequent talks with him, and B. M.'s experience in the mobilization of industry, asked if I could not be loaned to him to draw up such a bill . . . Mr. Baruch readily assented and I went over to Ray's office that afternoon. Indeed I never went back to New York from that day to the end of my service except to get my clothes and rarely even so much as saw my own family.[8]

An aside on Bernard Baruch's influence is in order. The "adviser to Presidents" maintained a unique position as businessman-consultant to occupants of the White House right up to his death at ninety-five in 1965. His high point of influence was with Woodrow Wilson, who became a close friend and sent him on to the Versailles Treaty discussions after his service on the War Industries Board. From that point on his advice poured forth for the benefit of later Presidents but was probably more often neglected than adopted. A great favorite of the newspapers, he was generally sounded out on important issues, particularly economic ones. Baruch's courtly presence and aggressive public relations contributed to his public image as an important man. Few people would have the style to become a crony of Winston Churchill as Baruch did, or to invent his final triumph of homespun celebrity, the man whose office was a bench in New York's Central Park. Baruch's power emanated from his supply of campaign funds as well as his accumulated wisdom and influential friends. He carefully nurtured allegiance from a dozen or so important Southern Senators and Congressmen, making his support for legislation a consideration in the White House.

FDR was not particularly beholden to Baruch, who came close to trying to stop him in the pre-convention struggles of the 1932 nomination. In addition FDR regarded the old Wilsonian as a more or less disapproving superior of his Navy Department days who might now interfere with his need to be his own man. Finally Baruch was indelibly connected with Wall Street. No matter how carefully Baruch later rationalized his career as a speculator, there was an awareness that he was not really an industrialist but instead a shrewd trader who had the immense foresight, like Joseph P. Kennedy, to cash in his chips months before the great crash. At any rate, Baruch's advice was deliberately unsought by Roosevelt for the first few months after the inauguration, a slight which would be keenly recognized by the veteran politician especially when, as he told Moley on the night of the election, "I gave two hundred thousand dollars."[9] As might be expected, Baruch had his detractors. Justice Brandeis, whom FDR revered, had no use for him. When Jimmy Warburg was told that Baruch was scheduled to head the American delegation to the London Economic Conference, he refused to serve under a man he felt had profited by bear runs on the market leading to the crash.[10] As it turned out Baruch was not designated and no doubt FDR was later delighted to reward him indirectly as a result of the lordly loan of Hugh Johnson negotiated by the astute Moley. Actually Baruch's conservatism, especially his tiresome demands for a balanced budget and preservation of the gold standard, were out of step with FDR's developing thought. Still his conservative influence would be reassuring to the business world whose support was so essential for NRA.

Johnson soon learned that several other experts had been working on an industrial recovery bill. With FDR's approval, Moley had asked Jimmy Warburg to examine the various proposals on file and to check out additional experts. The conscientious Warburg produced an elaborate memorandum on April 4 entitled "Industrial Rehabilitation by Reemployment" which emphasized either government loans to industry or government subsidies to start up industry in return for a later share of the profits. Moley and FDR decided more thought was needed and the Warburg report was shelved.

Meanwhile an alarm was sounded on April 6 when a young Senator named Hugo Black of Alabama saw the Senate pass his bill for a thirty-hour week. For most people who worked by the hour, a six-day week and an eight or nine-hour day were considered normal and even enlightened hours. Black's proposal rested on an untried economic theory. Technological progress had created a labor surplus and the only way to restore jobs and purchasing power was to share the work week among more workers. Although about fifty years early in his technological deductions, Black's prediction of an immediate gain of six million jobs as a result of the thirty-hour week was enticing. It enlisted the unexpected support of the American Federation of Labor and an ominous threat of a general strike from AFL President Green if the bill did not pass. The bill did not contain a minimum wage provision, which Black thought would be declared unconstitutional on an interstate basis. Besides New York state had just passed a minimum wage law and a half dozen other states were about to do so. Black argued that with so many more people employed, the tight labor market would enable workers to bargain for better wages, which a revived industry could then afford to pay.

Just as the Thomas Amendment to the Agricultural Adjustment Act forced FDR to do something about inflation, the Black bill threat accelerated the hasty improvisation of the NRA legislation. FDR and his associates were genuinely shocked at the rigidity of the bill which in retrospect and with a few amendments would probably have done as much good as the NRA bill with far less commotion. They thought it would only create a disaster, increasing the costs of business and dividing available wages into the hands of more workers, each with threadbare purchasing power. Secretary Perkins was delegated to stall the bill in the House by providing amendments. When she came up with extending the thirty-hour week to forty hours in exceptional cases and emergencies along with a government board to impose minimum wages when they fell below a fair living standard, the employers roared in protest. If there were to be wages and hours controls, stated Henry I. Harriman, let it be done only through the voluntary codes of business associations rather than compulsory federal legislation. In the White House, FDR decided that an omnibus industrial bill placating all interests had to be passed quickly. Moley was instructed to bring in a bill and the news was leaked to the newspapers on April 14 that something akin to the War Industries Board for reviving industry, along with a public works program in the billions, was in preparation.

While Hugh Johnson was dashing off his version of the NRA, efficiently reducing it two sheets of yellow foolscap, he learned that FDR had typically given the assignment to still others, including Senator Wagner and John Dickinson, Assistant Secretary of Commerce. When Johnson complained, FDR called a meeting of the principal architects at his office in the White House. There they sat and argued, Johnson, Dickinson, Madame Perkins, Wagner, Donald Richberg, enlisted as Johnson's deputy for labor matters, and Lewis Douglas, defending the budget by objecting to the proposed public works expenditures. In a famous incident used by historians to illustrate either FDR's administrative ingenuity or his willingness to sponsor hodge-podge legislation, the President genially ordered the disputants to lock themselves in a room and not come out till they came up with a single proposal. After a few days and nights of wrangling, a bill was produced which Roosevelt accepted and sent to Congress on May 17.

Meanwhile FDR explained to his millions of radio listeners in his second Fireside Chat on May 7 how careful they must be in using words: "It is wholly wrong to call the measures we have taken government control of farming, industry and transportation. It is rather a partnership . . . not partnership in profits, for the profits still go to the citizens, but rather a partnership in planning, and a partnership to see that the plans are carried out." Nor did FDR neglect his partners in the United States Chamber of Commerce, a few blocks away from the White House. To their annual convention, early in May, he sent a message calling on business "to prevent over-production, to prevent unfair wages, to eliminate improper working conditions." These were reasonable enough requests from one principality to another, and the business executives were only too glad to strike a radical pose. Over half the speakers on the agenda came out for more government direction of industry. If we want to be saved, one speaker noted, "we must make substantial concessions to what we have in the past classified as the more radical school of thought."

V

In analyzing the NRA forty years after the fact, one is reminded of a chase. Perhaps that is too frivolous a concept for a serious situation but the elements are there. It is as though we are seeing once again a Keystone two-reeler, with continual chases and pratfalls. First the chase to get the big ten basic industries signed up with codes in a period of only three months. General Hugh Johnson, nicknamed "Ironpants," pursues them relentlessly, a screeching Blue Eagle himself, crisscrossing the country in his private Army transport plane, armed with a desk bolted to its interior. When the codes were finally hammered out by an industry and approved by Johnson, they had to be signed by President Roosevelt. One day Johnson ran into the White House, handed the President three codes to sign and then tore out again to catch his Army plane. "He hasn't been seen since," the President beamed. Or take the hide and seek with Henry Ford. Ford is reported to have said of the Blue Eagle, "Hell, that Roosevelt buzzard, I wouldn't put it on the car," as he refused to have anything to do with the code.[11] Under the NRA rules, a majority vote in his industry made it mandatory for Ford to join up. The law gave the President power to punish Ford by denying him a license to stay in business. Johnson was afraid to test the licensing power, which was actually never used, having doubts himself about NRA's constitutional credentials from the beginning. When he resumed his pursuit of Ford by suggesting the American people "would crack down on him," it turned out that Ford had outdistanced him by observing all of the code anyway, even better than some of his competitors.

Perhaps the heart of the chase was in the escalation of prices. Industries took to the once-forbidden price-fixing like ducks to water. Minimum prices were considered patriotic enough. They prevented chiselers from operating and presumably made it possible for industries to adopt the type of wages and hours required for code approval and increased purchasing power. But with antitrust suspended and production quotas permitted, profit-hungry industries from steel producers to dry-cleaning establishments were setting minimums too high, or raising prices without concern about overproduction or competition. FDR had warned about prices when he signed the bill on June 16, 1933. "If we now inflate prices as fast and as far as we increase wages," he said, "the whole project will be set at naught." By the beginning of 1934 Johnson was on the run from antitrusters like Senator Borah and Senator Nye who charged the NRA was breeding monopoly pricing. As he maneuvered for position, his flanks were threatened by the NRA's own Consumers Advisory Board. Led by the vigorous Mary Rumsey, Averell Harriman's sister, the Board charged the consumer was being squeezed by price concessions granted too willingly by Johnson as the reward for code-making. Johnson was a bold enough economist to realize that some price inflation at the bottom of a depression was well worth the gamble for increased production and employment. Still, with new jobs coming in as low as thirty cents an hour, he knew that public opinion, which he needed on the side of NRA, required the capture of runaway prices. "If I had only nine words with which to address you," he hoarsely pleaded to a National Dry Goods Association audience, "I would rise here and say, 'Keep prices down — for God's sake, keep prices down.'"

Indeed the chase was typical of Hugh Johnson's furious work day. It might be an emergency flight to quell a strike or to bluff an employer into submission over NRA's union provisions. There was always a running battle of words with NRA critics and review boards. It could be time for one of his frequent escapes from the burdens of his office, sadly aggravated by over-drinking. Or it might be an attempt at ambush by his exasperated and ambitious subordinate, Donald Richberg. Finally the NRA itself was overtaken by the horse and buggy riders of the Supreme Court. The conviction of the Schechter brothers for selling sick chickens and violating other NRA codes was "delegation running riot," Justice Cardozo aptly observed.

VI

Inevitably the NRA was used as an example of monstrous bureaucracy and as a vindication of the free market. Yet when wages and price controls and even rationing were imposed in World War II, under old NRA leadership such as Johnson's deputy, Leon Henderson, they worked. The NRA was passed as a two-year measure, clearly indicating its emergency nature. There is no question, however, that both Roosevelt and Johnson hoped it would be renewed and perfected as the American way between monopoly and cutthroat competition, the old order having collapsed into stagnation so tragically. Ironically one of the elements that proved unworkable was the appeal to the conscience of business, to what is now called corporate responsibility in the areas of ecology and inflationary restraints. Johnson, his head chockful of crusades and battles, made the mistake of appealing to business to curtail profits and open its doors to unions for the good of the country. Yet he really had no power to impose such conditions, other than publicly breaking the swords of the errant knights of business. One can admire his dedicated substitution of jawboning and cheerleading under such circumstances but must recognize there was little chance for staying power.

In brief, individual reforms have always worked well for American business, as evidenced by the securities acts of 1933 and 1934, the "death sentence" for utility holding companies in 1935 and the eventual wages, hours and union protection laws. To expect the great engine of American business, however, to forego profit maximizing after the moral exhortation and emergency wore off was naive and actually impractical. Aside from wartime, the choice for maximizing industrial results then and now seems to be either indirect stimuli from Washington coupled with reform regulations or a shift to outright nationalization. That the United States has chosen the former path, with all its achievements and faults, is certainly due in some measure to its unique peacetime experiment with a hybrid structure of the NRA type.

Thus a review of some selected incidents from the NRA may hold valuable lessons. It should be noted that competition received a rehabilitation as a result of the NRA's failure. Yet government was not the real enemy of competition as much as business itself. Government consistently claimed it was giving business just what it wanted, the right to control prices and restrict production, and business trotted right down the alien path. For a while it appeared that big business particularly was flirting dangerously with the corporate state experiment of business-government monopolies, which tends to assumption of political power in the fascist philosophy. Perhaps it was just as well that the whole experiment floundered when it did with minimum casualties and some valuable side benefits. Perhaps also the idea of a dangerous philosophy is too theoretical for what may have been just a giant chase by a slightly mad General in the pragmatic, non-ideological arena of the New Deal.

Hugh Johnson's first great disappointment came when Roosevelt decided at the outset to take the $3.3 billion public works program provided by the NRA away from him and place it in the hands of the careful Secretary of the Interior, Harold Ickes. Johnson had been counting on a flood of Public Works Administration money to provide enough new jobs and purchasing power to help business absorb the wage increases of the codes through increased volume. His businessman-economist adviser, Alexander Sachs of Lehman Brothers, had strongly emphasized the necessity of such a joint undertaking while helping Johnson draft his version of the NRA bill. It meant spending the money quickly, the way Harry Hopkins would do with billions of relief funds, but FDR decided otherwise. Instead of orchestrating the whole economy, Johnson was left only with the wages, hours and production quotas of the codes. True to his nature, the honest Ickes strained his funds through the most careful screen, barely getting off the ground before the NRA was on the way out. In hindsight it was a strange mistake in casting. Ickes would have done well cautiously gaining bridgeheads in wages, hours and prices. Johnson would have been a great disbursing agent for the one sure remedy learned from the depression, pump-priming through rapid spending on public works programs. "He's ruined me," Johnson cried out about FDR to Secretary Perkins. Johnson had no illusions about his job. "It will be red fire at first and dead cats afterward. This is just like mounting the guillotine on the infinitesimal gamble that the axe won't work."

Still factory production had risen from an index of 56 in March to 101 in July and there had also been a Roosevelt boom in the stock market. The stage was set for action and Johnson irresponsibly predicted six million new jobs by Labor Day. As it turned out, smart businessmen were merely trying to get ahead of the expected wages and price increases of the inflationary new Administration and there would be a painful break in July. By that time, however, Johnson had brought in his first victory.

Three weeks after the law was passed, a textile code was adopted and approved. Code drafting procedures were kept admirably open ("We'll operate in a goldfish bowl," Johnson promised) and every businessman observed the fascinating development. First there were informal pre-hearing conferences in which the chief issues were developed. The trade association or "institute" represented the industry at the conference and a Johnson deputy along with an Industrial Advisory Board, a Labor Advisory Board and a Consumers Advisory Board, all government appointees, represented the NRA. The final stage was a thoroughly publicized hearing held in Washington, where all parties might feel the presence of the beleaguered Administration in a time of crisis. Everything was brought into the open and placed on the record. The law contained a provision that if no code could be agreed upon, the President himself could impose a code. FDR rarely invoked this power, as he too felt the baleful eye of the Supreme Court observing the proceedings. Finally the document would reach the hands of General Johnson. If it contained a reasonably improved wages and hours schedule for all employees and allowed unions the right to organize without resistance (the famous Section 7a which entered the law haphazardly and became the Magna Charta of unionism), Johnson would present it to FDR for signature. It was a type of pageantry and medieval oath-taking American businessmen had never imagined in their wildest dreams. For consolation they recognized that this was a time for experiment and that business interests generally dominated the code-making process.

The textile industry was more than ready to take the plunge. For years its trade association had tried to get industry-wide agreements and drive out the sweatshops. It was an industry that suffered from over-production and nineteenth century labor conditions. The association had a code ready the day NRA became law, complete with better wages, shorter hours and collective bargaining provisions. The minimum wages pointed to the end of a venerable institution in Southern cotton mills, child labor. Why not eliminate it by specifically naming it an unfair trade practice, Johnson asked. At first the mill magnates refused. Johnson reminded them of the limits on production and price-chiselers now sanctified by the law. At a final emergency meeting, the owners agreed to outlaw child labor by name. A roar of applause burst forth in the hearing room and a whole nation marvelled at the new way of doing business. For decades unions and child labor reforms had met a stone wall of opposition. The terrible strike at the Gastonia, North Carolina mills had happened only four years earlier. "It makes me personally happier than any other one thing which I have been connected with since I came to Washington," the President announced.

People who recall the Blue Eagle, however, remember its sticker on the windows of every kitchen, movie screen, bootblack stand, in barber shops, funeral parlor ads, on price tags and packages, wherever one looked. This was the result of Johnson's own brainstorm, a plan that galvanized the entire country into participation but also drew the NRA into an impossible mire of small business and service industry disputes. The others of the big ten did not bowl over so easily as cotton textiles. A standoff between a newly aroused labor and a somewhat revived business stalled the other codes week after week. Johnson came to Roosevelt with plans for a blanket code, to be called the President's Reemployment Agreement (PRA), which would call only for wages and hours agreements along with Section 7a, until the rest of the code apparatus could be adopted. This would bring in the local storekeepers who weren't involved in interstate commerce, or industries too fragmented to get together and submit a code. It would apply pressure on the big nine (coal, petroleum, steel, automobiles, lumber, garments, wholesalers, retailers and construction) to come to terms on the grounds that they could afford to raise wages if the rest of the country were similarly engaged. Even Tugwell, the least businesslike person to sit on the special cabinet committee to whom Johnson was supposed to report, saw cracks in the idea. Others urged Johnson to go after the big boys first and leave the small fry for last, or even out of the picture completely. By this time Johnson was a force of his own, in some ways the personification of the New Deal, crowding the President for daily headlines. FDR gave him his blessings.

A nation starved for action and leadership swallowed Johnson's ballyhoo with abandon. Artists, writers, public relations experts and celebrities joined in the promotion, led by the General himself as he stumped the country. It was something everyone could be in favor of, somewhat like the response to today's environmental crisis. Roosevelt started it off with his third Fireside Chat and within days copies of the PRA were mailed to millions of employers throughout the country, bearing the newly designed Blue Eagle. An employer who signed promised to employ no one under sixteen years of age (ending the newsboy profession temporarily, since practically every newspaper enlisted), to pay a minimum wage of \$12 or \$13 a week, to keep prices down and to keep to a thirty-five hour week in the factories and a forty-hour week elsewhere. According to NRA records, over 2.3 million employers signed up, covering 16 million workers. In addition the General enlisted the housewives of America to sign a pledge of their own, turning their wrath on dissenting husbands and pledging to buy only Blue Eagle goods. With the American housewife behind NRA, Johnson warned, "May God have mercy on the man or group of men who attempt to trifle with this bird." NRA opened offices all over the country and eventually there were five thousand employees on its payroll.

It was the summer and fall of NRA. The temptation to ridicule it would overlook the pathetic and touching faith the whole country — even Herbert Hoover signed the consumers' pledge — put in another of a long line of economic nostrums. Mass movements, whether Peter the Hermit's or General Johnson's, usually result in people being disillusioned and the NRA was no exception. Still the nation has rarely seen such an outpouring of goodwill for a peaceful cause. Perhaps it was fun to have parades again, to see newsreels of bathing beauties with NRA eagles stencilled on their sun-tanned backs, or high school students forming the symbols on their football fields. The PRA gave a psychological lift to the country and broke the log jam on codes. By the end of the year one thousand had been submitted and the big nine had each exchanged signatures with the President.

VII

By mid-1934, the NRA had run out of good wishes and was on the defensive. The first test would be how much reemployment Johnson could claim for it. He had stated in November 1933 that three to four million people were back at work due to NRA. To support this, he had asked Harry Hopkins' new Civil Works Administration, a work relief program that preceded Hopkins' WPA (not to be confused with Ickes' PWA) to put some people to work to ascertain the correct figure. For perspective, it should be remembered that in mid-1934, about one out of every seven Americans, over 18 million people, were receiving either direct relief or work relief and the total would rise to 20 million by the time WPA got underway in early 1935. CWA itself was creating a massive contribution of four million work relief jobs during its brief emergency existence in the terrible winter of November 1933 to February 1934, operating for the most part with a billion dollars appropriated by FDR from Ickes' hoard of PWA money.

At any rate the CWA work reliefers, earning the prevailing wages of $12 or $13 a week as against the typical direct payments of $6 or $7, made the survey and totalled up a score of 2,750,000 new jobs for NRA. Johnson refused to accept this figure and criticized the statistical methods. Washington correspondents asked several times for details of the CWA report but they were never released. Meanwhile the American Federation of Labor called the figure absurdly high. Its economists said it should be only 1.7 to 1.9 million. Even if Johnson's figures were true, his critics stated, there was no increase in purchasing power because total wages from private employment, based on Department of Labor statistics, hadn't gone up. The argument was similar to that attached to Senator Black's thirty-hour week, that the same wages were being divided among more people. It wouldn't be so bad, said the critics, if these wages were accompanied by a lower cost of living, but even that had gone up five per cent in the past year. Johnson was not going to lose the battle of statistics and his counterattack in a February 27, 1934 speech makes sense:

> If I have no money to buy a beefsteak dinner, does it make much difference to one whether it costs $1.00 or $1.05? I say — and I think the three million employed will all agree — that I will take the $1 and buy liver and bacon with it. The claim of all this criticism (that purchasing power among wage-earners has not increased) even before we consider its truth, is cruel, cynical buncombe . . . NRA reemployed three million people who were without jobs before and added $3 billion to the annual wherewithal of workers to live. It must be remembered too that all this happened during a downward cycle of production when without NRA we would probably have a fresh deluge of unemployment.

The final judgement is that about 2.5 million people were reemployed in the first half of NRA, an achievement widely heralded by Johnson and Roosevelt and an economic stimulant that carried on to the next year. The psychological stimulus, of course, was equally important. Still the increase in jobs to that extent was insufficient vindication for NRA's fatal structure of red tape and bureaucracy, along with the constant charge of monopoly pricing. The brickbats began to fall from some of NRA's most ardent supporters. A program that was intended to please business, government, labor and consumers in equal proportions could just as easily irritate each faction. By the end of 1933, code violations were widespread, taxing the abilities of the hastily recruited local compliance boards. People as diverse as Hearst and Walter Lippmann found the centralized controls excessive. The defection of Harriman and Swope must have been particularly painful to Johnson. Six months ago business had been 100 per cent behind NRA, Harriman observed, but now practically every representative group of businessmen questioned the whole program. Swope proposed in November 1933 that the government get out of the NRA business completely and turn it over to a super-body of trade associations organized by the United States Chamber of Commerce. Yet if NRA worked at all, it worked best for big business, where millions of workers were employed in key industries. Its chances would have been markedly improved if it had shied away from America's typically conservative and cantankerous small businessmen.

Thus Eugene R. Grace, president of Bethlehem Steel Corporation, the second largest unit of the steel industry, announced in January 1934 that "a sounder basis has been developed for industry out of these hard times than it has enjoyed at any time during the post-war period." Businessmen had ceased to fear that the NRA was a cloak for the ultimate socialization of industry, Grace stated, and considered it a proper policy "to pay the maximum wages which the profits of a business will bear." Coming down to the nub of the situation, Grace was particularly enthusiastic about "the banishing of speculation in industrial prices . . . the selling of steel in 1932 and for the years preceding had all of the confusion of the selling of rugs in a Turkish street fair."[12]

Bethlehem Steel may have been happy with a monopolistic pricing situation that let it concentrate on service to its customers but this did not necessarily apply to the rug merchant in Dubuque, Iowa who had to beat out the local department store to make a living. Having signed up practically the whole country in his blanket code campaign, Johnson now ruled a fantastic collection of codes, practically all of which had seen the dominant interests or chains cut themselves in for a round of price-fixing of one kind or another. The compliance problem centered on small business and Johnson later estimated that over 90 per cent of the violations came from the small service establishments. In fact he rued the day that he had ever gone beyond wages and hours for small industries, especially since every consumer could relate price controls to his own experience. Was it really necessary to have a code for the Dog Food Industry, the Curled Hair Manufacturing Industry, the Horse Hair Dressing Industry or, for that matter, Code No. 348 for the Burlesque Theatre Industry of New York?[13]

The Supreme Court only killed a Blue Eagle already shot down by the Cleaning and Dyeing Code, Johnson mourned after his exile from NRA. When the code was adopted for this industry in the spring of 1933, it seemed a most enlightened proposal for eliminating the cutthroat competition that had turned the industry into a vast sweatshop offering tremendous bargains for those with an extra suit to clean but little purchasing power for employees. The code established minimum wages and a minimum price for cleaning a suit at seventy-five cents. Behind the steaming press machines, however, there were some rugged enterprisers without the business statesmanship of Eugene R. Grace. About a year later one cleaning chain cut the price to forty-five cents and started a price war. In protest against these violations, the non-warriors locked up their establishments in order to bring about intervention by NRA's reluctant officials. The following from General Johnson's press conference of February 10, 1934 illustrates the futile story of NRA. It makes one wish the Supreme Court would have approved wages and hours legislation in 1933 instead of later and let prices bobble competitively on top of the resulting increased purchasing power. (It all seems so clear now, of course, but then we don't have an answer to our contemporary problem of solving unemployment during a period of runaway inflation rather than deflation.) The General speaks:

> If you get down below the price level (of seventy-five cents) there's lots of volume that would not exist except

> at that price. One firm (the offending chain) pays Code wages, observes Code hours and turns out as good stuff as anybody turns out anywhere. They clean suits for, I think, forty-five cents. We have only one case of that kind (where standard service is rendered for forty-five cents) and we've combed the woods. The rest of them (the other price cutters) don't clean the clothes, they run them through. In one case they run clothes through their mechanical establishment eight times as fast as what you'd call high-grade cleaning. That raises the question: if people want to have a low-grade cleaning service, are they not entitled to it? Just as soon as you get the price below a certain level, the volume comes in, but if you get it above that level, people clean their own stuff, or don't clean it. It happens that the business done by these chain operators is probably three per cent of the cleaning business (in New York City) but they are threatening all the rest of the cleaning business. You are in a real dilemma as to what is the proper and economical thing to do in a case of that kind.[14]

One way to solve the dilemma was to get the NRA out of the pricing business but disengagement was not so easy. When Johnson issued a ruling in March 1934 that allowed minimum price-fixing only in "emergencies," the protest from industry was so vehement that he had to relent and amend it to apply only to new codes. Still business got the message and minimum price provisions began to settle down at reasonably competitive levels. The NRA, however, had already been tarred as a monopolistic instrument for its production restraints — even new machines were forbidden in some industries — and the question of increased goods and services rather than less as a means of creating jobs had to be faced. Leon Henderson, Johnson's chief economist, was most articulate in advancing this theory of increased production.[15]

Honestly puzzled by the criticisms of antitrusters like Borah and Nye and the advocates of business expansion as against scarcity, the always resilient FDR appointed a Review Board in March 1934 to investigate monopolistic tendencies in the codes. Clarence Darrow, the famous criminal lawyer who had defended Eugene Debs in the 1894 railroad strikes and duelled with Bryan over evolution in Dayton, Tennessee, was named chairman with the naive blessings of Johnson and Richberg. At age seventy-seven, as independent as a man could be, Darrow accepted the honor as his last case and tore into the NRA. After four months and sixty hearings, Darrow passed the verdict that NRA was an instrument of monopoly. Bring back the antitrust laws, the old attorney advised, and restore competition. On the other hand, he added in a footnote, unregulated, vicious competition wouldn't do either and perhaps some socialism was in order. Johnson howled in protest and Washington rocked as the two masters traded insults at their press conferences. With socialism out of the question, labor leaders like John L. Lewis joined Johnson in denouncing a return to unfettered competition. Many business leaders began to see the irony of their price-fixing position and to weary of NRA overall, particularly for its charter to union activity. The effects of the Darrow review, the antitrusters in Congress and NRA's own obstreperous, price-conscious Consumers Advisory Board, now dominated by a young economist named Paul H. Douglas, changed the course of NRA in its second and final year. Even before the Supreme Court decision, the NRA began retreating to a position of a combination wages and hours authority and labor relations board. Its administrators held price-fixing and production restraints in growing disapproval. FDR himself had arrived at the same conclusion but hoped the basic NRA program would be renewed for another two-year term.

VIII

The decline of NRA was accompanied by the personal decline of Hugh Johnson. Overworked, overexposed, unstable and increasingly absent on alcoholic binges, he was obviously a candidate for replacement by FDR. Johnson claims that he offered to resign five times. Apparently the soft-hearted President could not face the issue and let him linger on until September 1934, when he finally accepted Johnson's resignation and placed NRA under a board rather than one man. No administrator or cabinet officer of his like has been seen in Washington since that day, although Leon Henderson assumed a similar image as OPA chief in World War II. The nearest in bombastic language would be Vice President Agnew but Johnson looked and acted the way he talked as Agnew does not. No government official ever paid such public attention to businessmen, now flattering them, now scolding them or demoting them militarily in the style of Thorstein Veblen: "Away, slight men! You may have been Captains of Industry but you are Corporals of Disaster!" Only one other philosopher of business, Adolf Berle, searcher for the corporate conscience, would think of investing business with the qualities of knighthood.[16] For Johnson, the NRA was "a holy thing," a blend of the cross and the sword. "This conference is as important as the Council of Nicaea or the Treaty of Verdun," he once told an audience of 4,000 government and industry representatives. The subtle, intellectual Berle would have blanched at Johnson's explanation of how he might discipline a code violator:

> As happened to Danny Deever in Kipling's regimental hanging — NRA will have to remove from him his badge of public faith and business honor (the Blue Eagle card) and "tykin' of his buttons off an' cut his stripes away" and break the bright sword of his commercial honor in the eyes of his neighbors — and throw the fragments — in scorn — in the dust at his feet.

IX

A fever chart for the life of NRA as well as the romance between FDR and the business community can be found in the annual meetings of the United States Chamber of Commerce. As far back as 1931 the Chamber, bewildered by the depression, had officially endorsed "the philosophy of a planned economy," under the leadership of men like Henry I. Harriman. In 1933, aware that the NRA was being drafted partially in response to the suggestions of its own leadership, the Chamber gave a standing ovation to FDR, who appeared personally to call on its members to join in a partnership "to prevent over-production, to prevent unfair wages and to eliminate improper working conditions." In 1934 its enthusiasm was waning, particularly because of Section 7a, which the Chamber had strongly opposed in Senate hearings at the time the bill was passed. Still in 1934 NRA was endorsed by the Chamber for continuance by a four to one vote. Now in April 1935 the situation had entirely changed. FDR had already sent word to Congress that he would like to see NRA extended beyond its June deadline for two more years. He acknowledged the need for revisions such as a turn away from monopolies and price-fixing as well as the elimination of borderline industries from code regulations. To abandon NRA, however, "would invite a return to industrial and labor chaos," he warned. Even the friends of NRA were becoming faint-hearted in the face of the agency's internal feuding, mushrooming bureaucracy and wavering philosophy. The shrill insistence of labor leaders for its retention did not impress business leaders.

FDR was not invited to the Chamber's annual meeting in 1935 since it had been decided to use the occasion to disown the New Deal. New leaders, representing the smaller businessmen who had special grievances against the NRA, were in the saddle. Now the sharpest voice came from Silas Strawn, a Chicago attorney who was also counsel for the National Association of Manufacturers. Strawn had been president of the Chamber in 1931 and at that time endorsed Swope's planned-business scheme as "excellent." In April 1934, Strawn displayed an emotional animus against the New Deal which was indicative of his changing mood. One William Wirt, a Gary, Indiana school superintendent who had achieved some prominence as a founder of the inflationary Committee for the Nation, was now making headlines with revelations of a Red conspiracy on the part of FDR and the Brain Trusters. Reporting on a dinner party held at the home of his former private secretary in Washington, Wirt quoted some of the guests who had shared with him their knowledge of secret plans to deliver America to Stalin via an unwitting FDR. Of interest to businessmen is how the news was given to the world. James Rand, president of Remington Rand, testifying against the 1934 Securities Exchange Act, took the occasion to read into his Senate Committee testimony Dr. Wirt's statement, rocking the news media accordingly. Eventually Wirt himself was put on the stand before a Special House Committee to investigate his charges. Wirt foolishly dissolved them into thin air but not before Silas Strawn had publicly praised Wirt "as the type of man needed to save this country from the intellectual jackasses in Washington."[17]

Two days before the Chamber meeting, the unpredictable FDR in a Fireside Chat had offered the nation a blanket invitation: "Feel free to criticize" the New Deal programs, he suggested. Silas Strawn's response on behalf of the Chamber was overwhelming. "We have floundered along for two years . . . We have a right to know where we are going. Businessmen are tired of hearing promises to do constructive things which turn out to be only attempts to Sovietize America." In such a mood the most important association in American business hammered through resolutions opposing the New Deal. Social Security legislation proposals must be dropped since there were "doubts to its propriety as well as its constitutionality." The proposed utility holding company act "would violate fundamental principles." Marriner Eccles' proposed Banking Act "would amount to little short of political dictatorship." Senator Wagner's proposed labor act, on hand to make Section 7a permanent law, would be "encroachment on the right of contract." The AAA should be thrown out and last but not least, business' own handiwork, the NRA, "must be allowed to expire in June."[18]

Thus the Chamber regained its course after following false winds. It would not stray again for the rest of the New Deal. The State Chambers followed suit. FDR's own New York Chamber soon circulated a pamphlet deploring "the billions of dollars of the people's money" which Congress had appropriated to "the political accident in the White House . . . to juggle with as suits his whims." Alfred P. Sloan of General Motors received cheers from the Michigan Chamber when he stated: "We are not going to tolerate further interference in recovery . . . We must liquidate the panaceas and discard quack theories."[19]

In fact most of the leading spokesmen for American business were winding up for the voyage to the Liberty League. The president of the National Association of Manufacturers told its annual meeting in 1935 that industry must enter politics "to rid the United States of the New Deal." From the joint war against the depression, business leaders solemnly veered off to a war to defend capitalism.

In the White House, FDR's mood was sad and frustrated, at least for the time being. Aware that he was considered a traitor to his class, he felt that the businessmen were the real traitors. Often he used the story of the man saved from drowning who was now infuriated because no one would dive in for his silk hat. He had friends on the business side to whom he could relate his grief. His Business Advisory Council issued a report condemning the U.S. Chamber's action and recommending a two-year extension of NRA. The Council, of course, was representative of big business, an important section of which had philosophically embraced the concept of big government as the inevitable partner of big business in the new "mixed capitalism." In retrospect, FDR, seeking to help "the forgotten man," never found support for his economic theories from the small businessmen as he did from the small farmers. On the other hand, he did enjoy strong support from members of the Council such as Henry I. Harriman, Gerard Swope, Winthrop Aldrich of the Chase National Bank, Walter S. Gifford of American Telephone and Telegraph, Averell Harriman of Union Pacific, Myron Taylor of U.S. Steel, Robert E. Wood of Sears Roebuck and particularly Thomas J. Watson of IBM. To Watson, FDR complained about the intransigence of businessmen and their official associations towards reforms. "Our own Chamber of Commerce in New York has a one hundred per cent record of opposition to things like factory inspection, excessive hours, elimination of child labor, old age pensions, unemployment insurance — year after year the same old story," FDR poured into Watson's sympathetic ear.[20]

X

Quite a different group of businessmen were destined to become the agents for the judicial destruction of the NRA. The Schechter Live Poultry Company of Brooklyn had been fined $5,000 and one of its principals sentenced to three months in jail for non-compliance with NRA codes late in 1934. They had been found guilty of eighteen wage and hour and trade practice violations of the Live Poultry Code in the U.S. District Court. Their conviction was upheld by the Second Circuit Court of Appeals on April 1, 1935, with the esteemed Justice Learned Hand sustaining the constitutionality of the NRA's authority. The Circuit Court did reverse the lower court's conviction for the wages and hours violations on the grounds that the Schechter employees themselves were not engaged in interstate commerce even though the chickens crossed state lines. The other violations, however, such as filing false sales and price reports and selling diseased poultry, were confirmed.

The Administration was on guard for such a critical case and hurried conferences took place between Johnson, Richberg, Attorney General Cummings, Frankfurter and FDR himself, away from Washington for a week's fishing on Vincent Astor's *Nourmahal.* The government lawyers had backed away from appealing an Alabama lumber code violation to the Supreme Court only a short time before, not wishing to test the production restrictions in the lumber code. Now the NRA officials felt they must face up to the Schechter decision and appeal to the Supreme Court for a reversal of the wages and hours decision of the Circuit Court. Otherwise the effectiveness of their compliance actions would be destroyed. Their hand was being forced at any rate by the counsel for the Schechter brothers, recently augmented by an eminent lawyer from one of Wall Street's most prestigious firms, who publicly announced he was taking the case for his clients to the Supreme Court. Thus the "sick chicken case" became national news as a test for the continuation of the NRA. Joseph Schechter had asked for sympathizers to help with legal fees which he later claimed were "$60,000, every nickel I had."[21] Even allowing for his tendency to exaggerate (it would be $180,000 in today's currency), his place in history was assured.

Reports of the bizarre case have the nine old justices rocking with laughter as they explored some of the trade practices of the live poultry industry. Donald Richberg, assisting Solicitor General Stanley Reed, a future Supreme Court Justice, argued desperately in terms of constitutional precedent and social needs. The Schechter counsel contended that "if the government could regulate live poultry, it could regulate all businesses, and carried to its logical conclusion, the concept would ultimately find Congress in charge of all human activity."

On Monday, May 27, 1935 the Justices filed into Court and delivered a stunning, unanimous decision against NRA. This was not a five to four decision with Justice Roberts the swing voter, as had been expected. The conservatives were intent on restraining excessive delegation of power by Congress to the President and the NRA. The liberals, led by Cardozo and Brandeis, were set on restraining the government from excessive centralization of power. The size and scope of the great business experiment was offensive to all of the Justices, regardless of the emergency. Technically the Court found the Schechters' business was intrastate, even though the chickens came from out of state; hence the federal government had no authority to regulate working conditions in that firm or in the hundreds of thousands of similar firms subject to NRA.

Roosevelt was shocked by the unanimous decision. "Well, where was Ben Cardozo?" he asked, "and what about old Isaiah?" his pet name for the prophet-like Brandeis. As unsympathetic as Brandeis was towards the claims of big business, he clearly rejoiced in the ending of NRA. It represented an excessive centralization of power in government which he consistently rejected, resting his hopes for reform in specific laws and regulatory agencies. For still different reasons, John M. Keynes, often identified as a statist by business spokesmen, also lauded the NRA decision. He too was against excessive government ambitions in economic organization, feeling confident that the economy could best be stimulated by indirect pressures such as raising and lowering taxes, insuring mortgages and government spending, if only FDR would listen to him. FDR had already absorbed some of the Keynesian approach in shifting towards the concept of increasing production rather than restricting it, of pump-priming through government spending rather than encouraging business through reducing competitive hazards. In addition, his experimental nature had not committed him all the way to NRA.

It is often said that the real test of a good executive is how he handles the decisions that go sour and in the case of NRA FDR acquitted himself well. At an unusual press conference two days after the decision, FDR radiated confidence and good humor. With Mrs. Roosevelt knitting away at a sock in the background, FDR lectured the "horse and buggy Court" on a level of high argument. If the Court were going to interpret interstate commerce so narrowly, he maintained, how could there be control over any national economic problem, save perhaps transportation which was obviously an interstate matter? For the time being he seemed content to try to bring the court back to reas n for future cases. After all, the best elements of NRA could be resubmitted in terms of specific laws. There was no hint of the bad temper and judgment that would lead him to the Court-packing attempt of 1937. One suspects that FDR was more angry at the business community which had proved so anxious to thwart him than the Court itself, a conjecture that is supported by his belligerent anti-business stance in the 1936 campaign. NRA was expendable and a good deal of recovery had been extracted from it. It was time to turn to other matters, such as the $4 billion WPA work relief program.

Even the Schechters were converted by the President's imperturbable good humor and leadership. Joseph Schechter asked a reporter after the Landon defeat: "I wonder if it would be possible to congratulate President Roosevelt through the newspapers and tell him that the sixteen votes in our family were cast in his favor?"[22]

XI

In the end, how should we evaluate the NRA? The conventional judgment is to write it off as a peacetime failure for business recovery which should not be repeated again. There were other ways to create the two million jobs which it only helped bring about. The concept of scarcity as against more goods has never regained popularity. Like "plowing under" farm products, it seemed immoral. America became committed to an ever-increasing gross national product as a guarantee of business prosperity, although today's concern hopefully emphasizes the quality of the product rather than the quantity alone. Obsolescence, fashion, advertising, consumer credit and welfare government are all calculated to meet the prospects of over-production rather than restrictionism.

The disrepute of price-fixing has never been proven satisfactorily. There is no reason to believe price-fixing is the natural accomplice of production restrictions and outright monopoly as was argued so continually by NRA critics. We have long ago admitted that a good deal, perhaps the majority of our prices, are either supported by government, through rate-fixing, subsidies or tariffs, or "administered" by a delicate adjustment among businesses themselves, where such businesses, for example, cigarets, automobiles and banking, are "oligopolies," subject to price leaders in each industry. Japan is a notable example of a country furiously — and successfully — bent on producing more and more goods where prices are largely controlled by giant cartels of the type feared to be implicit in the NRA experiment. Even the political power of such modern mercantilist firms seems to be defused in modern Japan.

Ironically price-fixing in relation to antitrust prosecutions persists as a hazard for all venturesome business executives in America. Antitrust made a great comeback after the NRA as a New Deal counterbalance to the power of big business. In turn Republican Administrations seem to have been more diligent than Democratic ones in using antitrust prosecutions and threats to keep competition, at least for the choice of products if not for prices, reasonably alive. The spectacle of the GE and Westinghouse executives being sent to prison for price-fixing in 1961, for doing exactly what Gerard Swope advocated both in and out of NRA, reminds us how uncertain national economic policy has been in this respect.

The final charge against NRA, therefore, is reduced to its being a case history of proving that, short of wartime conditions, direct controls don't work as well as indirect controls. With this goes the accessory charge that excessive national economic planning at the wrong levels quickly falls of its own weight. The object of NRA was to create jobs, which is never a wartime concern, so it is best to judge NRA as a peacetime measure, regardless of the severity of the depression. Most economists would agree that purchasing power, rather than price and production arrangements, is what business needs when recession strikes, along with confidence on the consumers' part even more than on the part of business. With minimum wages and maximum hours long established on generous terms by federal legislation, wages and hours no longer have utility for increasing purchasing power. Thus there remains practically nothing to be salvaged from the NRA experience, even when we agree on the charges.

Yet there were real benefits derived from NRA aside from the psychological stimulus and few million jobs resulting from General Johnson's impressive short-run tactics. NRA provided a great workshop, haphazard though it was, for permanent social reform. Arthur Schlesinger, Jr. summarizes it eloquently:

> The more enduring achievements of NRA lay not in the economic but in the social field. Here NRA accomplished a fantastic series of reforms, any one of which would have staggered the nation a few years earlier. It established the principle of maximum hours and minimum wages on a national basis. It abolished child labor. It dealt a fatal blow to sweatshops. It made collective bargaining a national policy and thereby transformed the position of organized labor. It gave new status to the consumer. It stamped out a noxious collection of unfair trade practices. . . .
>
> More than this, NRA helped break the chains of economic fatalism which had so long bound the nation. The Blue Eagle campaign changed the popular mood from despair to affirmation and activity. The psychological stimulus gave people new confidence in their capacity to work out their economic salvation. . . . It accustomed the country to the feasibility of government regulation and taught people to think in terms of national policy for business and for labor.[23]

XII

What happened to Hugh Johnson? He became a syndicated newspaper columnist and eventually an anti-Roosevelt man, not a Roosevelt hater of the Westbrook Pegler type, but a notable FDR detractor.

The bid to become a United Press columnist came as a result of his defense of FDR in a great public spat with Huey Long and Father Coughlin. In March 1935 Johnson was scheduled to speak at a Waldorf Astoria dinner sponsored by *Redbook* magazine to launch the serialization of his forthcoming book *The Blue Eagle from Egg to Earth*. It took courage to take on the two demagogues. The lawyer and the priest were gathering tremendous political power and no prominent politician had cared to tilt with them. Long was the dictator of Louisiana and a disgrace to the Senate with his cornpone swagger and threats, boasting that he would soon be President on a "Share the Wealth" and "Every Man a King" platform. Father Coughlin was a money crank, anti-Semite and hypnotic-voiced radio attraction who constantly denounced FDR on Sunday afternoons to millions of listeners. Now they seemed to have made a pact to exploit the masses of poverty-stricken and unemployed throughout the nation. With Bernard Baruch, Tugwell, Owen D. Young, George N. Peek and assorted friends gracing his head table, Johnson performed admirably as he ripped into the alliance "between the great Louisiana demagogue and this political padre":

> You can laugh at Huey Long — you can snort at Father Coughlin . . . but this country was never under a greater menace . . . stripped to the facts — and whether consciously or not — these two men are raging up and down the land preaching not construction but destruction — not reform but revolution — not peace but a sword. I think we are dealing with a couple of Catilines, and that it is high time for somebody to say so.[24]

The Kingfish stormed back at Johnson in the Senate and on the radio. Father Coughlin lashed at "the General of generalities . . . a chocolate soldier . . . the sweet prince of bombast. . . ." After casting aspersions about Johnson's personal habits and maligning Bernard Baruch, Coughlin still proclaimed his hopes in FDR. In a strange sequel to this incident, which must have exasperated Johnson, FDR found himself lunching with Father Coughlin at Hyde Park on September 8, 1935 along with Joseph P. Kennedy, who had brought Coughlin to see the President in an attempt at reconciliation. The luncheon was interrupted by the news that Long had been shot down in the statehouse at Baton Rouge by a young doctor whose father-in-law was a disappointed office seeker. Long died on September 10, a few days after his forty-second birthday. A year later Coughlin was calling Roosevelt a "Communist in the White House" as his own third party crashed to defeat, removing him from public life.

Johnson had one more service to render FDR after the scourging of Long and Coughlin. Quite unexpectedly he was announced in July 1935 as the WPA Administrator for New York City, destined to receive a substantial share of Harry Hopkins' $4 billion work relief fund. The General was less than enthusiastic about his non-salaried position. "The President said he wanted me to take the job . . . I'm a soldier and I do what I'm told to do . . . It feels like hell!" His fellow newspapermen speculated as to why he took it. Johnson felt he belonged in the President's Cabinet, they reasoned, and one good turn might generate another.

There was no call from FDR, however, and so he settled down to his *Hugh Johnson Says* column which he had been writing the past year for the *World Telegram* and thirty other papers. Satisfying his public image as a sulphurous, tough old cavalry officer with a curiously overblown style of literary invective, Johnson met his deadlines until his own obituary was recorded in 1942. For several years he had been one of the most outspoken critics of the post-Johnson New Deal and even took credit for helping launch the Willkie candidacy in 1940. In that campaign he warned his readers that Roosevelt's reelection would mean "the last of democracy as we have known it," and condemned FDR for leading the United States along the path to war. Hugh Johnson ended up a Rink-Stink after all, bitter and foresworn of his one-time hero in the White

House. There is no record of FDR striking back at the misplaced soldier-businessman who had done so well and so poorly in the cause of business recovery. One hopes that in spite of the rift, Hugh Johnson treasured to the end the sentiments of his "Dear Hugh" letter from FDR of September 25, 1934: "I repeat what I have often said to you — that I am happy not only in our friendship and your loyalty, but that in a time of great stress and fear your courage, enthusiasm and energy were a very potent factor in restarting a stalled machine."

Footnotes

[1] Hugh S. Johnson, *The Blue Eagle from Egg to Earth* (New York, 1935), p. 133.

[2] *Ibid.*, p. 405.

[3] *Ibid.*, p. 47.

[4] *Ibid.*, p. 107.

[5] Broadus Mitchell, *Depression Decade: From New Era Through New Deal, 1921-1941* (New York, 1947), p. 231.

[6] William E. Leuchtenberg, *Franklin Roosevelt and the New Deal* (New York, 1963), p. 37.

[7] New York *Times*, April 28, 1933.

[8] Johnson, *op. cit.*, p. 193.

[9] Raymond Moley, *The First New Deal* (New York, 1966), p. 338.

[10] James P. Warburg, *The Long Road Home: The Autobiography of a Maverick* (New York, 1964), p. 125.

[11] Sidney Fine, "The Ford Motor Company and the NRA," *Business History Review*, XXVII (1958), p. 362.

[12] *Literary Digest*, February 3, 1934, p. 38.

[13] *Fortune*, "The Business of Burlesque A.D. 1935," February 1935.

[14] Jonathan Mitchell, "The Versatility of General Johnson," *Harper's*, October 1934, p. 593.

[15] Leon Henderson to the author, 1966; also Arthur M. Schlesinger, Jr., *The Politics of Upheaval* (Boston, 1960), pp. 388-389.

[16] Irving S. Michelman, *Business at Bay* (New York, 1969), p. 262.

[17] George Wolfskill and John A. Hudson, *All but the People: Franklin D. Roosevelt and His Critics, 1933-1939* (New York, 1969), pp. 98-99.

[18] Rinehart J. Swenson, "The Chamber of Commerce and the New Deal," *Annals of the American Academy of Political and Social Sciences*, May, 1935, p. 136.

[19] New York *Times*, September 26, 1935; November 26, 1935.

[20] Schlesinger, *op. cit.*, p. 273.

[21] Cabell Phillips, *From the Crash to the Blitz 1929-1939* (New York, 1969), p. 230.

[22] *Ibid.*, p. 492.

[23] Arthur M. Schlesinger, Jr., *The Coming of the New Deal* (Boston, 1959), pp. 174-175.

[24] *Newsweek*, March 10, 1935, pp. 5-7.

Chapter 5

The Pangs of Labor

"Give 'em everything," the exasperated, senile seventy-eight year old Henry Ford instructed his major-domo, a sinister, near-thug named Harry Bennett, in June 1941.

The United Auto Workers, coached and subsidized by the phenomenally successful CIO, were on the brink of their final victory. General Motors and Chrysler had been captured early in 1937 after the sit-down strikes but Ford had outwitted and outgouged the tough, young UAW for five violent years.

Until now Bennett and old Henry could muse upon the former's career as union-buster with satisfaction as they target-practiced in Bennett's basement office or out on the range, away from Edsel, the nominal company president who advocated recognition. ("Who is this man who has so much control over my husband and is ruining my son's health?" Clara Ford asked tearfully.)[1]

Bennett was indeed a man of parts, more likely to be found in a Renaissance palace than in modern Detroit. Yet a Machiavelli was possible enough in a corporation with a tyrant at the top, especially a tyrant with one foot firmly planted in a previous century. Pint-sized, bow-tied and baby-faced, Bennett was endowed with a gangster's shrewd intelligence. He was a natural for a role by Jimmy Cagney. After joining the Navy at age seventeen, he boxed with the best in the fleet and then hired out as a "security" man for Ford in 1916. His frustrated ego resulted in a book in 1951 entitled *We Never Called Him Henry*, a choice which perfectly caught the cynicism and contempt of the author, even for his benefactor. "The reason I stayed with Mr. Ford for thirty years," he wrote, "is because I always did what he wanted me to." The many who admired and pitied Edsel, locked in tragic embrace with Henry, must have winced at Bennett's crow of triumph: "During the thirty years I worked for Henry Ford I became his most intimate companion, closer to him even than his only son."

As might be expected, Ford Motor Company in the thirties was down at the heels compared with its great days of industry leadership and the inspired doubling of wages to $5 a day in 1914. Wages in 1937 lagged behind those of GM and Chrysler. Most notorious conditions of all were the frantic "speed-up" on the assembly line and the degrading police-state surveillance of workers for disloyalty, both enforced by Bennett's 3,000 man Service Department. The company was leaderless and its employees racked by fear and insecurity, above and beyond such a condition inherent in the depression itself. Even the friendliest of critics assign Ford low marks for its record in the thirties, generally relating its decline to the Byzantine policies and paranoia of its one-man owner. Ernest Breech, who later was called in by Henry Ford II to help save the company, recalls regarding Ford with "contempt and pity" from his competitive position at General Motors.[2] There were some redeeming factors. The plants were spotless, well-lighted and ventilated. There was a core of great engineers and technicians who kept going regardless of the confusion at headquarters. Negroes were fairly generously hired (although some said only to be exploited in the worst jobs or used as strike breakers) and ex-convicts and the handicapped were greatly helped. Employee benefits were hardly the topic of the day when bankruptcy faced most manufacturers and workers were desperate for any kind of job at all. Still Ford hired, fired and promoted without regard to seniority. It was adept at other specialties, such as laying off high-wage men at the model change shutdown period and then rehiring them at beginners' rates all over again. This particular practice evoked a touch of character, or at least of candor, in Harry Bennett. "If I had been one of the men in the shop," he wrote, "and this had been done to me, I'd have been in sympathy with the union myself."

But Bennett was not one of the men in the shop. In the wake of the GM victory and the validation of the Wagner Act by the Supreme Court in April 1937, Henry bluntly notified Edsel and Charles Sorensen, his production boss, to keep out of union matters. These would now be the complete responsibility of his trusted ally. Bennett responded with all the pugnacity of his flawed temperament, managing to stall off the UAW, the National Labor Relations Board and the course of history itself until receiving his reversal of orders in June 1941.

The swaggering little tough, who always carried a gun and kept lions and tigers for pets, had a score to settle with agitators. When the "hunger marchers" staged their demonstrations in 1932, the Ford plant at Dearborn was a well-publicized objective. Bennett met them at the gates as head of plant security. Egged on by Communist leaders as well as hunger pangs, the crowd shouted "We want Bennett." Bennett thereupon announced himself and was greeted by a rain of slag. Falling to the ground, he dragged down and grappled with Joe York, a nineteen-year old Young Communist League organizer. York was instantly shot to death by the police and Bennett was saved after being knocked unconscious by the mob. With this kind of basic training, Bennett grimly held up his end of the war for Ford Motor Company. There was, for example, the Battle of the Overpass at the Rouge plant on May 26, 1937, when young Walter Reuther and Richard Frankensteen, UAW organizers, passed out handbills at the gates and were mercilessly kicked, beaten and stomped upon by a collection of Bennett's boxing and wrestling goons, all duly recorded by photographers and denied by Ford spokesmen. It was as though the Wagner Act and NLRB never existed, although of course the UAW finally brought Ford to surrender through these new instruments of government.

Meanwhile, having won the day at the Rouge plant in Dearborn, Bennett engineered bloody reprisals against union organizers at Ford plants in Dallas and Kansas City, running up a list of Wagner Act and civil rights violations that no company lawyer could hope to defend successfully. Finally, as the government cases ground out against Ford and court appeals were upheld against him, the stubborn old man began to face the inevitable. Now World War II was in the air. War orders were already being withheld from a company which refused to deal with unions. Henry Ford was personally unpopular for his isolationism and the company's sales position had slipped substantially. Some damaging NLRB hearings were scheduled to take place. Most important of all, manpower shortages had taken the fear out of Ford employees and they were ripe for organizing. The UAW had terminated most of its bitter internal fights for power, which Bennett had adroitly encouraged, even to the point of personally corrupting the hapless Homer Martin, UAW president for most of the thirties. A strike in April 1941 resulted in an epic agreement whereby Ford for the first time agreed to allow an NRLB vote on union recognition. Edsel had summoned a final reserve of courage to force Henry to this position, two years before his own death.

When the employees voted almost unanimously for union affiliation, Henry was crushed. According to Sorensen, it was "the greatest disappointment he had in all his business experience." Bennett then spent twelve days giving the UAW everything it wanted, including an unprecedented dues check-off and the closed shop, obligating all new employees to join the UAW. When the contract was shown to Henry for approval, he made a last show of protest. "Shut the plant . . . let the union take over," he shouted at Sorensen and Edsel on June 19, 1941 and stalked out.

Still on June 20, a smiling Harry Bennett signed the contract in Washington with Philip Murray, the CIO president (John L. Lewis had resigned over FDR's defeat of Willkie), and R. J.

Thomas, UAW president. What had happened is revealed in Sorensen's *My Forty Years With Ford*, published in 1956. It is one of those engaging commentaries that reduce history for a moment to human terms. After leaving Sorensen and Edsel, Ford went home and told Clara, who thereupon told him she was leaving him. "What could I do?" Ford asked Sorensen. "I'm sure now she was right . . . I'm glad I did see it her way. Don't discredit the power of a woman."[3]

What happened to Bennett? Henry Ford II, Edsel's son, was relieved of Navy duty in 1943 to help run the great plant. In 1945, with an assist from Clara Ford and Mrs. Edsel Ford, who threatened to sell her stock, he convinced his grandfather to step aside and make him president. This happened on September 21, 1945 and within a month Bennett, who had carried in his pocket an unsigned codicil to Henry's will naming him a trustee for Henry's stock for a ten-year period, was out.

II

Most of the interesting writing about trade unions takes us back to the great birth-time of the CIO industrial unions in the thirties. Today's union affairs seem boring and domesticated compared with the heroic clashes of forty years ago. Contemporary union leaders are considered non-relevant by youth, for example, for whom one Ralph Nader is worth a dozen Meanys or Woodcocks. Hardhats are suddenly old hat, on the wrong side of Vietnam, civil rights, the SST and long hair. Union leaders, except for the convicted Jimmy Hoffa and some brawlers in the United Mine Workers, are viewed by the young as sedate, and, for the most part, old. The ultimate irony is the sight of union presidents more distinguished and conservative looking than their counterparts in industry. They are political vacuums, without ideology, the sociologists tell us. They cause "cost-push" inflation, some economists tell us, mindlessly coming up for their rounds of wage increases by conditioned reflex. In between they make news by running off with the union funds or granting questionable loans to Las Vegas hotelmen. There seem to be no replacements for the great labor reporters like Louis Stark and

A. H. Raskin of the *New York Times*, or Howard Brubaker of the *New Yorker Magazine*. For that matter, neither the *New Yorker* nor *Fortune* devote anywhere near the space to labor matters they did in the thirties and forties. A successful musical comedy like *Pins and Needles*, coming out of the International Ladies Garment Workers Union, and full of topical humor about the split between John L. Lewis and William Green, is inconceivable today. Yet with the bouncy union ladies themselves, along with cloakmakers and truck drivers from the shops, actually playing the parts, *Pins and Needles* was a hit for three years. There was a command performance for the Roosevelts at the White House in 1938. Altogether the show grossed $1,500,000 in hard, depression dollars. Its dramatic counterpart a few years earlier was Clifford Odets's *Waiting for Lefty*. Lefty, chairman of a taxi-drivers' strike committee, never shows up in this virulently class-conscious drama, as he has been killed, presumably by the bosses. The play was a solid Broadway success. The bosses in their orchestra seats must have shared a tingling awareness that the taxi boss, whoever he might be, was probably called "Righty," as they watched the play end with the chant: "STRIKE, STRIKE, STRIKE!!"

III

The bosses are important in the history of this period because in most of the great showdown cases, company presidents personally marshalled their forces and called the plays. Today as a result of the Wagner Act and the establishment of corporation industrial relations departments, these men would be pretty much kept offstage. If we examine their attitudes and decisions in the light of their beliefs and the great social changes swirling about them, we can broaden our understanding of one of the stormy passages of modern capitalism. But first a review of the significance of labor's victory is in order.

The fact is that the successful accommodation of labor in the thirties was a great and narrow escape for capitalism. In retrospect, the time for labor to emerge as a major institution in American society, in many ways equally powerful to employers, had arrived and was not to be temporarily held back as it was immediately following World War I. First of all, there was the festering sore of the great depression, now recognized as being tolerated only once for modern capitalist democracies. Capitalism simply was not working when thirteen million were unemployed in a population of 125 million. Psychically, if for no other reason, the working class — or the unworking class as veterans of the depression would remember themselves — had to be given some inner satisfaction to make up for the dreadful breakdown of the system. The right to vote Hoover out and FDR in was not enough reward in this respect. Neither was the painfully slow resumption of employment throughout the pre-World War II period. One should not expect that this inner need was appreciated by corporation presidents faced with sit-down strikes and other assaults on their plants organized on an industry-wide basis. Nor for that matter were FDR and the New Dealers themselves particularly interested in psychic income for the employees of big business. Actually FDR found the labor wars a constant threat to his first priority of restoring employment. It may be only the kind of armchair deduction that historians make years later — yet today it seems highly credible that the by-product of labor's successful bid for union recognition, namely increased status and self-respect, was a major victory for capitalism. Lloyd K. Garrison, first Chairman of the National Labor Relations Board under Public Resolution No. 44, preceding the Wagner Act, recognized this function while engaged in the pragmatic repair work that makes such later theorizing possible. In testifying for the formalization of the NRLB under the proposed Wagner Act in 1935, he stated: "I am for it as a safety measure, because I regard organized labor in this country as our chief bulwark against Communism and other revolutionary movements."[4]

A second factor to bear in mind in this overview of the rise of labor is to note it as an inevitable response to the march of technology. The significant factor in America's economic landscape has been the emergence of mass production involving hundreds of thousands of employees on assembly belt lines. Not everyone was destined to work in the big factories. In fact some of the gloomier predictions of the economists of technology such as Thorstein Veblen and philosophers such as Charlie Chaplin (in his film *Modern Times)* have been softened by the recent statistics showing over half of all employees are now in service businesses and occupations. But the giant plant blossomed here as nowhere else, bringing with it all sorts of little murders known as the speed-up, the stretch-out, the kick-out, favoritism, industrial hazards, unskilled occupations, thought control, alienation, anonymity, insecurity and the like, all depending for their amelioration on bosses who in turn were at the mercy of the competitive system. John L. Lewis recognized the obsolescence of the old AFL system of unions based on crafts in the face of this development and so he huffed out of the AFL with his CIO. To be effective, the new unions in the mass production industries had to recruit members straight across the face of the industry, skilled or unskilled, in so-called industrial unions. That way they would have the power to deal with the mass employers. In a sense, big business created the condition which made big unions possible, or if one is more comfortable with an abstract agent, technology was to blame. The results, of course, were on the whole beneficial. Politically, for example, we have come to accept the idea of big labor being a "countervailing force," in J. K. Galbraith's terms, offsetting the power of big government or of big business, again easing capitalism into the twentieth century.

A third factor to reckon with is that the power of organized labor had a tremendous affect on purchasing power. The continual pressure for more wages and benefits created a vast change in the proportion of families with "middle class" purchasing power, able to buy the autos and refrigerators pouring off the assembly lines. Most economists now agree that in the twenties we did not spend ourselves into a depression. In fact a case can be made that we saved profligately, and thus underconsumed. Of course, the trouble was that income was so poorly distributed, both regionally and by occupation, we were unable to match our productive capacity. Again employers of the thirties would probably react to such a claim on behalf of unions with a beady eye. They weren't trying to pay the

The Archives of Labor History and Urban Affairs, Wayne State University

The young men who took on General Motors and won union recognition. Strike leaders arraigned before Judge Edward D. Mallory are (from left) Victor Reuther, Robert Travis, Roy Reuther, Maurice Sugar, Henry Kraus, on January 16, 1937. Walter Reuther was also a key strike leader.

Wide World Photos

South Chicago, Illinois, May 30, 1937, near Republic Steel plant. Ten strike demonstrators were killed and forty wounded by bullets.

Wide World Photos

A meeting of titans. Myron C. Taylor, former board chairman of U.S. Steel and John L. Lewis, former CIO chief, shake hands in 1941. Together they had ended the steel strike in 1937.

Underwood & Underwood

Gerard Swope. He won the confidence of both capital and labor. An ardent New Deal supporter, he negotiates a strike settlement on behalf of the NRA in 1933. From left, George Berry, Pressmen's Union president, Swope, Louis Kirstein and Thomas Moses, president of Frick Coal Company.

Wide World Photos

Dalton Trumbo and John Howard Lawson, two of the Hollywood Ten, leave Pennsylvania Station in New York City to start one-year prison terms for contempt of Congress. June 9, 1950.

Dore Schary. The Hollywood producer-executive was critized by both the left and right during the HUAC hearings. He is shown here in 1956 on MGM's *Teahouse of the August Moon* set with Adlai Stevenson and Marlon Brando.

John Henry Faulk. The blacklisted TV performer whose libel suit broke the back of this tactic. At the Algonquin Hotel, New York City, during the trial with Louis Nizer, his attorney. June, 1962.

Robert S. McNamara. The Ford President turned Defense Secretary who had second thoughts about the arms race and Vietnam. August 5, 1964.

lowest wages. Henry Ford had shown the way about purchasing power in 1914, minimum wages and hours legislation were on the whole acceptable and excessive wages would be dissipated in inflation and the loss of export markets. In fact, the wage demands of the new union contracts in the thirties were generally very reasonable and usually passed right on by management in the form of price increases. The strikes were essentially for union recognition, the one thing big business wanted to withhold.

On the subject of purchasing power, incidentally, it is often thought that when Congress passed the Full Employment Act of 1946, with its mandate for the forces of government to encourage and promote full employment, purchasing power made its first appearance as a government ward in legislation. Senator Wagner in his second and successful try at passing the Act bearing his name (1935) took pains to mention purchasing power as a specific aim of the Act in Section 1, its declaration of policy. A redistribution of income through the establishment of collective bargaining would raise those at the bottom and remove inequities in the wage structure, the declaration stated. This would benefit society as a whole by creating mass purchasing power to even out the business cycle. This concept, later heavily identified with J. M. Keynes, was a novel one. Purchasing power was not particularly accepted by academic economists as having any pump-priming power in the workings of the economy at this time. Historically, of course, the wage demands of unions, along with advertising and consumer credit, did become a tremendous factor in sustaining the record period of prosperity after World War II. This was particularly so when management was able to increase productivity, or output per man hour, through more machine efficiency, and thus hold prices to a reasonable level. When that condition stopped, the unions found themselves in their present dilemma as a primary engine of inflation.

A fourth general result of the triumph of labor was the new relationship it established with the federal government. Viewed in a broad perspective, the essentially pro-labor stance of the New Deal Administration actually dealt a body blow to the American Communist movement, at least for those who had done their homework on Marx. A basic tenet of Marxism is that the state under capitalism must turn out to be the instrument of the ruling class, exploiting the workers on behalf of this class. Yet here was a government trading off the sponsorship of collective bargaining as the price for a business-programmed NRA, then passing the Wagner Act with its NLRB agency authorized to police and judge industry on labor's behalf. Add to this the La Follette Committee, admirable though it was in investigating unfair employer practices, almost shamefacedly serving as an agency of the CIO's organizing campaigns,[5] and the domestic Communists must have been perplexed. Still one should not underestimate the ability of the Communists to swallow pills of policy changes on a moment's notice nor should one expect the employers of the thirties to subscribe readily to our vision of forty years later. The Communists after all were a major factor in the labor wars of the thirties and cannot lightly be dismissed.

It is amusing, however, to note how seriously and openly the Communists expounded their theory at the Senate hearings in 1934 on the Wagner Act. In this pre-Cold War period, a time when all ideas seemed to be welcomed in the marketplace, Senator David I. Walsh of Massachusetts, chairman of the Senate Labor Committee, cordially invited them to express their views on the bill. The Communist-dominated Trade Union Unity League gravely took the stand and joined in the opposition so vigorously advanced by the National Association of Manufacturers. The bill presupposed an impossible identity of interest between government and the working class, the TUUL spokesman maintained. In capitalist America, government intervention in labor relations could only be for the purpose of oppressing the workers and preventing their right to strike. The bill's real objective, he maintained, was to save capitalism, depress labor standards and promote company-sponsored unions. The speaker did not discuss the absence of genuine unions in Communist countries.[6]

On a more serious level, the New Deal legislation placed government firmly in the business of promoting unions and more particularly of sponsoring the right of unions to force elections on collective bargaining upon employers. This was a fundamental shift from a prior history, involving all three branches of the government, which at best assumed that although unions were legal, the contest between business and labor was an essentially private matter. In a situation somewhat analogous to the rights of Negroes before the Civil Rights Act of 1957, the rights of unions were available but only to the extent that employers would grant them, by fair means or foul.

When one tries to empathize with business leaders who found adjustment to the new social forces a traumatic experience, it may be helpful to note that many liberals as well as conservatives were caught off balance by the new position of the state. For years, the American Civil Liberties Union had seen the state, particularly the federal government and often its Supreme Court, as the source of deprivation of civil rights and liberties. The suspensions of freedoms in World War I and the aberrations of Attorney General A. Mitchell Palmer and his "Red Scare" after the war come to mind. For this reason, many ACLU leaders felt it was desirable to resist any increases in power for the Leviathan in Washington. Some nervously objected to FDR's early New Deal legislation and Roger Baldwin, the ACLU leader, opposed the Wagner Act for a brief moment on the eve of its passage.[7] In short order, however, the ACLU recognized that civil liberties were now likely to flow from Washington as a prime source and it made a quick about-face. Meanwhile it had jumped into the labor movement with an alacrity that annoyed the business world. An example of the ACLU's lingering fear of the state, however, occurred over a Ford-NLRB altercation in 1937-1938 when, to its credit, the ACLU defended the distribution of Henry Ford's anti-union "Fordism" messages on the grounds of free speech. Even the traditional leadership of the AFL, such as its mossback vice-president Matthew Woll, had looked askance at federal bounties such as wages and hours legislation and unemployment insurance when first advanced, fearful of a state bearing gifts. The business leaders were not alone in their discomfort over the new role of the federal government.

Thus the rise of labor in the thirties reflected an irresistible need of disillusioned American laborers to have their status recognized as equals at the bargaining table. Technology itself had framed the shape of the new industrial unions that would accelerate the attainment of this status for employees in mass production. An unexpected by-product would be unprecedented prosperity for capital as well as labor through increased purchasing power. Finally American capitalism confounded the dire forebodings of Marxian theory when the federal government, somewhat haphazardly, committed itself positively to the cause of unionism and indirectly to the civil liberties movement.

IV

The characters in the labor war were king-size. On the business side, however, Henry Ford is only of passing interest. True enough, Ford will always make any list of America's ten greatest businessmen, or three greatest, for that matter, but Ford on labor is not very enlightening. When the issue came to a head, he was already an unbalanced man, burdened with manias of persecution and conspiracy. A poorly educated person, to whom history was "bunk," Ford placed the blame for his rejection as peace envoy in World War I, his defeat as Senatorial candidate in Michigan and his humiliation as an anti-Semite on the unions and bankers, to name a few of his special enemies. He did have a philosophy of sorts about unions — what could the union do for his employees that they could not do for themselves? But Ford was already a legend, even to himself, in the thirties, unable to hear his employees' response. He was the genius who had put America on wheels and had become one of the richest men in the world in the process, assuming Ford Motor Company was not actually bankrupt at the time, as Ernest Breech and Robert McNamara had reason later to believe. Besides, Ford's attitude towards unions was not shared by the Company president, Edsel. Indeed, Henry Ford on the couch might have admitted he was against unions because Edsel was for them. All in all, he is not a satisfactory witness for the conflict.

Instead a selected group of company heads with the saving qualities of intellect and ambivalence — the facility to see a bit of the other side of the question — are more rewarding. They are all from the ranks of big business, where the confrontation took place. Even today only about twenty per cent of America's employees actually belong to unions. As industrial unions go, however, so go wages, prices and employee benefits in general. Big business and its unions undoubtedly set the style and tone of the American economy. American capitalism is basically defined in terms of its mass production enterprises.

Our candidates are Ernest T. Weir of National Steel, Gerard Swope of General Electric, Myron C. Taylor of U.S. Steel and Tom M. Girdler of Republic Steel. Weir brought the NRA and its Labor Board to defeat in an early show of defiance. Swope was an FDR supporter who practically delivered GE to the United Electrical Workers on a silver platter. Taylor, a born diplomat, made the momentous decision to give John L. Lewis the crown of Big Steel. Girdler, least attractive of the four, then fought a bloody rear-guard action for Little Steel in a last-ditch defense of his threadbare beliefs.

In the background, of course, was a presence, FDR, his great self-confidence and sense of proportion allowing him to intercede ever so reasonably as the drama unfolded. FDR was a man who could take the measure of labor leaders and business leaders in equal stride. His record during the turbulent years of labor unrest show FDR at his best.

Yet it is not FDR against whom these four horsemen of industry should be measured as much as the labor leaders themselves, men whose destiny surfaced with the charter to labor given by the New Deal. The new breed of labor chieftain was as tough, capable, fanatic and self-disciplined as the best in the corporations. He was the equal of any good capitalist entrepreneur, capable of multi-million dollar organizing budgets, grandiose membership goals and general staff decisions based on the opposition's weaknesses, supply lines, balance sheets, public opinion exposure and similar strategies that would have made old Samuel Gompers flinch in disbelief. Such men were John L. Lewis and Walter Reuther.

Lewis, who died in 1969 at age eighty-nine, was easily the most colorful and important man in American labor history. Yet his great deeds were practically all accomplished in a stunning performance between 1933 and 1937. Section 7a of the NRA bill, originally Lewis's idea, committing the government to intervention on behalf of collective bargaining, had been accepted by FDR, his advisers and the Congress of the Hundred Days as a bid for labor's support in the great business and government partnership of the NRA. The fire of the magic section burned in the middle-aged Lewis's brain as he recognized its possibilities. If ever a man grabbed his second chance in life, it was this descendant of Welshmen who himself had been in the coal mines as a youth. He too had feared the embrace of the state and had voted for Hoover in 1932 as he presided over the remnants of his tattered and depleted United Mine Workers. Now Lewis saw the government as labor's patron and realized the time had come to lead the AFL into a new career of industrial unions, such as UMW already was, among the other basic mass production industries.

First he had to revive his UMW, down to 100,000 from a former membership of 500,000 in the twenties. "The President wants you to join the union!" the UMW organizers clamored to new prospects and union dropouts. If pressed, they acknowledged they meant John L. Lewis and not FDR but in the very month the NRA was passed, June 1933, over 128,000 members signed up in Pennsylvania alone under Lewis's inspired direction. Next he took on the captive mines owned by the steel companies. Steel had been a stronghold of anti-unionism ever since U.S. Steel crushed its strikers in 1919 by starving out the dissidents to its twelve-hour day. Only a small percentage of coal came from these mines but a great principle was at stake. In a warmup for the later battle with steel itself, the UMW challenged men like Taylor, Weir and Girdler for their coal mines. "President Roosevelt is not a UMW organizer," growled the managers of U.S. Steel's Frick mines as they offered instead one of the new company unions guaranteed to outwit Section 7a by the industry's best lawyers. Where such maneuvering failed, company guards shot at "rioters," causing several deaths. Carefully exploiting Roosevelt and the NRA's Hugh Johnson, who feared their recovery plans would be smashed by an extended strike, Lewis pulled out 100,000 captive miners until he received sufficient union recognition for the times in January 1934. UMW membership soared to 400,000 once again with practically every employed miner a member.

This was just a sample of Lewis's momentum. In a brief period, he had built the UMW into the nation's largest union and now he had a power base from which to challenge the conservative leadership of the parent AFL. Drawing men like Sidney Hillman and others sympathetic to industrial unions to his side, Lewis challenged the AFL leadership to cut him loose for organization in other industries at the famous Atlantic City convention in October 1935.

By now the NRA was dead but its labor charter lived on stronger than ever in the Wagner Act. Over the years Lewis had supplemented his seventh grade education by reading deeply in the classics. Part of the enjoyment of reviewing labor history is to come across the oft-quoted light and shade, bombast and lament with which this great force of a man impaled his enemies or announced his dreams. Yet in between lines, he was truculent, vengeful, spoiled, a very complex person. At this convention his many sides came into play. "Heed this cry from Macedonia that comes from the hearts of men. Organize the unorganized and in doing this make the American Federation of Labor the greatest instrument that has ever been forged in the history of modern civilization to befriend the cause of humanity." But the old sultans of the AFL would have none of that and led the convention into defeating Lewis by a vote endorsing the craft position once again. Towards the end of the convention, Big Bill Hutcheson, who presumably was big with such a nickname, put Lewis down a peg as they argued in the aisles, whereupon the six-foot, 225-pound Lewis socked him squarely in the face and knocked him to the ground. "He called me a foul name," Lewis explained to President Green on the platform. The next morning Lewis and his followers established the CIO, to work within the AFL for the time being on behalf of industrial unions. It was an ominous day for corporate management in steel, autos, textiles, rubber, glass and other big industries. The CIO was able to commit millions of dollars to organizing drives, to be paid back to the UMW from the dues of the new members. Where money was less important, manpower and brain power were contributed. Lewis soon moved onto the national stage, his UMW contributing a half-million dollars to FDR's Presidential campaign of 1936. FDR, who would not be allowed to accept such a gift under today's Taft-Hartley law, never trusted Lewis, who left him for Willkie in 1940, after requesting the Democratic Vice Presidency for himself. The old lion of labor kept in the news by baiting both FDR and Truman with wartime coal strikes. He retired in 1960, acknowledged as a labor statesman by some of his ancient corporate enemies, who gave him a bound set of Shakespeare, possibly in memoriam of his poetic insults against them, at a pleasant farewell banquet. Although Lewis brought CIO membership to approximately four million as the thirties closed, his monument in the UMW today is a faction-ridden union of 150,000 members, its ranks depleted by labor-saving machinery and other awesome social changes that have affected coal-mining regions. Still, 67,000 pensioners now live on UMW funds.

While industrialists watched John L. Lewis with mingled horror and admiration, quite a different personality was cutting his teeth in the labor wars of the auto industry. Walter Reuther, who died in an airplane crash in 1970 at age 63, headed a modern UAW with 1.6 million members. As president of the CIO, he had led the CIO back to the arms of the AFL in 1955. He then took the UAW out of the AFL-CIO in 1968 to stand alone. Ostensibly the AFL was still too conservative for Reuther who, nurtured on working class Socialism, kept a purer liberal faith than Lewis ever cared to follow.

The striking thing about the labor leaders who toppled General Motors for the UAW-CIO in early 1937 is their extreme youth. When the competing, fragmentary auto unions finally banded together in the summer of 1936 under the UAW-CIO banner, representing only 30,000 members in the entire fear-ridden industry, the majority of their officers and executive board members, including president Homer Martin, were under thirty-five. Walter Reuther, representing a Detroit local, was twenty-nine. Yet he and his two younger brothers, Roy and Victor, were soon to be in the thick of the GM sit-down strike, which many labor historians feel was the most significant labor conflict in the twentieth century. The photos of Walter Reuther of that time show a young redhead something like the boy next door. He is a world away from the sixty-one year old bony-faced, dapper, spatted Alfred P. Sloan, Jr., who was the arch-critic of FDR and the New Deal, even though GM was enjoying a great year in 1936, sales having tripled from 1932 to 1.4 billion and net profits after taxes being twenty-seven times greater at $240 million. More incredible is the photo of Roy and Victor posting bond upon their arrest in Flint, Michigan on January 16, 1937 at the height of the strike. Their hair brushed back, ties neat, vests and watch chains showing, they and Robert Travis, the twenty-seven year old strike boss, smile with becoming embarrassment. Such youthful presumption rankled GM executives far below the remote Sloan. When Travis and Roy Reuther visited Arnold Lenz, manager of the Flint Chevrolet plant in November 1936 to complain about illegal discrimination against union members, Lenz gave them a dressing down. He knew from GM's elaborate spy system that the Flint locals were pitifully weak. GM had just increased wages and announced a year-end bonus, Lenz reminded them, and he would fire any worker wearing a union button in his plant. Scolding his young adversaries for having "a lot of piss and vinegar in their blood," he recalled that in his native Germany union workers in the foundry where he worked had burned his legs with hot metal because he refused to join their organization.[8] No doubt Lenz would have given a thousand to one odds that these young men would not capture GM within three months for the UAW, let alone actually steal a Chevrolet plant from behind his back, but then anything could happen on the labor front in the thirties.

V

The Reuther brothers were also by-products of German trade unionism. Valentine Reuther, their father, was a German immigrant who was an ardent Socialist and trade unionist. He became an organizer for the United Brewery Workers and then president of the Ohio Valley Trades and Labor Assembly. The boys, literally born into the labor movement, received from their father a tradition of hard work, respect for craftsmanship and the concept of the union as an instrument for social action. The dinner table at the Reuther household was an intellectual forum where each of the boys developed a gift for oratory. Eugene Debs, a labor leader who went to jail for his principles, was an icon in this household. Walter led the way from the family house in Wheeling, West Virginia to Detroit where he became a skilled tool and die maker for Ford and took courses in economics at Wayne University at night. The sober young man spent his vacation in 1932 campaigning for Norman Thomas in the true spirit of his family inheritance. Covering his car with Thomas stickers was inappropriate for a Ford employee and he was fired. With characteristic foresight he then drew out all his money from a Detroit bank just before it closed. There was enough to pay for the passage of Victor and himself to Europe and off they sailed. First they said goodbye to Roy Reuther, busy manning his duties in the Briggs plant strike kitchen. While his brothers were at sea, Roy and other pickets were pushed against an iron fence. Roy thus acquired an ankle scar for life, an omen of the physical wounds all three would suffer in their careers.

After bicycling through England, Walter and Victor visited the family home in Germany. There they witnessed the grinding heels of the Nazi stormtroopers as people like their father were arrested. Young and curious, they went on to Russia, the enigmatic home of the workers' revolution, which FDR had recently recognized, largely in the interests of export markets for America's struggling capitalists. Walter Reuther worked sixteen months in the Ford *autostroy* at Gorki. Ironically this plant had been authorized by old Henry whose security men had fired Walter for socialism and whose grandson, Henry II, was prevented by the Administration from building a new joint-venture auto plant in Russia in 1971. At the Gorki plant, Reuther was an excellent Stakhanovite, leading enough speed-ups to win medals as a Hero of Production. He also wrote letters to the *Moscow Daily News* on how to improve industrial techniques. There were other Americans working in the Gorki plant. Henry Ford was high on Stalin's list of what was good in America. In the fall of 1931 over 100,000 applications for jobs in Russia were received by Amtorg, Russia's trade agency, in response to an ad for skilled workmen.[9]

Murray Kempton has a rather special observation to make as to why Walter Reuther did not succumb then and there to Communism: "At Gorki, Walter Reuther was a master workman and his Russian colleagues were apprentices beside him. He could hardly believe that a people with so much to learn about toolmaking had quite so much to teach him about social tactics."[10] It is more likely that Walter Reuther was simply too independent a man to wear the collar of the Communists and too strong a democrat to accept their dictatorship. He did work hand in glove with the Communists in the early UAW days as they were among the ablest and most militant union leaders. He was not, however, taken in by the myth that beguiled so many earnest young men, including Kempton himself for a brief period, in the thirties. In addition, he had a relentless ambition to achieve high office in unionism. Thus by 1938 he had dropped his socialism to campaign for Governor Murphy's reelection. The New Deal had shown him a middle way for the working class.

The brothers ended their global wanderings by way of China and the Pacific. Arriving in Detroit in late 1935, Walter got a GM job under an assumed name but soon was spending full time in UAW organization work. A review of the activities of the three Reuther brothers in the GM strike will point up the new type of leadership that would emerge in the UAW and CIO as John L. Lewis gradually left the stage.

VI

The UAW strategy was to strike the GM plant in Flint as the key to the GM empire. Flint's group included Chevrolet's massive operations, Buick's basic production facilities, the Fisher Body plants and the AC Spark Plug Division. On the other hand, Flint was a company city. with GM's 40,000 employees supplying 80 per cent of its total jobs. This offered the prospect of an unfriendly police force and the usual citizens' committee — in Flint's case it would be called the Citizens Alliance — which could summon all the forces of the Establishment, such as the newspaper, radio, merchants, most of the clergy, as well as employees demanding the "right to work" — on the side of GM in a showdown. From the union point of view, automatic response to such committees was to cry "vigilante" or "unfair labor practices." Still a management out to win could hardly be expected not to use all its resources. Ever since James H. Rand, Jr. cracked a strike in upstate New York in May 1936 with such strategy, known as the "Mohawk Valley Formula," its use was always considered. Fortunately in Flint the patient intercession of Governor Murphy, along with the steady hand in the White House, kept the Citizens Alliance from physical confrontation with the strikers.

The UAW wanted only one thing, recognition, the company having met the wage factor in anticipation of the strike. If it won at GM the entire auto industry would eventually succumb, bringing a vast number of new members into the UAW-CIO, as well as opening the door to industrial unionism in every other big industry. The UAW had no real desire to negotiate the issue, being convinced that a bold strike was the only way it could deal from its weak membership position, which in turn reflected the anti-union tactics of GM. Thus the union demanded *exclusive* recognition as the price for ending the strike, evading the issue of the NLRB elections until the last minute, not being sure that NLRB legislation would be held constitutional after all. GM, for its part, was acting on the hope that the Wagner Act would be invalidated by the Supreme Court. Fearful that the unions were radical and would assume intolerable power, GM was in no mood to make an offer of elections, which in retrospect it might very well have won at that point. Instead it held out for the unacceptable "proportional" representation, along the lines of a precedent established by a conciliatory FDR himself, in order to get the auto industry enrolled in an NRA code, back in the experimental days of 1934.

Now bolstered by FDR's landslide victory and the brilliant initial success of the CIO, the unruly young strike strategists, quite independent even of John L. Lewis, were spoiling for premature action. Only the payment of the Christmas bonus and inauguration of the new, liberal Governor, Frank Murphy, swept in on FDR's coattails, held back the UAW as the year ended. Meanwhile, the technique had been selected, one that would electrify the nation and paralyze GM — the sitdown strike.

Walter Reuther and Homer Martin had observed a brief sit-down strike work at Goodyear early in 1936. They had gone to Akron to help their brothers in the rubber union celebrate. The role of the CIO was critical in the Akron success, providing a dress rehearsal for the Flint engagement. About two months later, the first mass sit-down strikes in history took place in France. Americans wondered at the newsreel photos of auto workers waving defiance from the Renault and Citroen plants. The basic demand in France as in America was for union recognition. The French premier, Leon Blum, refused to use force to evict the illegal sit-down strikers, setting an example that the UAW strategists were sure Frank Murphy would follow. William Knudsen, the GM president, who was more interested in his machines than in the claims of either side, visited France in the summer of 1936 and was warned by French industrialists that it could happen in America. "No," he announced to the press, "that could not happen in the United States. The people would not stand for it."

By December, Walter Reuther had guided his Detroit Local 174 through a successful sit-down strike at the Kelsey-Hayes plant. This was his first claim to fame under fire. Ironically he owed a good deal of his success to the Ford Motor Company's absent-minded pressure on Kelsey-Hayes to settle quickly so that Ford's production wouldn't be unduly delayed. One might think, incidentally, that the Big Three automakers would seek strength in their own solidarity. Actually, in their fierce competitive spirit, they realized that what was bad for General Motors was good for their own sales. Ford ran its own world and had good reason to believe the union would not raise its head there for many years. Chrysler enjoyed the best labor relations among the three and kept its own counsel. (The unreal world of the sit-down strike is revealed in the memory of Augustus M. Kelley, the book publisher. When the sit-down hit Chrysler immediately after GM caved in, he was awakened by the midnight visit of Chrysler president K. T. Keller to the home of his father, Nicholas Kelley, Chrysler attorney. Keller explained to the frightened little boy: "Some nasty men have taken away our factory!")[11]

At any rate, by now the UAW had experience with all the logistics involved in a sit-down strike, for example, discipline and respect for property within the plant, food from the outside, thousands of organized pickets to keep the gates secure, a womens' marching auxiliary to shame the bosses and finally the songfests that gave the revivalist touch to the inspired labor movement of those days. Aware that the political climate was for a charmed moment on its side and assured by the La Follette Committee that soon the lid would be blown off on GM's elaborate payments for anti-union espionage (GM spent $839,764 for labor detective agencies alone between January 1934 and July 1936),[12] only a touch of what de Gaulle would call audacity was needed to tie up the giant manufacturer.

On December 30, 1936, two Fisher Body plants were occupied by about four hundred sit-downers who were to stay there for six weeks until the strike ended. Coordinated with a few other strategic strikes, including a key plant in Cleveland, the strike eventually idled 136,000 GM employees, costing the company 280,000 cars valued at $175 million. The Reuther boys each had an important role to play. In an episode involving a rush by Flint police to empty the smaller of the Fisher plants, occupied by only a hundred sit-downers, young Victor Reuther distinguished himself inside the union sound car by blaring music and an inexhaustible supply of encouragement for his colleagues in the plant and on the picket lines. A rain of debris was poured on the police as they shot at the plant windows and finally retreated. In labor parlance such battles achieve titles. This one is known as "The Battle of the Running Bulls." The police then had a higher farm pedigree than now in the pursuit of their often dismal duties. As a result of this battle,

Governor Murphy had to call in the National Guard, which, to his credit, he kept firmly under control.

For a touch of humor, however, a high-spirited maneuver of Roy Reuther and Robert Travis should be recounted. By now the conflict had risen into the hands of the first team. FDR, loath as he was to become personally involved, was negotiating behind the scenes with Secretary Perkins, Governor Murphy, Alfred P. Sloan, Jr. and John L. Lewis. Lewis had grandly assumed the position of UAW spokesman, having sent the unpredictable Homer Martin on a trip to keep him out of the way. In spite of these pressures, negotiations had broken down badly as January drew to a close. Meanwhile, GM had decided to force the issue by applying for a court injunction. If granted, it would put tremendous pressure on Governor Murphy to order evacuation of the Fisher Body plant. It was time for a spectacular countermeasure to put the union on the offensive once again.

Travis and Roy Reuther decided to capture still another plant, Arnold Lenz's Chevrolet No. 4, producer of a million engines a year and considered one of GM's most important units. If Fisher Body had to be evacuated, at least Chevrolet could still be knocked out, with its vital flow of engines. The strike leaders realized that a direct attack on Chevrolet 4 would be disastrous, considering its size and heavy concentration of guards and tear gas assigned by Lenz. The young conspirators called a meeting of about 150 Chevrolet stewards and foremen for the purpose of listening grievances to discuss with Lenz, whose plant was still working at considerable capacity. At this meeting, slips were handed to a selected thirty who were given the honor of being invited to a secret midnight meeting. Travis and Reuther took care to include a number of GM "stoolpigeons." At the meeting plans were detailed for the takeover of Chevrolet No. 9 the next day in the confusion of the shift change. Of course, the action was a decoy which Lenz swallowed. On February 1, some UAW stalwarts carried out their assignment in No. 9 by attempting to shut down the machines and engaging in a fight with non-strikers and Chevrolet policemen who had been mobilized for the occasion. Meanwhile, another UAW crew took over Chevrolet No. 4 during its brief unguarded period. Hundreds of outsiders then appeared at No. 4 from Detroit and Toledo, led by Walter Reuther, who barricaded the entrance with heavy objects moved into position by cranes and trucks with more or less military precision.

The sequel of the strike is well known. Governor Murphy, backed by FDR and Lawrence Fisher of Fisher Body, simply refused to follow the letter of the law at the expense of bloodshed. In doing so, he became a temporary national hero before sentiment turned against the unions for their continued sit-downs, which eventually were declared illegal by the Supreme Court in the *Fansteel Metallurgical Case* in 1939. Murphy was defeated for reelection in 1938 but became Attorney General and then a Supreme Court Justice.

Murphy's final task was to work on Lewis while the President worked on General Motors as the great conflict inched toward settlement on February 11, 1937. The ultimate details revolved on how long GM would give the UAW what amounted to exclusive bargaining rights — without benefit of an election — yet not actually calling the rights by that name. The term was settled at six months and the victory was UAW's, since *de facto* recognition as well as the absence of reprisals swept the workers into UAW membership in sufficient numbers to win elections after the Wagner Act was upheld the following April. As Lewis held out majestically, Murphy, by the best reports, is said to have announced in no uncertain terms that he would enforce the court injunction. They did meet with their formidable eyebrows to eyebrows, but Lewis's version, as contained in a speech to the 1940 UAW convention and in a friendly biography, is somewhat different. It is typical of the theatrics which must have driven Lewis's corporate adversaries to distraction as they reaped the whirlwind of the irresistible labor movement for which they were so poorly prepared:

> "You want my answer, sir? I give it to you. Tomorrow morning, I shall personally enter General Motors plant Chevrolet No. 4. I shall order the men to disregard your order, to stand fast. I shall then walk up to the largest window in the plant, open it, divest myself of my outer

> raiment, remove my shirt, and bare my bosom. Then when you order your troops to fire, mine will be the first breast that those bullets will strike!"
>
> Then Lewis lowered his voice, "And as my body falls from that window to the ground, you listen to the voice of your grandfather as he whispers in your ear, 'Frank, are you sure you are doing the right thing?' "
>
> Governor Murphy, white and shaking, seized the order from Lewis's hand and tore out of the room.
>
> The order was not issued and the next day General Motors collapsed and capitulated. . . .[13]

VII

"I am what Mr. Roosevelt calls an economic royalist," Ernest T. Weir wrote for *Fortune* magazine in October 1936, a month before the election he hoped would retire FDR to Hyde Park. "I have personal means; I am chief executive of a large corporation; I am opposed to the policies of this Administration. I deny that these things make me an antisocial force." It was a time for trading insults and for losing one's sense of perspective, in accordance with the traditional rites of Presidential elections. FDR had started it by using the phrase at the beginning of the 1936 campaign, his romance with business having faded with the failure of NRA and the emergence of the Liberty League, not to mention his own aristocrat's pleasure in twitting the men of business who now so generally opposed him. FDR did not mention names, Weir admitted, but he was sure he was on the list. He did not think it very appropriate for FDR, who had never met a payroll, to belittle businessmen.

Ernest Weir could have made a credible case against FDR on conservative grounds but much of the anti-business sentiment against FDR at the time was directed at the President personally. Weir does raise the basic issue of the shift of power from businessmen in their own fields to the central government through a proliferation of laws and regulations. The possibility that the times called for such a shift is not pursued, however, and the reader is left with a comparison of FDR and George III that is not quite convincing. Still a rather attractive picture of Weir himself comes through, as he describes how he took over an antiquated, bankrupt tin-plate mill in Clarksburg, West Virginia and built it up to the $675 million National Steel Company with 23,000 employees in the preceding thirty years. Ownership and independence were the goals of this entrepreneur, who came from a family too poor to keep him at school and who had worked from the age of fifteen. "I was born a commoner," he wrote in the *Fortune* article, contrasting himself with FDR and his silver spoon, "have lived a commoner and am still a commoner." In fact he was uncommonly able in business and at age thirty had left his job as a U.S. Steel plant manager to go in for himself. His salary for 1936 was $160,000. "We had to fight each inch of the way. Every dollar I have today has come from that plant and the larger company that grew out of it." He died in 1957 at age 81, running his company almost to the end. Eisenhower's Secretary of the Treasury, George M. Humphrey, resigned to succeed Weir as Board Chairman. The Humphrey family's Hanna Mining had owned a controlling interest in National Steel for some time. Just as he wanted to maintain independence of unions, Weir had wanted to avoid dependency for his ore supplies and so had brought in the Hanna interests. Thus the antecedents of National Steel go back to Mark Hanna, who, a generation earlier, was notably more conciliatory towards unions than Ernest Weir.

In searching for a clue to Ernest Weir's classic rugged individualism, one comes across a strange reading habit, an extraordinary devotion to *David Copperfield*. He said he had read it more than one hundred times and that he kept a copy of it in each of his five homes,[14] presumably in case he needed a quick brush-up. Aside from identification with David's poverty-stricken origins, the clue cannot be pushed too far. Dickens was a social reformer who probably would have been on the side of the unions.

The fact is that Weir won his case against FDR and the New Deal not in the pages of *Fortune* but at the very outset of the Administration, when most businessmen were willing to give FDR a fair try. Eugene Grace and the other steel masters had found NRA's monopoly price-fixing features very much to their liking. Weir, however, was a maverick in his own industry, always ready to cut prices or raise wages when least expected, a truer disciple of free enterprise than his competitors. Not that any of them were particularly happy about the affiliations they were supposed to make under the NRA. Secretary Perkins, FDR's first lady cabinet member — and Secretary of Labor of all posts — recalls with a sense of humor a 1933 meeting of steel company presidents for the purpose of discussing the proposed steel code of the NRA. Since the NRA represented labor as well as industry and steel was not an organized industry, the Secretary brought in president William Green of the AFL. When six steel company presidents, including Ernest Weir, Tom Girdler and Eugene Grace, walked into the room and were greeted by the mild and friendly Green, they recoiled as from the plague, backing into a corner like "frightened schoolboys," according to the secretary. She explained in effect that Green had come to praise the code and not to bury anyone. The presidents were so concerned about the encouragement for new acts of defiance the steelworkers might receive from such a meeting that Green finally left in disgust.[15] In such a fragile atmosphere, Weir went along with the steel code, hopeful that Section 7a would not bother him at his Weirton mills where he lived and worked near his employees in a condition of hard-nosed, enlightened paternalism. A long-time opponent of unions, he did take the precaution, as advised by the National Association of Manufacturers, to establish a company union in 1933 — just in case.

Meanwhile, since Section 7a produced a rash of strikes for union recognition, a policy had to be developed for the NRA's guidance. A National Labor Board was established by FDR at the request of the NRA, experimental in nature and without effective legal power. Senator Wagner was its chairman. There were three members from labor and three from industry, the latter being Gerard Swope of GE, Louis E. Kirstein of Filene's and Walter C. Teagle of Standard Oil of New Jersey, all in all an impressive delegation from industry with peer authority in big business circles. The NLB worked very nicely, helping to settle hosiery mill strikes in Pennsylvania and John L. Lewis's major captive coal mine strike in the fall. On December 23, 1933, FDR, little anticipating the tremendously bitter labor clashes that would disturb the New Deal, wrote to Felix Frankfurter: ". . . strikes are so extraordinarily few that I am almost worried by their scarcity. Bob Wagner's board has done a wonderful job."[16]

On the day after the NRA bill was signed, William Green sent a telegram to the venerable head of the Amalgamated Association of Iron, Steel and Tin Workers, known as "Grandmother" Tighe, to start an organizing drive in the steel industry. Tighe's timid union had only 4,800 members and $27,000 in the treasury, beneath the notice of John L. Lewis when he later took over steel organizing activities and certainly no threat to Weir. Yet in October 1933, by some strange surge of life, the Amalgamated had led 10,000 Weirton workers on strike for recognition. The AFL leaders were nothing "but a bunch of racketeers involving only a handful" of his employees, Weir stated. Still, rather than fight the strike, he accepted NLB mediation. This involved a return to work without reprisals and a secret election for the choice of either the AFL union, the company union or no union at all, under the procedures being established by the NLB. The election was scheduled for the second week of December.

After the men had returned to work, Weir had a change of heart and repudiated his signed agreement with the NLB. He lamely explained to his employees that purchasers of Weirton products had threatened to stop buying from him if he recognized the outside union. On the other hand, he would carry out the elections but only for designation of representatives who would bargain on behalf of the company union. The Amalgamated would not be on the ballot. Senator Wagner held an emergency meeting on December 7, asking if the company really intended to resist the government. "If that's the way you take it, yes," was the answer. General Johnson sent a hot wire to Weir on behalf of his threatened Blue Eagle. Weir paid no attention and announced the elections for company union representatives in his mills, which, of course, were held without NLB supervision.

In February 1934, NLB attorneys asked Weir's representatives once again to permit an NLB election. The government people were told NLB would not be allowed to step on the plant property and would receive no cooperation at all. It was now time for General Johnson to strip the plant of its Blue Eagle and the government filed suit immediately for violations of the NRA Act. A Federal Judge refused to grant the government an injunction on a technicality and the case was appealed to the Supreme Court. Before it was ever heard, the NRA was struck down in the Schechter decision of May 27, 1935. Ernest Weir had brought the NRA, or at least the NLB, to its knees. His defiance for a year and a half gave heart to other reluctant employers and diminished the impetus of the NRA. Senator Wagner stored the lesson in his tenacious mind and set about preparing a government labor law based on tight procedures, with particular concern for elections and the virtual end of company unions.

What eventually happened at the National Steel plants? They were the only company the CIO could not organize. Inevitably Weir's company union tactics would result in unfair labor practices charges under the Wagner Act. Weir fought an NLRB 1937 case for thirteen years until finally in August 1950 he was ordered to dissolve his company union and keep hands off until an election would be held three months later. That gave the CIO three months to go in and organize. When the votes were counted, Ernest Weir's workers had decided by majority vote to select the new company union listed on the ballot.

Weir was no less intransigent with his fellow steel masters. In 1941 he gave his employees a ten cent hourly raise while U.S. Steel was holding out against the United Steelworkers for seven cents. The others had to fall in line and in doing so bitterly accused Weir of raising the rate in order to keep the Steelworkers out of his plants. "In view of the country's booming earnings," he answered, "we felt the men should share the improvement." He next helped sabotage U.S. Steel's plan to raise prices and publicly supported Leon

Henderson's pending wartime price freeze, marching out of the American Steel Institute in acknowledgement of the opposition of his fellow members.

Weir met controversial issues head on in the postwar period, having expanded his range of reading and inquiry considerably. He had never ridden the Communist issue in his fight against unions, his basic position being an unwillingness to dilute the powers of management beyond company unions. Still he may have surprised many fellow industrialists during the cold war period by publicly advocating friendly relations with Russia and calling for America to take the lead in disarmament. "Why not negotiate with Russia?" was his position in articles and pamphlets, much in keeping with the thinking of Cyrus Eaton, the Cleveland industrialist who shares many of Weir's qualities. It is an unusual ex-Liberty League opponent of FDR and the CIO who would write in *Harper's* in 1953: ". . . much as we detest Communism there are millions throughout the world who do not regard it as bad or necessarily associated with the terrors of the Stalin regime. These people also forget Communism, like all ideas, is a thing of the mind and spirit and that things of the mind and spirit have never been eradicated by force. Bad ideas must be fought with better ideas; bad systems by demonstrations of better systems."[17] Besides, this independent-minded devotee of *David Copperfield* just didn't like seeing the West German steel mills doing all that business with Russia.

VIII

Gerard Swope of GE was unique in his ready acceptance of unions and collective bargaining. In 1926 this most imaginative and unflappable of industrialists came to the conclusion that sooner or later America's basic industries, including GE, were going to be unionized. Having analyzed the situation, he then decided to do something about it. Accompanied by his close friend and chairman of the board, Owen D. Young, Swope did the unimaginable. He met secretly with William Green in New York in December 1926 and suggested that the AFL try to win over GE's quasi-company unions, then known as Plans of Representation. He made it a condition that the AFL would organize on the basis of one industrial union for all of GE. Swope could read the future better than most men and he simply did not want to deal with numerous craft unions. As far as Swope could see, the meeting had proceeded cordially but he never heard from Green again. One can imagine Green's reaction as he walked away with his secret. Relatively open-minded about industrial unions, Green could hardly be expected to present GE's terms to fossils like Bill Hutcheson who dominated the AFL's governing council. It remained for John L. Lewis to mount that issue.

What manner of man was this Gerard Swope who fished in such dangerous waters? All the reports about his business genius place him on a pedestal. In a confidential poll of industrialists in 1937 to choose the "best brains" in management, Swope ranked first, followed by Alfred P. Sloan, Jr., Walter C. Teagle, Myron Taylor and Walter S. Gifford of AT & T. The vote was taken at the height of labor unrest in America when one would think Swope might have been nominated as "traitor to his class" in the Roosevelt fashion. What is clear about Swope is that he was the smoothest of men, gifted with the talent for getting away with things denied most mortals. Bernard Baruch spotted him early and brought him to Washington from his vice-presidency at Western Electric (then unconnected with GE) to be his assistant on the War Industries Board. There Swope demonstrated his persuasiveness both with industrialists and the generals. An example of the durability of this talent took place in the summer of 1935 when Swope was FDR's good friend and in the thick of practically every New Deal business-related board or committee. An agitated salesman called from Weirton, West Virginia. "Ernie Weir thinks you are the devil and won't give us any business," the salesman is reported to have said. "I found, as is often the case, that our gentleman was entirely wrong in his assumption," Swope recalled. "I called up Weir and went to see him — and we had a very lovely hour together. I have great respect for him — and he gave us the business."[18] Apparently

Gerard Swope not only was smart but could charm the birds out of the trees.

He was born in 1872 in St. Louis, Missouri, the son of Jewish immigrants from Germany. His younger brother, Herbert Bayard Swope, was equally well-known as a great reporter and newspaper editor of the New York *World.* The reporter, however, was what is today known as a swinger, his pals including Harpo Marx, Alexander Woolcott and Heywood Broun, the famous columnist who became a union leader himself as president of the American Newspaper Guild. Gerard, on the other hand, was not easily turned from the business at hand. Part of his legend is that he would answer certain people who remarked "What a fine day" with "What's so fine about it?" He not only possessed an analytical mind but an obsessed one in relation to his associates at GE. One of the most original of these was T. K. Quinn, the renegade from big business who resigned as a top-ranking vice-president and the acknowledged heir apparent to Swope himself. In books such as *I Quit Monster Big Business*, T. K. Quinn recalls a Gerard Swope who was less than perfect. When he reprimanded T. K. for postponing a Sales Committee meeting scheduled for the day of Quinn's father's funeral, T.K. accelerated his plans to go into business for himself, which he did in 1936. Quinn's father, incidentally, was a scarred veteran of the labor movement. In his writings, T.K. recalls how difficult it was for the son to be on the side of GE's "reactionary" labor policy, illustrating how even Swope's liberalism was all a matter of degree.[19]

Swope graduated from M.I.T. in 1895, in the same class with Alfred P. Sloan, Jr. While working in Chicago for Western Electric he moved into Hull House in the Chicago slums. There, under the tutelage of Jane Addams, his social conscience was undoubtedly reinforced, as it was for many others of the New Deal who had crossed her path, including Frances Perkins, a resident there in the early 1900's. At Hull House Swope also met his wife, a student of Professor John Dewey at the University of Chicago.

In 1909, when Western Electric sold its power apparatus business to GE, Swope was offered the chance to come along with the package. "I'm no chattel," Swope said, "I'll stay where I am." Such independence can make a company hunger for a man and GE's president Coffin finally lured him after the war with the presidency of GE's international department. In 1922, after three years of overseas travel, Swope was made president of the corporation and Young chairman. As "Mr. Inside" and "Mr. Outside" they presided over GE's great growth years, including the tremendous expansion in consumer appliances. During the years of Swope's presidency, lasting until 1940, strikes were avoided at GE.

A man as well-organized as Gerard Swope had no trouble balancing a life in public affairs with his careful attention to GE. The various welfare programs he encouraged at GE had their counterpart in the experiments that would eventually produce the welfare state. In the early days of the depression, he was a strong advocate of a massive public works program but was unable to convince his friend Herbert Hoover to go along with it. The "Swope Plan" for encouraging employment through a government-business partnership also was tabled by Hoover but was a forecast of the NRA Act, in the drafting of which Swope was active. Meanwhile along the way he had urged federal programs for workmen's compensation, old age pensions, unemployment compensation, government insured mortgages and the like. He also participated in shaping the Social Security Act in 1935. A Democrat, he was very much in evidence during the New Deal and must have restored FDR's waning faith in communicating with the indispensable business community of the distressed country.

As a member of Senator Wagner's premature National Labor Board during the NRA days, Swope made an essential contribution to the body of common law that was being established to accompany the birth pangs of government-favored labor. This was the concept of secret elections for determining the choice of unions or no union at all. What appears to be a commonsense application of the democratic system was not so obvious in those days when employers feared letting the camel put its nose under the tent in the first place. In one of the first cases brought before the NLB, the Berkshire Knitting Mills of Reading, Pennsylvania had refused to deal with a union organizing committee which claimed it was entitled to recognition. A nasty strike with some violence followed as the hard-headed Pennsylvania Dutchmen on the sides of both labor and management locked horns. At a meeting held in Washington before the NLB, the representative of the employers claimed he had no evidence that the union represented the workers. Secretary Perkins quotes Swope: "I have a suggestion. Let them vote on it. We'll have a free election by secret ballot and every employee of yours can vote whether he wants to be represented by the union or not. That's fair, isn't it? Then you'll know."

The manufacturer was determined not to fall out of the trees so easily. "Why should they vote?" he asked.

Swope's firm-jawed, intense face clouded as he put away his flute. "Because this is America and that's the way we do things here," he snapped, apparently with enough authority to settle the issue.[20] The "Reading Formula," involving calling off a strike, rehiring without discrimination and holding a secret ballot election became an essential part of strike settlement technique and of course found its way into the Wagner Act.

Swope was perfectly aware that GE itself would be faced with a demand for union recognition and readily consented to the request for an NLB election at the Lynn, Massachusetts plant in the fall of 1933. He was not surprised when the employees voted for an independent union to replace the company union and predicted to his associates that would inevitably be the outcome in each plant in spite of GE's record of paternalism. A more significant test came in September 1936 when the United Electrical Workers asked for an election in Schenectady, the most important of GE's plants. It was a time when the government and its NLRB were distinctly out of favor with industrialists who hoped that the Wagner Act would soon be declared unconstitutional. GE readily agreed to the request and the UE won the plant. Now the UE pressed for a company-wide agreement. This was too much for Swope's subordinates who pressured him to hold to a system of one plant at a time. They particularly did not want him to meet personally with the UE president, who had asked for such a meeting, on the grounds that

GE's bargaining power would be diminished by according the union such prestige. Swope had just returned from a vacation where he had time to reflect on the fall of GM that had recently taken place. In a reminiscence that reveals how Swope enjoyed talking to himself rather than others on such weighty matters, he stated: "I went home on the subway and read in the paper that Chrysler had agreed to meet Lewis and the other people, and I said, 'Swope, it isn't time for you, a little king, to say you won't meet with anybody.' So I called our managers together the next morning and I said, 'I think you are all wrong; I have never objected to meeting anyone . . . and I can't begin now.'"[21] While they sat there, he thereupon phoned James B. Carey, the UE's young president, and set up a meeting.

Carey at the time was all of twenty-five years old, a scrappy Irish-Catholic from a family of ten children, typical of many labor leaders of the thirties. Their gift of rhetoric and belief in the pro-labor encyclical of Pope Leo XIII may have accounted for their prominence in the movement. Carey had earned his spurs not only as an organizer from his Philco days in 1933 but also in fighting the fierce resistance of the AFL's craft unions as he drove for a radio and electrical workers' industrial union. With John L. Lewis's encouragement he had grouped his unions together to form the UE in 1936 and was promptly expelled from the AFL. Carey suggested to Swope that he bring along his secretary but the circumspect executive thought it would be better to come alone.

As it turned out, the secretary was not a blonde, but Jules Emspak, secretary-treasurer of the UE. He had joined up with Carey a year earlier, representing the independent GE local at Schenectady that had preceded the victorious UE. To add to Carey's burdens, Emspak was a Communist. The old man and the young man got along famously and Swope agreed to recognize UE throughout GE by elections or other satisfactory methods. "You seem to know all about me from the age of six," Carey is reported by Swope's biographer to have said at the meeting. "No, from the age of two," Swope one-upped him. But if Swope's intelligence reports had been accurate on Carey, how about Emspak? The fact is, Swope must have known all about Emspak. The GE college education fund had loaned Emspak the money to go to Union College in Schenectady before employing him. Emspak, and for that matter, other Communist leaders, were not reticent about their Communism and the unions fought about such matters publicly. In the UE's case, the Communist leadership was actually to gain the upper hand for a brief period. This happened when a group of machinery locals headed by James B. Matles affiliated with the UE in 1937. They had once been a part of the Communist-dominated Trade Union Unity League, which was now infiltrating the established unions, following the current Communist policy. Matles was named director of organization of the UE and between himself and Emspak gradually assumed control of the union through strategic staff appointments. Nevertheless the young non-Communist who sat alone with Swope in early 1937 worked in harmony with Emspak and Matles as they built the UE to over 130,000 members. The accord lasted until the servile adherence to the party line on foreign policy by Emspak and Matles forced a rupture during the period of the Hitler-Stalin pact. Readers of the *UE News*, such as the writer, who then lived in Pittsfield, Massachusetts, a GE city, found it a lively paper. The Emspak-Matles group opposed aid to Britain in 1940 and opposed FDR's bid for a third term. Carey castigated them in his personal "President's Column" and was especially eloquent when they did a back flip after Hitler invaded Russia. Carey was no match for these veteran in-fighters, however, and in 1941 they put up another good Irishman, Albert J. Fitzgerald ("I am no Communist," he said) as their hand-picked candidate against Carey. Fitzgerald won and Emspak and Matles controlled the UE until after World War II. In his retirement as honorary president of GE, Gerard Swope maintained his calm at these wondrous events, even putting in a good word for the conduct of the post-Carey union. How does one explain this detachment when other industrialists were rushing to the barricades on such an issue? Certainly Swope knew about the Communists in the UE. Perhaps his overseas experiences contributed to his sophistication. As urbanely cynical as a Roman emperor, Swope may also have thought of the wizard in the GE laboratories in Schenectady he had inherited for a few years from president Coffin, Charles P. Steinmetz. The crippled genius made a big show of voting Socialist and indulging in other eccentricities, like offering his services to Lenin, while endowing GE with discoveries worth hundreds of millions. At any rate, Swope did not take the conspiratorial threat of Communism at face value as did so many others who confused unionism and Communism. One employed Communists at that time and could hardly not expect to find them in the unions. On trade union issues there was very little difference between the goals of the CIO and the Communists in the thirties. It was possible, if one had enough faith in the democratic system, to tolerate Communists in the labor movement and trust in the good sense of the electorate, including the electorate of the unions themselves, to eject them from power, if necessary. Perhaps these thoughts passed through Swope's mind as he met with Carey. At any rate, neither the old gray fox who had risen to the heights of the business world nor the bantam rooster who was pledged to unionism saw fit to rush at each other's throats over the issue of Communism.

IX

Since so many prominent industrialists felt the Communist issue was a justification for resisting unionism, its position in American labor in the thirties may well be reviewed. In so doing, it would be helpful to distinguish between the attacks on FDR and the New Deal as "Communistic" and the facts of Communist infiltration in the labor movement itself.

As for FDR and the New Deal, the charge of Communism, a good deal of it coming from the most respectable business quarters, reflects little credit upon supposedly rational minds. The best that can be said in its defense is that FDR provoked passionate resentment among the business class he alternately wooed and scorned with all the vividness of his strong personality and politician's bag of tricks. Feeling attacked as a class and genuinely resenting government intervention in business, the business community often responded with the epithet of Communism rather than the dialogue of debate. The catalog of their denunciations, from high and low quarters, from country clubs and country stores, is well-documented in such studies as George Wolfskill's and John Hudson's *All But the People* and is somewhat difficult to believe from today's vantage point. In order to move on to the case of labor, the reader is urged to concede that FDR and the New Deal were not Communist-inspired, nor for that matter Communist-duped, regardless of the short-term Communists like Alger Hiss who gravitated in and out of government agencies in the thirties. Men like FDR, Raymond Moley, Harry Hopkins, Harold Ickes, Adolf Berle and Rexford Tugwell, the last-named the most utopian-minded of the insiders, clearly made a conscious, deliberate choice for the "middle way" at a time when democratic capitalism was in one of those death throes predicted by Karl Marx. Whether or not they saved capitalism while they were busily trying to feed people, get them back to work and improve their security, is for history to decide. As far as Norman Thomas was concerned, one institution they didn't save was Socialism. "In a word, it was Roosevelt," was Thomas's explanation of what happened to the decline of his non-Communist bid for state ownership of production and cradle-to-grave security.

Adolf Berle, as near a house philosopher as the New Deal possessed, was exasperated by the charges of Communism. "We certainly refused to take advantage of the economic collapse to set up state socialism (let alone Communism) or to intrigue within the government to prepare for such a development," he wrote in 1964. "For once in history, the pragmatic, socially-minded reformists won."[22] "It is just possible," he had earlier reminded such critics, "that all the social inventiveness of the world was not exploded between the poles of Adam Smith and Karl Marx."[23] Finally there is the rough treatment received by the New Deal from official Communist sources. Arthur Schlesinger, Jr. quotes from the *Daily Worker* of the early thirties showing how every aspect of the New Deal was derided and scorned by the faithful. "The New Deal is striving toward fascism and war in order to hold the workers in industrial slavery. . . . The claws of the Blue Eagle are the grasping hands of the parasite rich. . . . Every move, every act of the Roosevelt regime strengthens the powerful lever of the exploiters crushing the masses to the ground."[24]

Yet American Communism was about to experience a show of strength and glamor it would never experience again. There was no Smith Act to harass it. The government regarded the party as a nuisance but not as a threat. Communists were eligible for jobs in a government too preoccupied with individual security to care much about internal security in a peacetime setting. Reports about actual conditions in Russia were confused but there was no doubt that Russia was the avowed enemy of Hitler and Franco and the ally of no one particularly offensive to Americans. The times conspired to give the conspirators their place in the American sun and they did not muff the opportunity.

One of the zany aspects of the domestic party was its post-1934 line of wrapping itself in the American flag. For the latter half of the thirties, the Communists attempted to project an image as American as apple pie. A reasonable explanation is that Moscow knew eventually it would go to war with Hitler and so encouraged domestic parties to make a "popular" or "common" front with their host countries against the day when sides would be chosen. Whatever the reason, the Communist Party-USA cheerfully followed suit, toning down its anti-capitalism and emphasizing the Mayflower antecedents of Earl Browder and other heresies. Although actual party membership never exceeded 50,000, the united front movement was extremely successful, involving millions of Americans in causes and organizations that suited the party line. Exploiting the depression, the rise of Hitler and the basic appeal to conscience implicit in Communism, the party thus exerted considerable influence on American life of the thirties. Guided by brainy and zealous leaders, the front organizations attracted major support, first in the peace movement and then in the anti-fascist movement, especially among intellectuals, artists, writers, college students and liberals in general. This could hardly be termed a triumph for Communism since even those duped about the sponsors of the fronts were in sympathy with the objectives. The fronts of course collapsed with the Hitler-Stalin pact. When Hitler invaded Russia, the Communists turned again and became model patriots in World War II.

The shift in policy in 1934 affected the Communists in the labor movement as well. Popular front strategy required the abandonment of the separate trade union movement typified by the Trade Union Unity League in favor of boring from within the AFL. With a publicity that seems so strange for a supposedly secret party, Jack Stachel, the party's top labor official, announced in 1934: "Our basic task is to win the millions in the AFL."[25] The CIO, of course, with its militancy, its drive for unskilled workers and its dynamic, tradition-breaking John L. Lewis, was more to the party's liking and soon its best labor men showed up in CIO ranks.

On the whole, what manner of men were these Communist union leaders who shocked the sensibilities of the industrialists so greatly? Here we are on difficult ground. A middle class businessman feels he can understand the lapse of a professor, a minister, a Hollywood writer or similar type who was in and out of the movement in the thirties. But the party labor leaders were mostly non-intellectuals. Nor were they necessarily the foreign-born radical that one can visualize dominating a union like the Furriers in the big cities. In many instances, they were the hard-handed working stiffs who felt above all a genuine antagonism for bosses, men who had often been beaten up or starved out in their earlier careers. They could be the blood cousins of the old International Workers of the World — the Wobblies — veterans of jailings and floggings in the copper mines, lumber camps and lettuce fields, the unique native-American proletariat John Dos Passos romanticized in *The 42nd Parallel.* They might also be men, or the sons of men, who had been prosecuted and jailed under the criminal syndicalism and anarchy acts that erupted in most states in the "Red" scare after World War I. Lint-heads in the Carolinas textile areas, miners from the backwoods of Kentucky, skilled mechanics in Detroit, Spanish-speaking migrant workers in California, sharecroppers in Arkansas, homeless seamen on the West Coast, truckdrivers in Minneapolis, all showed up in the Communist ranks in the thirties. How many were true revolutionaries and how many were finding a home and a cause — perhaps revenge — in the union halls?

The rank and file Communists, of course, are unstoried, as always. From the reliable labor historians, however, we can take the measure of a few of the leaders. Harry Bridges of the West Coast longshoremen received affirmation from the Supreme Court in 1945 that he had never been a Communist. Yet he worked with them and ardently advocated the class struggle consistently enough to qualify for the honor. Defiant, honest, incorruptible, living in a cheap apartment or sailors' hotels, he was a natural waterfront leader. He had been arrested on a picket line and was a Wobbly for a brief period before finding his career as a union leader in San Francisco. Of a trade union family in his native Australia, he read up on the history of labor and protest movements in the Public Library while on relief during the depression. When the NRA offered Section 7a, Bridges led his longshoremen into a strike for recognition that paralyzed the West Coast and had Governors wiring to FDR to put down the insurrection. It finally evolved into a bitter general strike that almost shut down San Francisco for four days in July 1934. A general strike, practically unknown in America, with its threat to cut off all essential services could very well be a revolutionary tool. The community reaction was so strong the general strike collapsed after some violence and a giant scare. Bridges's union, however, gained recognition as part of the settlement and the archaic, somewhat barbaric "shape-up" was replaced by the union hiring hall. The strike illustrated the need for a national labor policy that would force negotiation, now that 7a had opened the door. The immediate effect, however, was to alert employers across the nation of the actions of the Communist party, which had been instrumental in bringing on the general strike. Bridges nonchalantly accepted the characterization of "Marxist" but never that of a Communist Party member as he ruled his longshoremen for the next thirty-eight years.

In Minneapolis another violent confrontation in 1934 called attention to a most unusual family affair of Communists in the trade union movement. Six Dunne brothers, sons of devout Irish Catholics, were active radicals and four of them were among the earliest Communist party members. Ray, the leader in the Minneapolis truckdrivers' strike, was once a lumberjack and had been arrested in California for making a Wobbly speech. Between 1921 and 1933 he was a model employee for a Minneapolis coal company, indulging in his political activities after hours. In 1934 he felt it was time to unionize his fellow truckdrivers in spite of Minneapolis's organized freeze-out of unions. The three Dunne brothers at hand in the struggling local soon had thousands of drivers on strike for union recognition. Minneapolis was an important terminal city where truckdrivers were a critical labor target. The employers formed a "Citizens Alliance" to break the "Communist-led" strike and then deputized a "citizens army" as the sense of class strife mounted. On May 22, a riot occurred and two of the citizens were killed, one a corporation vice president who was also attorney for the Alliance. The strike continued sporadically until July, when both strikers and police, itching for an incident, produced a barrage of fire by the police on an unarmed strikers' picket truck and into the gathering crowd. Sixty-seven persons were shot, many in the back, and two died. Young Eric Sevareid, on leave from the University of Minnesota and covering the story for the *Star*, recalls his father exclaiming: "This is revolution!" To the young reporter, it seemed the shooting must be fascism, an example of the gap produced by the social crisis.

Minneapolis was a typical American city brought to chaos and dissension over labor's pangs. It now fell under martial law as Governor Olson, himself an avowed radical, brought in the National Guard. In August its agony ended with the employers recognizing the union. Ray Dunne's local won agreements from 500 Minneapolis employers in the next two years, in spite of Dan Tobin, head of the Teamsters Union, who continued to brand the local as Communist, just as he had done during the strike itself. (The Teamsters now number two million, the nation's largest.) The fact is Roy Dunne and his brothers had broken with the Communists in 1928 and more exactly were members of the Trotzkyists, a Communist splinter movement opposed to Stalin. Minneapolis was one of the few places where the cocktail circuit at least knew the exact difference between a Trotzkyite and a Stalinist. Americans at large had been offered still another example of Communist leadership in the labor movement.

For a third example of a Communist in labor take Wyndham Mortimer of the UAW. At age fifty-two, when he quietly slipped into Flint to stir up the GM strike, he was the old man of the UAW's inner circle. A Welshman from a coal-mining family in Pennsylvania, he had caught the approving eye of John L. Lewis, who had no qualms about using Communists in the CIO-sponsored drive the UAW would undertake. Mortimer's worldly experience, like that of the others, was gained with his hands. He had worked in coal, steel and railroads as well as automobiles. He was dedicated to industrial unionism but was also a confirmed Communist. This was the type of man whose dossier must have been spread across the desks of GM's top executives as they pondered their next move in 1936. GM was quite expert in surveillance. One of the Pinkerton operatives testified before the La Follette Committee that Wyndham Mortimer as well as Walter Reuther and others were shadowed from the start for GM's Detroit office.[26] Renegade Pinkertons swore to the Committee that their firm alone had no fewer than fifty-two undercover men supporting the practically defunct UAW unions with their dues. One became president of a Chevrolet local in Flint.[27] A man as skilled as Mortimer, with his disciplined dual allegiances, was well-suited to match wits with the corporation. Finding the Flint local down to 200 members and riddled with spies, he spent the summer of 1936 creating a new undergrcund union. The Flint workers were afraid to hold open meetings for fear of being reported and fired. Mortimer visited their homes and cellars at night, listing their grievances and signing them up. A weekly letter mimeographed in Detroit was mailed to 5,000 homes in Flint. From such strange beginnings, within six months GM's sit-down strike would triumph over the giant corporation, an incredible David and Goliath feat — except that its time had come.

Amidst all this derring-do, the UAW itself was split with rivalry and factionalism, reflecting the unruly high spirits of its leaders and the tenacious bid for control by the Communists. President Homer Martin, a recent national hop, step and jump champion and a reverend to boot (he was called "The Leaping Parson") feared the power of Mortimer, his first vice-president. Martin had previously denounced Mortimer as a Communist at UAW council meetings and now eased him out of the Flint command. Mortimer was allowed to name his successor, however, and he chose Bob Travis, who brought the union into the open and marshalled the victory. Was Travis the clean-cut American boy he appeared to be? According to informed reports, "he firmly shared Mortimer's political views."[28] At the same time, young Henry Kraus, a Communist writer, came to Flint to edit the Flint UAW newspaper, completing the strike leaders' roster with Mortimer, Travis, Roy Reuther and Victor Reuther. If ever a corporation had a perfect right to cry "Communist and Socialist!" it was GM during the Flint sit-down strike. That it didn't may have been because the four youngsters knocking at its gates simply didn't look sinister enough. Incidentally, the UAW was to go into decline during the recession of 1938. Memberships and dues fell precipitously and it had to borrow funds from other unions to stay alive. It was failing at Ford and losing favor with the public, as well as members who wanted to work, because of its inability to prevent "wildcat" sit-down strikes. Finally John L. Lewis and the CIO had to step in to force peace on the fighting factions, as Homer Martin charged his enemies with Communism more vociferously than GM had raised the issue against the UAW. Rebuffed by Lewis, Martin then led a splinter group into the arms of the AFL. Finally he gave up unionism in 1940 to accept a completely furnished home from an unlikely patron, Henry Ford's Harry Bennett. R. J. Thomas succeeded him as UAW-CIO president, followed by the long and successful reign of Walter Reuther, one of the few statesmanlike figures produced by the American trade union movement. Reuther fought the Communists in the UAW to defeat after becoming president in 1947. One of his die-hard opponents was his old comrade in arms, Wyndham Mortimer, who charged Reuther with being a tool of the employers.[29]

X

For still another measure, one can examine the scope of Communism in the CIO, the NLRB and the La Follette Committee, each an agency that raised the temperatures of employers facing unions.

John L. Lewis was utterly cynical about the Communists. He had ruthlessly suppressed them in the UMW during the lean years preceding the New Deal. He now welcomed them as experienced organizers for the CIO drive. At his right side was Lee Pressman, the brainy general counsel who admitted in 1950 he had become a party member for one year in 1934. Pressman broke with the CIO in 1948 to support Henry Wallace. He was succeeded by Arthur J. Goldberg, the future Secretary of Labor and Supreme Court Justice, who was more in keeping with the CIO's new anti-Communist stance. Len de Caux, the *CIO News* editor in the thirties, was generally assumed to follow the party line at Lewis's headquarters.

Of the forty large CIO unions at the height of the Communist penetration in 1941, about twenty, involving 18.9% of the total CIO membership, were considered controlled by Communist officers. Only one was a large union, the UE, with 133,000 members led by the Emspak-Matles-Fitzgerald group. There remains the question of whether these officials really had the power or the will to impose their political ideas on their membership. At any rate, their influence was sharply reduced after World War II. This occurred even before the passage of the Taft-Hartley Act in 1947, which required a non-Communist affidavit from elected union officials in order to engage in collective bargaining. As for Lewis, few believe he took his political cues from any man, especially a subordinate. For him, the Communists were the running dogs of his own goals. When David Dubinsky, who was more interested in Hart, Schaffner and Marx than Karl Marx, objected to the policy of allowing Communists in the CIO, Lewis retorted: "Who gets the bird, the hunter or the dog?"

The NLRB, operating much as the SEC now does for Wall Street, was a special target for business criticism. Immediately after the Wagner Act passage, a committee of distinguished lawyers representing the American Liberty League declared the Act unconstitutional. Chaired by Earl F. Reed, Ernest Weir's attorney who had outmaneuvered the NRA labor provisions, the "National Lawyers' Committee" reversed the usual custom of accepting a law as law until reversed in the courts. "When a lawyer tells a client that a law is unconstitutional it is then a nullity and he need no longer obey the law," Reed announced to the press, infuriating the newly appointed Board. Corporation attorneys soon tied up the Board's uncertain powers with close to one hundred temporary injunctions, a tactic that did not cease until the law was validated. To add to its woes, the AFL went after the NLRB's scalp as avidly as did the National Association of Manufacturers, on the grounds that NLRB favored CIO unions when jurisdiction was a question. The business community had the pleasure of hearing AFL vice-president John P. Frey and AFL counsel Joseph Padway attack the NLRB almost from the start, not hesitating to level the charge of Communism against Board members suspected of favoring the CIO. In June 1938, Frey testified before the Dies Un-American Activities Committee that the Communists had captured both the CIO and the NLRB, perhaps straining his credibility under the circumstances.

It turned out there was Communist influence in the NLRB. The Board's secretary, Nathan Witt, was a Communist, one of the Harold Ware group, including Lee Pressman and Alger Hiss, who had joined a Washington cell while working in the Department of Agriculture in the early New Deal days. Whittaker Chambers, also a member, testified about the group before a Congressional Committee in 1948 and in his book *Witness*. Pressman added his evidence about Witt, once his closest friend, in 1950, leaving no doubt that there had been the opportunity, in the early NLRB days, to favor both the Communists and the CIO, insofar as Witt was concerned. FDR and his level-headed Secretary of Labor Perkins were determined to restore balance to the Board rather than expose the Wagner Act itself to crippling amendments. A few changes in Board members and the exit of Witt sufficed to pull the Board through the crisis of its early years. Even in the Board's beleaguered condition of those years, *Fortune*, representing the business community, had some good things to say about it. Once one accepts the principle of encouraging collective bargaining as a national labor policy, *Fortune* observed, the National Labor Relations Act (Wagner Act) and its Board should remain the law of the land. Recognizing that the Board was "conducting a staggering experiment in human relations under three overworked men who received $10,000 a year apiece" and a group of amazingly young staff lawyers who often faced violence at local hearings, *Fortune* counselled patience. It reminded its readers that the NLRB was acting out its part in "one of the greatest mass movements in our history. . . ."[30]

The La Follette Committee was as biased against big business as the various Un-American Committees have been against their special victims. The Committee arrived on the scene after labor had received its formal charter, the Wagner Act, from a friendly Congress and government. Labor did not need the Committee to achieve its goals. The forces of unionism, along with the requirements of the Act, which Senator Wagner had drafted with the experiences of the NRA in mind, were strong enough for success. In turn business certainly could have done without the public rattling of its skeletons. It interred them as swiftly as possible once the Act and the Board prevailed. The net effect was a morality play, in which business was shown to have presented its worst side in resisting unionism, particularly in its decision to flout the law of the land. The resistance was not limited to harmless tactics such as company union activity, which became illegal only with the Wagner Act. It included invasions of civil liberties, which had been illegal since 1787. Such a program was not only doomed to failure but once exposed to the Committee limelight, it would force the automobile companies, for example, to capitulate to keep their share of the consumers' market, among other considerations.

Congressional investigating committees, with their immunities, national publicity and dramatic response to current issues, are considered a generally useful and ingenious activity of the legislative branch. Inevitably after the books are closed, each committee faces its own charges of political motivation and bias. These committees were particularly active in the New Deal years, when confrontation rather than consensus suited the mood of the times. Each committee exaggerated the villainy of the object of its investigation. The Pecora Committee exposed Wall Street, the Nye Committee pilloried "the merchants of death," Senator Black's Committee denounced the lobbying of the utilities magnates and now the La Follette Committee would shame the flint-hearted capitalists with their hired goons and thugs. In this context, the element of Communism in the La Follette Committee is a factor to consider as we try to weigh the choices of American business leadership in the thirties.

The Committee arose, incidentally, from the missionary zeal of an unusual citizen named Heber Blankenhorn, an NLRB examiner who was frustrated by the initial sandbagging of the Wagner Act by most employers and their attorneys. A man who recognized that a Senate investigation was the next best thing to Supreme Court approval, Blankenhorn persistently buttonholed Senators who might sponsor one. In this endeavor, he had the support of two of the three Board members. He was also fortified by his own long experience as a professional observer of strikebreaking and intimidation of unions. A relatively unrecognized hero of labor's cause, Blankenhorn was a middle-aged man who, like John L. Lewis, found an old goal attainable in the new turn of events. He had supervised a Commission of Inquiry for the Interchurch World Movement following the steel strike of 1919, which had been ruthlessly suppressed by management with the general approval of a radical-frightened populace. The two-volume report detailed widespread violations of civil liberties but it soon gathered dust, perhaps in the feeling that the churchmen had best keep to their own affairs. The clergy, however, were not going to be put down so easily and in 1932 the Federal Council of Churches joined with the American Civil Liberties Union in deploring the abridgment of liberties directly connected with the attempts of labor to gain bargaining rights. In May 1935, 250 prominent clergymen issued on interfaith call to the Senate Judiciary Committee to launch an investigation of similarly deprived civil liberties. A month later the Central Conference of American Rabbis echoed the appeal. Meanwhile Blackenhorn himself was assigned to conduct an investigation for the NLRB in the fall of 1935 on the extent of industrial espionage, armed strikebreakers, factory arsenals and the like. With evidence in hand, the wiry, balding, bespectacled investigator, wearing his old army trenchcoat, was a familar figure in Washington as he stalked Senators who might lend a name to this hot potato. Although his predictions were overenthusiastic (he once estimated to Senator Wagner that nearly 100,000 labor spies were at work and he detected roots of fascism that just weren't there),[31] his motives were pure enough and he was not a Communist. One can imagine his gratification when Senator La Follette finally accepted the command and, after several months of hearings and delays, the Senate voted the Committee into existence on June 6, 1936.

The NLRB gained a new lease on life from the Committee. On May 18, the Liberty League lawyers had received confirmation of their constitutional insight when the Supreme Court in the *Carter* decision held unconstitutional the labor provisions of the Guffey Act, which had guaranteed collective bargaining for the coal industry prior to the Wagner Act. With the shadow of the *Schechter* and *Carter* decisions over its head and a new rain of injunctions on its hands, its prospects for prosecuting, judging and punishing recalcitrant employers looked bleak. For the time being the Board became practically an adjunct of the La Follette Committee, its investigators and lawyers spending their time feeding information to the Committee. Perhaps more inappropriately the Committee, coinciding with the CIO's great march towards industrial unionism, served as its office for war information. By investigating and publicizing the four anti-union practices that had repressed labor for decades, espionage, stockpiling of munitions, strikebreaking and intimidation by company police both on and off plant premises, the Committee gave invaluable aid to the CIO. Its timing and hand-in-glove coordination with the CIO were essential factors in the defeat of General Motors and the capitulation of U.S. Steel. In turn its conclusions might have gathered the dust of preceding investigations had not the tremendous vitality of the CIO drive accompanied its life-span. One example will suffice. On December 18, 1936, as the sit-downs started, John L. Lewis announced that the UAW would demand a collective bargaining agreement with GM. On December 19, the Committee announced it would inquire into labor conditions in GM plants and their officers and records were subpoenaed. Though the hearings did not actually start until four days after the strike ended, GM's misdemeanors took much of the sting out of the illegal appropriation of property by the sit-downers.

To what extent was the fine hand of Communism involved in the La Follette Committee? Jerold S. Auerbach, who has written a recent definitive history of the Committee, concludes that, for all its good work, it abandoned neutrality to exaggerate a condition of class warfare on the part of industry.[32] Soon right-wing groups, John P. Frey of the AFL and various business spokesmen levelled charges of Communism against the Committee. While the charges seemed irresponsible and malevolent in the thirties, again history has revealed a body count of Communists. Whittaker Chambers testified that Committee counsel John Abt and chief investigator Charles Kramer had been in the Ware cell while previously employed in the Department of Agriculture. Lee Pressman, who recommended Abt to the Committee, confirmed this in 1950. Gardner Jackson, a supporter of lost causes from the days of the Sacco-Vanzetti case, who had helped Blankenhorn obtain Senatorial support, has recalled for the Columbia Oral History project that he believed John Abt "brought into the staff quite a good many Communists." Also that La Follette subsequently told Jackson that he, La Follette, had "been hoodwinked at the time the . . . staff was set up . . . having taken on fellows he now, looking back, realized were active Communists."[33]

Thus the busy Communists were represented in the CIO, the NLRB and the La Follette Committee. At the time they were a legal party but only in the CIO would they act openly. In government, though they could be hired, they were generally not wanted and went underground if they hoped for career advancement. The business leaders who had to face the demands of unions may be assumed to have possessed a good deal of information about their presence.

Did their presence justify either resistance or acceptance? Did their influence discredit the agencies they had infiltrated?

XI

In the summer of 1936, John L. Lewis dispensed $1 million of UMW funds in equal portions. One-half went to the Roosevelt campaign against Landon and one-half was a payment to "Grandmother" Tighe's anemic steelworkers' union on condition it become part of the CIO's Steelworkers Organizing Committee (SWOC), which would spend the money organizing the steel industry. Philip Murray, a trusted UMW lieutenant of Lewis, was designated to head the drive. He immediately took space in the Grant Building in Pittsburgh, where many owners and their attorneys had office suites. The pleasant, courtly Mr. Murray would meet his opponents in the elevator, tip his hat and comment on the weather until the doors opened and contact was broken. Murray would run a tight ship as he laid siege to the main goal, U.S. Steel. There would be none of the factionalism and premature strikes that marked the UAW experience. High-powered attorneys like Lee Pressman were brought in, along with researchers and publicity men. The strategy included persuading the company unions themselves to join the SWOC or at least "to bite at the heels of management." This move was spectacularly successful. In addition ethnic groups were cultivated through their lodges and religious organizations. Finally the government was exploited through the NLRB and La Follette Committee. It is estimated that over $2,500,000 was spent in the first year alone.[34] Yet all the elaborate preparations, so far as U.S. Steel was concerned, were made unnecessary by the personal decision of a man who was also busy that summer, preparing to go on vacation.

Myron C. Taylor at sixty-two had more in common with Murray than Lewis. Like Murray he was thoughtful, courtly, a bit stiff and sad-eyed. He would cap his career after leaving Steel by becoming FDR's personal envoy to the Vatican with the rank of Ambassador, the first such envoy since 1868. Philip Murray, a devout Catholic, kept the encyclical of Leo XIII, the "Workingman's Pope," on his desk. It must have given him cause for reflection to consider that Taylor's greatest diplomatic feat before presenting his credentials at Rome was a series of secret meetings with John L. Lewis at the beginning of 1937.

Myron Taylor set sail for Europe on June 27, 1936, his destination his villa near Florence that once belonged to the Medici. Two days later, the American Iron and Steel Institute published a newspaper notice rejecting the SWOC's demand for a "closed shop." Its members would resist outsiders, it proclaimed, and would continue to bargain collectively with its own "representation plans," ignoring the NLRB's dim view of company unions. It promised to protect its employees and their families from "intimidation, coercion and violence." Taylor had gone on record against this manifesto by his trade association colleagues who no doubt were glad to see him take leave. In fact he was prepared to do some deep thinking of his own under the Italian skies. He was keenly aware that the days of the blood and brimstone labor philosophy of his predecessor, Judge Gary, and certain of his contemporaries, were numbered. It wasn't just a matter of an open shop versus a closed shop, which SWOC had not in effect demanded. It was a matter of continuing tactics that resulted in Steel becoming an enemy rather than a friend of labor. Continued enmity indicated war, or more likely, a lost war.

Taylor was a very independent man. He differed from most of the other steel company executives by not being a steel man. His entry was as a professional manager, experienced in law, textile mills and banking. As a professional manager he was also different, having made a fortune of $20 million before stepping into Steel. A small town boy from upstate New York, he had made his fortune by picking up distressed textile mills, renovating them and then selling out with a sharp sense of timing. In his short banking career he had been the key man in merging the Guaranty Trust Company with the National Bank of Commerce, creating a $2 billion institution and bringing him into the inner circles of big banking. When the bankers and the Morgan interests searched for a businessman-statesman to succeed Judge Gary at Steel, he accepted the position in 1932 as a kind of knighthood for his distinguished business career. It was a foregone conclusion that he would rule on his own terms for a temporary period, without submerging his life or his emotions in the company. Now that the company was prospering for the first time since he took over, he was anxious to consolidate his gains and move on. His attitude towards labor had started in a conservative manner. As soon as the NRA indicated a defensive strategy of company unions was called for in 1933, he hired a national expert in that endeavor, Arthur H. Young, as vice president of industrial relations. Young quickly led the steel industry into furious activity in this direction, performing his job only too well, as it turned out. Taylor did make some efforts to eliminate the old espionage system but they were generally scuttled by the men below him in the 200,000 employee company.

The statesman took over from the businessman as he pondered the choice in his villa. In that ancient setting one might speculate that Myron Taylor yielded to his sense of history as against the fighting spirit of his colleagues in the Institute. Here was a case of a detached capitalist recognizing the outside union as a social force capable of producing a social crisis. In the tradition of the English conservatives, he decided to invite the rebels into the mainstream rather than lose out altogether. The thought is not so fanciful, as Lord Runciman, President of the British Board of Trade, was on his way to Washington and would be there during the fifty days of the Taylor-Lewis negotiations. Britain had $7 billion of armament money to spend and could hardly be expected to grant contracts to companies unable to guarantee production. Thus Taylor's idealism received its proper dash of materialism.

Never a man of many words, Taylor finally came up with a precise 100 word statement, to be known as the Taylor formula for industrial peace. In May 1937 *Fortune* stated it "packed more dynamite than any 100 words ever written by a U.S. industrialist."[35] It simply said what the Wagner Act said about the right of employees to collective bargaining, with a specific proviso prohibiting the closed shop, although the words used were "right to work," a phrase that would gather force in later years as the pendulum swung back against labor. Armed with his memorandum, Taylor returned.

In the short run he would determine if Arthur Young's company unions deserved further support. If not, he would break from the prevailing doctrine of the Institute in favor of his formula and he set about preparing Steel's board of directors for the heresy.

The forces against this decision were considerable. Soon after Taylor returned from Europe, a movement got under way among a number of big industrialists for the formation of their own "united front." Representatives of the threatened General Motors and the belligerent steel independents were the instigators. Taylor went so far as to attend a meeting of the united front. When he was told that the time had come to put up capital for a do-or-die fight, he arose and disowned the proposition completely. He stated that any such concerted action would only be treated as a capitalistic conspiracy to gang up on labor.[36] This was enough to break up the united front until it reappeared in Little Steel.

The next act took place in the dining room of the Mayflower Hotel in Washington on January 9, 1937. As Myron Taylor escorted his wife to a Saturday afternoon luncheon, he bowed to greet Pennsylvania's Senator Joseph F. Guffey and John L. Lewis at another table. Having seated Mrs. Taylor he thereupon returned to Senator Guffey's table and shook hands all around. This act was later regarded by writers and other romantics as some kind of mystic portent of an accommodation to be reached by the three estates represented therein, government, labor and business. History is made by personalities as well as events, however, and when Lewis ambled over after lunch, he was introduced to Mrs. Taylor for the first time. In a twenty minute conversation the old charmer is reported to have conquered her and become a bosom friend of Taylor himself. At least enough to have set up the first of a half-dozen secret meetings in Taylor's Mayflower suite, starting the very next day, a Sunday on which neither man customarily worked. The nerve of both men was considerable. Lewis was in a fighting mood, blasting Alfred P. Sloan, Jr. and FDR as well. Taylor was inviting the wrath of his own colleagues as a backslider and meddler. Briefly, Taylor offered to recognize SWOC for all of Steel but without a closed shop or dues check-off. It was implied that the GM strike would have to be settled on similar terms.

The meetings proceeded from Washington to Taylor's New York townhouse, as Lewis moved back and forth from Detroit and the GM strike. A hitch came when some steel independents got wind of the conversations and demanded that Taylor join them in a wage increase instead of recognition. Taylor refused to accept this reasoning and on March 2, Benjamin Fairless of Steel's Carnegie-Illinois plant and Philip Murray signed a preliminary contract to open the bargaining. STEEL BOWS TO LEWIS'S UNION was the typical newspaper headline.

The independents immediately announced their own substantial increase, which had to be met by the Steel negotiators. Then as now Steel was not reluctant to pass on the increased costs through price raises, leading Marriner Eccles, the clearsighted Chairman of the Federal Reserve Board, to call to FDR's attention that the price boost greatly exceeded the wage costs. As far as Taylor was concerned, recognition was the key issue. In an unusual report to stockholders for the year 1937, Taylor elevated his decision above business considerations alone:

> I have taken it as a part of my duty as a trustee working for the ultimate good of the army of stockholders and workers who together compose the Corporation to arrange, to the best of my ability, full cooperation between the Corporation and whatever national administration happened to be in power. The lines of interest of the Corporation considered as a whole and of the public considered as a whole must run parallel — for the Corporation cannot exist except as it serves the public. . . .

As an afterthought, the man of business power added a plaintive note as he announced his retirement in this report: "These have been turbulent years, and no man knows the full significance or the permanency of the social changes that have come about."

XII

Tom Girdler was one of the production heroes of World War II. Carrying on as chairman of Republic Steel, which he had headed since 1929, Girdler went to San Diego in 1942 to turn out a prodigious stream of aircraft as chairman and chief executive of Consolidated Vultee. Labor's old villain, the intransigent leader of "Little Steel" in its bitter, wasteful, last stand against outside unions, had changed careers at 65. He never changed his mind about unions, however, even when forced to recognize the SWOC, by then the United Steelworkers, in 1941.

His own villains are enumerated in *Boot Straps*, an autobiography written in 1943. They include "every Communist cell among the subversive allies of CIO leadership." Also the La Follette Committee, the National Labor Relations Board and on occasion the National Committee of the Democratic party, comprising "a group of conspirators" in a "cold-blooded plot" to harm not only Republic Steel Corporation but "the whole capitalistic economy of the United States as well."[37] Which only proves that clear-cut political analysis is not a requirement for a production genius.

It is difficult to make a fair assessment of Tom Girdler because of the exaggerated stereotype that comes across from his book and other public statements. *Fortune* gave him a generally bad press. He was "the avatar of the old-style, unsocialized competitive order," is about the best they can say for him.[38] It noted that the Aliquippa plant of Jones & Laughlin under his direction had been known as "Little Siberia." Girdler corrected the record in his autobiography: "It was a benevolent dictatorship." Cyrus Eaton, the Cleveland industrialist who assembled Republic Steel and hired Girdler away from J & L to be its chairman in 1929, quickly parted company from him, philosophically as well as financially. In what surely was a reference to Girdler, Eaton later recalled "the classical example of managerial folly . . . found in one especially vain and strutting corporation head who some years ago announced that he would retire from business before he would let his plants be organized. He wasted twenty million dollars of his stockholders' money in a futile fight against a strike for union recognition."[39] Of course, by that time Eaton was the great and good friend of John L. Lewis, who had characteristically called Girdler "a heavily armed monomaniac with murderous tendencies, who has gone berserk." Dwight MacDonald, writing a profile of the steel masters in the thirties, described him as a gnomelike, restless person who, with his black-rimmed glasses, resembled the comedian Bobby Clark. Our biased survey of Girdler's style can end with a quote from *Boot Straps*. In the middle of the Little Steel conflict, with John L. Lewis's "Communist-trained agitators" trying to create "civic disorder, the basic tool of revolutionists," Girdler writes he turned to his vice president and said: "Only Oliver Warbucks can fix it."

The fall of U.S. Steel was a call to action. "I won't have a contract, verbal or written," announced Girdler, "with an irresponsible, racketeering, violent, communistic body like the CIO and until they pass a law making me do it, I am not going to do it."[40] His fellow steel men applauded him and made him president of the Iron and Steel Institute on May 27, 1937, symbolically taking the leadership away from U.S. Steel. Only the day before, the Little Steel strike had started. It would involve nearly 200,000 workers, paralyze a dozen industrial communities and earn a reputation as one of the bloodiest and costliest of America's labor feuds. Yet the Wagner Act had been approved by the Court on April 12 and on May 20, Jones & Laughlin, a typical Little Steel Company, had voted three to one for the SWOC in an NLRB election.

The handwriting on the wall was not accepted by Girdler. There were still Bethlehem, Youngstown Sheet & Tube, National, Armco, Republic and Inland, led by men who felt the CIO had to be stopped in the interests of American industry, perhaps in the interests of America itself. Wages were not the consideration since these companies had already matched Steel's settlement. Their lawyers were realistic enough to point out the law required them to bargain with the SWOC but noted they did not have to sign an agreement even if an agreement were reached. (This was true until the H. J. Heinz case of 1941.) Thus they could withhold written recognition. If the unions struck rather than negotiate on such terms, they would fight the strike through a community-supported back-to-work drive along the lines of the Mohawk Valley technique. If the strike were defeated, the union theoretically would be smashed. The tactics on both sides were so stubbornly technical that FDR was caused to issue his famous "a plague on both your houses" statement when Murray pleaded for government help after the Memorial Day tragedy of May 30, 1937. Lewis's retort to FDR was equally bad-tempered. "It ill behooves one who was supped at labor's table . . . to curse with equal fervor and fine impartiality both labor and its adversaries when they become locked in deadly embrace."

The Girdler forces were counting on their estimate that the SWOC, having made insufficient progress in their plants, had attempted a premature strike. Public sentiment was turning against the CIO in the aftermath of the sit-down strikes and FDR's maneuvers for packing the Supreme Court. With the grievance identified as an insistence on a written agreement, the union started out in a bad light. There was great company exposure to NLRB action from supporting company unions as well as the inevitable misrepresentation, violence and false propaganda connected with instigating the "back to work" movement. In spite of the exposure, it was decided that it would be well worth it to buy time and weaken the union. The strategy worked. Governor Davey of Ohio, after bringing troops into Youngstown to prevent violence, decided three days later on June 25 that the "right to work is sacred." The troops were now used to protect returning workers and it was too late for the disbanded pickets to organize all over again. A mediation board sent along earlier by Secretary Perkins and FDR had produced only scorn from Girdler, even after a personal phone call from FDR himself. Girdler could not understand how one of the mediators, the labor expert Charles P. Taft, son of the former President, could have such a poor understanding of the facts. Perhaps because work was often unimportant to sons of rich families, he surmised, they could not understand why other men so highly prized the right to work.[41]

No review of labor in the thirties can fail to discuss the Memorial Day incident, known by labor as the "Memorial Day Massacre," outside Republic Steel's South Chicago plant a few days after the strike began. By chance a Paramount news photographer had taken footage of the conflict, which Paramount, in a strange burst of self-censorship, decided to suppress as being too inflammatory. The La Follette Committee tracked down the film, held hearings and soon built a damaging report around it. The famous scenes have a chill contemporaneity. One recognizes the upraised clubs of inflamed police carrying out orders, or lack of orders, inadequate for the social crisis involved. Retreating in a sprawling tangle are typical workers in holiday white shirts, panic-stricken. The caps, suspenders and old felt hats they wear create an atmosphere of the thirties but the civil violence is all too familiar.

Fortune called it an incident "as savage as any in the dark annals of American labor struggles."[42] Ten were killed and forty wounded by bullets. The gunfire was generally from the back. The low-keyed Senator Thomas of Utah, a former college professor who shared the direction of the La Follette Committee, issued his own supplementary report: "The encounter of May 30 should never have occurred. Police and marchers defended their actions on the basis of right, but those who died were not martyrs to a cause. . . . The use of police officers in such a way that they seem allied with either side of a labor dispute destroys their effectiveness as peace officers representing the public."[43]

Briefly, two thousand strikers, their wives and sympathizers had gathered on a sunny Sunday afternoon at SWOC headquarters across the field from the Republic factory gates. Speakers rallied them in support of the strike and attacked the alleged restrictions on peaceful picketing. At the conclusion of the speeches, a motion was made to establish a picket line in front of the plant. Led by the American flags both sides so frequently called upon, the marchers straggled towards the plant in a holiday mood. Inside were about 1,300 loyal workers on the Sunday shift. The Chicago police, numbering 264, discussed picketing with the leaders. The inevitable stick or club was thrown at the police and in moments the confrontation degenerated into chaos.

Captain Mooney of the police testified the battle was one "between us and the Communists." Girdler, who bore no direct responsibility for the tragedy, accepted the Communist thesis readily. "This crowd was being organized to force its way into our steel plant to drive the men out." The marchers were "playing parts in a drama written, directed and produced by revolutionists."[44] The La Follette Committee rejected the contention that the marchers intended to storm the plant, citing among other reasons the presence of women and children in their ranks. "Women and children form the usual screen behind which hide assassins seeking to embarrass society by provoking its guardians," explained Girdler in *Boot Straps*.[45]

Still, when Girdler himself appeared before the La Follette Committee a year later, he was the victor over the CIO. All the devious policies and rationalizations of the employers and their citizens' associations were spread on the record but the day's battle had been won. The citizens' groups seemed to be unanimous in their belief that they were fighting in the front lines against Communism. The La Follette Committee report in turn exaggerated the threat of these groups as a possible "super-government" of local tyrants. Girdler briefly testified and accused the La Follette Committee of raking over "the dead ashes of past disputes, in search of the minutest mistakes made by industry." It was as near as he came to admitting error.

The victory of Little Steel in the field was eventually snatched from it in the courts. The Republic Steel case broke all NLRB records for days of hearings and pages of testimony. In October 1938, the order came down to reinstate over 7,000 strikers with back pay. It found Republic guilty of just about every anti-union offense. Republic's appeal was turned down by the Supreme Court in 1940 and it finally signed with the union on August 13, 1942. Girdler had few comments to make, now being involved in the heart of war production. How does one finally evaluate this harsh, simplistic, able man who lacked the intelligence even of Daddy Warbucks? Perhaps the key is in his final *Boot Straps* statement: "A terribly *disorganizing* influence is at work at the base of all industry in America. . . . The boss is no longer the boss."[46]

XIII

At the White House, FDR also was wrapped up in the larger war. His presence had animated the gains of labor, although in a passive manner. FDR was not a labor activist. His concept was one wherein government reforms and regulations would benefit all classes, without labor having to take so much in its own hands. He had not originally grasped the significance of Section 7a for collective bargaining and his personal concession of proportional representation for the auto industry in the NRA days was a block in the progress of that concept. He was a reluctant supporter of the Wagner Act at the outset and held back for at least a year before encouraging it. Yet he did intervene with a sure touch in the coal mine and GM strikes and skillfully withheld intervention in the San Francisco and Little Steel strikes. He was noticeably silent about the Memorial Day incident but it is possible he recognized that the antagonists should now be resolving their differences in the courts, a national labor policy having been established. He refused to pick up the Communist scare and his confidence that the American worker would not shift politically to that position, as happened in Europe, was confirmed.

On April 15, 1937 at an off-the-record press conference for newspaper publishers and editors, FDR discussed the great labor turmoil philosophically. He explained that he had withheld public condemnation of the sit-down strikes on the grounds that labor itself would soon move away from them. The crisis, caused in part by the attitude of employers towards the Wagner Act, would blow over. "It will take some time, perhaps two years, but that is a short time in the life of a nation." Similarly, unions would clean house and produce leaders who saw the whole picture. The nation must adjust to collective bargaining, FDR said patiently. It would learn by experience and ultimately "we are going to get a workable system."

Footnotes

[1] Allan Nevins and Frank Ernest Hill, *Ford, Decline and Rebirth, 1933-1962* (New York, 1962), p. 138.

[2] *Ibid.*, p. 265.

[3] Charles E. Sorensen, *My Forty Years with Ford* (New York, 1956), pp. 268-272.

[4] Irving Bernstein, *Turbulent Years* (Boston, 1970), p. 332.

[5] Jerold S. Auerbach, *Labor and Liberty: The La Follette Committee and the New Deal* (New York, 1966), pp. 160-161.

[6] Bernstein, *op. cit.*, p. 195.

[7] Auerbach, *op. cit.*, p. 27.

[8] Sidney Fine, *Sit-Down: The General Motors Strike of 1936-1937* (Michigan, 1969), p. 119.

[9] William E. Leuchtenberg, *Franklin Roosevelt and the New Deal* (New York, 1963), p. 28.

[10] Murray Kempton, *Part of Our Time* (New York, 1955), p. 277.

[11] Augustus M. Kelley to the author, October, 1970.

[12] Auerbach, *op. cit.*, p. 113.

[13] Saul Alinsky, *John L. Lewis* (New York, 1949), pp. 97-147.

[14] Ernest Dale, "Ernest Tener Weir: Iconoclast of Management," *California Management Review*, Vol. I, No. 3, Spring, 1959, p. 24.

[15] Frances Perkins, *The Roosevelt I Knew* (New York, 1946), Ch. 18.

[16] Max Freedman, *Roosevelt & Frankfurter: Their Correspondence, 1928-1945* (Boston, 1967), p. 183.

[17] Ernest T. Weir, "Why Not Negotiate with Russia?" *Harper's*, December, 1953, pp. 66-71.

[18] David Loth, *Swope of G.E.* (New York, 1958), pp. 250-251.

[19] Irving S. Michelman, *Business at Bay* (New York, 1969), p. 158.

[20] Loth, *op. cit.*, p. 229.

[21] *Ibid.*, p. 257.

[22] Adolf A. Berle, "Intellectuals and New Deals," *The New Republic*, March 7, 1964, p. 21.

[23] *Newsweek*, February 16, 1948.

[24] Arthur M. Schlesinger, Jr., *The Politics of Upheaval* (Boston, 1960), pp. 190-191.

[25] Bernstein, *op. cit.*, p. 270.

[26] *Ibid.*, p. 517.

[27] Auerbach, *op. cit.*, p. 112.

[28] Bernstein, *op. cit.*, p. 522.

[29] Frank Cormier and William J. Eaton, *Reuther* (New Jersey, 1970), p. 245.

[30] *Fortune*, "The G— D— Labor Board," October, 1938, pp. 52-123.

[31] Auerbach, *op. cit.*, p. 31.

[32] *Ibid.*, pp. 152-153.

[33] *Ibid.*, p. 167.

[34] Bernstein, *op. cit.*, p. 453.

[35] *Fortune*, "It Happened in Steel," May, 1937, pp. 91-180.

[36] *Ibid.*, p. 176.

[37] Tom M. Girdler, *Boot Straps* (New York, 1943), p. 368.

[38] *Fortune*, March, 1938, p. 73.

[39] Cyrus Eaton, "A Capitalist Looks at Labor," *University of Chicago Law Review*, April, 1947, pp. 331 ff.

[40] *Fortune*, November, 1937, p. 168.

[41] Girdler, *op. cit.*, p. 357.

[42] *Fortune*, November, 1937, p. 172.

[43] Auerbach, *op. cit.*, p. 128, *fn.*

[44] Girdler, *op. cit.*, pp. 251, 253.

[45] *Ibid.*, p. 251.

[46] *Ibid.*, pp. 449-450.

Chapter 6

The Un-Americans

In October 1947, the Hollywood Ten, a group of eight writers, a director and a producer, gained a certain immortality by defying J. Parnell Thomas and his House Un-American Activities Committee. They took the First — not the Fifth — Amendment as the basis for their refusal to answer "Are you now or have you ever been a member of the Communist Party?" Their reasoning was that such an inquiry into their political beliefs violated freedom of speech and assembly and was also far removed from the legislative ends of a Congressional Committee. The full House and the Supreme Court thought otherwise. On November 27, 1947, Thomas asked his fellow Congressmen for a citation of contempt against each of the "unfriendly" witnesses and was rewarded by an overwhelming vote, typically about 346 to 17 of those voting. Accepting this as traditional courtesy among Congressmen, the Ten, after grand jury indictments and appeals, waited two years for the Supreme Court to save the day in a typical Hollywood finish. In a five to four decision in June 1950, the Supreme Court refused to review the case and soon the ten, all of whom were or had been Communists,[1] found themselves in Federal prison, mostly for a year, the maximum sentence for contempt.

The Ten were only a forerunner of things to come. In 1951 the Committee hauled Hollywood to Washington once again, this time for mass testimony of subpoenaed and voluntary witnesses. Altogether 90 prominent Hollywood people testified in the 1951-1952 hearings compared with only a few dozen who testified out of 43 called to Washington for the brief two-week 1947 session. Of the 1947 group, the majority were "friendly" witnesses, including such figures as Jack Warner, Mrs. Lela Rogers (mother of Ginger) and Adolf Menjou, who confirmed the Committee's fears about Hollywood's infiltration. The nineteen witnesses who announced they would not cooperate were dubbed "unfriendly." Eight of the "unfriendlies" were not called to the stand. That left eleven, of which ten went to jail. The eleventh was Bertolt Brecht. Contemporary playgoers who feel that business expense accounts are rarely so well expended as when used for superior fare like *Threepenny Opera* and *The Caucasian Chalk Garden* should note that Brecht testified "no" in answer to the question. Though not contradicted by the undercover agent who read off the party cards on the Ten, Brecht in disgust packed off to East Berlin where he became an open Marxist while continuing as one of the theatre's leading figures. Another German expatriate, the great philosopher-novelist Thomas Mann, descended from a long line of Lübeck businessmen, suffered similar anguish over the hearings. He was never called before the HUAC, being too Olympian even to have considered joining a group of swimming pool comrades for cocktails, let alone Communism. Yet he supported the high-minded Committee for the First Amendment from the start in 1947 and eloquently denounced the House Committee's procedural deficiencies as a repetition of the tactics of smear and guilt by association that preceded Hitler. Finally when the Mundt-Nixon Bill (now known as the McCarran Internal Security Act) was passed in 1950 in its original unconstitutional form, Mann left his Pacific Palisades home to live in Europe as a reproach to his adopted country.

These were some of the elements of the anti-Communist hunts of the forties and fifties, involving great talent and inner decisions, great tragedies and fears. One stream of inquiry sought to remove subversive Federal employees from their jobs, a reasonable and necessary enough endeavor, especially in relation to "sensitive" positions during a cold war and espionage period, which finally erupted into the inane ugliness of McCarthyism. The other stream sought to flush out the Communists in movies, radio and television, with some side excursions to schools, unions and the churches. Into this stream eagerly paddled a succession of second-rate HUAC Chairmen, equating even the shadow of Communism with clear and present danger, and attracted not in the least by the glamor and sex appeal of Hollywood.

Here the national security was assuredly not at stake, if one excludes the low level of taste films often seek. The specific area where harm might be done, propaganda, had already been spread on the screen for the whole world to see for the price of a ticket and hardly needed an investigation to ferret it out, as the 1947 hearings clearly revealed. Stymied in this direction, the 1951 investigations turned towards a self-appointed morality exercise of exposure and humiliation, of blacklisting and absolution courts about as un-American as anything in the nation's history. Only remotely clutching to the fiction of legislative ends, this phase of HUAC deliberately scourged and put out of work not only present or long-ago Communists but approximately three hundred others, great and small, who had signed petitions (including that of the Committee for the First Amendment), supported the wrong union, enrolled in actors' workshops, attended anti-fascist or peace rallies or just had the finger pointed at them by an old friend.

It is very likely that the HUAC could have been restricted to a sensible and useful area had it not been for the misguided, servile acquiescence of businessmen in Hollywood, on Madison Avenue and in a small chain of supermarkets in Syracuse, New York. There is probably no greater example of inexcusable response to a crisis situation than the inglorious performance of a good many top-level movie, radio, advertising and TV executives in response to the HUAC witch-hunts. The failure to stand firm in the heat of the crucible was particularly offensive since it turned out that very little in the way of money or profits was really at stake.

II

Power in Hollywood in 1947 rested with the movie moguls. Men like Jack Warner, Spyros Skouras, Barney Balaban, Harry Cohn, Samuel Goldwyn and Louis B. Mayer were authentic emperors, ruling their star systems, unworried about proxy wars or investment bankers and still enjoying the great financial successes of the pre-television days. They had come through the war in fine fashion, movies being considered essential for the morale of defense workers as well as the armed forces. This would include wartime films written by the Ten such as *Action in the North Atlantic* and *Sahara* (John Howard Lawson), *Thirty Seconds Over Tokyo* (Dalton Trumbo), *Pride of the Marines* (Albert Maltz), *Objective Burma* (Alvah Bessie) and similar flag-wavers that one used to see on the late late show.

In developing the argument that the moguls acted without distinction and possibly without honor, one can reluctantly grant their right to fire the Ten (specifically they fired the five who were under contract or let their contracts expire and announced a refusal to employ any of the Ten until they "purged" themselves of contempt and "declared under oath" they were not Communists). This could be justified by the rationale that an instrument of Congress deserves cooperation at the least, however offensive its procedures. The Ten, it might be assumed, were publicly exposed as unworthy representatives of a business highly sensitive to public approval and thus had lost their usefulness to their employers. The legal rights of the moguls in this respect were supported by court decisions handed down against some of the Ten in contract violation suits. Ring Lardner, Jr., for example, prevailed in a lower court on a breach of contract suit against Twentieth Century Fox but was reversed by the Federal Court of Appeals. As one might anticipate in a Hollywood contract, a bagful of escapes is itemized for employers to fall back upon. In Lardner's case, his silence before J. Parnell Thomas constituted "moral turpitude" to the appeals court.[2] (One of the grim bits of humor in this transaction occurred when Lardner entered the Danbury Federal prison in 1950. There he found Thomas, already serving time for padding the public payroll.)

Employers dominating a cultural medium of immeasurable impact, however, cannot fall back on legalisms as the last word. If we excuse their withdrawal from the ten contentious witnesses who consciously sought martyrdom and were short on candor, can we justify their tacit approval of the blacklisting of hundreds of others caught in a careless, spiteful dragnet? Can we accept their expulsion of talented actors and writers who, beginning with the 1951 investigations, refused to inform on friends even though ready to confess their own affairs with Communism? To what extent can the moguls be excused for recognizing the legitimacy of special "clearance" agents such as Roy M. Brewer, a vigilantist union boss, and George Sokolsky, a self-appointed confessor for errant Hollywoodians?

When one searches for justification for the employers' overreaction, the suspicion grows that these moguls simply decided to curry favor with the feared Committee, to win points against further harassment by casting out all traces of Communism, regardless of incidental damage to civil liberties and plain decency. In one area only, the content of films, was there any parallel to the need to resist Communist infiltration as called for in sensitive government agencies. The business of film-making is so fragmented and divided among so many cooks that this danger simply didn't exist, as any intelligent film-goer with a reasonable memory can attest for himself. Even the Ten could have kept on writing the films they did write — and which several of them are of course now writing once again — with their political fantasies no more likely to intrude on the screen than their sexual fantasies. Yet the moguls caved in rather than hold out for a judgment based on content and withheld employment, a matter in which they alone held the final decision. Certainly they were not in a mood to accept the tongue-in-cheek advice offered by the irascible Dalton Trumbo in his statement to HUAC in October 1947:

> Let every businessman in America clearly understand that if this Committee can usurp the rights of management in one industry, it has established the precedent by which it can usurp the rights of management in all industries. Modern history reveals many instances abroad where workers in private industry have resolutely defended the rights of management against the encroachments of a corporate state. I am certain they will make such a defense in this country against the attempt with which this Committee is presently engaged.

The announcement signifying the capitulation to HUAC by the owners came on November 25, 1947 and is known as the Waldorf Statement. On November 24, fifty members of the Association of Motion Picture Producers, the Motion Picture Association of America and the Society of Independent Motion Picture Producers met in New York's Waldorf Astoria to plan their strategy. The meeting was dominated by the big studio heads whose trade executive and spokesman was Eric Johnston. Johnston, high-domed and articulate, his pouchy eyes making him a look-alike for the comedian Fred Allen, represented the progressive, younger forces of business in those days. He had been brought to Hollywood to create a brighter image than that of his predecessor, the old-fashioned politician Will Hays. A dynamic success as an electrical appliances wholesaler in the Northwest, he had been catapulted into the presidency of the United States Chamber of Commerce in a similar refurbishing role for that stereotyped organization. Now as Hollywood's spokesman he put down HUAC with just the proper amount of statesman's courage and defiance. "Hollywood is weary of being the national whipping boy for Congressional committees," he announced when Thomas leaked press releases about the impending investigations after having sent staff members to Hollywood in May to gather preliminary information. Although a major cooperative witness heard in executive session at the Biltmore Hotel had been Jack Warner, one of his bosses, Johnston continued: "We are tired of having irresponsible charges made again and again and again and not sustained. If we have committed a crime we want to know about it. If not, we should not be badgered by Congressional committees."[3]

Johnston was scheduled to be one of the first witnesses at the Washington hearings and the group of non-Communist, top-drawer Hollywood figures who had launched the Committee for the First Amendment took great heart from what appeared to be a common cause between themselves and their unpredictable, emotional, rags-to-riches bosses. *Variety* quoted an open letter from Johnston to members of Congress during the first week of the hearings which couldn't have been more to the point: "Too often, individuals and institutions have been condemned without a hearing or chance to speak in self-defense; slandered and libeled by hostile witnesses not subject to cross-examination and immune from subsequent suit or prosecution."[4] Even on blacklisting, which in the long run was the major offense of the owners, Johnston was early on the side of the angels. In a conference called on October 18, 1947 at the Shoreham Hotel in Washington, headquarters for the "unfriendlies," Johnston was challenged on this subject by their attorneys, Bartley C. Crum and Robert W. Kenny, former Attorney General of California. The newspapers had reported Thomas to the effect that the producers had agreed to establish a political blacklist throughout the entire motion-picture industry. Johnston is quoted as having said: "That report is nonsense! As long as I live, I will never be a party to anything as un-American as a blacklist, and any statement purporting to quote me as agreeing to a blacklist is a libel upon me as a good American!"[5]

Paul V. McNutt, a nationally prominent former Indiana governor who had been called in by the owners as special counsel (along with James F. Byrnes, already an ex-Secretary of State and about to become a Supreme Court Justice), was also present at this meeting and echoed the brave sentiments. McNutt's presence was particularly significant because he was a past National Commander of the American Legion, a potent force at the time and the most feared pressure group threatening the box-office on the issue of Communism. Aside from warning the industry that a blacklist would be indefensible legally, McNutt on October 23, three days after the hearings started, issued a lashing statement against HUAC itself: "It became apparent by the Chairman's questions that the purpose of the hearing was to try to dictate and control through the device of the hearings what goes on in the screens of America. It does not require a law to cripple the right of free speech. Intimidation and coercion will do it. Freedom simply cannot live in an atmosphere of fear. The motion picture industry cannot be a free medium of expression if it must live in fear of a damning epithet 'un-American!' whenever it elects to introduce a new idea, produce a picture critical of the status quo, or point up through a picture some phase of our way of life that needs improving."

Yet by 1952 the Legion was driving full steam ahead to make Hollywood finish its housecleaning and a craven group of owners, already corrupted by years of unofficial blacklisting, was treating with the Legion as an equal. Again a delegation representing eight major movie studios, headed by Eric Johnston, went to Washington in March 1952, this time to placate National Commander Donald R. Wilson and former National Commander James F. O'Neil, director of publications, whose magazine had just published 66 names of tainted Hollywood personalities. The taint consisted of being subject to "Communist influences," not even card-carrying itself. Since seventeen of the 66 gained this distinction in the article for no other reason than having signed an *amicus curiae* brief for the Ten, one would think the moguls would have fought back. But this was already the era of McCarthyism and what little backbone the moguls retained was further eroded by the genuinely bad financial times finally brought on by television and the antitrust decisions requiring the divestiture of their movie theatres. All they did was plead for mercy and ask for instructions on the housecleaning. They were rewarded with a formal letter listing 300 haphazardly selected names as a starter which they dutifully added to the unacknowledged but largely operative blacklist. Thus the Legion, whose waning membership now gets excited about fish-fries and possibly by adult movies, once rode herd on the moguls.

IV

Hollywood itself did not present a united front to the investigations, a fact which must be weighed before passing judgment on the Waldorf Statement. There were splits in the ranks of the stars and creative people as well as among the bosses.

When sides are chosen in Hollywood, at least in the days when Hollywood was still unafraid to be counted on a vital issue, the list of names, reflecting a caste system of household gods, is all important. The Committee for the First Amendment, hastily assembled as the 1947 hearings opened, was as impeccably prestigious as an earlier group, the "Committee of 56," sponsored by the Hollywood Anti-Nazi League. This group, in December 1938, had petitioned the President and Congress to apply "economic pressure" against Germany in recognition of her "aggressive attitude" towards other nations. The signers of the December 1938 petition, a masterpiece of understatement considering what was going on in Germany at the time, included celebrities from Groucho Marx and Jack Warner at one end of the spectrum to Spencer Tracy, Fredric March and Edward G. Robinson at the other. Ironically, the Anti-Nazi League *was* manipulated to a significant degree by the high-riding American Communist Party of the Peoples Front days. After it flip-flopped during the Soviet-German non-aggression pact period, to the dismay of the non-Communist liberals who had supported it, prior sympathy with the League became another nail in the blacklist coffin for a good many of its supporters. If this nightmarish torturing of reason seems appalling, then the similar inclusion of the Committee for the First Amendment falls into perspective. Committee signers like Gene Kelly and John Huston were cited for this offense in the published 1947 Report of California's Tenney Un-American Activities Committee, a discredited local product which had gained a new lease of life from the HUAC headlines. Soon Committee for the First citations found their way to the dossiers of offenders listed by *Red Channels*, *The American Legion Magazine* (and its newsletter *The Firing Line*) and *Counterattack*, the leading exposure publications of the non-government vigilantists. To top it all, Attorney General

Tom Clark soon listed the Committee as a subversive organization on the "Attorney General's list." (This unworthy security device, later declared by the Supreme Court to be a non-admissible source of evidence, is now generally disregarded. It was an outgrowth of President Truman's loyalty review executive order of March 1947, when the hysteria affected the judgment of the White House itself — perhaps the best plea for exoneration the moguls might make.)

William Wyler, one of the founders of the Committee, later stated: "Of course the Attorney General said it was a Communist front and apparently a front organization is what the Attorney General decides. But this was *not* a Communist front organization. There may have been some Communists in the group but then there are probably Communists in any organization. The point is, they did not run the Committee and a Communist-front organization is one that is run by Communists. We ran the Committee and we were not Communists."[6] Another founder, screenwriter-director Philip Dunne, has personally confirmed this to the author, emphasizing that the Committee was basically a protest against the irresponsible proceedings of the HUAC and that care was taken to avoid sponsorship of the Ten themselves. For additional name-dropping, one can note on this Committee Gregory Peck, Henry Fonda, Kirk Douglas, Van Heflin, Eddie Cantor, Katherine Hepburn, Paulette Goddard, Myrna Loy, Billy Wilder, Danny Kaye, Humphrey Bogart and Sterling Hayden. The last two give an indication of the great confusions that reign when celebrities, let alone ordinary people, are held responsible for their passing enthusiasms. When Bogart, one of the twenty-eight Committee members who had gone to Washington to form a cheering section for Eric Johnston and the rights of Hollywood in general, saw the Ten orate, declaim and then refuse to answer "the question" outside the Committee chambers, he had second thoughts about political positions for actors. He later renounced his participation in the Committee and took Lauren Bacall along with him. Another pratfall occurred when Sterling Hayden arrived at the Capitol to find a Washington newspaper claiming he was a Communist. The Committee leaders were about to raise funds so Hayden could sue for libel when he suddenly recalled he had been a Party member for six months in 1946. Hayden was immediately blacklisted. The full story of his obsequious clearance in 1951, involving the laborious turning of wheels by the noted Hollywood lawyer Martin Gang, which finally gave Hayden the opportunity to win favor in the eyes of HUAC and his bosses by naming names of friends before the Committee in March 1951, is a typical one of this period. As one thinks about Bogey and Hayden, the first with his genteel New York background and the second with his subdued intellectual profile, the heartbreaking absurdity of the investigation, exemplified by the experiences of the pseudo-tough guy on the one hand and the pseudo-Marxist on the other, becomes painfully apparent.

Hayden's pain, though primitive, was permanent, it turned out. Businessmen are generally reticent about their emotional crises. Thus, it would be futile, for example, to try to measure the remorse or anguish the moguls suffered, if any, as they presumably protected their stockholders. Artists are a different breed. Besides, only the artists were faced with the trauma of informing, which soon became the seamy underside of the HUAC investigations. There is no need to pass judgment here on the few namers of names. Some were illustrious personages, such as Clifford Odets, Elia Kazan, Lee J. Cobb, Budd Schulberg and Edward Dymytryk, each numbly rationalizing his action in terms of the confused knowledge of the times about the Communist menace. Others such as Sterling Hayden seem to have been simply expedient, following the cynical clearance advice of their lawyers, agents and, in Hayden's case, psychiatrists as well. In that framework, here is Hayden's afterthought of a dozen years later, as revealed in his autobiography *The Wanderer*, in 1963. It is a reminder to the business community of the hollow victories it helped HUAC obtain:

> Not often does a man find himself eulogized for having behaved in a manner that he himself despises. I subscribed to a press-clipping service. They sent me two thousand clips from papers east and west, large and small, and from dozens of magazines. Most had nothing but praise for my one-shot stoolie show. Only a handful—led by

> *The New York Times* — denounced this abrogation of constitutional freedoms whereby the stoolie could gain status in a land of frightened people.

Altogether five hundred persons, including about every eminent figure in Hollywood and four United States Senators, lent their names to the Committee. For a while, the headlines were running in their favor as talented radio writers like Norman Corwin produced nationwide broadcasts during the hearings under the title "Hollywood Fights Back." Notables from Thomas Mann to Leonard Bernstein joined in these broadcasts. Some of them, such as Joseph Cotten, Edward G. Robinson and even Lucille Ball, later had to run the gauntlet of demeaning "clearance" rituals before they could count on steady employment. Equally important for stiffening the resolve of the moguls at this critical time was the condemnation of the hearings by major newspapers and mass magazines. "Some attempt was made to show that Communism was being permitted to creep into films but in each case the attempt dissolved into the ludicrous," stated the New York *Herald Tribune*.[7] "Is it un-American to ask a man if he is a Communist?" speculated *Life*, deliberately reversing the Committee's thrust.[8]

Still the HUAC had prepared its case rather well. If we would fairly put ourselves in the shoes of the moguls as they edged toward the Waldorf Statement, we must hear some evidence from the cooperative witnesses. This will be of particular interest to businessmen as the witnesses offered some staunch if dim-witted defenses of capitalism against its subverters.

J. Parnell Thomas had selected as anti-Communist witnesses not liberals like Fredric March and Melvyn Douglas, who were qualified even though their first concerns were anti-fascist, but instead some representative members of the Motion Picture Alliance for the Preservation of American Ideals. The Alliance was a militantly anti-Communist group established in 1944 to combat the impression that "Hollywood was dominated by Communists, radicals and crackpots." There were similar splits between conservatives and radicals in the Hollywood labor unions, the Screen Writers Guild and the

Screen Actors Guild. In retrospect, these were the arenas where Hollywood's ideological battles should have been fought out, assuming the alternative of a witch-hunting HUAC augmented by collaborating owners willing to impose a blacklist. Emmet Lavery, testifying at the 1947 hearings as president of the Screen Writers Guild, was the voice of reason in this respect: "Let me break the suspense immediately," he testified, "and tell you that I am not a Communist. I never have been. I don't intend to be. . . . Under our existing contract with the producers and our existing constitution, it would be next to impossible to remove anybody from our Guild for political belief, private political belief or action . . . If any individual members are guilty of indictable offenses that are clearly sedition or treason, let a proper complaint be brought to the FBI and an indictment sought by a Federal grand jury and action taken accordingly." He was not afraid of Communist activity in the Guild, he added, since they could not take over. He did not believe in making martyrs out of them but thought they should be opposed by open democratic means.

If Lavery was pure reason, there were others who were not. Alliance founder Rupert Hughes, a screenwriter who had called Lavery a Communist, warned that where there was "a little drop of cyanide in the picture, a small grain of arsenic, something that makes every Senator, every businessman, every employer a crook and which destroys our beliefs in American free enterprise and free institutions, that is Communistic!" Mrs. Lela Rogers, not an artist but something of a den mother to the Alliance through her concern for her daughter Ginger's exposure to scripts by writers like Theodore Dreiser, was quickly shuttled from the stand by HUAC's chief investigator Robert Stripling in favor of the tough-minded Ayn Rand. Miss Rand, who today is still going strong with her combination of talent and unabashed faith in rugged men motivated by a pure dollar sign, was then best known for her success *The Fountainhead*, which starred Gary Cooper, also an Alliance witness. The profit motive, incidentally, had been working quite well at the time to bring together Hollywood's opposing factions. An outstanding film like *For Whom the Bell Tolls*, for example, had a script by the liberal Dudley Nichols in a story glorifying the Spanish anti-fascists. Gary Cooper was a credible Robert Jordan in this film under the expert direction of Motion Picture Alliance director Sam Wood, also a witness at the hearings.

But Ayn Rand would not tolerate such an accommodation. Drawing on her authentic escape from Bolshevik Russia in 1926, she delivered a 4,000 word scene-by-scene analysis of Louis B. Mayer's wartime *Song of Russia* which came to the conclusion that anything good said or pictured about contemporary Russia was Communistic. Her testimony was buttressed by Robert Taylor, star of *Song of Russia*, who according to the newspapers drew a mob of frantic women attempting to gain seats in the hearing room. Taylor related his patriotic reluctance to play the leading role and received cheers from the audience. Mayer himself plaintively testified that the film was made in 1942 and obviously was a friendly gesture to a wartime ally. Even so it was only a boy meets girl romance, he pointed out, with a chance to use the music of Tchaikowsky. Ayn Rand's harsh standards seemed to surprise the HUAC Congressmen and interrogators. She had previously supplied the Alliance with a "Screen Guide for Americans." This published pamphlet included guidelines such as "Don't Deify the Common Man," "Don't Glorify Failure," and "Don't Smear Success." Some of the moguls, used to traditional concepts of heroes and villains, may have wished for protection from friends when they read her injunction that "every decent man in the motion picture industry . . . has a moral duty to throw into the ashcan where it belongs every story that smears industrialists as such." Even the Bible, that convenient work in the public domain so often produced on film, expressed reservations about rich men getting into Heaven too easily.

One more witness on film content will suffice. A screenwriter named William C. Moffitt, then screen reviewer for *Esquire* magazine, charged the Communists with having inspired "the most dangerous censorship that has ever occurred in the history of the motion picture industry and in the history of motion picture thought." The following is directly from the hearings transcript (Moffitt asked to be allowed not to name films):

> *Mr. Stripling:* Mr. Moffitt, then, without naming any specific pictures, could you give us some examples of the techniques that have been employed?
>
> *Mr. Moffitt:* Well, I gave you one, of the confusion of the class war with the war against Nazi Germany. There is also the campaign against religion, where the minister will be shown as the tool of his richest parishioner . . . There has also been the party line of making the returned soldier fear that the world is against him, that the American principle is against him, that business is against him, that the free-enterprise system is against him. You will see picture after picture in which the banker is presented as an unsympathetic man, who hates to give the GI a loan . . .[9]

If the reader is experiencing the eerie feeling that he has seen that scene somewhere either at the time of its heart-warming postwar success, or again and again on TV, he is right. It was Sam Goldwyn's *The Best Years of Our Lives*, starring Fredric March. Is there any better index to the quality of these hearings than that William Wyler, director of *The Best Years*, announced on a nationwide broadcast five days later that he feared it was a film he "would not be allowed to make today"?

V

Jack Warner confirmed his reputation among a good many of his employees by his eagerness to cast out the devils in his shop. Asked if he stood by his previous secret testimony, he said he couldn't be sure whether the writers he had named were Communists but they were surely "un-American," judging from the things they had tried to slip by him into their scripts. Eight writers had already been fired or allowed to wait out their contracts with no work. On the other hand, he now casually withdrew four of the guilty ones from his secret testimony.

In an opening statement Warner read his lines well: "Ideological termites have burrowed into many American industries, organizations and societies. Wherever they may be, I say let us dig them out and get rid of them. My brothers and I will be happy to subscribe generously to the pest-removal fund. We are willing to establish a fund to ship to Russia the people who don't like our American system of government and prefer the Communistic system to ours."[10] In cross-examination, his tendency to incoherence plagued him. Of two of his withdrawals, the Epstein twins, he stated: "The Epstein brothers worked on a picture called *Animal Kingdom.* As I recall — that was aimed at the capitalistic system — not exactly, but the rich man is always the villain. Of course, those fellows getting $2,000 or $3,000 a week aren't rich men. I don't know what to call them. Both of these fellows work together . . . The rest of the time, they are always on very good American films. As I said, they do it in a joking way. The rich man is always the villain, which is as old as the world itself."[11]

But for the blacklisted writers, it was no joking matter. In spite of Warner's statement at this hearing that he would not join in any attempt to blacklist his fired writers, the fact remains that three of the four withdrawals named by Warner still were unable to find work in Hollywood as late as 1956. This is on the authority of John Cogley, former editor of the Catholic journal *Commonweal* and later religious editor of the *New York Times*, who published an on-the-scene analysis of blacklisting for the Fund for the Republic in that year. Cogley notes that this occurred even though the three subjects were not called up in any of the HUAC hearings or listed in any of the HUAC Annual Reports.[12] Possibly their talent withered on the vine precisely in 1947. Since the blacklist was unofficial and clandestine, one could make it on the wings of rumor as well as through the vigilantist guide-books.

Robert Stripling pushed Warner hard in an effort to prove *Mission to Moscow* (1943) was a propaganda film that had been produced under pressure from the White House. The picture was based on Ambassador Joseph E. Davies's memoirs of 1936 to 1938 and was for the most part a faithful rendition of the best-selling book. Warner stuck to his guns and deprived the Committee of its best chance to show that film content had been infected by subversive activities. Without confirmation from a credible witness,

Stripling's parting shot fell flat: "I don't see that that is aiding the war effort, Mr. Warner — with the cooperation of Mr. Davies or with the approval of the Government — to make a picture which is a fraud in fact."[13] Stripling also failed to prove propaganda in his examination of other friendly witnesses who had been called to testify about Communist infiltration, notably Leo McCarey, a prominent director and James K. McGuinness, supervisor of scripts at MGM.

For high drama, the appearance of Dore Schary, a non-conformist representative of the owners, stands out in this play within a play of twenty-five years ago. Dore Schary was the thinking man's Hollywood producer, urbane, intelligent, compassionate and dedicated to civil liberties. Yet he was tough-minded enough to stand off an assortment of tyrants from Howard Hughes to Louis B. Mayer in his tour of the Hollywood corporate jungle. In 1959 he left Hollywood for New York where he became an independent playwright and producer as well as National Chairman of the Anti-Defamation League. As with so many at the hearings, Schary came face to face with some hard decisions. On balance his conduct was meritorious, although he was destined to be buffeted with bruises from the Ten. As head of production at RKO, then controlled by the remote Floyd B. Odlum, Schary qualifies as a businessman, or at least as a boss — though without power of stockholdings — faced with a moral crisis. Businessmen inevitably face several such crises in a lifetime, the decision to knife or not to knife a friend on one's ladder, to meet or not meet at the antitrust gathering, to transmit or not transmit the payoff, to steal or not steal the trade secret, to lobby or not lobby against the public interest. The more ambivalent, intellectual and inner-directed the man, the more tormented his decision. At any rate, in Schary we can view the young mogul in love with his job in the movies but still clinging to old-fashioned concepts of justice and fair play. A more interesting case history, one might assert, than the cocksure, power-based Jack Warner or the doctrinaire, obsessed John Howard Lawson.

Schary had come to Hollywood fortified with the durability of his hard-working Newark family of caterers (affectionately described in his book *For Special Occasions*). Like them, he was making it in America with taste and energy. A special ingredient of his character was a strong sense of social responsibility, now enlarged by his distinction as a writer and top executive. The Roosevelts were his demigods, their hold on him finally finding expression in his *Sunrise at Campobello*. Like the Roosevelts he was secure enough to scorn hysteria in the certainty that the resilient forces of democracy were better stretched than pilloried. With only a precarious high school education, he had climbed ahead swiftly. Unafraid of commitment, he had early enough put his name on lists, for example, the Hollywood Independent Citizens Committee of the Arts, Sciences and Professions. This Committee was a division of the Progressive Citizens of America and its main object at the beginning was FDR's re-election in 1944. Later the Committee followed Henry Wallace down the alien path of 1948 but without Schary. With Ronald Reagan, Olivia de Haviland, John Green and others, Schary had formed an anti-Communist group within the Independent Committee before moving on to other causes, such as a strong commitment to Adlai Stevenson.

With such credentials, as well as having just made the socially conscious *Crossfire*, Hollywood's first major treatment of anti-Semitism, Schary moved in a rather select circle, with many suitors anxious to count him on their side. He presented the HUAC interrogators with a ringing declaration in favor of hiring on the basis of merit: "Up until the time it is proved that a Communist is a man dedicated to the overthrow of the government by force and violence, or by illegal methods, I cannot make a determination of his employment on any other basis except whether he is qualified best to do the job I want him to do." Chairman Thomas, taken aback by Schary's adroit hedge against accepting the Communist label itself as proof of subversion, demanded: "Therefore, assuming X is a great artist, assuming also that he is a Communist, you would not hesitate to rehire him?" Schary pushed the burden of proof back into Thomas's lap: "I would not hesitate to rehire him if it was not proven that he was a foreign agent. I would still maintain his right to think politically as he chooses." This two-tier system of Communism, one benign and one malign, was too much for Thomas. Comparing Schary with a sleeping Rip Van Winkle, he took him off the stand.

Before proceeding to the Waldorf, the activity of two modest figures at the hearing, Ronald Reagan and Richard Nixon, should be noted for historical interest. Reagan was president of the Screen Actors Guild and a staunch anti-Communist member of the Motion Picture Alliance. Still this handsome young man, who before the war had been a highly-charged New Dealer, spoke with measured good sense when placed on the stand. Asked for his opinion concerning proposals that the Communist Party be banned by law — precisely the kind of question the Committee should have been concentrating on — Reagan's answer was completely consistent with Dore Schary's employment conditions:

> Fundamentally I would say in opposing those people that the best thing to do is to make democracy work. In the Screen Actors Guild we made it work by insuring everyone a vote and by keeping everyone informed. I believe that, as Thomas Jefferson put it, if all the American people know all of the facts they will never make a mistake.
>
> Whether the party should be outlawed I agree . . . is a matter for the Government to decide. As a citizen I would hesitate, or not like, to see any political party outlawed on the basis of its political ideology. We have spent 170 years in this country on the basis that democracy is strong enough to stand up and fight against the inroads of any ideology. However, if it is proven that an organization is an agent of a power, a foreign power, or in any way not a legitimate political party, and I think the Government is capable of proving that, if the proof is there, then that is another matter.[14]

The presence of Richard Nixon is significant since in the long run he was the only Congressman who found HUAC membership not to be a road to political oblivion. The freshman from California did not have too much to say in the 1947 hearings. When Adolf Menjou surprisingly advocated keeping Communist writers on the job so long as their propaganda was clearly labelled as such, Richard Nixon amiably agreed. "If we refuse to allow a Communist picture to be made and advertised as such," said Nixon, "we would be falling into the same error that we criticize the Communists for in Russia."[15] By 1948, however, Nixon had warmed up to his HUAC duties. In that year, his relentless support of Whittaker Chambers against Alger Hiss won him fame that eventually carried him to the White House.

VI

Eric Johnston finally was called upon by Thomas in the second week and made a spirited defense of the industry. He challenged the Committee to screen the films instead of talking about them. He defended the right of free speech and told the Committee that he was not going to let it dictate what sort of films Hollywood should make. There was no reason to believe at this point that the moguls, clearly the winner on the propaganda count, would not be fairly lenient with their employees, including the Ten, who represented considerable talent if not tact. Certainly the subsequent years of blacklisting in the hundreds would then seem far-fetched.

Johnston's testimony ended on an ominous note as Thomas complained that Johnston had promised the full cooperation of his Motion Picture Association of America. "I just wouldn't want to tell the kind of cooperation that we have been getting," grumbled Thomas after Johnston's statements. Then Stripling crashed down on Johnston by naming one of his top assistants as having once been a member of the Communist party.[16] (This irrelevant, ruthless display of immune power was of course repeated by Senator McCarthy, to his regret, against an assistant to attorney Joseph Welch in 1954.)

Without giving his reasons, Thomas suddenly terminated the hearings on October 30, with many witnesses still uncalled. In his remarks to the press, he promised to reopen the hearings soon with conclusive evidence of Communist content in the films. At best it was a retreat.

The fifty most important members of the industry, encamped in the Waldorf a month later with Johnston, McNutt and Byrnes, received news on the first day of their meeting that Thomas had won his contempt citations from Congress for each of the Ten. The press was still running strong against the Committee's tactics (with the notable exception of the Hearst papers) and the independent-minded President in the White House was known to have little sympathy for those who would knock the New Deal while taking on Hollywood. In addition, there were strong dissidents within the Waldorf, notably Darryl F. Zannuck, Samuel Goldwyn, Walter Wanger, Eddie Mannix and Dore Schary. Zannuck's boss, Spyros Skouras, however, had already publicly announced that Twentieth Century Fox's board had passed a resolution to fire either acknowledged Communists or persons refusing to answer questions before the HUAC. Schary would similarly find himself overruled by Floyd B. Odlum, the RKO chairman. When the Board of Directors of RKO called a special meeting for the firing of Scott and Dymytryk, Schary asked that the minutes record his vote against it. He also told Odlum he would not execute any orders to fire them. Odlum respected Schary's position, defended it against the critics of the far right and issued a statement in defense of Schary's behavior. In spite of this, Schary became the unique target of criticism from both the left and the right.

Since the statement issued from the Waldorf on the second day was in effect the first public announcement in modern American industry relating to firing for political beliefs, it bears reading in full.

> Members of the Association of Motion Picture Producers deplore the action of the ten Hollywood men who have been cited for contempt of the House of Representatives. We do not desire to pre-judge their legal rights, but their actions have been a disservice to their employers and have impaired their usefulness to the industry.
>
> We will forthwith discharge or suspend without compensation those in our employ and we will not re-employ any of the ten until such time as he is acquitted or has purged himself of contempt and declares under oath that he is not a Communist.

> On the broader issue of alleged subversive and disloyal elements in Hollywood, our members are likewise prepared to take positive action.
>
> We will not knowingly employ a Communist or a member of any party or group which advocates the overthrow of the Government of the United States by force or by any illegal or unconstitutional methods.
>
> In pursuing this policy, we are not going to be swayed by hysteria or intimidation from any source. We are frank to recognize that such a policy involves dangers and risks. There is the danger of hurting innocent people. There is the risk of creating an atmosphere of fear. Creative work at its best cannot be carried on in an atmosphere of fear. We will guard against this danger, this risk, this fear.
>
> To this end we will invite the Hollywood talent guilds to work with us to eliminate any subversives; to protect the innocent; and to safeguard free speech and a free screen wherever threatened.
>
> The absence of a national policy, established by Congress with respect to the employment of Communists in private industry, makes our task difficult. Ours is a nation of laws. We request Congress to enact legislation to assist American industry to rid itself of subversive, disloyal elements.
>
> Nothing subversive or un-American has appeared on the screen. Nor can any number of Hollywood investigations obscure the patriotic services of the 30,000 Americans employed in Hollywood who have given our Government invaluable aid in war and peace.

Legally of course the moguls were on firm ground, in spite of a California law prohibiting such firing, since Communism, thanks to President Truman's loyalty review order as much as anything else, had achieved sufficient definition on its own as being a state of disloyalty. Besides, bosses can fire for any reason they want, subject to minor restrictions such as employment contracts, union agreements and possibly conspiracy to deprive people of their livelihoods. What was involved was basically a moral, not a legal decision. Finally, the statement should be read with the insight derived from our knowledge that when the hysteria finally died away, the statement was simply forgotten. Men like Dalton Trumbo (who never purged himself) and Ring Lardner, Jr. (who admitted in 1961 that he had been a half-hearted Party member for a brief period — not under oath but in the *Saturday Evening Post)* are working today as busily as ever. Since the statement itself was never withdrawn, one is suddenly frozen with the apprehension that this momentous document, affecting stands of conscience, personal values, reputations and careers, was simply tailored to meet the demands of the times. No one really cares about the political beliefs of Hollywood writers today, either at the box-office or in Jack Warner's office, so now the statement is an anachronism. For citizens seeking absolute truths on which to base decisions, such relativism is a chilling example at best. America's cyclical bouts of hysteria from Salem on, however, have always substituted emotion for reason and law. The moguls at least recognized this, revealing their embarrassment in that next to last paragraph of the statement, which asks Congress to pass laws covering its dubious work rather than pressure one industry to come clean before a Congressional committee.

Now Dore Schary returns to center stage. As a former member of the Screen Writers Guild and advocate of employees' rights at the hearings, he had been chosen to discuss with Guild members the new policy on behalf of the owners. "We seek to acquaint you with the intent of the producers' statement," he telegrammed its members on November 27, "and to reassure you that our action is designed to protect the industry and all those engaged in it and to disavow any intention of a witch-hunt." A certain amount of courage must be awarded to Schary for even appearing on such a dismal task before approximately four hundred men and women writers including six of the Ten. Though he had defended two of the Ten at the hearings, RKO's producer Adrian Scott and director Edward Dymytryk, they had of course immediately been fired in accordance with the statement. Schary gamely tried to enlist the support of the Guild for the owners' position, although stating that he himself had not agreed with it. It was not just a matter of relating the producers' stand on the Ten, which Schary did not ask them to condone, but also of informing them that people suspected of being Communists were also ineligible for work on the same terms.[17] The unhappy emissary repeated that he did not expect them to condone this either but asked for a closing of ranks to restore Hollywood's good name. Presumably Schary meant that since the producers would not "knowingly employ a Communist," the unfriendly witnesses who had not been called to testify, for example, would somehow have to clear themselves before they could work again. The vagueness of such a position was an omen of the widespread blacklisting that was to follow, a condition which Schary, of course, personally deplored. After he left the meeting, Schary and his colleagues were colorfully denounced by the indestructible Trumbo and the Guild voted practically unanimously to demand an end to the spreading blacklist.

Schary's predicament as a business executive came from that part of his makeup that made him a dissenter in the first place. Now to please Trumbo and his other critics, nothing short of the grand gesture of resignation would suffice. Since he was an anti-Communist to start with, this kind of sacrifice may have been asking too much. Fellow executives may speculate for themselves what they would have done in his place. Lillian Ross, a reporter for *The New Yorker* magazine, pursued the point a few weeks after the Waldorf statement. She quoted the young executive as answering that he had been faced with the alternative of joining up with the producers, including the stand taken by RKO, or quitting his job. "I don't believe you should quit under fire," Schary told her. "Anyway, I like making pictures. I want to stay in the industry. I like it."[18] No one else, it should be noted, including the most ardent members of the Committee for the First Amendment, saw fit to resign either. Still Schary had exposed himself to inconsistency. On December 4, 1947, Schary was scheduled to receive the Anti-Defamation League's first "Humanitarian Award" for being executive producer of *Crossfire*. Since Scott and Dymytryk had produced and directed the film, Schary tactfully declined to accept the award in person. Eric Johnston accepted it on Schary's behalf.

Ironically this man who incurred the wrath of the Ten found himself under attack by a vigilante group after leaving RKO to become head of production at MGM. A nondescript organization called The Wage Earners erupted in Los Angeles in 1951. Its pickets paraded with signs reading: "Please do not patronize. This is an MGM picture. Dore Schary Boss of MGM. See House un-American Activities Report. . . . See California Tenney Committee Reports." Schary filed suit for libel and the picketing was soon stopped by court order.

Within the motion picture industry Schary constantly sought to break the blacklist system while suffering the conscience pangs of being a part of the establishment that carried it on. When *Moulin Rouge* was being picketed by the American Legion in 1952, he unsuccessfully proposed a head-on confrontation with the Legion by attacking them with a trailer film to be shown along with the feature. The owners preferred to outflank the Legion on that issue by using the powerful Roy M. Brewer to "clear" Jose Ferrer and John Huston, whose connection with the film offended the Legion's "guilt by citation" standards.[19] In doing so, they helped confirm Brewer in his unprecedented role as clearance boss as well as union boss. Soon Brewer crossed the line, becoming an executive at Allied Artists.

VII

There is a widespread theory that the real reason the moguls capitulated to the HUAC was because the bankers gave them an ultimatum to do so. This would suit the purposes of the moguls indeed and no denials of the theory have ever been issued. Dore Schary, fresh from the Waldorf, noticeably did not offer such a handy defense in his explanation to the Writers Guild.

Yet the theory has gained wide currency and is repeated in the literature on the subject. "It was genuinely agreed . . . in the financial circles which control the industry, that something had to be done," writes Cogley in discussing the Waldorf statement.[20] In turn he quotes Ed Sullivan, then a Broadway columnist: "Reason that Hollywood big shots rushed to New York and barred the ten cited by Congress was forecast in my Nov. 1 column: 'Hollywood has been dealt a body blow that won't please Wall Street financiers, who have not less than $60,000,000 in picture companies.' Wall Street jiggled the strings, that's all."[21] Alvah Bessie, one of the most bitter of the Ten and the least likely to grant a refuge to the moguls, picked up the theory at face value in his 1965 *Inquisition in Eden:* ". . . the producers, whom Eric Johnston swore would never institute a blacklist, were called into the Waldorf-Astoria Hotel in New York by the boys who really run the industry (the financiers) and told where to head in."[22] Walter Goodman, in his full-scale review of HUAC, *The Committee* (1964), a book which scoffs at the Committee and the Communists with equal vigor, picks up the theme: "The decisive pressure came from the New York financial interests on which the Studios relied."[23] Finally, Martin Gang is represented in Cogley's book as having advised a screenwriter seeking clearance: ". . . certain organizations did have lists of names and had announced that they would picket any theatre showing pictures on which any of these names appeared. Since such picketing would result in loss of income as a result of diminished attendance, the banks had come to the decision not to lend money for the production of any pictures which used people whose names were on any of these lists. Since studios could not produce pictures without financing from banks, they were therefore unable to employ anyone on these lists."[24]

To a writer-businessman, bank pressure of this type in the Hollywood of 1947 does not seem credible. The balance sheets of the big companies show debt ratios that would have allowed them to produce *The Communist Manifesto* had they so desired. The big studios were flush, arrogant and independent. Most of them had negotiated long-term financing for their debt structure which made interference on individual films all the more remote. The $60,000,000 referred to by Ed Sullivan was equity capital, owned by hundreds of thousands of happy stockholders concerned only with their dividends and current stock prices. Bank of America was the major lender to the industry but the First National Bank of Boston and the Chemical, Bankers Trust and Chase of New York were also important, often participating in loans with Bank of America. Within this context, the writer has checked with veteran Bank of America and other bank officers. They are unanimous in deriding this theory.[25] The independent producers, incidentally, who were the most likely to take a chance on employing blacklisted writers and actors, were then the specialty of Security Pacific National Bank in Los Angeles. Security's former chief lending officer to the film industry has also confirmed that the banks were simply not involved in any such decisions.[26] Martin Gang has stated to the author that he is completely misquoted by Cogley's anonymous screenwriter and that the banks were not a party to such action then or later. Finally Dore Schary has told the author that the theory is totally false. (Thus the moving finger of history writes, scratches out and moves on.)

What then, were the real reasons for the Waldorf Statement and the widespread blacklisting for which it set the inevitable pattern? The most obvious answer is that the top bosses decreed it out of fear of the Committee, of Communism and of the box-office in that order. These moguls were for the most part unsophisticated men of limited vision and culture, nickelodeon tycoons unable to face a moral crisis with style during a period of hysteria.

Yet the war in Korea, the "loss" of China and the rash of spy revelations that helped bring about McCarthyism, when hysteria peaked, were still around the corner in 1947. The tycoons were also natively shrewd men whose Waldorf Statement shows they were aware they were running temporarily with the forces of repression and thus against the American tradition. Was there perhaps another factor in 1947 that tipped the scales when they could have swung either way? One can suggest that since the majority of the fifty at the Waldorf were Jewish, they were just plain embarrassed by the number of Jews among the unfriendly witnesses. Of the nineteen such witnesses called to Washington in 1947, thirteen happened to be Jews. So, of course, were a great many of the actors, writers, directors and producers in and out of causes later deemed

Communist-front or for that matter the Party itself. What attracted these talented, imaginative people to Communism would require a separate sociological study. Mixed with the quest for social justice, especially during the depression, one would find the inheritance of European Socialism and intellectualism as well as the laggard reaction of the democracies to Franco and Hitler in the early days of fascism. Probably too there was a dash of glamor and a sense of belonging in the secrecy and discipline of the Party and of course there was the guilt related to high earnings for the commercialization of their talents.

This speculation need not be pursued too far lest it lead to the stereotyped thinking suggested on the part of the moguls. The fact is no matter how many Jews happened to go in and out of Communism in the thirties and forties only the insanity of anti-Semitism can equate Jews and Communists as a magnetic alliance. If Jews or other minorities ever reach total tolerance in America, it will be when each is judged on his own merits, habits, manners and all, as is the case for the majority. In just a few years, the unveiling of Whittaker Chambers, Elizabeth Bentley, William Remington and above all Alger Hiss, the most unbelievable WASP candidate imaginable, pointed out to Americans how many mansions the Party contained, no doubt adding immeasurably to the nation's hysteria as a result. The labor movement also had a more than generous share of authentic Americans among its Wobblies and Commies. And writers as rooted as Theodore Dreiser, Sherwood Anderson, Lincoln Steffens, Edmund Wilson and Granville Hicks had announced for Communism in the thirties rather than vote for Roosevelt.[27] In 1947, however, the Jewish moguls, primitives that they were in many respects, could very well have been so horrified by the bad conduct of their Jewish hired hands that they were persuaded to take the upright J. Parnell Thomas's advice and turn their backs on them and their friends completely. Dore Schary has told the author of a meeting of the moguls wherein one Warner, it doesn't matter which, stated that if he found out his own brother were a Communist, after what this country had done for them, he would put a rope around his neck and deliver him to the authorities.

Schary recalls suggesting that for one's own brother an alternative would be to try to find out what happened and then help him mend his ways but he found no keepers across the conference table.

To close the matter, one should remember that Spyros Skouras, a prime shaker at the Waldorf, and Howard Hughes, who took over RKO early in 1948, could not have been bothered by this problem. Hughes, then as now, defies analysis. The Ten actually thought he was going to be their patron for a while and fly them to Washington in his Constellation.[28] His own brushes with Congressional committees were well known. Hughes, however, outdid his fellow moguls in housecleaning. The *New York Times* of April 7, 1952 quotes Hughes in an outright affirmation of blacklisting for "sympathy" alone. "RKO will operate on a curtailed production basis for an indefinite period," said Hughes, "in a drastic move to strengthen a political screening program to prevent employment of persons suspected of being Communists or having Communist sympathies. . . . All studios have at their disposal information concerning the people who have been connected with one or more of the well-known Communist-front organizations." The news story also contains a ludicrous account about troubles in his script department that would lead one to believe the best writers had to be congenital radicals. The *Times* quoted Hughes as asserting that "every one" of eleven stories, selected as best for filming out of 150 read by the studio over a period of six months, had to be discarded because "information concerning one or more persons involved in the past writing of the script or original story showed that these writers were suspected of Communist ideas or sympathies." Dore Schary had left RKO in 1948 to become head of production at MGM. Speaking from the vantage point of his new career as independent producer and civil rights champion, Schary recently considered once again the moral dilemma confronting him in 1947. "At first I thought of quitting, and then when I thought of the actions of these fellows, I said to myself, 'I don't really want to be part of their bag.' I sensed that a lot more trouble was coming. I felt that I would rather be in a position of some authority to fight it off, which, over a period of time, proved to be a wise decision. I saved a number of people from getting smeared and blown out of work."[29]

VIII

The trouble came indeed, culminating in the 1951 hearings. This time the HUAC chairman was John S. Wood of Georgia, who had once observed that the activities of the Ku Klux Klan were "an old American custom." Wood's tenure was noted for repeated forays against the labor movement as well as against Communism in Hollywood. Under his regime HUAC's published annual reports featured names unearthed during the year's investigations, including those offered without proof by cooperative witnesses.

The 1951 hearings were not in the least interested in propaganda — in fact, Hollywood had already turned to producing a spate of anti-Communist films by that time. Instead HUAC was devoted to exposure as the sure way to punish Communists and their sympathizers. Exposure would also cut off the funds which Hollywood was pouring into the Party coffers. A good word can be said for exposure through properly motivated and conducted committee investigations. Raised to the level of "prescriptive publicity," in the phrase of the political scientist Earl Latham, it contributes to the legislative process.[30] Whenever Congressional committees, however, work on Communism, the results rarely seem worth the effort. (The ability of the government to cope with treason and revolution in a normal fashion is considerable enough. Yet the HUAC is still with us, under its new name the House Committee for Internal Security.)

By 1951 the actions of the moguls in relation to HUAC were thoroughly disreputable. As with all corrupting habits, use itself had institutionalized blacklisting, deadening the capacity to be shocked. In addition, the political and financial climate insured that no changes would arise. The alarms induced by Korea, spies and Senator McCarthy were exacerbated by the flowering of television. Movie attendance of 80 million a week in 1946 was on its way to 46 million a week in 1953. Aggravated industry leaders now played the anti-Communist game all the way, freezing out those who took the Fifth Amendment and placing the burden of guilt on anyone named or cited by indiscriminate informers and agencies. Performers who had not been associated with the Party but were suffering from work-depriving rumors, such as Edward G. Robinson, Jose Ferrer and John Garfield, actually appeared in Washington at their own request to go through a show of shriving. Everyone's sensibilities hardened a degree in those years including the professionals themselves. The Actors Guild condemned its members who took the Fifth Amendment and showed little concern about the blacklist or even the grey list. Members of the Writers Guild, heirs to Kafka and his tales of nightmare trials, were too battered by internal dissension to keep the issue alive.

The taking of the Fifth was a nightmare experience for witnesses at the 1951 and subsequent hearings. A later decade of citizens saw the gangsters taking the Fifth on TV without feeling much about it either way, recognizing the witnesses did not want to incriminate themselves. But taking the Fifth at the HUAC hearings was quite a different matter. A Supreme Court decision in 1950 *(Rogers* v. *U.S.)* had decreed that once a witness admitted he had been a Party member he could not refuse to answer the next question (name your friends in the Party). Yet to start out with the Fifth itself, because it provoked the suspicion of Communism and demonstrated non-cooperation with a Congressional committee, was a guarantee of unemployment. Larry Parks came prepared to admit he had been a Communist. No doubt he was also prepared to repent publicly, perform anti-Communist deeds and get a clearance, his commitment, like that of practically all the others, having been strictly a temporary conversion. But he was not prepared to become an informer. As the first witness to take such a stand in 1951, he made a desperate plea: "Don't present me with the choice of either being in contempt of this committee and going to jail or forcing me to really crawl through the mud to be an informer, for what purpose? I don't think this is a choice at all. I don't think this is really sportsmanlike. I don't think this is American justice. . . . I think it will impair the usefulness of this Committee to a great extent because it will make it almost impossible for a person to come to you, as I have done, and open himself to you and tell you the truth. So I beg of you not to force me to do this." Congressman Walter, later to be a chairman of the Committee, expressed sympathy. "How can it be material to the purpose of this inquiry," he asked, "to have the names of people when we already know them? . . . Why is it so essential that we know the names of all the people when we have a witness who may make a contribution to what we are trying to know?" His colleagues differed and Parks was told in effect to name names, which he did, or face a citation for contempt. Now that the smoke has cleared, there are those who say the Committee was bluffing and would not have pressed jail on a person who refused to name names, so one need not have taken the Fifth in the first place. Yet how does one justify even the bluff of jail for not informing? What should we tell our children about informing?

Lillian Hellman, the distinguished playwright of *The Little Foxes* and *Watch on the Rhine*, met the issue when subpoenaed to appear in 1952. Granted that her eminence gave her economic protection denied most others in the same predicament, as well as the fact that Broadway alone dismissed blacklisting as a straw man for its box-office, Miss Hellman's letter to Chairman Wood is provocative (she later took the Fifth):

> I am most willing to answer all questions about myself. I have nothing to hide from your committee and there is nothing in my life of which I am ashamed. I have been advised by counsel that under the fifth amendment I have a constitutional privilege to decline to answer any questions about my political opinions, activities, and associations, on the grounds of self-incrimination. I do not wish to claim this privilege. I am ready and willing to testify before the representatives of our Government as to my own opinions and my own actions, regardless of any risks or consequences to myself.
>
> But I am advised by counsel that if I answer the committee's questions about myself, I must also answer ques-

tions about other people and that if I refuse to do so, I can be cited for contempt. My counsel tells me that if I answer questions about myself, I will have waived my rights under the fifth amendment and could be forced legally to answer questions about others. This is very difficult for a layman to understand: But there is one principle that I do understand: I am not willing, now or in the future, to bring bad trouble to people who, in my past association with them, were completely innocent of any talk or any action that was disloyal or subversive. I do not like subversion or disloyalty in any form and if I had ever seen any I would have considered it my duty to have reported it to the proper authorities. But to hurt innocent people whom I knew many years ago in order to save myself is, to me, inhuman and indecent, and dishonorable. I cannot and will not cut my conscience to fit this year's fashions, even though I long ago came to the conclusion that I was not a political person and could have no comfortable place in any political group.

I was raised in an old-fashioned American tradition and there were certain homely things that were taught to me: To try to tell the truth, not to bear false witness, not to harm my neighbor, to be loyal to my country, and so on. In general, I respected these ideals of Christian honor and did as well with them as I knew how. It is my belief that you will agree with these simple rules of human decency and will not expect me to violate the good American tradition from which they spring. I would, therefore, like to come before you and speak of myself.

I am prepared to waive the privilege against self-incrimination and to tell you everything you wish to know about my views or actions if your committee will agree to refrain from asking me to name other people. If the committee is unwilling to give me this assurance, I will be forced to plead the privilege of the fifth amendment at the hearing.

At any rate, our basic concern is with blacklisting by employers. This applies not only to the relatively small core of Communists who the author believes should not have been prevented from writing and acting *by general edict*, but more particularly to the hundreds of do-gooders and petition-signers caught in the web of reaction in a time of hysteria. Eventually the more durable and talented of the Ten found their way back, beginning with Otto Preminger's courageous announcement in 1960 that he was hiring Dalton Trumbo as scriptwriter for *Exodus*, picketers be damned. A remarkable ordeal and trial, however, involving a non-Communist hastened the end of blacklisting in the entertainment industry. It also helped certain members of the business community and the American Legion to regain their senses. For that story, we go to New York and John Henry Faulk.

IX

It was 1952 and Joseph Cotten was flying into Syracuse, New York. He was in the private plane of his sponsor, Seabrook Farms, accompanied by the firm's president, C. F. Seabrook, its lawyer and its advertising agency head, Peter Hilton of Hilton and Riggio. Cotten was the star of Seabrook's radio series, "The Private Files of Matthew Bell." They were on their way to see Laurence A. Johnson, a supermarket owner who was terrorizing a good portion of the radio and television industry. For Seabrook, sales and profits were at stake. For Hilton, fifteen per cent of his half-million dollar account. For Cotten, the cold sweat of facing a tormenter who could keep him from earning a livelihood in his profession. Hilton had already asked MCA, the show's producer, to cancel it. MCA had refused and pushed for the trip to Syracuse.

Johnson, an aging businessman gone berserk on the subject of Communism, did not often grant audiences. His was the power of the letterhead, the telegram and the phone call. As a crafty poison-penner, he instinctively realized that the medium was as important as the message. In turn his leverage on Madison Avenue was magnified coming from Syracuse, a major marketing area on all the data charts but somehow mysterious to the men in Manhattan.

The assault on Cotten had started on the red, white and blue letterhead of Johnston's staunch ally, the American Legion Post No. 41 of Syracuse. In this instance the letter was signed by Johnson himself, although normally the signature would be that of John R. Dungey, Chairman of the Anti-Subversive Committee of that organization. Sometimes Johnson in his cat and mouse game with the glamorous people of the entertainment world would have three telegrams fired on the hour, the first from Johnson's Supermarkets, the next from the Legion and the final from the Veterans Action Committee of the Syracuse Supermarkets, Francis W. Neuser, Commander. Neuser was Johnson's fruit and vegetable buyer. This group, too, had an imposing red, white and blue letterhead.

When it was all over — approximately ten years later when John Henry Faulk received a $3.5 million libel award against Johnson and his co-defendants — responsible businessmen must have sighed with disbelief at their fear of this grocer from Syracuse. Why did they let Johnson and his professional consultant, Vincent Hartnett, tyrannize them? Major manufacturers, able to give the back of their hands to union demands and stockholder complaints, rushed Johnson's harsh letters to their frightened agencies with demands to "do something," rather than throw them in wastebaskets. The networks, experienced in standing up to the FCC and the White House itself, basely played the blacklist game, institutionalizing it with "security officers" who either cleared with Hartnett (at $5.00 to $20.00 per name) or kept their own kangaroo court files of listed artists. The show packagers, particularly those like David Susskind and Mark Goodson, showed up better than the others. True free enterprisers, respectful of talent, they dragged their heels as best they could, fought when they could and told all, as the networks would not, at Faulk's great symbolic trial. The ad men, most precariously perched of all those on the business side, mutely accepted their inglorious, trapped position between sponsor and artist as another ulcer. There was enough talent to go around. "Why stick your neck out?" was the prevailing doctrine on Madison Avenue. Yet the matter at hand concerned one's livelihood.

The simplest explanation for the sad showing of these businessmen is fear. Not only fear of losing money but fear of being smeared as pro-Communist. This was one of the insidious aspects of McCarthyism in the years 1950 through 1954, namely that if you spoke against the anti-Communists, you were likely to get the accolade yourself. McCarthy used this tactic, HUAC used it and Johnson and Hartnett used it, in their case to the point of their own undoing over Faulk. There seems to be no other fear which has gripped Americans so irrationally and so out of proportion as Communism. What logically should have been a fear of Russia as the other great world power, with particularly dangerous ambitions being shown in Korea, was transmuted into a phobia normally reserved for something unclean like the bubonic plague. In that atmosphere, hundreds of entertainers — the most naive and trusting of political scholars to start with — were harassed for being "tainted," with only supergrocers and vigilantists able to cleanse them. One suspects in addition a sexually-oriented sadism in the passion of these new Puritans to corner and humiliate the beautiful and the handsome.

The four supplicants drove from the airport to Johnson's office, in the rear of one of his supermarkets. As Hilton told the story at Faulk's trial in 1962, there were stiff formalities as introductions were made. Since it was about noon they adjourned to a nearby restaurant. Mr. Seabrook opened negotiations by assuring Johnson that he personally was against anything that might be tinged with Communism. He cited the record of Seabrook Farms in the war and indicated he would not knowingly support anything which might foster or help a known Communist. Having established credentials for the firm, he then turned to Hilton who made a peace offering. In effect, if Johnson would lay off Cotten, every third commercial would be changed to an institutional message praising America and the need to protect its freedoms.

Johnson thought this was a good idea and turned to Cotten, who had been described in his letter as advancing the cause of "Stalin's little creatures," crawling over Seabrook products. Johnson had also made it clear in his letter that Seabrook faced boycott not only by Johnson's six supermarkets but by his friends in the

National Association of Supermarkets, of which he was an official.

Cotten recited at length the work he had done during the war and submitted letters testifying about entertaining the troops, speaking at war bond dinners and the like. Cotten had not been called before the HUAC and had never been charged with present or former Party affiliation. His problem was being identified with a "front" organization cited by HUAC in one of its reports. He explained to Johnson that this membership was casual and brief and had long preceded the period cited in the HUAC report. According to Hilton, Johnson replied cryptically he had only the record to go by and he had to make his judgment as to who was American and who was not American by the record.

They left after lunch and on the way to the airport passed a Johnson supermarket, whereupon Johnson asked if they would like to see it. Naturally they acquiesced and suddenly Cotten found himself besieged by customers who obtained his autograph while the kindly, white-haired Johnson beamed on approvingly. To his disgust, Cotten realized he was being paraded like a captive animal by Johnson.

Seabrook was not satisfied and cancelled the show at the end of the first thirteen-week segment. In addition, he fired Hilton and Riggio as his agency for having led him into the scrape. The only beneficial result was that Hilton was encouraged to add his testimony towards the careful building of the case that would prove Johnson capable of conspiring with Hartnett and Aware, Inc. to libel and keep out of work John Henry Faulk.

X

Of all the unlikely candidates for Johnson and Hartnett to take on, Faulk was certainly a poor choice. A native Texan, a former University of Texas teacher, collector of folk songs and Negro sermons, he had a daily talk and music hour on WCBS radio and was a rising television star on panel shows when lightning struck him in 1956. His personality clearly emerges in his own book, *Fear on Trial*, and in *The Jury Returns*, by his famous counsel,

Louis Nizer.[31] Forty-two at the time, he wore tweed jackets and smoked a pipe as a professor would. When he spoke, it was with the Texas accent and picturesque idioms of the country South. Apparently he was something of a literate Will Rogers type at that phase of his career. Unfailingly courteous and genial in manner, he carried the memory of his civil-rights-minded lawyer father as one of the foundations of his spirit during the agony of the trial. His idol was Professor J. Frank Dobie, the noted Texas educator, after whom he had named one of his three children. His achievements included a Julius Rosenwald fellowship and a Rockefeller Foundation fellowship. His recordings and collections of Negro sermons are now in the Library of Congress.

He tried to enlist immediately after Pearl Harbor. Rejected for blindness in one eye, he joined the Merchant Marine and saw convoy duty in the Atlantic. Then he joined the American Red Cross and became Assistant Field Director in Egypt. By 1944 he was able to enlist in the Army for limited service as a psychiatric social worker. A lecturer as well as entertainer, he had appeared before the Daughters of the American Revolution, Yale, Harvard, Fordham and churches of all denominations. His chief subject was "The American Heritage." His family town was Austin. He was an intimate friend of Sam Rayburn, who knew him from childhood, and of Lyndon Johnson. In 1955, two years before he was fired by WCBS, Mrs. Lyndon Johnson offered him the vice-presidency of her Texas radio stations. Faulk resigned to accept and was asked to stay by his superiors at CBS, including Frank Stanton, the president. They prepared a letter for him, withdrawing his resignation and resuming his contract, which became evidence in his trial.

Why did Johnson and Hartnett pick on this paragon of Americanism as a man for a blacklisting object lesson? He hadn't even made *Red Channels*, the bible of radio-TV blacklisting, which Hartnett collaborated on in 1950 for *Counterattack* and its parent organization, American Business Consultants. Given a second time around, Hartnett failed to include Faulk in his supplemental *File 13*, listing more performers with alleged Communist-front affiliations. Finally, as Nizer made Hartnett admit on the stand, he never found

Faulk's name mentioned in any of the HUAC reports and he had never seen him at the front meetings Hartnett covered professionally.

The answer is simply that Johnson and Hartnett overreached themselves. They thought they were immune from suit. After all, they had brought the biggest and most glamorous stars to bay and Faulk was small fry. There were always disclaimers at the top of each exposure publication to the effect that the authors relied on the sources quoted and were making no charges of their own about Communism and the person cited. So much for libel. As for blacklisting, employers had the right to hire and fire as they wished. They could count on the networks and ad agencies not to testify about conspiring together for joint action in that respect. Certainly no one in the industry was going to challenge the sponsors, transfixed as they were with audience ratings for their huge expenditures.

If extra pressure were needed, Hartnett and his followers had good friends in the HUAC, ready to subpoena entertainers who challenged them. All in all, the type of law suit involved would be costly, would take at least three or four years and would fly in the face of Hartnett's rights under the First Amendment. Besides, veterans organizations and a good portion of the public seemed to approve of their endeavors. Johnson carried letters of praise from sponsors and even a letter of apology from a CBS television president for having allowed comedian Jack Gilford to appear on an Arthur Godfrey show. Hartnett regarded himself as a patriot even while making a living out of his specialty. The blacklisting itself was unorganized, varied from station to station and was amenable to purging under certain circumstances. The times were running with the Hartnetts and Johnsons.

Faulk challenged them and their friends in the area of union activity. As a result, they decided to dig up enough about him (rather sloppily, it turned out) to punish him, including probable unemployment. The surprise was not so much that they picked on him with his clean background as the fact that Faulk decided to fight back as a matter of principle. He started the suit while he was still employed by CBS radio. He had, however, lost several radio sponsors and all his TV spots immediately after the attack.

On the basis of this damage, he genuinely and idealistically hoped to stop the ugly practice, little dreaming he would face the five years of total unemployment in his field that would lead to the huge verdict. Even then, he probably would not have won his case without the brilliant, painstaking advocacy of his attorney, Louis Nizer, who had previously conquered Westbrook Pegler in a famous libel suit involving Quentin Reynolds.

XI

Every radio and television performer has to belong to the American Federation of Television and Radio Artists, a union known as AFTRA. Faulk joined the union in 1946 when he first went on the air but had never been very active in its affairs. In 1953 an organization named Aware was incorporated "to combat the Communist conspiracy in entertainment-communications," something of a counterpart to the earlier Motion Picture Alliance in Hollywood. By 1955 Vincent Hartnett was a director of Aware and the source for most of its exposure bulletins. From the point of view of Faulk, Aware had turned into a vigilante committee, carelessly blacklisting performers for pro-Communist activities or records. A pro-Aware faction soon dominated the board of directors of AFTRA and several members served as officers of both organizations, including distinguished performers such as Vinton Hayworth and Bud Collyer.

According to Faulk and his associates, only fear of the consequences kept the members at large of AFTRA from denouncing Aware and ejecting it from union affairs. Fear has its own fever chart and in March 1955, in the wake of Senator McCarthy's deflation, the membership at a stormy meeting was presented with a petition to condemn Aware. Minutes of the meeting were introduced into Faulk's trial and they reveal a high level of concerned debate among people often regarded as superficial in their emotions and principles. Actor Leslie Barrett told of receiving harassing letters, beginning in December 1954, from Vincent Hartnett asking if he were not a man in a certain photograph, in Hartnett's possession, marching in New York's May Day parade of 1952. Barrett went to the FBI, denied he was in the parade and had his lawyer so inform Hartnett. "Is this lawyer the same Harvey L. Klein who is listed as having signed Communist Party nominating petitions in 1939-1940?" wrote back Hartnett, his bulldog tenacity reaching into fifteen-year old files for the irrelevant attack. The lawyer's outraged denial was submitted to Hartnett. Whenever Barrett found himself out of work, thereafter, he was tortured by self-doubt as to whether his talent or Hartnett's pen was the primary cause. (Hartnett admitted at Faulk's trial that there never was a photo.) On the other hand, Godfrey P. Schmidt, a prominent lawyer and Catholic layman who was president of Aware and had once acted himself, argued in favor of the Aware bulletins being circulated throughout the industry: "A man has the right as an American citizen to recognize the peril of this day, to recognize that the Communist conspiracy has encircled its coils about all of the decency behind the Iron Curtain and is trying to subvert this country too. . . . Every single line of this is the unchallengeable truth, and the best proof of it that none of you dare, if you feel aggrieved, bring it to court, as you could."

As a matter of fact, no one did dare bring the matter to court for all the reasons of expense, apathy, the common conspiracy in the industry itself, fear of being smeared and the like. The big stars generally managed to clear themselves outside of court. A young actress such as Elaine Eldridge, cited in an Aware bulletin for once belonging to the Actors Studio, for signing a petition to save the life of one Willie McGee and for agreeing to teach — it never happened — for the National Committee of Arts, Sciences and Professions, could not even dream of court action. That is why the confluence of events that brought a stubborn Texas Wasp and a brilliant New York Jewish lawyer into the toils of the law was so significant. But homage must also be paid to the businessman from Syracuse. The Aware bulletins were adroitly libel-proof, at best worth a nominal six-cents verdict to a plaintiff. Similarly Hartnett as a renderer of services couched in pseudo-research jargon was reasonably immune. It takes two people to conspire, however, and when Johnson was caught hands down conspiring with Hartnett and Aware to defame Faulk and keep him out of work, the jig was up for respectable blacklisting. More to the point, Johnson, the reputed millionaire, became liable for large damages for his actions, making all concerned take a fresh look at the practice.

Aware fought back at the insurgents in AFTRA, aided by HUAC hearings the following summer in New York, during which fifteen AFTRA members, most of them signers of an anti-Aware petition, were subpoenaed. Eleven of this group took the First or Fifth Amendment. In spite of this, a mail referendum of the entire membership produced a two to one vote condemning Aware, thus confirming a prior victory at the membership meeting of May 24. On Fire Island, John Henry Faulk discussed the matter with his neighboring vacationers, the CBS newsman Charles Collingwood, Collingwood's wife, actress Louise Allbritton, and Orson Bean. They decided that the membership was ready to throw out the Aware crowd if the proper opposition slate could be assembled. They rounded up Garry Moore, Faye Emerson, Janice Rule and other well-known performers for a total of thirty-three candidates for the board. They were extremely careful to avoid identity with the far left faction and accordingly named themselves the "Middle-of-the-Road" slate. In their press releases and appeals for support they stressed they were opposed to both Communism and blacklisting.

In December 1955 they were swept into office with a grand flourish, winning twenty-seven of the thirty-five board seats. The board then elected Collingwood president and Faulk second vice-president. Faulk had obtained the largest of the Middle-of-the-Road votes. The New York newspapers, particularly the influential columnists Jack Gould of the *Times* and John Crosby of the *Herald Tribune*, hailed the victory. On the other hand, Ed Sullivan, then a widely read columnist for the *Daily News*, expressed dismay. Sullivan had praised *Red Channels* from the day it was launched and would prove an implacable foe for the Middle-of-the-Roaders, who would be routed out of office at the next annual election. Their defeat was not only an expression of fear at what was happening to John Henry Faulk but an evidence of how strong the anti-Communist animus was in AFTRA as late as the middle fifties. On the other hand, Actors Equity, led by president Ralph Bellamy, denounced Aware in 1955 and never retreated.

Meanwhile the board of Aware met in December 1955. Its secretary took minutes destined to be subpoenaed by the diligent Nizer. They supported the charge that the attack on Faulk was over union power, not to mention Hartnett's earning power, and thus all the more discreditable. A "run-down" was to be made on the Middle-of-the-Road winners with particular emphasis on "the worst people on the slate." A special bulletin was to be issued against Faulk, Collingwood and Bean. The meeting then turned to the men from Syracuse, helping to nail the difficult conspiracy charge: "Mr. Milton is to contact Messrs. Neuser, Johnson and Dungey re coming down from Syracuse. . . ."

XII

Reports on trials run the risk of abundance, especially six-year cases involving thirty-five witnesses for each side. With the responsibility of the business class as our special point of view, we will select our own cast to evoke the flavor of the trial and to highlight the issues involved. There will be Tom Murray, heroic ad agency man in an age supposed to have no heroes. Then Mark Goodson because his authority and knowledge about blacklisting, coupled with his distaste for it, were a mighty force in convincing the jurors to decree monumental penalties. Kim Hunter will take the stand to show us how base a villain Hartnett was, how commercial in spite of his patriotic calling. Next Jack A. Wren, because he was a "security officer" for Batten, Barton, Durstine & Osborne and got religion right on the witness chair. Finally, CBS will be examined and found to be a network of inconsistency, timidity and complicity, ultimately forcing its organization men to shame themselves before their colleague and moral superior, John Henry Faulk.

First, Bulletin 16, the instrument providing the foundation for a record $3.5 million jury award to Faulk, should be examined. Dated February 10, 1956, it cited Bean for a recent satire against HUAC and took issue with Collingwood's January defense of the

Middle-of-the-Roaders against the HUAC's criticism. The main entry was reserved for Faulk. A key paragraph preceded the charges against him:

> John Henry Faulk was further quoted as saying that "all (Middle-of-the-Roaders) were chosen for their opposition to Communism as well as their opposition to AWARE." In most cases, this may well be true. But how about Faulk himself? What is his public record?

The final two questions were essential in saving the case from dismissal on the usual grounds that no charges of Communism and thus no libel were involved. In the pre-trial skirmishes, the appropriate judges ruled these two questions produced a charge of Communism by innuendo. (A similar case brought by actor Joe Julian against *Red Channels* was to be dismissed by New York's Judge Saypol just after Faulk filed suit, no cause for libel being seen.) Now come the seven charges:

1. According to the Daily Worker of April 22, 1946, "Jack Faulk" was to appear at Club 65, 13 Astor Place, N.Y.C.— a favorite site of pro-Communist affairs.
2. According to the Daily Worker of April 17, 1947, "Johnny Faulk" was to appear as an entertainer at the opening of "Headline Cabaret," sponsored by Stage for Action (officially designated a Communist front). The late Philip Loeb was billed as emcee.
3. According to the Daily Worker of April 5, 1948, "John Faulk" contributed cabaret material to "Show-Time for Wallace," revues staged by the Progressive Citizens of America (officially designated a Communist front) in support of Henry A. Wallace's candidacy for the presidency of the U.S. Although Wallace was the officially endorsed candidate of the CP, by no means all his supporters were Communists or pro-Communists. What is in question here is sup-

port of any candidate given through a Communist-front setup.

4. A program dated April 25, 1946, named "John Faulk" as a scheduled entertainer (with identified Communist Earl Robinson and two non-Communists) under the auspices of the Independent Citizens Committee of the Arts, Sciences and Professions (officially designated a Communist front, and predecessor of the Progressive Citizens of America).
5. Vol. 3, Nos. 1 & 2, of the Bulletin of People's Songs (officially designated a Communist front) named Faulk as one who had sent greetings to People's Songs on its second anniversary.
6. "Johnny Faulk" was listed in a circular as an entertainer or speaker (with Paul Robeson and two others) to appear at "Spotlight on Wallace" to be held in Room 200 of the Jefferson School of Social Science on February 16, 1948. The Jefferson School has been found by the Federal Government to be what it is, the official training school of the Communist conspiracy in New York.
7. "John H. Faulk" was a U.S. Sponsor of the American Continental Congress for Peace, staged in Mexico City, September 5-10, 1949, as shown by the official "call." The Congress was later described by the HUAC as "another phase in the Communist world 'peace' campaign, aimed at consolidating anti-American forces throughout the Western Hemisphere."

Innocuous as these may now seem to many people, especially in view of their origin in a fight for union power, the seven allegations were deadly. First of all, Aware had extraordinary police powers in the industry and its ten-year old citations were as lethal as newly-minted ones. Secondly, the Bulletins were mailed to where they could do the most harm. All television and radio networks, their news departments and top executives were on the list. Leading newspapers and editors of their radio and television departments, advertising agencies, sponsors, grocers' associations, newspaper columnists, government investigating committees were included — one can imagine the rest. A public with an abhorrence of Communism and an industry deriving its revenue from advertisers utterly dependent on public approval created a precarious mix for Faulk. After his borrowed time ran out at WCBS, he became an economic pariah, unemployed in radio and TV until the winning of his case in 1962.

What about these charges? The court ruled the defendants failed completely to establish the truth of any of them as a defense against libel. They also denied the defendants the excuse of reliance on sources such as "officially designated a Communist front" on the grounds that HUAC, Tenney Committee and Attorney General's lists had no standing as judicially determined findings. Still, assuming they were pro-Communist enterprises, Faulk denied in court that he had ever attended meetings other than Item 4 and no proof was established otherwise. As an example of the malice that brings a libel to life, the preparation of Item 4 can be mentioned. The "program" Hartnett referred to was obtained by Nizer from Hartnett's own files. It turned out to be the program of the First Anniversary of the United Nations, the honorees being the U.N. Security Council and the sponsors including the American Bar Association, the National Y.M.C.A. and similar organizations. Secretary of State Stettinius was an honored guest. CBS had broadcast the event and asked Faulk to entertain that evening, which he did with Art Carney and Eddie Mayehoff.

About the only true charge was Item 3. Faulk testified he had contributed material and had been paid for it. He had never been a member of the Progressive Citizens of America. Actually, Hartnett, in pre-trial examination, commenting about the poorly researched seven items, stated: "I was once sold a barrel of false information." At that point, he and Godfrey Schmidt were ready to issue a letter recommending Faulk as a loyal American to prospective employers in order to drop the matter. Faulk decided to pursue the suit but the decision had already been made by the appearance of a new law firm for the defendants, that of Roy Cohn and Tom Bolan. Bolan took over from Schmidt, withdrew the peace overtures and fought tenaciously to the end.

XIII

The conspiracy between Johnson and Hartnett might never have been proven without a letter from Dungey to one of Faulk's sponsors and the non-conformist reaction of ad man Tom Murray to the episode. Johnson never reached the courtroom, pleading sickness and making himself hard to find. This was an important defense strategy, it having been claimed no connection existed between the Bulletin and Johnson and thus with Faulk's troubles. Judge Geller had warned the jury that unless connection could be established, Johnson could not be implicated. In pre-trial examination, Johnson had even denied influence over the deeds of the Legion post, well aware that any money verdict would be aimed at his capacity to pay.

The missing link was provided by Thomas D. Murray, former vice-president of Coca-Cola and at the time a senior account executive at Grey Advertising, in charge of Hoffman Beverage, a Pabst subsidiary, one of Faulk's radio sponsors. In March 1956, the very month of the Bulletin, the scrappy old grocer had phoned Tom Murray. On the witness stand, Murray, described as a gentle, disheveled, sincere type, first praised Faulk as one of his best producers, both from the Coca Cola and Hoffman days. He then testified as follows:

> MURRAY: First Mr. Johnson identified himself as Larry Johnson of Syracuse. He said that he owned several supermarkets and had influence over a number of others in central New York State. He gave me an indication of the total gross volume of food business that was done in the area and it was most impressive. It ran into the millions. I believe the figure was eighteen to twenty million dollars annually.
>
> He then said, Mr. Johnson then said that he felt it was a disgrace that our company was using a Communist, John Henry Faulk, to advertise its products.
>
> I replied that I had no such knowledge about Mr. Faulk. And he said, "Well you had better get in line because a lot of people along Madison Avenue are getting in line

> and the display space which the Pabst Brewing Company has in the stores that I either own or control is what he called "hard-won space."
>
> THE COURT: What do you mean by "hard-won"— w-o-n, or o-n-e?
>
> MURRAY: W-o-n. In other words, it had been difficult to achieve status that Pabst Brewing Company had in a display sense within his stores. That happens to be a very accurate statement, by the way.
>
> NIZER: Now we will come back to what hard-won space is, but would you be good enough to finish the conversation for us.
>
> MURRAY: I will. I said I could not accept a telephone implication of this kind. I felt that there were legal ways of establishing whether or not Mr. Faulk — Mr. Faulk or for that matter, anyone else — was a Communist, and that I had no intention of firing or recommending the firing of a man who was a first-rate salesman for our product. Then he (Johnson) said, "How would you like it if your client were to receive a letter from an American Legion Post up here?"
>
> And I said that I was a veteran myself and that I could not believe that the American Legion would lend itself to what I considered to be an obvious blackmail attempt, and he said, "Well you will find out."

Murray told his boss, Samuel Dalsimer, about the call. Dalsimer, having experienced a traumatic "Stalin's little creatures" bout with Johnson in 1952 over Amm-i-dent's "Danger" series, immediately dispatched Murray to catch Johnson at his hotel and placate him. "After the way you spoke to me, I want nothing to do with you," snapped Johnson, turning his heel on Murray in the hotel lobby.

Perhaps it was just as well, since the wheels started to turn in Syracuse and Dungey's letter promptly arrived. Placed in evidence at the trial and supplementing the hearsay phone recital of Murray, the letter was accepted by Judge Geller as a certification of Johnson's responsibility. The letter to the president of Pabst is quoted in full, first to make businessmen ponder at how such pennyweight pressure could frighten a billion dollar industry and second, to give an example of the fighting technique of the Johnson-Hartnett axis:

> Dear Mr. Perlstein:
>
> These are indeed trying times not only in the field of international politics but also in the TV and radio field. For International Communism to succeed in bringing the rest of the world under the yoke of their conspiracy they must gain complete control of the airwaves. The Communists are working around the clock to accomplish this. They must also raise money to finance their operations. As an example four Communist Fronts in the entertainment field raised over a million dollars for the Communist cause.
>
> The American Legion for years has realized the efforts that Communists are exerting in the field of entertainment and has gone on record not to support programs that feature Communists or individuals who have supported Communist causes.
>
> Therefore, we respectfully call to your attention one of your salesmen, John Henry Faulk, whose program comes through WCBS Radio, New York City—5:05 to 6 P.M., Monday through Friday.
>
> We are enclosing data from publication *Aware* on a John Henry Faulk and would like to know if this is the same John Henry Faulk who has this WCBS program.
>
> We of the American Legion sincerely hope that you will look into this situation and will be waiting a reply since we want to have our facts straight as to the person in question and his sponsor. . . .
>
> Very truly yours,
> John K. Dungey, Chairman
> Anti-Subversive Committee
> Onondaga County American Legion
> 1842 Bellevue Avenue
> Syracuse, New York

The letter carried the notation that copies had been sent to Mr. L. A. Johnson, Mr. Francis W. Neuser, Commander of a Post of Veterans of Foreign Wars and Mr. Wayne Murphy, National Americanism Commission, American Legion, Indianapolis, Indiana.

Murray's contribution should not be underestimated. He appeared willingly as witness for the plaintiff, breaking the code for an industry that preferred to let sleeping dogs lie. Other ad executives refused to act as witnesses and in a very real sense, Tom Murray was placing his career in advertising on the line, the winning of libel trials being notoriously remote for plaintiffs. In cross-examination, he gave Bolan little satisfaction:

> BOLAN: When Mr. Johnson said to you that Mr. Faulk was a Communist, didn't you ask him what the basis of his statement was?
>
> MURRAY: I said I had no knowledge myself of Mr. Faulk being a Communist.
>
> BOLAN: But you didn't ask Mr. Johnson what the basis —
>
> MURRAY: Mr. Johnson had not qualified himself as an authority on such subjects. I thought he should be back wherever he comes from, selling baked beans, to tell you the truth. By what right does a grocer call me up and tell me so and so is a Communist, "get rid of him." I don't mind admitting I was kind of sore.

Murray's testimony was backed by Dalsimer, executive vice-president of the $60 million agency. Dalsimer, a top official in the Anti-Defamation League, openly recounted the Amm-i-dent story and expressed his contempt for the blacklisting process, which had never before been aired in such an important forum. The performance of these ad men had a lasting effect on the jury's comprehension of blacklisting and the culpability of the missing witness.

Mark Goodson was equally effective. Goodson-Todman was the acknowledged leader among the television producing firms, having created shows such as "What's My Line," "I've Got a Secret," "The

Price is Right," "The Name's the Same" and "Stop the Music." At the time of the trial, they were running thirty-two half hour shows a week on major television networks and had won thirty-five awards. Anything this handsome, elegant impresario of TV would say on the subject was bound to embarrass sponsors, networks and his own organization as well. Most of Goodson's shows were on CBS, the livelier and more experimental of the two major networks. Since it was vital for Faulk to prove that his separation from WCBS, even though eighteen months after the Bulletin, was connected with the Aware attack, Goodson's testimony about his troubles with CBS was a breath of fresh air for the plaintiffs. Strangely enough the following information was inadvertently elicited by Bolan:

> GOODSON: Yes, "The Name's the Same" did not have a clearance system, although I pretty much followed the CBS policy. So if somebody were not cleared by CBS I would tend to avoid using that person on "The Name's the Same" on ABC, just because I wanted to keep our company out of trouble, I suppose.
>
> In the case of Judy Holliday, which was the incident that we discussed, I had tried for some time to persuade CBS that Judy Holliday should be used. They said their list indicated that she had a questionable background and that they would not go into it. Then we were approached by her agent, William Morris, and were told that George Sokolsky, a political writer, had been meeting with Miss Holliday and had determined in his judgment that she was a good American and had done some other behind-the-scenes business of which I was not aware, and they asked whether we would be willing to use Miss Holliday on "What's My Line." I said we would be very happy to, but they had to check with CBS. They went to CBS. CBS looked at the various documents and they said "Go ahead and use her," which we did.
>
> So, just a few weeks later — we had no reaction from that at all from Mr. Johnson or from anybody. A few weeks later we decided to use Miss Holliday on "The

> Name's the Same," but in that particular show we billboarded it in advance. The guest star on "What's My Line," as you know, because of the fact that it is a mystery, the person comes on as a surprise. If there is going to be any protest it is after the fact. In this particular case we announced Miss Holliday in advance and we began to get mail very quickly and after this performance of Miss Holliday, which was practically a duplicate of what she had done on CBS, we got a call from Clark Swanson who said we could never use Miss Holliday again because "we have been threatened by the Laurence Johnson organization."
>
> * * *
>
> Now, since they (CBS) had also rejected Oscar Hammerstein, Richard Rodgers, Moss Hart, Jerome Robbins, and an entire list of other famous people, we figured we ought to come back and find out why —
>
> * * *
>
> They said we could not clear Miss Holliday and I said, "Why?" I got on the phone personally on this one and I said, "Will you please tell me why we can't use Judy Holliday?" And he (the CBS executive) said, "She is just a bad actor." That was one of the standard phrases at that time to indicate, to give you the word that this person was on a blacklist. And I said, "But can't you tell me why?" He said, "I don't want to go into it but she has a questionable background and we just can't clear her now." That was where I heard "questionable background."

Bolan bravely tried to retrieve the ball by asking for the reason these people were on the supposed blacklist in the first place. Goodson replied:

> Mr. Bolan, all I can say is there were no differentiations made between Communists, Communist sympathizers, those who had lunch with Communist sympathizers, those who knew somebody who had lunch with Communist sympathizers, and so forth, but there was one over-all list and the differentiation was not made for us.

Goodson did not try to pin the blame on any one source. The buck simply passed around and around. Can one say the sponsor, the place where the money came from, bore the greatest responsibility? "A sponsor is in business to sell goods," Goodson commented at one point. "He has no interest in getting involved in causes. . . . The favorite slogan along Madison Avenue is 'Why buy yourself a headache. . . . There are a lot of other performers. Why bother with this one?'"

Still, should not power centers like big business and big networks be concerned with due process, the right to be confronted, the right to work, the overzealousness of vigilantes? Do all social crises have to end obliquely, McCarthyism in the censure of the Senate for "breaking the club rules," blacklisting in a six-year lawsuit that only a Nizer could win?

XIV

Nizer had learned in his pre-trial examination of Hartnett of pressures exerted on Kim Hunter. For six years, Paul Martinson, Nizer's associate, had asked her to give testimony against Hartnett in the Faulk case, without success. The attack by Hartnett and his associates had come in 1949 after she had achieved stardom as Stella in *A Streetcar Named Desire*. Later she earned an Oscar in the motion picture version of this play. From about 1950 through 1954 she had been practically unemployed in her profession and had just gotten back through an accommodation with Hartnett. The whole experience had been so traumatic, however, that she could not discuss it without bursting into tears. She definitely did not want to get involved and jeopardize her career once again.

Kim and her husband were old friends of Faulk and he finally prevailed upon them to meet with him in Martinson's office as the opening day of the trial approached. They were accompanied by her lawyer and public relations man who strongly advised against appearing after hearing Martinson out. When all was said, the decision was left to Kim. As Faulk reports, she spoke quite solemnly: "I have decided I'm going to testify. I want to be part of this trial. I'm going to do it for your sake, Johnny, and on behalf of my children and my profession and my country."

What was involved was no less than admitting to the world that she had compromised her deepest principles by turning into an anti-Aware critic solely to please Hartnett. Imagine the effect on the jury as Nizer led Kim Hunter through the maze of her experiences with the blacklist. Fighting hysteria a good deal of the time, she told how in 1953 she had asked William Dozier, a CBS executive producer, for help. Dozier referred her to Roy Brewer in California, who thereupon shuffled her case back and forth with his twin in the East, Hartnett. Along the way her public relations man, Arthur P. Jacobs, had opened negotiations directly with Hartnett on May 12, 1953, pointing out she had appeared in the stage version of Arthur Koestler's anti-Communist *Darkness at Noon*. Hartnett wrote back that he would issue a report on Miss Hunter but there would be a fee of $200. Kim testified she refused the payment as a matter of principle. Then Nizer read a letter to the general counsel of the ABC network on October 7, 1953 from Hartnett stating, "In my opinion, you would run a serious risk of adverse public opinion by featuring on your network Kim Hunter." It seemed to be almost a case of no pay, no clearance.

Eventually the Brewer-Hartnett contact came into play and a beaten actress went through the degradation of purging and confession usually thought to be the specialty of the Kremlin. Her affidavit to this end was read to the jury by Bolan presumably to show how far she had once strayed but the jurors coldly received it as a case example in their education about self-appointed brainwashers. She admitted she had gone to a 1947 meeting on behalf of the Hollywood Ten (which she now regretted). She had allowed her name to be used in connection with "world peace" by the National Council of Arts, Sciences and Professions, but had never attended a meeting. She signed a petition in aid of Willie McGee, seeking justice in the Mississippi courts. She had recently sent five dollars to the New York *Post* for reprints of Oliver Pilat's article "Blacklist—The Panic in TV-Radio" (which she now realized was promoted by a faction of the AFTRA union "so radical . . . as to be considered pro-Communist"). For these transgressions, she sought absolution on the grounds of repentance and because "Theatre people . . . incline to be gullible, sentimental and . . . politically naive. . . . They are often fair game for the . . . Communist-inspired operations. I was no exception. . . ."

The worst was yet to come. The Brewer-Hartnett therapy treatment required positive deeds of anti-Communist action in addition to literary exercises. Having enjoyed the sensation of working again, she received a phone call from Hartnett shortly before the May 24, 1955 meeting of AFTRA in which the anti-Aware resolution would be voted upon.

> MISS HUNTER: The substance of it was that he said to show — kind of show my good faith, that I was truly a loyal American and not pro-Communist, that affidavits were not sufficient, that I should by all rights do something actively anti-Communist and did I object to do any such thing, and I said, "No, certainly not."
>
> He asked me then if I knew about the Aware resolution, the resolution to condemn Aware that was pending within our television union at AFTRA and I said yes, I know about it.
>
> And he said, well one way that I could show a strong anti-Communist stand would be to go to that meeting and speak up in support of Aware, publicly, in front of everybody.
>
> I said, "Mr. Hartnett, it would be very difficult for me to speak in support of Aware because I am not in support of Aware, Incorporated."
>
> He said, "Well, it wouldn't be necessary to support Aware, Incorporated, as such, and, in fact it wouldn't even really be necessary for you to go to the meeting, if you would be willing to send a telegram that could be read before the meeting publicly, speaking, saying in so many words that you are against this resolution to condemn Aware."

> I said, "Mr. Hartnett, I will do my best to form a telegram."

In a trembling voice, Miss Hunter later testified that since then she had worked frequently. Nizer then drew the conspiracy knot between Hartnett and Johnson by quoting from a letter to Johnson subpoenaed from Hartnett's files: "She (Kim Hunter) assured me she would do so and if she comes through tomorrow right at the AFTRA meeting as she promised she would do, you will hear the comrades shrieking all the way from New York to Syracuse. The Kraft situation seems to me to be very much improved, Larry. . . . You and your associates have done wonders. Sincerely, Hartnett."

XV

When John Cogley published "Volume II, Radio and Television" of his *Report on Blacklisting* in 1956, the name Faulk never appeared. Ironically the opening of the great case missed the deadline for the book's publication. Jack A. Wren, however, received the full treatment as "security officer" at BBD&O. "To the performer who wants to be cleared for work, Wren's name buzzes through the industry grapevine," wrote Cogley. "He and BBD&O are mentioned more frequently than any other individual or agency."

Cogley's reports are strangely unsatisfactory, viewed from the seventies, because of their passion for anonymity. One tries to understand his view that if blacklisting were a form of invasion of privacy, then the victims and even friendly informants should be spared further identification in a report on blacklisting. When Cogley was rewarded for his efforts by being hailed before the HUAC (and charged with having an ex-Communist researcher), he found to his annoyance that several of his "X" and "Y" informants would not come to his aid when the HUAC denied the validity of his study. With this in mind, here is Cogley's report on Wren by a "New York public relations expert":

> Somewhere along the line I may find George Sokolsky is involved. I go to him and tell him that the Legion official thinks this boy is all right. If I can convince Sokol-

> sky then I go to Victor Riesel, Fred Woltman (New York *World-Telegram and Sun* staff writer) or whoever else is involved. When I've gotten four "affidavits" from key people like these, I go to Jack Wren at BBD&O and to the "security officer" at CBS.
>
> I wait a few days, then I telephone Wren. He may say to me, "You're crazy. I know 15 things this guy hasn't explained." I ask him, 'What are they?' and he says, "He didn't come clean." So I send for the guy. . . .
>
> I call Wren back and he says, "When your boy is ready to come clean I'll talk to him." In that case we've reached a dead end. My boy has been cleared but he can't get a job. I know cases where victims have sat around eight to ten months after "clearance" before they got work.[32]

One can assume that with this kind of publicity, Wren might have felt somewhat hostile to critics of the system. After all, if people like himself did not pick up the burden in an unfair case, as he frequently did, what other recourse was there for the entertainer?

Now Jack Wren in 1962 was given by Vincent Hartnett as the reliable source who had told him about Faulk's appearance at the "notorious" Jefferson School of Social Science, Item 6 of the Bulletin 16 on Faulk.

The formidable Nizer produced Wren as a surprise rebuttal witness to this important testimony. Wren denied telling anything to Hartnett, in effect calling him a liar. Cross-examined by Bolan, Wren, to his credit, was a reformed "security officer:"

> BOLAN: Mr. Wren, what were your duties at BBD&O in late 1955?
>
> WREN: Well, my duties, among other things, was to protect our clients against false charges made that we loaded our shows with Communists, by Vincent Hartnett who made these charges against us, who wrote poison pen letters behind our backs to our clients, wrote to our officers accusing us of loading our shows with Communists.

* * *

> BOLAN: Did you ever send any communications to Mr. Hartnett at any time?
>
> WREN: It is entirely possible I sent communications to Mr. Hartnett in the early fifties, especially when Mr. Hartnett was engineering picket lines around our clients' shows, and I had to treat with him as a merchant treats with a racketeer who sells protection.

XVI

The role of CBS is a mixed one, involving good deeds and misdeeds, as one might expect in a great corporation employing creative people and ruling part of the air. President Stanton and Chairman Paley are still at CBS but most of the others have left the scene. "A fundamental principle of a free society is now at stake," Stanton announced in 1971, as CBS found itself on the receiving end for "The Selling of the Pentagon."

The big concern in the late forties and early fifties was over the slant of the news commentators rather than the problems of blacklisted performers, or so it seemed at the time. This may explain why Stanton and Paley were silent on the Faulk matter, presumably concentrating on major matters such as the waves produced by the controversial Edward R. Murrow, their network star. Perhaps their silence was simply related to the fear of losing sponsors. At any rate, only men in their position could have resisted the pressures directed at the sponsors with appropriately organized counterpressures and this they failed to do.

Murrow had launched his nightly 7:45 radio broadcasts, heard by at least two to three million people, in September 1947, after a few restless years in the executive suite as a corporate vice president. Never able to refrain from editorializing, even if only by his tone of voice or raised eyebrow, Murrow consistently violated the CBS official position about objectivity. Of the HUAC investigations of Hollywood, he came right to the point: "Movies should be judged by what appears on the screen, newspapers by what appears in print and radio by what comes over the loudspeaker. The personal beliefs of the individuals involved would not seem to be a legitimate field of inquiry, either by government or individuals."[33]

Murrow himself, sitting on the employer's side of the table, had made a hard decision involving talent only a few months earlier in 1947. It concerned William L. Shirer, the man with whom Murrow had pioneered CBS coverage from Europe a decade earlier and on through the war. Shirer was a top performer, admired for his sharp analysis of the news, but his subdued, slow voice lacked dramatic content. Shirer's sponsor decided this voice was not selling enough shaving cream and Murrow, as corporate vice president in charge of the news division, shifted him to another time period at a substantial reduction of income and importance. Though Shirer had eighteen months to go on his CBS contract and Murrow urged him to stay on, he resigned. Shirer charged in effect that he had been gagged, presumably for his liberal views such as his opposition to the new Truman Doctrine of "containing" Communism. Murrow suffered the experience of seeing the cantankerous left picket CBS as an expression of its animosity to the network and Murrow himself. According to Alexander Kendrick, Murrow's biographer and a CBS commentator for twenty years, Murrow personally felt that Shirer was no longer doing his best work, was too "ivory-towerish" and that the sponsors had the right to choose the kind of program they wanted.[34] The nagging question of whether or not sponsors thus controlled the news, when applied to a man of Shirer's stature, had to be sidestepped as a dilemma of commercial broadcasting. Murrow's total record in respect to advancing democratic procedures, of course, was overwhelming, reaching its high point with the decision to impale Senator McCarthy, with Paley's approval, before tens of millions of viewers on the evening of March 9, 1954, often called "television's finest hour."

The Shirer incident of the radio days has its parallel in the Faulk case. Nizer could not afford to let the jury hold CBS harmless in spite of the eighteen months of extended employment accorded Faulk. The thrust of the Faulk case was to implicate CBS as well as the defendants, regardless of CBS's position that Faulk's talent was declining at the time of his difficulties with the Aware bulletin. Nizer had no trouble convincing the jurors that blacklisting as a general practice flourished at CBS. Yet in the particular case of Faulk as with Shirer, some sympathy should be extended to the business side, censured as it is whenever a borderline separation takes place. There is a possibility that Faulk's bosses were planning to shuffle him about or even terminate him on the basis of performance, considering the rapidly shifting field of entertainment, whether or not they were reading their rating figures correctly. There is also the tantalizing thought that had they not fired him at all, the jury would have been hard put to measure his damages in any significant amount. A great trial, as in the Sacco-Vanzetti case, needs a martyr. Still, even with CBS muddying up the waters, Faulk was clearly libelled and gravely hurt economically by the vigilantist conspirators.

Murrow was a strong supporter of Faulk from the start and Collingwood in addition was one of Murrow's team. As Faulk relates the incident, he was about to file suit in June 1956 but was $7,500 short of the modest $10,000 retainer Nizer had established. Murrow at this point phoned him to express pleasure that the suit was being filed. He quoted his close friend Carl Sandburg who had sent word on the matter: "Whatever's the matter with America, Johnny ain't." Faulk told Murrow that the CBS executives had advised him not to sue and that he needed the $7,500, which Murrow immediately put up himself. "Let's get this straight, Johnny . . . I am investing this money in America," said Murrow. "Louis Nizer *must* try this case. These people *must* be brought into court. This blacklisting racket must be exposed. This is a very important suit. I don't know whether you even realize how important it is."[35]

Thus spoke the top personality of CBS who, as a corporate executive, like Dore Schary in Hollywood had participated in decision-making he personally abhorred. As a board member of CBS from 1949 to 1956, Murrow was not only well aware of the CBS "security officer" engaged in continuous political screening but certainly participated in establishing the "loyalty oath" procedure which CBS, alone of all the networks, installed in 1950. Faulk, incidentally, had signed this oath as well as another required of him in 1955 as an AFTRA officer under the provisions of the Taft-Hartley Act. Armed with a third non-Communist affidavit prepared by his CBS bosses for their sales force after the Aware attack, Faulk still became unemployable, a comment on the one-way street such oaths apparently travel. (The CBS oath vanished as McCarthyism expired and the Taft-Hartley oath provisions were repealed in 1959.)

In CBS's defense, one might say the depth of its reactionary record was somewhat in proportion to the height of its daring programming. An oft-quoted *Fortune* magazine article tells how Paley and Stanton, as heads of the upstart network after the war, took the lead in promoting lively and controversial news and entertainment formats that set the pace for the industry, as Murrow's brilliant career illustrates. CBS in effect was so active in hiring and raiding talent and promoting new shows it invited criticism from all sides. "CBS and blacklisting have become almost synonymous," concluded Cogley in his 1956 report, on the grounds that the big test for security clearance was whether or not one could make it on that network.[36]

In this context, Sam Slate and Carl Ward took the stand in 1962 as defense witnesses as the eleven-week trial drew to a close. Nizer and Faulk had hoped they would not appear, on the assumption that they would have let Bolan know they were hostile to his cause and he would thus be afraid to subpoena them. Sam Slate was a close friend of Faulk and had been program director at WCBS at the time of the Bulletin. When promoted to station manager a short time thereafter, he apparently attended a party given in his honor by Faulk in Faulk's apartment. This occurred in May 1957 and Nizer and his wife were also guests. At this party, Slate made the staunch and perhaps foolish declaration that no matter what happened in regard to the rumored possibility of Arthur Godfrey's taking over part of Faulk's time, Faulk had "nothing to worry about." While Faulk was on vacation in Jamaica with his family in July 1957, his agent was notified by Slate that Faulk had been fired. Sam Slate had also dined with the Faulks and columnist Murray Kempton the night before the departure for Jamaica.

Neither the party conversation, the presence of the Nizers nor the pre-vacation dinner with Kempton could be recollected by the hapless witness under Nizer's booming questions. As for blacklisting, "Mr. Nizer," Slate answered, "I never blacklisted anyone from appearing on CBS shows and to the best of my knowledge this was not done."

Slate declared the reason Faulk was terminated was because of his sliding ratings and general programming changes. Nizer was unable to elicit any admission that the blacklisting forces were a factor. He therefore relied on the generally bad impression Slate made on the jury — he could hardly make himself heard most of the time — to convey the idea that here was an organization man at work, unable to tell the whole story or call his soul his own. Faulk reiterates this point of view in his book, although protesting compassion and understanding for his one-time boss.

Carl Ward, station manager of WCBS at the time of the firing, also offered little on Faulk's behalf while whitewashing CBS of any tainted motives in letting Faulk go. Ward did assert, however, that even though publication of Bulletin 16 did not affect Faulk's employability at CBS, it definitely would make him less employable elsewhere. Precise and unattached to Faulk personally, Ward's testimony was neutral in its effect. Now a veteran of thirty years with CBS and a top network executive, Ward candidly reminisced about the case with the author in 1971 on a high floor of the new CBS building in New York. He noted that neither Faulk nor Nizer had ever approached him about appearing as a witness for Faulk, apparently indicating they recognized the possibility that Faulk would have been terminated anyway and had been kept on for most of the time because of CBS's embarrassing position. Performers do eventually terminate, he noted, and even though Nizer produced an effective rebuttal to the tricky subject of Faulk's ratings, he was on his way out when the trouble started. Ward recalled also that some of Faulk's radio sponsors made a point of sticking with him as a protest against the attack, which was a further reason for the period of grace. He stated he recalled no terminations for blacklisting in his CBS radio experience although there obviously was a bad case of it in the industry and he was delighted to see Faulk win the suit. The decision to fire, he claims, was not handed down from above and he and his associates were all surprised when the case assumed such national importance. He feels that he and Slate were not subpoenaed by the defense as friendly witnesses. It was a matter of Bolan's case being so desperate, anything was worth a gamble. In 1971 he had not seen Slate or Faulk for years and did not know what they were doing.

From a litigation point of view, Faulk would have been better off had he been fired immediately, although this seems hardly possible due to the influence of Collingwood and Murrow. It is a tribute to Nizer's ability, as well as the general villainy of the defendants, that the huge verdict was granted in spite of the dubious generosity of CBS. Kendrick and Murrow apparently had their own reservations about the conduct of Slate and Ward. Perhaps news commentators are by nature cynical on such matters. Kendrick writes:

> The testimony which held the most painful meaning for Murrow, as he watched the trial closely — though he was by then no longer in broadcasting but had become director of the United States Information Agency — was that of two WCBS executives, one of them a close friend of Faulk's. Instead of testifying to the blacklisting pressure and the boycott threats exerted against broadcasting, as they could very well have done, they appeared for the defense, that is, for the blacklisters. They solemnly asserted that Faulk had not been discharged by CBS for Communist sympathies, but because his audience ratings had decreased. In cross-examination they conceded that what in fact had happened was that the ratings of the CBS station itself had decreased in the highly competitive New York market, and that Faulk's loss was considerably less than the station's own.[37]

Nizer was making his summation to the jury as the six year case approached its end. He had asked for compensatory damages of one million dollars, based on Faulk's loss of past and future earnings, and punitive damages of two million dollars, as a measure of the punishment deserved for the offense and as a deterrent against its repetition. He felt he must hammer away at the missing defendant Johnson, the reputed millionaire who had avoided appearance due to medical disability. Nizer scorned the excuse:

> NIZER: He had this esophagus condition ten years ago, and five and six years ago when he was crushing Mr. Faulk.
>
> The only trouble with him inside is guts, not esophagus, and he should have appeared here and defended himself. . . . There is nothing the matter with his esophagus. May I have a recess at this time?

The judge ordered the recess. As Nizer turned to sit down at the counsel table, a young lady rushed into the courtroom and thrust a note at Bolan. Bolan glanced at the note, turned white and handed it to Nizer. It read: "Laurence Johnson has just been found dead in a Bronx motel."

The denouement to this stunning news need not be drawn out. Judge Geller arranged for the estate of Laurence Johnson to be substituted as a defendant but stipulated that no punitive damages could be awarded against the estate as a dead man cannot be deterred from repeating an offense. The jury was admonished not to speculate on the cause of Johnson's death. Weeks later it was determined to be related to his esophagus condition but why he had driven from Syracuse to the motel remained a mystery, at least to Nizer and Faulk.

Finally the jury paraded in, but only to ask a question: "The jury would like to have a clarification on the subject of awards for punitive damages. . . . Is the jury allowed to award more than the amounts requested by the plaintiff?"

The amazed judge answered in the affirmative and as the jury filed out, the Faulk supporters expressed their unconfined joy at this omen of success. The jury came back with an award for compensatory damages of one million dollars against Aware, Inc., Hartnett and the estate of Johnson, along with one and a quarter million dollars of punitive damages against each of the first two defendants.

The hopes for a substantial collection from the estate of Johnson were dashed when its attorneys proved the net assets were only a fraction of the million dollar assessment against it. Under those circumstances a settlement of $175,000 was accepted by Faulk and paid by the estate. (Faulk netted $75,000 after expenses and still collects about $1,000 a year from Hartnett.) Aware Inc. and Hartnett appealed to the Appellate Division where they received a unanimous condemnation for "a vicious libel, deliberately and maliciously planned and executed with devastating effect upon the plaintiff, all without a semblance of justification." The court however, reduced the overall damages to $550,000, which did not affect the settlement already made for $175,000. The Court of Appeals unanimously held for Faulk and finally the United States Supreme Court refused to review the case. Blacklisting in radio and television stood condemned in a stack of tribunals. An uneasy public, a mortified communications industry and a cautious group of sponsors simply walked away from the unnecessary, un-American practice. The times were no longer running with the vigilantists.

As for John Henry Faulk, he lives in Austin, Texas now, busy polishing a one-man show *(Pear Orchard, U.S.A.)* which has been a local hit and which he hopes to take on tour. Since the trial he has been writing and lecturing, mostly as a humorist. In his opinion, blacklisting is just about dead.

Who was to blame? Everyone shared in it but the centers of business power, the movie moguls, the corporation presidents, the communications tycoons and their boards of directors were probably most guilty. They could have refused to recognize the illegal, unauthorized meddlers in their businesses. They should have used their high positions and inside knowledge to cry out against the invasions of due process, fair trials, the right to be confronted, the right to work, all being trampled in their own vineyards.

On the other hand, were they only giving a fear-ridden public what it wanted? Is it possible that reforms come only after abuses bring us back to our senses? Perhaps, but somewhere along the line individual responsibility must emerge. As George Orwell has reminded us, cowardice is as great a threat as official tyranny. Charles Collingwood testified at Faulk's trial:

> Well, it really depends, Mr. Nizer, on how much guts the sponsor has, the network and the station, whether they have got enough guts to stand up to the pressures which are brought against them, or whether they don't. The time of which we are speaking in most cases they didn't have very much guts.

Footnotes

[1] Walter Goodman, *The Committee* (Baltimore, 1969, Penguin Edition), p. 301. Eric Bentley, in *Thirty Years of Treason* (New York, 1971), writing as a critic of HUAC, acknowledges Goodman as "the principal historian of HUAC." Bentley does not go so far as to affirm the Ten were "all card-carrying members of the Communist party" (p. 945). Yet he claims Bertolt Brecht, on whom he is an authority, erred in asserting in 1950 that "most" of the Ten were not Communists (p. 206). Lawson, Trumbo, Lardner and Dymytryk have publicly announced past membership.

[2] John Cogley, *Report on Blacklisting, Part I—Films* (The Fund for the Republic, 1956), pp. 174 ff.

[3] *Ibid.*, p. 3.

[4] *Ibid.*, p. 9.

[5] Alvah Bessie, *Inquisition in Eden* (New York, 1965), p. 193. Also, Cogley, *op. cit.*, p. 10.

[6] Cogley, *op. cit.*, p. 8.

[7] New York *Herald Tribune*, November 1, 1947.

[8] Cogley, *op. cit.*, p. 1.

[9] Bessie, *op. cit.*, p. 199, qu. from *Hearings Before the Committee on Un-American Activities, House of Representatives, Eightieth Congress, 1947.* Also, Robert K. Carr, *The House Committee on Un-American Activities 1945-1950* (Ithaca, 1952), p. 67 fn.

[10] Carr, *op. cit.*, p. 10.

[11] *Ibid.*, pp. 21-25.

[12] Cogley, *op. cit.*, p. 16.

[13] Carr, *op. cit.*, p. 62.

[14] *Ibid.*, p. 60.

[15] Cogley, *op. cit.*, p. 14.

[16] Goodman, *op. cit.*, p. 217.

[17] Bessie, *op. cit.*, p. 226. Also Cogley, *op. cit.*, p. 75.

[18] Cogley, *op. cit.*, p. 75.

[19] Dore Schary to the author, 1971. Cogley, *op. cit.*, p. 158.

[20] *Ibid.*, p. 21.

[21] *Ibid.*, p. 23.

[22] Bessie, *op. cit.*, p. 221.

[23] Goodman, *op. cit.*, p. 218.

[24] Cogley, *op. cit.*, pp. 90-91.

[25] Tom Deane, former senior vice president of Bank of America, to the author, 1971.

[26] George Yousling, former vice president of Security Pacific Bank, to the author, 1971.

[27] Arthur A. Ekirch, Jr., *Ideologies and Utopias—The Impact of the New Deal on American Thought* (Chicago, 1969), p. 89.

[28] Bessie, *op. cit.*, p. 190. (Henry Rogers, public relations counsel to the Committee for the First Amendment, who flew to Washington with the Hollywood celebrities for the hearings, advised the author in 1971 that they flew in a TWA plane and that Hughes picked up *that* bill.)

[29] Bernard Rosenberg and Harry Silverstein, *The Real Tinsel* (New York, 1970), qu. from a taped interview with Dore Schary, p. 143.

[30] Earl Latham, *The Communist Controversy in Washington from the New Deal to McCarthy* (New York, 1969), pp. 373 ff.

[31] John Henry Faulk, *Fear on Trial* (New York, 1963). Louis Nizer, *The Jury Returns* (New York, 1966). Quotations from the trial transcript are taken from these books unless otherwise noted.

[32] John Cogley, *Report on Blacklisting, Part II—Radio-Television* (The Fund for the Republic, 1956), p. 90.

[33] Alexander Kendrick, *Prime Time* (Boston, 1969), p. 308.

[34] *Ibid.*, p. 295.

[35] Faulk, *op. cit.*, p. 49.

[36] Cogley, Part II, *op. cit.*, p. 125.

[37] Kendrick, *op. cit.*, p. 302.

Chapter 7

The Military-Industrial Complex

The speaker was concluding his remarks to a group of editors and publishers. The place, San Francisco, across the bay from his Piedmont high school years and Phi Beta Kappa days at Berkeley. The date, September 18, 1967. Secretary of Defense Robert S. McNamara had already gone dovish on his tragic boss Lyndon B. Johnson and only the formalities of his easing out to the World Bank remained to tie them together. The brilliant Secretary of Defense with the steel-trap mind could no longer make it as Secretary for War. The élite technocrat, the textbook epitome of the new manager for twentieth century big business, spoke from the humanist side of his organized intelligence:

I do not view man's history with that degree of cynicism,

> but I do believe that man's wisdom in avoiding war is often surpassed by his folly in promoting it.
>
> However foolish unlimited war may have been in the past, it is now no longer merely foolish, but suicidal as well. It is said that nothing can prevent a man from suicide, if he is sufficiently determined to commit it.
>
> The question is what is our determination in an era when unlimited war will mean the death of hundreds of millions — and the possible genetic impairment of a million of generations to follow?
>
> Man is clearly a compound of folly and wisdom — and history is clearly a consequence of the admixture of those two contradictory traits.
>
> History has placed our particular lives in an era when the consequences of human folly are waxing more and more catastrophic in the matters of war and peace.
>
> In the end, the root of man's security does not lie in his weaponry.
>
> In the end, the root of man's security lies in his mind.

It was as if Dr. Spock or Dr. Wald had momentarily taken over Defense from the ex-president of Ford. Not that an American Secretary of Defense has to be a missile-rattling Dr. Strangelove, but he should have faith in the nation's weaponry. Nuclear weaponry, along with the rest of the defense establishment, costs us about $75 billion a year. The least a business-minded country expects is its money's worth when sums like that are involved. From his practical side, McNamara would tell us that we have had that, too, in the form of deterring Russia from a first strike against us for twenty-five years. It's just that the failure in Vietnam not only dashes careers but calls for new audits of old untouchables. The military-industrial complex, once praised as the arsenal of democracy when we needed it in World War II, invites re-examination of the role of industry.

II

To attack the military-industrial complex is to attack both a traditional foe and friend of the American system. By and large Americans acknowledge their military heroes and often elect them Presidents, but for militarism itself the country has little taste. As for business, however, there is no other estate in American life to compare with it in long-run power and popularity. From Yankee traders to millionaire Governors, the captains of industry and their descendants are most highly regarded citizens. Ours is a business civilization. Our only class distinction is monetary. Businessmen and their allied lawyers populate our Congress, provide our Mayors and have given us all ten Secretaries of Defense, with the exception of General George C. Marshall who was in a class by himself. Some sixth sense, perhaps a fortunate one, keeps the public from electing successful businessmen to the Presidency, but when it comes to a civilian keeping in line that new bureaucracy, the cold war Joint Chiefs of Staff, a first class industrialist is a favorite choice.

With an industrialist typically heading Defense, is the path opened to a conspiracy wherein industry profits by war or more to the point, by peacetime defense budgets running at six to eight per cent of the gross national product? Before examining the possibility of even inadvertent complicity, for example, the self-perpetuating monster argument, one should call as an expert witness Dwight D. Eisenhower.

No matter how much defense advocates like the American Security Council point out that Ike ate some of his words later on in the famous farewell address of January 17, 1961, the fact remains it is the most ringing indictment of the dangers of a military-industrial pact in American history. J. K. Galbraith wrily notes that all critics of the complex, including himself, gingerly wrap themselves up in this impeccable speech before sallying forth and the present writer is no exception:

> Until the latest of our world conflicts, the United States had no armaments industry. American makers of plowshares could, with time and as required, make swords

> as well. But now we can no longer risk emergency improvisation of national defense; we have been compelled to create a permament armaments industry of vast proportions. Added to this, three and a half million men and women are directly engaged in the defense establishment. We annually spend on military security more than the net income of all United States corporations.
>
> This conjunction of an immense military establishment and a large arms industry is new in the American experience. The total influence — economic, political, even spiritual — is felt in every city, every State house, every office of the Federal government. We recognize the imperative need for this development. Yet we must not fail to comprehend its grave implications. Our toil, resources and livelihood are all involved; so is the very structure of our society.
>
> In the councils of government, we must guard against the acquisition of unwarranted influence, whether sought or unsought, by the military-industrial complex. The potential for the disastrous rise of misplaced power exists and will persist.
>
> We must never let the weight of this combination endanger our liberties or democratic processes. We should take nothing for granted. Only an alert and knowledgeable citizenry can compel the proper meshing of the huge industrial and military machinery of defense with our peaceful methods and goals, so that security and liberty may prosper together.

The alert and knowledgeable citizenry has fallen down on the job, some say, and for a very good reason. It simply cannot comprehend the magnitude, and therefore the need, of the fantastic weapons called forth by defense experts in an age that can send a man to the moon. In turn the citizens expect their delegated representatives, the Congress, to exercise veto power by either funding or not funding the billions requested. The Congressmen, for a variety of reasons, ranging from national security to local employment, have funded a trillion post-world war II defense dollars by practically unanimous vote. Until the unpopularity of the Vietnam war made the defense budget debatable, Congressmen voted the funds as if for motherhood, leaving undistinguished, seniority-ridden Armed Services and Preparedness Committees the task of absorbing the impossible defense budget homework. Senator Fulbright himself, Chairman of the Senate Foreign Relations Committee, confessed to a Congressional inadequacy that makes the lobbying of defense contractors of secondary significance:

> Many times appropriations bills, requests and authorizations for amounts of from $10 billion to $50 billion have been submitted to the Senate, and a very perfunctory statement has been made about them.
>
> There has been literally no debate.
>
> I do not believe that I have ever voted against one in my life. I rarely read one. I rarely tried to cut one.[1]

Finally in 1970, history was made when the anti-ballistic missile program (ABM) was thoroughly debated in the Congress and just missed being scrapped altogether (Secretary McNamara had testified *against* its adoption in 1967) by one Senator's vote. This was the year when a balky Congress cut $5.3 billion from the Administration's defense budget. As the fiscal year 1970 ended, however, supplements had brought it up to $77 billion and Secretary Laird served notice that another $80 billion would be requested for the year beginning July 1, 1972. (It was passed at $75 billion.)

It would appear that the military establishment and the Congress are the senior partners in the complex after all. Even Eisenhower reserved his special scorn for the military mind he knew so well, rapping its knuckles instead of the businessman's:

> Words like "essential" and "indispensable" and "absolute minimum" become the common coin of the realm, and they are spent with wild abandon. One military man will argue hotly for a given number of aircraft as the "absolute minimum," and others will earnestly advocate the

> "indispensable" needs for ships, tanks, rockets, guided missiles, or artillery, all totaled in numbers that are always called "minimum." All such views are argued with vigor and tenacity, but obviously all cannot be right.[2]

III

Still the industrial arm, though junior in the enterprise, cannot be let off so easily. The Eisenhower days are viewed as a dim anachronism at this point, when a $40 billion defense budget was all Ike and his economical Treasury Secretary Humphrey would allow the Services to squabble over. Khrushchev's atomic bomb and then his Sputnik changed the rules of the game and made it possible for John F. Kennedy to campaign against the Republicans on the basis of a spurious "missile gap" they had supposedly handed over to the Russians. Industry was then invited to join in the Kennedy strategy of providing whatever was needed for adequate national defense ("national security" are the words usually used), without any budget limitations and, of course, at the lowest possible cost. This strategy in practice is based on the most conservative estimates of Russia's nuclear attack potentialities, aggravated by Russia's shroud of secrecy as that country pores over our reams of disclosures. Thus was opened the door to the Doomsday nuclear weapons race which depressed Robert McNamara in San Francisco.

Supplementing the great new sales opportunity for America's defense contractors was the Kennedy-McNamara-Rusk strategy of "flexible response." Since the new team figured quite correctly that nuclear weapons were immobilized in a balance of terror (at a possible three to one ratio in favor of the United States), then a million men with non-nuclear weapons for themselves and their pact allies should be placed all over the world to contain Russia and put out "brushfires." It is all too easy to deride this posture now that Vietnam has discredited American might and Russia shows signs of willingness for a *détente.* In the sixties, Russia's hard truculence appeared to justify the strategy and the Berlin and Cuban missile crises confirmed it. Our defense machine was ready and waiting for the escalation in Vietnam. The worldwide strategy was firmly accepted, with high and low profile variations, by Presidents Johnson and Nixon.

Vietnam, inflation and the incredibly sophisticated nuclear weapons such as ICBM's and missile-launching submarines, raised the defense budget from $50 billion in the mid-sixties to the 1970 peak of $77 billion. Many people are surprised to note that the cost of Vietnam has averaged "only" $25 billion a year in its peak years. Of this sum, no more than half is expected to be released through budget reductions when the war ends. This leads to the conclusion that short of major disarmament, a defense budget at least in the $50 billion area could stay with us indefinitely. One-half to one-third of the giant expenditure will continue as payments to defense contractors, led by those hapless monsters, General Dynamics and Lockheed. Since the fear of the complex as it relates to industry ought to be based on its scale, that is, the amount of dollars involved in annual defense contracts, the charge of unwarranted influence, power and harmful impact on the economy is not going to disappear with peace in Vietnam.

IV

One charge that can be dismissed summarily is the "Merchants of Death" tag-line.

It is a charge which has appeared in most of the war-making countries, usually in the backlash of postwar revulsion. It received its widest notice in American history with the exposures of the Senate's Nye Committee in the 1930's. Predictably, glaring examples of profiteering in World War I's munitions industries, as defense contractors were then known, were uncovered by the Committee. General Douglas MacArthur, then Army Chief of Staff, helped set the scene by testifying before Congress in 1931 about "profiteering by unscrupulous contractors," a military point of view engaged in today only by the unsinkable Admiral Rickover. Excessive profits are an inevitable product of war, however, and the government is probably as much to blame as the suppliers. The surprise element of the Nye investigations turned out to be the then current international sales activities of the munitions makers, flushed out intentionally by the isolationist-minded Senators on the Committee. Here the munitions makers were caught at their professional tricks, including bribery of foreign government officials, using government ships and planes for sales demonstrations, hiring ex-officers, employing lobbyists to scuttle disarmament conferences and similar exercises in enterprise.[3] To top it all, two competing groups were selling planes and bombs to both sides of the war in Manchuria despite the fact that the United States had condemned the Japanese aggression against China. While one should not condone such activities, the government was quite capable of stopping them. It is worth noting that the Nye Committee concluded it could not determine a conspiracy to start either World War I or a war in the thirties on the part of business, regardless of the bad conduct that admittedly is a hazard of the profit system.

The fact is such a conscious conspiracy and the power to bring it about have so far been outside the American experience. It is conceivable that mammoth armament companies could ally with paranoid generals to provoke a war for their combined benefits. The nearest conceivable candidates we have in this category are the few defense giants doing over 80 per cent of their business with the military, led again by General Dynamics and Lockheed. These companies are owned by New York Stock Exchange shareholders, however, and not by an American version of the House of Krupp. The desire to start a war should hardly be added to the present woes of their Boards of Directors. The classic relationship between the war lords and the munitions lords that once prevailed in Germany, Italy and Japan involved a national mystique and aristocracy unknown to America. Even the wily Rothschilds, who sold arms to both England and France, or Shaw's Sir Andrew Undershaft, the urbanely cynical father of Major Barbara, whose munitions profits went to her Salvation Army, are distinctly European products. Indeed the only true example of the integrated military-industrial state at this point of time happens to be Russia, although that country has not committed any of its soldiers to an extended shooting war in the past twenty-five years.

This is not to say that a very unwholesome association with death and violence cannot be charged to contemporary America. The Quakers standing at vigil in public places remind us of complicity in at least a million deaths all told in one wretched Asiatic country since the Europeans withdrew in 1954. Still our defense industrialists can counter that they are no more responsible for this than the auto industry is for death on the highways and that they would gladly see our statesmen keep all weapons in storage along with the nuclear warheads.

One ought not leave the "Merchants of Death" accusation without soberly reflecting on the fact that post-war America has become the world's leading dealer in arms. Since 1950 we have dispensed, through foreign aid or plain give-away programs, $36.5 billion of military equipment and weapons, including 7,000 fighter planes and over four million carbines and rifles. This activity, which flows from the present concept of national security and a commitment to alliances such as NATO, raises some hard questions, aggravated by the experience in Vietnam. Did we make it possible for Pakistan and India to go to war, for example, and have we enabled repressive regimes in Latin American and Greece to stay in power only with their American weapons? As usual, the Russians are the ultimate instigators of our arms activities in a good many of the approximately fifty countries we deal with, the theory being that if we don't arm them, the Russians will. Though the Russians are running a fast second in foreign arms trafficking, they too have paid penalties. The Indonesian Army, using Russian weapons to frustrate a Communist takeover in 1965-1966, slaughtered some 200,000 Indonesian Communist Party members in the process.

It was in response to such dilemmas in the current use of power that a majority of the Senate finally rebelled against our post-war tradition of massive foreign aid in late 1971. Senator Frank Church of Idaho, while denying a return to isolationism, explained his vote as follows:

> The major preoccupation of the present foreign aid program is the massive disbursement of munitions which we either give away or make available at bargain basement prices. We ply half a hundred foreign governments with

> our weaponry. Most of the world has become a dumping ground for ships, tanks and planes, which we label as excess to our needs. Easy credit is available at interest rates well below the cost of money to the U.S. Government. The Military Assistance Program has become a preposterous scandal. It should be drastically curtailed, not enlarged.

The businessman, of course, does not establish foreign policy. No Basil Zaharoffs or other mysterious agents are enlisted by the Pentagon or the State Department to conduct this sorry business. The government for that matter has found itself unable to pass a domestic fire-arms control bill for the good of its own citizens. At any rate, one should not rake over the old charge of "Merchants of Death" without acknowledging a common responsibility for the deadly games still being played.

V

While we are about it, we can strike at another myth attached to the defense industry, the danger resting in the size of the individual producers. It should not be a matter of alarm that defense business is largely done by big business. The size of the orders and the complexity of the product alone would insure this result, whether for the Defense Department, the Space Administration or the Atomic Energy Commission. (The costs of the latter two, incidentally, are not included in the defense budget.) The statistics show that year in and year out approximately 50 per cent of military procurement goes to the top 25 companies doing defense business and close to 70 per cent to the top 100 companies. The percentages were practically the same in World War II, indicating no changes in this type of concentration. For years, the top five prime contractors have included Lockheed, General Dynamics, McDonnell Douglas, Boeing, Grumman, American Telephone & Telegraph Company and General Electric, each doing $1 billion to $2 billion of the total $30 billion to $40 billion of contracts involved. Since defense accounts for 80 per cent of aircraft industry sales and 35 per cent of electrical industry sales, the grouping of the top five is understandable. Less expected is the fact that America's biggest giants, the companies with over $1 billion in assets, do not dominate the defense market. They share only 25% of the defense contracts handed out to the top 100 suppliers, indicating that the great majority of big business is not the creature of the war machine nor even highly dependent upon it.[4]

The size of our producing units is always a matter of concern, as our antitrust actions constantly remind us. We tend to view absolute size as a threat to competition and a dangerous accumulation of power, either of market power or of financial power. It is not the size of the individual firms engaged in defense that warrants alarm. A Justice Department that can calmly order International Telephone and Telegraph to divest itself of subsidiaries with a billion dollars of sales primarily because ITT was getting too big can do the same to a defense contractor if necessary. It is the pervading influence of the total defense expenditure that really matters.

We can start with the observation that the military establishment, with its great purchasing power, is the largest single feature, although hardly the dominant one, of our economy. According to Bureau of Labor Statistics figures for 1967, there were approximately 7.4 million people depending on defense paychecks of one kind or another. This figure is often mistakenly used by critics of the complex to assert that "one out of ten of the nation's labor force" is so employed.[5] Eliminating the 3.3 million people in the armed forces and applying the remainder to the employed civilian labor force, which in 1967 was 73 million, the figure is closer to one out of eighteen. Secretary Laird announced in August of 1971 that the Nixon Administration cutbacks in procurement since 1968 had resulted in a reduction of about 2.3 million jobs in the Defense Department and its related industries, thus supplying a reason for that much unemployment in the nation while he was about it. This would bring the civilians employed in defense down to one out of forty in relation to our current civilian labor force. The difference is not so important when we are still contemplating a $75 billion defense budget. Yet the casual escalation of these employment figures by widely-quoted experts illustrates the difficulties of dealing with the problem, loaded as it is with figures and weaponry even Congressmen cannot understand.

The critics would be on firmer ground if they emphasized the substantial percentage our recent annual defense procurement of $20 to $30 billion, including $7 billion a year for research and development, bears to our gross manufacturing product of $500 billion. (The 1972-1973 procurement legislation request is for a comparatively low $22.7 billion.) It is enough, with its secondary effects on the subcontractors and other businesses depending on its momentum, to have sent a shiver through the nation when Lockheed faced bankruptcy due to a calamity in the 10 per cent civilian end of its business. Here was the complex stripped to its ultimate absurdity. It had developed so many constituents depending on its payroll — employees, unions, scientists, banks, states, shareholders and politicians seeking reelection, to name a few, that the business of government almost had to stop until its fate was settled. The fact that Lockheed had received $10 billion in vital defense orders in the last seven years was hardly noticed. It could be making widgets, in the opinion of the majority of its constituents, so long as it kept its doors open.

VI

Is the defense industry then just a gigantic public works program, amenable to demobilization as occurred so quickly after World War II? Obviously it is not. A twenty-five year institution of such dimensions cannot be replaced so easily. On the economic side, there is no pent-up demand for civilian goods, for example, to ease its transition. Even if this could be solved by substituting obviously needed public priorities, the suggestion of unilateral disarmament is a political impossibility and perhaps suicidal as well. The Russians are thus shaping our defense budget, far more than the lobbying defense contractors, just as we are influencing Kremlin decisions on guns or butter. Their defense budget is now reported to be about half of ours, although presumably they are getting more bang for their ruble, without unions, the profit motive or other distractions. On the other hand, they are spending $10 billion a year on military research and development, according to Dr. John S. Foster, Jr., director of research and engineering in the Defense Department. Dr. Foster is concerned. "It is absolutely essential," he recently stated, "that the free world be technologically superior to the Soviet Union."[6]

Even the most distinguished critics of the complex falter when coming to grips with the budget reductions that are the only immediate way to diminish the weight of this value-eroding, lopsided, inflationary diversion of our resources. J. K. Galbraith, in his book *How to Stop the Military*, sees no conspiracy, either on the part of business or of the military. He enumerates all the self-serving procedures that keep the pot boiling, the 2,000 former high-ranking officers reported to be in defense industry, the spreading of the contracts and bases in Congressional backyards, the think-tanks giving civilian status to defense preparations, the accomplices in the universities, the public relations men selling the Pentagon, the career men advancing the cause of their Services, in short, a self-perpetuating web of bureaucracy basking in the climate of a cold war foreign policy. Somewhat reluctantly, he finally places the buck at the door of the Presidents and of Congress. Noting one ray of hope, that the nation's mood is changing, he advocates that now is the time to apply pressure on Congress to stand up to the incessant overkill demands of the military — by eliminating $5 billion for each of the next three years for a total reduction of $15 billion.[7]

Just as Galbraith sees room only for a starter, so does the National Urban Coalition. In its recent study entitled *Counterbudget: A Blueprint for Changing National Priorities*, this organization, supposedly on the very antennae of the domestic crises affected by defense spending, proposes gradual defense budget reductions from $60.2 billion in fiscal 1972 to a level of $50 billion for the years 1973-1976.

Similarly a long-awaited, major report of the Brookings Institution on *Setting National Priorities: The 1972 Budget* analyzes the "defense options" in depth. It challenges the "full redundancy" of our three-way nuclear strategy of superiority in missiles, bombs and submarines, and notes that this "triad" might be reduced to a "diad." The lowest option they feel they can offer the Administration is one for $69.5 billion in the fiscal year 1972, followed by *increases* to $75.5 by 1976, without Vietnam but with a volunteer army. Was it possible that tough-minded Harry Truman was dreaming when he clamped down an absolute lid of $14 billion for his defense budget of 1949?

VII

Perhaps it is time to leave these moderate critics and hear from the moralizers, the passionate critics who simply know from their insides that something besides the Russian intransigence is wrong in this matter. Vietnam, of course, makes them eloquent and it is hard to discern where their fury about the war and the indictment of the complex starts and stops. They warn us that if we prepare for war we will get war, or at least the bleakness and spiritual destruction of the garrison state. To the extent that books are weapons, hopefully these jeremiads stimulated our power structure to gamble with Russia more aggressively at the Strategic Arms Limitation Talks (SALT) in Helsinki. Some of the best in this vein are *The War Profiteers* by Richard E. Kaufman, Senator Proxmire's skilled defense researcher, *The Weapons Culture* by Ralph Lapp, *The Economy of Death* by Richard J. Barnet and *The War Business* by George Thayer. At a more profound level of discussion there is Adam Yarmolinsky's *The Military Establishment*, a major study commissioned by The Twentieth Century Fund. Yarmolinsky served Secretary McNamara as Special Assistant and Deputy Assistant for International Affairs. The book explores the impact of the military establishment on American society and while it avoids the polemical treatment of the moralizers, the author and his distinguished team of collaborators cannot disguise their yearning for strong countervailing forces to offset the overweening military presence. Interestingly they find the military quite civilianized and the civilians militarized, a hybrid accommodation all the more dangerous for the best pluralist traditions of the country.

As for the military-industrial complex, these writers, while describing with distaste the intriguing of the contractors for their slice of the business, generally stop short of placing real blame on the business system. There is the usual listing of the dollar amounts awarded to the 100 largest contractors and all their subsidiaries as well as the list of universities receiving approximately a half-billion dollars a year for defense-related research. The latter of course are seen as particularly inappropriate, although Congress apparently would just as readily appropriate money to the same installations off-campus. More to the point, there is the recording of excessive waste, chronic cost overruns and cancelled contracts in the billions. The obverse of the coin, an absolutely efficient Pentagon without cancellations (which are mostly due to new technology) should not have appeal for sincere critics of the system.

Barnet personalizes his business criticism by flaying the economic and social backgrounds of the establishment men in Defense and related departments. For the period 1940-1967, he finds seventy important names from the ranks of big business or high finance, including eight out of ten Secretaries of Defense, seven out of eight Secretaries of the Air Force, every Secretary of the Navy, eight out of nine Secretaries of the Army, three out of five Directors of the CIA and three out of five Chairmen of the Atomic Energy Commission. Barnet concludes that these "National Security Managers," having built their careers on inherent conservatism, naturally tend toward an aggressive, heavily-armed, non-negotiating posture. One need not answer this power-élite argument, considering the distinguished public service records of these men, some of whom were as glibly attacked by Senator Joe McCarthy in a different context. Presidents have relied on such men as civilian administrators, particularly for Defense, ever since the days of Woodrow Wilson and World War I, when historically the military-industrial complex came to life.[8] Lately they have been joined at the National Security Council table by an intellectual élite without noticeable improvement.

Yet now that heavy defense expenditures seem to be entering a period of widespread disrepute, perhaps this civilian establishment is in need of fresh thinking. It has been noticeably deficient in producing many sentiments along the line of Secretary McNamara's deploring of the "mad momentum" of the arms race even in the early days when he was committed to it. The independent analysis of our defense needs commissioned by the Rockefeller brothers as a public service in 1958, the ensuing report of the Gaither commission and the Presidentially commissioned Fitzhugh report on the Defense Department of 1970 each are replete with rationalisms and operating reforms but also with fear of taking the first step towards any budget cuts. Similar establishment names appear as the sponsors of the Urban Coalition, the Brookings Institution and the Twentieth Century Fund reports already mentioned. A few dovish labor leaders, if there are any, and other representatives of our diverse society would seem to be welcome at this deadly level.

While Yarmolinsky is above such a biased view as Barnet's, he does indulge in some thought-provoking sociological analysis of the new military leadership. The new military officer is far removed from the General Patton type. The defense establishment has become so dependent on advanced technological resources and modern management techniques that a new type of "military manager" may eventually displace the "heroic leader" type. The centralization of civilian authority over the Pentagon began with President Truman's National Security Act of 1947 and reached its peak with the seven-year sojourn of Secretary McNamara. If only for self-defense, the military men settled down to learning systems analysis, programming and other civilian games with the eagerness of Harvard Business School students. Even with subordinates, the new military bosses are reported to be keeping their voices down and making suggestions rather than giving orders, much as a dean deals with his faculty. Career generals are further civilianized by the need to understand foreign affairs, now that war and defense have truly become instruments of foreign policy. At any rate, there now seems to be a formidable corps of highly educated and urbane officers who in their knowledge of science and geopolitics are among the best-trained men in the country. Possession of the Ph.D. degree is widely recognized as the key to the very highest ranks. As these handsome products swing through Congressional committee doors with their attaché briefcases, one can understand how many Congressmen, a great proportion of whom have service records, are horn-swoggled into giving them what they want. Professor Samuel Huntington of Harvard has also engaged in probing the military mind in his influential book *The Soldier and the State*. Huntington's scholarly research leads to the proposition that the professional soldier really is ready by the nature of his calling to accept civilian control. If we want to keep the generals in their place, he argues, we had better not give them too much civilian status and graces. Otherwise, they may have ambitions to master the state rather than carry out their duties as prescribed by the constitutional executive.[9] If a choice is to be made, there are those who would disagree with Huntington and maintain that civilian processing is the only way to keep these new paragons from blowing us up. Again it would seem that Congress and the President are where we should look for the proper exercise of countervailing force, certainly not to profit-hungry defense contractors. Harry Truman seemed to know how to put down General MacArthur, whose talents were adequate enough to master the Pentagon and Japan itself. Lyndon B. Johnson learned to distrust the military as a member of Armed Services Committees long before becoming President. "All the generals know," he said as President, "is spend and bomb." This was when he thought the world of his prize Cabinet specimen, McNamara, and before he desperately turned to General Westmoreland to support his losing cause in Vietnam.

VIII

Soviet critics of our military-industrial complex can be expected to attack it on ideological grounds. For example, they could use the Lenin version of the dangers inherent in such an alliance, namely that it exists to instigate imperialist wars of conquest for the creation of economic markets to take care of overproduction. Aside from the fact that America has an almost blameless record on colonialism, the theory has been consigned to the dustbin of history by Russia itself. Since World War II that country has been heavily engaged in demonstrating a new kind of non-Lenin imperialism involving political power over satellite countries. While America is constantly denounced as "imperialist" in the Russian press, there are few responsible critics who can make a credible case for it, unless one accepts the charge of world-policing, which is not essentially an economic issue. There are enough problems relating to our military-industrial complex, led by inadequately counterbalanced military power and gravely sidetracked domestic priorities, without adding the flimsy charge of market imperialism.

Still the businessman should be willing to stretch his mind by weighing some formidable home-grown charges of capitalist or business-instigated imperialism. Not the old dogma of Lenin about the inevitability of imperialist war-making nor even the American multinational corporations which so alarm France's Jean Jacques Servan-Schreiber with their skill and aggressiveness. Indeed not even the revelations of ITT's state department presumably meddling in Chile's elections, as was once our custom in the banana republics. For a forthright condemnation of American capitalism as imperialist beyond redemption, one must consider the thesis of the noted historians Joyce and Gabriel Kolko, highly respected and non-Marxist to boot.

In *The Limits of Power*, the Kolkos continue their prodigious and controversial analysis of foreign policy from the close of World War II through the fifties. They conclude unequivocally that our foreign policy was not only influenced by economic considerations, which one would reasonably grant, but also was obsessed with the idea of making the world safe for American capitalism. Why would Harry Truman, his advisors and successors, including Eisenhower, follow this line? Because they realized that without a subservient, non-Communist group of nations ready to trade with America, it would not be possible to maintain a level of employment and profits sufficient for American capitalism to survive. Thus the high levels of military preparedness, the exaggeration of the Russian threat to obtain Congressional defense funds, the formation of military alliances, the rebuilding of a strong Germany and Japan, the stretched-out war in Korea and, perhaps in their next book, Vietnam.

These are strong charges for the businessman to face with his fondness for those remains of capitalism he still perceives in the United States. Is our system of producing and distributing goods, after surviving world depressions and world wars, actually a built-in obstacle to our proposed goals of peace because of foreign trade factors? Is the military-industrial complex only a natural bit of conniving resulting from an endemic condition in our institutions themselves? Has capitalism reformed only domestically?

The Kolkos support their revisionist history with reams of government reports and extracts from Congressional hearings. If one seeks dialogue, however startling the conclusions, one should read their works for interpretative testimony about our cold war obsession. Surely there is an alternative explanation for our foreign policy, regardless of how inept it often seems to have been in these years. Can one really accept the idea of Truman and Eisenhower placing jobs and markets above all? The alternative explanation is the fear of Stalin's Russia as the other great super-power, especially after the devastating experience of being unprepared for the Germany of World War II. As for propping up defeated rightist nations, in many ways we now face more economic threats from West Germany and Japan than would have been the case had these nations gone to the Left. As for centrist nations, the United States has stayed neutral over the development of the European Common Market, now a trading group of 250 million people. If America is so irretrievably destined by its institutions and way of life to dominating economically the rest of the non-Communist world, why did President Nixon, the most capitalist-minded of our post-war Presidents, the man who wants America to be first in the world economically, initiate a low-profile anti-Communism during a period of rising unemployment? Why did Lyndon Johnson impose curbs on foreign investment?

In brief, our foreign policy does not begin and end with a crusade for capitalism, even though burdened with excessive fear of Communism. As for businessmen, they were probably as relieved as most of the rest of America when Khrushchev threatened to bury us economically rather than with bombs. The weak link in the Kolko thesis is in the assumption of motivations. One can hardly accept a primarily economic survival motivation as against a balance of power motivation on the part of Truman and Eisenhower, two Presidents whose formative experiences and instincts were certainly more military-minded than profit-minded. When the Kolkos write their final story on Vietnam, they will have a difficult time proving an economic calculus for that desolate nation as against a missionary, patriotic crusade reminiscent of the Spanish-American War.

One philosophical question may finally be considered as we examine the military-industrial complex. To what extent is the embrace of these institutions likely to strangle capitalism itself? Businessmen shy away from such an introspective question and go about their business of providing goods and services, considering it an honor and something of a duty to sell to the government. Still the question is not so far-fetched. It was one thing to see military expenditures reach 48 per cent of the gross national product in World War II and find capitalism, in terms of relatively free markets and independent business decisions, suspended for the duration. Now that our cold war with Russia compels us to engage in peacetime spending of 6 to 8 per cent of our gross national product on defense, with several key states critically dependent on such payrolls, are we socializing our economy? President Nixon's wage and price control actions of October 1971, for example, were strongly affected by the inflation resulting from a $23 billion budget deficit and a balance of payments problem, both substantially related to Pentagon spending. Democratic economists were quick to point up the irony of the Administration's decision. Extended controls would result in "Sovietization" of the economy, Walter W. Heller suggested. In doing so, he was matching the crocodile tears shed by J. K. Galbraith only a few weeks earlier when Lockheed was not allowed to expire under the laws of perfect competition, which both economists well realized had been abrogated at the turn of the century. In brief, capitalism can survive enormous defense spending, as it has so far, but other institutions suffer.

Allowing one more critic his stand, we can call on Columbia's noted Professor Seymour Melman, author of *Pentagon Capitalism.*

Melman's concern for capitalism does not spring from conservatism but from a fear of the military state. He sees the military power and the purchasing power of the Pentagon creating a state within a state, self-perpetuating and growing, deriving its authority from fear and misplaced patriotism. The complaint about the deprivation of domestic priorities and erosion of values caused by the Pentagon's conscription of talent and resources is familiar. The figures are also recounted in detail and rather than slight their significance, some not already listed ought to be mentioned here for the reader to weigh. The Department of Defense is the largest planned economy outside the Soviet Union. Its assets and inventories are the equivalent of about 10 per cent of the country's entire economy, however that is measured. Its Post Exchange (PX) system is third in retail sales behind Sears and the A&P. Over 60 per cent of all our scientists, engineers and technicians were working on defense-related projects, at least before the recession of 1970-1972. The Department owns 30 million acres of land and employs about half of all federal civilian employees. The industrial army of over 3 million employees cited by Melman is of course overstated by double if Secretary Laird's figures about defense-caused unemployment are accepted. It is just this kind of rapid swing in Pentagon infiltration that causes one to take its economic threat with a grain of salt. After all, the entire country was a military-industrial machine in World War II and both elements were almost completely demobilized within a few years. To speak of the Pentagon, as Robert L. Heilbroner does, as the "acknowledged master of the industrial core of the primary economic system"[10] is indulging in some sort of numbers game, however deplorable its immense influence on our foreign policy and domestic allocations.

Professor Melman has a more original contribution to make in analyzing defense firms as capitalist enterprises. He points out, as Kaufman and Yarmolinsky do, that many of the largest contractors receive a considerable portion of their capital from the Defense Department, including such items as $2 billion of government-owned furniture and office machines, $4.7 billion of materials and over $5 billion of plant and equipment, as reported in 1967. Add to this the billions of dollars in progress payments that have been made as frequently as on a weekly basis and defense contracting would seem to be quite a non-competitive, guaranteed-market, freely-financed plum. In fact, as Melman points out, there are risks not connected with the usual capitalist risk-taking. Defense business by necessity is the antithesis of capitalist enterprise, being managed and policed by a central management with the largest office staff in the world. These central managers control "profits," which are in effect a grant to the contractors generally measured as a percentage of costs and theoretically limited through the power of renegotiation and constant auditing. Watchdogs like Senator Proxmire and Congressional investigating committees also contribute some profit control by exposure. The Department in addition can cancel out for performance or technological changes, leaving the contractor overextended in plant and manpower, regardless of cancellation payments.

When Lockheed was going down for the third time, this fact of life about the largest contractors in the aerospace industry became more apparent to the public. In a sense, it was unfair to make scapegoats out of Lockheed's management in the capitalist tradition because the Pentagon controls the big decisions of contractors of this magnitude and not vice versa. Lockheed could hardly have been expected to pursue the efficiencies presumed to result from a policy of maximizing profits since its prices were negotiated and even its costs were regulated by Pentagon management. When it comes to allowing cost overruns to make sure some fantastically conceived, never fully-tested missile or aircraft will work, the Pentagon simply has to encourage and pay for such overruns. The same would apply to space administration contracts and atomic energy projects. This does not downgrade the immense need for efficiency and the type of contract that discourages cost overruns. Nor does it excuse the inane harassment of A. E. Fitzgerald, Air Force Deputy for Management Systems, when he reported $2 billion of *concealed* cost overruns on Lockheed's C-5A contract to the Proxmire Committee in November 1968. Cost overruns of 30 per cent are typical of defense contracts and the C-5A cargo planes at last estimate will cost about $60 million *each* as against the $22 million originally estimated. Reasons for overruns include "bidding in" at an unrealistic price in order to get "locked into" the contract, news from the Kremlin about the current competitive model and inflation itself, only the last of which is an inevitable capitalist risk.

At any rate, companies doing the bulk of their business with the Pentagon are far removed from enterprise capitalism and this fact should be calmly recognized. In the sense that Lockheed is something of a government arsenal, it was fitting that the government should guarantee its bank loans and keep it in existence. Some say it would be more fitting for Lockheed to become in fact a government arsenal rather than be financed by private banks and shareholders. So far the Defense establishment has resisted such an idea on the grounds that arsenals are less efficient and creative than private enterprise. One suspects that the Defense Department, committed to keeping us first in military might, prefers the civilian cloak of its Lockheeds and RAND's (a private research and development firm whose customer is the Pentagon and whose creator was the Air Force) as a more discreet apparatus for getting its funds from Congress. This thought could be reinforced by the advertising, the campaign contributions and the personal pressures on Congressmen available from the contractors.

IX

In what has been called Robert McNamara's "ordeal in the Pentagon," all the problems and challenges of this fateful government agency can be seen in human terms. McNamara is one of the most brilliant and interesting men ever to have come from business into government. Only the Pentagon job would have made him leave Ford after being its president for forty-two days. When the Kennedy scouts approached him after the election he expressed no interest but saw JFK as a matter of courtesy. Interestingly one of the questions he asked the President was whether he had really written *Profiles of Courage* by himself. The President proved it to McNamara's satisfaction. When McNamara observed that he had no experience in government administration, Kennedy remarked that there was no school for Presidents either. Obviously the sparks of rapport flew between the 43 year old President and the 44 year old auto executive. One of the few jobs with more power than president of the world's largest privately controlled enterprise was the Department of Defense. McNamara made up his mind, resigned from Ford, sold stock and allowed options to expire (while still netting out an after-tax estate of a million dollars) and went to work. Characteristically he sent out over ninety requests for precise information reports from startled agency heads within his first few weeks in office. For seven years he kept to a back-breaking work and travel schedule, staying in office three times as long as any of his predecessors and leaving his indelible mark on the Department.

Actually McNamara had been in government service once before. As a young Harvard Business School instructor with a flare for accounting, he taught Air Force officers statistical control and analysis and then went into uniform to carry out Air Force management missions himself. Under the leadership of Tex Thornton, who would later found Litton Industries, ten of these officers, soon known as "Whiz Kids," banded together to offer their services as a group to some ailing big business. Young Henry Ford II, having recently seized control of his shaky business from his senile grandfather, was sorely in need of bright young men and hired them *en masse*. McNamara was lured from teaching at Harvard with a $12,000 salary and Thornton drew the top amount of $16,000. The group also included Arjay Miller who would precede McNamara as president of Ford.

The Ford days were marked by a certain independence of life style. Even while competing for the presidency, McNamara chose to live in Ann Arbor rather than the traditional Ford enclave of Grosse Pointe, commuting the thirty-five miles daily in order to develop a social and intellectual life among the professors at the University of Michigan. In many ways the austere, plainly dressed McNamara, with his rimless glasses and slicked down hair, was the opposite in personality to Ford's current president, the flashy Lee Iaccoca. McNamara's best product was the stripped down, functional Falcon. His emphasis on merchandising safety as a Ford feature aroused industry antagonism on the theory of unmentionables. It may have been with some feeling of relief that having become number one at Ford, he could transfer with enthusiasm to the only mountains left to climb, the corridors of power and public service.

Administrations proceed from crisis to crisis and McNamara soon had his initiation in the Bay of Pigs assault. The error was engraved on his memory and he had no hesitancy as he left office seven years later to admit participation in its decisions as his biggest mistake. From it he learned to share JFK's cynicism about military advice. Announcing that he conceived of his job as that of a leader rather than as a judge of the conflicting positions presented by the Services, he forcefully accelerated their consolidation in his office as called for in the Defense Unification Act. Inevitably he reaped his award from men like General Thomas D. White, a former Air Force Chief of Staff: "I am profoundly apprehensive of the pipe-smoking, tree-full-of-owls type of so-called professional defense intellectuals who have been brought into this nation's capital. . . . I don't believe these professors . . . and other theorists have sufficient worldliness or motivation to stand up to the kind of enemy we face."

There were other generals, however, who responded to McNamara's demands for planning, programming, quantifying of costs and systems analysis of options with the eagerness of converts. From the point of view of budget totals, which is the connection with the military-industrial complex, an ironic result of McNamara's cold efficiency is that he gave respectability to the demands of the military. The Congress was now offered requests for more billions documented and rationalized as never before. Instead of the embarrassment of each Service scrambling for an edge in responsibility and glamor, the Department now presented a coordinated front. Budget requests were tied in with foreign policy considerations, data on industrial capacity and intelligence estimates. They were endorsed by the formidable presence of the articulate and self-composed Secretary who wore the mantle of being right-hand man to Presidents Kennedy and Johnson on practically all matters. Since the public itself, the elder statesmen and the Presidents also approved, the lobbying of defense contractors, or for that matter, the lobbying and propaganda of the Pentagon itself, were probably superfluous. At least that may be said to be the situation before the failure in Vietnam.

Not the least of the arguments in favor of big defense spending was the view of the government's Keynesian economists that not only was the world situation demanding an increase in defense expenditures but the money in effect was being pumped into the economy in a beneficial sort of way, sustaining employment. To cut down defense spending at such a time would not necessarily see the funds transferred to a "higher use" (today's neglected domestic priorities), claimed James Tobin, Yale professor and Kennedy economist. They would instead be used for superfluous private consumption compared to vital public programs, defense or non-defense.[11] The change in thinking about what to do with released defense spending — the "peace dividends"— in one decade could not be more marked.

In this context the change in McNamara's thinking, both on Vietnam and on the essence of security, is striking. In a sense, McNamara operated on two levels, one as the skilled managerial technocrat, harnessing America's largest enterprise and fighting the battles of weapons choice, Service rivalries and even crackpot Congressional appropriations of funds specifically not requested by himself and his Presidents. On the other level, he was the humanist, dreadfully aware that the whole premise of nuclear supremacy rather than parity might be wrong, or that the opinions of his friend Robert Kennedy should outweigh his concept of absolute loyalty to the boss.

Businessmen thirsting for adventure in Washington may be fascinated by McNamara's experience with the TFX (tactical fighter experimental) project as an example on the first level. The TFX, which became the F-111 "all purpose" fighter-bomber plane, pursued McNamara like an albatross throughout his seven years as Defense Secretary. It was marked at the outset by bitter in-fighting, particularly on the Navy's part, on the grounds that the Navy needed a lighter plane that could hover over and operate from its carriers, as compared to the type of plane demanded by the Air Force. McNamara was determined to effect the economies of a multiservice plane, convinced that the variable "swing-wing" design he found on the Pentagon drawing boards would save a billion dollars and put an end to what he saw as the irrational, tradition-bound system of separate planes. Meeting the problem head-on in his first year in office, he cracked down and asserted civilian dominance, ordering the Navy to accept, and the Air Force to develop, the single aircraft.

Enough has been written about the TFX controversy to insure at least another decade of misunderstandings and accusations, but some final results are incontrovertible. The Navy dragged and stalled in its specifications long enough to get Congress, with Pentagon support, to cancel out its entire production immediately after McNamara's departure in 1967. The Navy's F111B, incidentally, had by then reached a cost estimate of $8 million per plane, double the original estimate. At the time of the cancellation, the Navy had only seven test planes on hand and was already happily engaged in plans for its own F-14. The F-14 is expected to roll off production lines soon at $17 million per plane each, assuming it does not bankrupt Grumman Aerospace Corporation along the way.

Meanwhile the Air Force version suffered a series of test accidents and then a disastrous try-out in Vietnam, when three planes quickly crashed through malfunction or pilot error. The final Air Force order has been ingloriously reduced from 1400 to 526. The Navy's order had been for 300.

What caused the tremendous mistake? Taxpayers are offered an answer in Alain B. Einthoven's book *How Much is Enough?* Einthoven was one of McNamara's own Whiz Kids, serving in his thirties first as Assistant Controller and then as head of Systems Analysis. The Air Force and the Navy didn't use systems analysis, he writes, as it hadn't yet been installed. Hence they didn't specify adequately just what the defense contractor had to deliver. "It is typical of the ironies of the defense business," he states, "that McNamara was severely attacked later for overruling the Services, when, in fact, the troubles that were to beset the F-111 — very high cost, failure to meet technical objectives, crashes in testing, and weight growth in the Navy version — stemmed not from McNamara's decisions but from the unjustifiably demanding performance requirements set for the aircraft by the Services."[12] McNamara does not give in easily and when the planes failed to perform well in early tests, he stepped directly into the management process himself. In August 1966, he began a series of urgent Saturday meetings with aerospace executives and specialists from all over the country for the sole purpose of straightening out the F-111. The final programs to make the Navy's lady watch her weight were pathetically humorous, if one can forget the cost. The campaigns proceeded from WIP (Weight Improvement Program) to SWIP (Super Weight Improvement Program) to SCRAPE.

If the F-111 was McNamara's Edsel, Senator McClellan was his Ralph Nader. The crusty old Arkansas Senator clashed with the new Secretary over the industrial side of the complex, namely, the awarding of the contract to General Dynamics instead of Boeing. McClellan was Chairman of the Permanent Subcommittee on Investigations. One of his committee members was Senator Henry M. Jackson of Washington, a defense expert whose home state had just lost the contract with possibilities of reaching $7 billion, the largest ever awarded by the Pentagon. For nine months, the investigation of the TFX contract lingered on, descending into personality clashes and innuendoes and trailing off only after the assassination of President Kennedy.

McNamara and by implication the Kennedy Administration had some explaining to do. Jackson complained that Boeing's bid had been lower and that it was technically superior for the particular contract. The proposals had been submitted and resubmitted several times before the award on November 21, 1962. The final bids were $5.455 billion by General Dynamics and $5.364 billion by Boeing. On cost alone, McNamara might be absolved, since everyone realized that according to the unreal world of Pentagon, contractors bid in ridiculously low. The image used is "getting the camel's nose under the tent." Air Force analysts even then estimated the cost at least at $7 billion. As the hearings ground on they revealed that McNamara and the General Dynamics supporters were in the minority even in his own citadel. A mountain of support on the military side had developed for giving the contract to Boeing. More than 200 specialists had spent 275,000 man-hours appraising the designs and had decided in Boeing's favor.[13] McNamara, backed by his Air and Navy Secretaries and also by Deputy Defense Secretary Roswell Gilpatric, had overruled fifteen generals, six admirals and their hundreds of retainers. In addition he affronted McClellan and Jackson by refusing to delay the commitment after the award was announced.

It did not take long for critics to draw deductions about the political and industrial prizes at stake. One did not require a computer to note that General Dynamics needed a big contract to keep afloat. It had completed its B-58 bomber and had recently taken a loss of $425 million on commercial jets. Henry Crown, a Democratic party stalwart, was concerned with his massive investment resulting from merging his building materials corporation into General Dynamics. Columnists totaled up the electoral votes involved. Texas and New York, where General Dynamics and its participant Grumman would build the plane, carried sixty-nine; Boeing's Washington and Kansas plants were worth only seventeen and had not gone to Kennedy in 1960 anyway. Vice President Johnson was known to be a realist on the benefits of defense orders for his home state, the success of Texas in that field having risen spectacularly along with Johnson's own career.

Obviously McClellan and Jackson were treating McNamara as an adversary. A conflict of interest was charged in the case of Gilpatric, whose former New York law firm had become principal counsel to General Dynamics. McClellan claimed he should have disqualified himself from TFX. The Justice Department ruled that he was legally innocent of conflict of interest charges but the Committee's final report rapped him for lack of candor in its presence. Navy Secretary Fred Korth, however, was an easier victim. He had succeeded Texan John Connally straight from a Fort Worth bank presidency. General Dynamics owed the bank $400,000 and Korth had neglected to sell his stock before assuming command of the Navy. By the time investigators dredged up personal letters to business acquaintances on official stationery, the embarrassed President let it be known a resignation from Korth would be appreciated.

McNamara firmly denied White House political intervention. "Neither so-called nor actual socio-economic factors entered into the award," he testified, using a strained synonym for political-industrial influence. The final judgment is that McNamara and his supporters made their decision on non-political grounds, so far as this is possible. General Dynamics was chosen because they felt its capabilities were best suited for the single-plane concept. Reflecting on the matter as an insider, Yarmolinsky concludes that General Dynamics won because its specifications were based on the conviction McNamara would prevail whereas Boeing decided the Services would win out with separate planes. To add to the irony, McNamara later reflected that if Boeing had won, the TFX might have succeeded since the military would have at least started out with some enthusiasm for the project.[14] This suggests that the military subconsciously sabotaged the TFX, a sorry commentary on the whole process. A final comment is provided in a section of McNamara's Committee testimony pointing up that a businessman attempting to ride the defense behemoth pays dearly:

> McCLELLAN: I think we had better go on and try to make a record here and get the facts on the record, so there will be no further doubt about what the truth is.
>
> McNAMARA: Mr. Chairman, I know that that is your desire and intention and I hope that that is the result. I don't believe it will be. Last night when I got home at midnight, after preparing for today's hearing, my wife told me that my own twelve-year old son had asked how long it would take for his father to prove his honesty.[15]

X

According to a *Newsweek* article in the summer of 1971, the twelve-year old son was then a junior at Stanford and something of a campus radical. The McNamara of the World Bank is reported to be happily immersed in lending billions for peaceful development. Some say he is atoning for his part in Vietnam but McNamara's code keeps him noticeably reticent, even after the premature opening of the Pentagon Papers, which he himself had commissioned.

Two photo images have emerged on the American consciousness of McNamara's Pentagon career. One is McNamara at Harvard in November 1966, surrounded by taunting student hecklers, physically threatened and denied the right to speak. How could he explain the liberal businessman's predicament on the use of power, that it must be possessed in order to do good? How could he explain that it was no longer "McNamara's War," that the first years of his office had been years of disillusion, that now he was the one who restrained generals, limited bombing objectives, and made speeches that would cause an ordinary Defense Secretary to be thrown out of office? "We had freedom of speech in my days at Berkeley," was his barely heard comment. "I was tougher than you then and I'm tougher now," he added darkly and inconsequentially.

The second image is the man with the pointer, standing like a schoolmaster in front of the chart of statistics or the aerial view of Vietnam, lecturing, perhaps to Congressional Committees, LBJ, or frustrated generals. On the theory that knowledge is power, he was Faustian, handling the deadly figures with ease, steps ahead of any questioner, yet sensing his own convictions crumbling in the process. This is the image that reminds us of McNamara's greatest accomplishment, the plea to stop the strategic arms race at parity, symbolized by his constant pressure to hold back nuclear weapons from escalating over ABM deployment. On this note he stepped out of office, grudgingly yielding to his President on a "thin" ABM system, almost facetiously justified as a Red China deterrent. Hardly a victory for the disarmament people, but a high level of achievement in his limited area of maneuver.

As a background for discussing the ABM question, the most significant arms race development the nation ever considered in terms of potential cost and Russian reactions, one should go back to a

Defense Department chart. Here, using Pentagon figures, is a primer for businessmen to consider if they are called upon to help produce a "thick" ABM shield:

Number of Fatalities in an All-Out Strategic Exchange (Assumes No Soviet Reaction to U.S. Antiballistic Missile Deployment) (in millions)

	Soviet strikes first — United States retaliates		United States strikes first — Soviet retaliates	
	U.S. Fatalities	Soviet Fatalities	U.S. Fatalities	Soviet Fatalities
U.S. programs:				
Approved	120	120	100	70
Posture A	40	120	30	70
Posture B	30	120	20	70

The above table was used by McNamara in requesting his final budget before the House Appropriations Committee in 1967 for the fiscal year 1968. The "approved" ABM system is the one that had been approved to that date by Congress, costing over a half-billion a year to maintain and supported by over $4 billion in research and development between 1955 and 1968, under such names as Nike-Zeus, Nike-X and Sentinel. McNamara's position throughout his term had been to yield to the military on the research requests but to resist as long as possible increased deployment of the system (Postures A and B). He regarded such increases as the signal to Russia to escalate its offensive missiles in a fatal, wasteful race. Postures A and B would have involved deployments of "thicker" ABM's, costing $12 billion and $22 billion respectively, all possible to do from the accumulated research and development on hand.

What the chart says is that even if we deploy Posture B (about 52 lucky cities would be "locally defended" in addition to the continent itself), the Russians of 1967 could have taken thirty million American lives with a surprise attack. If we strike first (in the scenario our position is that we would never strike first) we would still lose 20 million Americans.

The Defense Department analysts are still running computer print-outs in this field of endeavor. Alain Einthoven's up-to-date figures for the 1970's culminate in what happens if 1, We go to Posture B and 2, This time the Kremlin *responds* by upping its defense budget to produce the latest in missile offense, for example, 500 mobile ICBM's accompanied by MIRV's (multiple nuclear warheads stemming off from the same missile) and "penetration aids" to foil our most advanced electronic scramblers. Then the score in millions of dead would be as follows:[16]

Soviet strikes first		United States strikes first	
United States retaliates		Soviet retaliates	
U.S. Killed	Soviet Killed	U.S. Killed	Soviet Killed
100	100	100	80*

*The reason the Soviet is "better off" if we strike first is that first strikes are against military targets and their sites are better dispersed.

Although the layman's mind boggles at these figures to the point of blackout, as they probably did for the Germans and their concentration camps, one conclusion seems clear. If we force Russia to the limit in offensive missiles by escalating our ABM, we will still lose half our population, regardless of which power strikes first. It isn't worth the money.

Just when Robert McNamara's pointer began to tremble is not certain but he reached his greatest eloquence against the arms race in the San Francisco speech with which this chapter opened. Already estranged from Johnson, as the Pentagon Papers now make clear, he even admitted that the United States, through missile gap fantasies and inability to judge Soviet intentions, had built a far larger nuclear arsenal than needed, reaping a whirlwind. "It is precisely this action-reaction phenomenon that fuels an arms race," he said, calling for an agreement first to limit and then to reduce strategic (nuclear) weapons. In the previous June he had met Premier Aleksei Kosygin with President Johnson at Glassboro, New Jersey and made the same request, admitting before the President that the ABM would only increase the costs and dangers for both countries. Kosygin was non-committal but it was one of McNamara's finest moments.

Still this Defense Secretary who had called for the great powers to find security not in weapons but in the minds of men and in the extension of economic aid to the have-not countries,[17] went along with his President, who, under tremendous pressure from the Congressional Committees, demanded support for a $5.5 billion Sentinel deployment system. Many say McNamara should have resigned over this as well as his disenchantment over Vietnam but McNamara's characteristic loyalty to his chief prevented him from taking such action.

The ABM system is still with us under the new name Safeguard. In turn Safeguard has a new "backstop," SDM (Site Defense of Minuteman), now in the prototype stage at a potential cost of billions, depending on SALT talks. But McNamara's reluctant and forced support for the present "thin" deployment helped bring on the great 1970 debate over ABM. This debate was a watershed for informed discussion, both in and out of Congress, among scientists, industrialists and the public at large, of the dangers and useless costs of the nuclear arms race. The advocates of defense spending reduction won a moral victory of the first magnitude, one that may have thawed the cold war and that is sure to accelerate as the country moves towards the inevitable reaction against the excessive militarism of its foreign policy.

XI

What should the verdict be for the "unwarranted influence and power" of industry as seen in the career of this auto executive turned public servant? McNamara himself showed little concern for the power of the complex, although as Secretary of Defense he could hardly have attacked it. In his final newspaper interview with the

Associated Press on leaving office, McNamara was asked if he shared Eisenhower's concern about the military-industrial complex. "I don't," he replied, "as long as the Secretary of Defense operates as he should, examining the factors of the problem and making decisions on his own analysis, regardless of the pressures applied to him." "If the President backs his Secretary," he added, "how can the military-industrial complex get to him?"[18] True enough, McNamara spent half his time fighting with his generals and Congressmen as he forced cancellations of obsolete or redundant projects involving billions of dollars. The lost profits of contractors did not deter him from discarding the Nike-Zeus ABM, the Skybolt missile, nuclear-powered aircraft, supersonic bombers, a one-man contraption for entering space called the Dyna-Soar and finally hundreds of defense bases. Yet the very existence of a complex spending $20 to $30 billion a year on procurement, supplied by profit-seeking contractors, means political pressures beyond the capacity of even a President to withstand. One of the reasons that impelled President Johnson to go along with his $5.5 billion Sentinel system was to protect himself against opposition party charges of failing to protect the national security. To the extent that this is so, states scientist Ralph Lapp, we may as well forget all our elaborate systems analysis about defense needs.[19] But here again it is Congress lobbying on behalf of the military-industrial complex rather than the other way around. In short, defense is too large, involves too many jobs and is based too strongly on a militarized foreign policy for Congress itself to stand up to it. We have not yet turned the country into an armed camp, as Eisenhower feared, but we have gone too far for too long a time in that direction.

If America is not an armed camp, the world itself is a deadly arsenal of strategic nuclear weapons. Entering the third year of SALT negotiations, the United States and the Soviet Union renewed their talks with a fairly accurate knowledge of each other's box-score in nuclear capacity. The consensus is that the United States still has the edge in deliverable warheads — about 5,800 to 2,500 — for a ratio of two to one against the old ratio of three to one. The Soviet Union, however, has completely closed the gap in launchers. Its land-based and submarine launchers, along with its nuclear bombers, have increased from 500 in 1965 to approximately 2000, exceeding the launching capacity of the United States. With a head start in MIRV, including a new cluster of ten warheads, instead of the previous three, for each Poseidon underseas missile as our latest announced breakthrough, we maintain warhead superiority with a lesser number of launchers. Adding to Pentagon fears, the 1971-1972 edition of the authoritative Jane's Weapons Systems states that "Russia now has the initiative in weapons technology" in spite of the billions we have spent to maintain supremacy. Meanwhile, the charts for population overkill are outdated once again. Each side can now destroy the other many times over in retaliation against a surprise first-strike.

Both countries have pressed ahead with strategic missile deployment over the past two years as though trying to beat a deadline. The U.S. looked upon its ABM and MIRV systems as "bargaining chips" at the SALT table. The Soviet Union claimed to seek "parity" through its giant SS-9 ICBM's and a furiously pursued submarine program. In SALT language, the great goal was a reduction in ABM's, preferably to "zero ABM," in the hope that each side would then stop escalating the MIRV's, the weapon that spins off in the sky like a fireworks display, with each component on its way to a targeted enemy city.

Certainly Americans should feel some relief as a result of the SALT accords signed in Moscow on May 21, 1972. For the first time the superpowers reached an agreement on the nuclear weapons targeted on each other's cities. The ABM portion of the treaty, limiting both sides to a two-site "thin shield" (we had plans for twelve and four under way) finally justifies Robert McNamara's contention that the ABM's were the most destabilizing factor in propelling the mad arms race. The balance of the treaty freezes major offensive weapons at levels already deployed or under construction for a period of five years. The permitted limits still allow a race for the Soviets to build more and bigger missiles, particularly mobile ICBM's, and for the U.S. to concentrate on its lead in MIRV's. Neither side need do so, however, and at least the bargaining table has been opened towards nuclear arms reduction.

If there is any good that can come out of the Vietnam experience, it will arise from the backlash against the excessive militarism and commitments of our foreign policy. This will in turn diminish the size and power of the military establishment to the point where business association with it, as in the atomic energy and space efforts, could be reasonably benign and non-dependent. Then perhaps the Russians, who of course are also excessively militaristic, will have reason to meet us half-way. They have already expressed interest in sharing the costs, or at least the technology, of atomic energy and space exploration and hopefully will extend this interest to a joint reduction of defense budgets. This assumes the initiative to bargain is somewhat more ours than theirs since we have insisted on being the stronger nuclear power for over twenty-five years. At any rate, until public opinion leans against the military and encourages Congress to take away a good deal of the money this great Caesar feeds upon, the entire nation, including the business community, will suffer from the pangs of misused power.

A bleak outlook? Not for the long run. Remember, each crisis detailed herein was poorly anticipated, though cast up by the times. Each peaked, then receded into history. On balance, our response to social crises, whether as businessmen or as citizens, has been reasonably good. Too often, however, we have escaped only by the skin of our teeth.

Footnotes

[1] Quoted by Joseph S. Clark, president of World Federalists, in "The Quest for One Vote," (Washington, 1970).

[2] *U.S. News & World Report*, May 29, 1953, p. 98.

[3] Richard F. Kaufman, *The War Profiteers* (New York, 1970) pp. 15-17.

[4] Adam Yarmolinsky, *The Military Establishment: Its Impact on American Society* (New York, 1971) p. 250.

[5] Richard J. Barnet, *The Economy of Death* (New York, 1969) p. 13; John Stanley Baumgartner, *The Lonely Warriors: Case for the Military-Industrial Complex* (Los Angeles, 1971) p. 8; Yarmolinsky, *op. cit.*, p. 8.

[6] *Fortune*, "Famine Years for the Arms Makers," May, 1971, p. 167.

[7] John Kenneth Galbraith, *How to Control the Military* (New York, 1969) p. 58.

[8] Paul A. Koistinen, "The Industrial-Military Complex in Historical Perspective: World War I," *Business History Review*, Winter, 1967, pp. 368-403; also "The Industrial-Military Complex in Historical Perspective: The Inter-War Years," *Journal of American History*, March, 1970, pp. 819-839.

[9] Samuel P. Huntington, *The Soldier and the State* (Cambridge, 1957) pp. 80-97.

[10] Robert L. Heilbroner, summarizing Melman's thesis in a review of *Pentagon Capitalism* in *New York Review of Books*, July 23, 1970, p. 5.

[11] Kaufman, *op. cit.*, p. 203.

[12] Alain C. Einthoven and K. Wayne Smith, *How Much is Enough?* (New York 1971), p. 263.

[13] Henry L. Trewhitt, *McNamara: His Ordeal in the Pentagon* (New York, 1971) p. 146.

[14] *Ibid.*, p. 153.

[15] Report of the Committee on Government Operations made by its Permanent Subcommittee on Investigations, Report No. 91-1496, 91st Congress, 2nd Session (Vol. II, pp. 445-446).

[16] Alain C. Einthoven and K. Wayne Smith, *op. cit.*, p. 190.

[17] Robert S. McNamara, *The Essence of Security* (New York, 1968) Preface, x-xi.

[18] *Washington Star*, February 4, 1968, p. 1.

[19] Ralph E. Lapp, *The Weapons Culture* (New York, 1968) p. 179.

INDEX

DATE DUE

GAYLORD			PRINTED IN U.S.A.